Text Analytics
with Python

A Practical Real-World
Approach to Gaining Actionable
Insights from your Data

Dipanjan Sarkar

Apress®

Text Analytics with Python: A Practical Real-World Approach to Gaining Actionable Insights from Your Data

Dipanjan Sarkar
Bangalore, Karnataka
India

ISBN-13 (pbk): 978-1-4842-2387-1   ISBN-13 (electronic): 978-1-4842-2388-8
DOI 10.1007/978-1-4842-2388-8

Library of Congress Control Number: 2016960760

Managing Director: Welmoed Spahr
Lead Editor: Mr. Sarkar
Technical Reviewer: Shanky Sharma
Editorial Board: Steve Anglin, Pramila Balan, Laura Berendson, Aaron Black,
      Louise Corrigan, Jonathan Gennick, Robert Hutchinson, Celestin Suresh John,
      Nikhil Karkal, James Markham, Susan McDermott, Matthew Moodie, Natalie Pao,
      Gwenan Spearing
Coordinating Editor: Sanchita Mandal
Copy Editor: Corbin Collins
Compositor: SPi Global
Indexer: SPi Global
Artist: SPi Global

Distributed to the book trade worldwide by Springer Science+Business Media New York, 233 Spring Street, 6th Floor, New York, NY 10013. Phone 1-800-SPRINGER, fax (201) 348-4505, e-mail orders-ny@springer-sbm.com, or visit www.springeronline.com. Apress Media, LLC is a California LLC and the sole member (owner) is Springer Science + Business Media Finance Inc (SSBM Finance Inc). SSBM Finance Inc is a **Delaware** corporation.

For information on translations, please e-mail rights@apress.com, or visit www.apress.com.

Apress and friends of ED books may be purchased in bulk for academic, corporate, or promotional use. eBook versions and licenses are also available for most titles. For more information, reference our Special Bulk Sales–eBook Licensing web page at www.apress.com/bulk-sales.

Any source code or other supplementary materials referenced by the author in this text are available to readers at www.apress.com. For detailed information about how to locate your book's source code, go to www.apress.com/source-code/. Readers can also access source code at SpringerLink in the Supplementary Material section for each chapter.

Printed on acid-free paper

This book is dedicated to my parents, partner, well-wishers, and especially to all the developers, practitioners, and organizations who have created a wonderful and thriving ecosystem around analytics and data science.

Contents at a Glance

Contents

About the Author

Dipanjan Sarkar is a data scientist at Intel, the world's largest silicon company, which is on a mission to make the world more connected and productive. He primarily works on analytics, business intelligence, application development, and building large-scale intelligent systems. He received his master's degree in information technology from the International Institute of Information Technology, Bangalore, with a focus on data science and software engineering. He is also an avid supporter of self-learning, especially through massive open online courses, and holds a data science specialization from Johns Hopkins University on Coursera.

Sarkar has been an analytics practitioner for over four years, specializing in statistical, predictive, and text analytics. He has also authored a couple of books on R and machine learning, reviews technical books, and acts as a course beta tester for Coursera. Dipanjan's interests include learning about new technology, financial markets, disruptive startups, data science, and more recently, artificial intelligence and deep learning. In his spare time he loves reading, gaming, and watching popular sitcoms and football.

About the Technical Reviewer

Shanky Sharma Currently leading the AI team at Nextremer India, Shanky Sharma's work entails implementing various AI and machine learning-related projects and working on deep learning for speech recognition in Indic languages. He hopes to grow and scale new horizons in AI and machine learning technologies. Statistics intrigue him and he loves playing with numbers, designing algorithms, and giving solutions to people. He sees himself as a solution provider rather than a scripter or another IT nerd who codes. He loves heavy metal and trekking and giving back to society, which, he believes, is the task of every engineer. He also loves teaching and helping people. He is a firm believer that we learn more by helping others learn.

Acknowledgments

This book would definitely not be a reality without the help and support from some excellent people in my life. I would like to thank my parents, Digbijoy and Sampa, my partner Durba, and my family and well-wishers for their constant support and encouragement, which really motivates me and helps me strive to achieve more.

This book is based on various experiences and lessons learned over time. For that I would like to thank my managers, Nagendra Venkatesh and Sanjeev Reddy, for believing in me and giving me an excellent opportunity to tackle challenging problems and also grow personally. For the wealth of knowledge I gained in text analytics in my early days, I would like to acknowledge Dr. Mandar Mutalikdesai and Dr. Sanket Patil for not only being good managers but excellent mentors.

A special mention goes out to my colleagues Roopak Prajapat and Sailaja Parthasarathy for collaborating with me on various problems in text analytics. Thanks to Tamoghna Ghosh for being a great mentor and friend who keeps teaching me something new every day, and to my team, Raghav Bali, Tushar Sharma, Nitin Panwar, Ishan Khurana, Ganesh Ghongane, and Karishma Chug, for making tough problems look easier and more fun.

A lot of the content in this book would not have been possible without Christine Doig Cardet, Brandon Rose, and all the awesome people behind Python, Continuum Analytics, NLTK, gensim, pattern, spaCy, scikit-learn, and many more excellent open source frameworks and libraries out there that make our lives easier. Also to my friend Jyotiska, thank you for introducing me to Python and for learning and collaborating with me on various occasions that have helped me become what I am today.

Last, but never least, a big thank you to the entire team at Apress, especially to Celestin Suresh John, Sanchita Mandal, and Laura Berendson for giving me this wonderful opportunity to share my experience and what I've learned with the community and for guiding me and working tirelessly behind the scenes to make great things happen!

Introduction

I have been into mathematics and statistics since high school, when numbers began to really interest me. Analytics, data science, and more recently text analytics came much later, perhaps around four or five years ago when the hype about Big Data and Analytics was getting bigger and crazier. Personally I think a lot of it is over-hyped, but a lot of it is also exciting and presents huge possibilities with regard to new jobs, new discoveries, and solving problems that were previously deemed impossible to solve.

Natural Language Processing (NLP) has always caught my eye because the human brain and our cognitive abilities are really fascinating. The ability to communicate information, complex thoughts, and emotions with such little effort is staggering once you think about trying to replicate that ability in machines. Of course, we are advancing by leaps and bounds with regard to cognitive computing and artificial intelligence (AI), but we are not there yet. Passing the Turing Test is perhaps not enough; can a machine truly replicate a human in all aspects?

The ability to extract useful information and actionable insights from heaps of unstructured and raw textual data is in great demand today with regard to applications in NLP and text analytics. In my journey so far, I have struggled with various problems, faced many challenges, and learned various lessons over time. This book contains a major chunk of the knowledge I've gained in the world of text analytics, where building a fancy word cloud from a bunch of text documents is not enough anymore.

Perhaps the biggest problem with regard to learning text analytics is not a lack of information but *too much* information, often called *information overload*. There are so many resources, documentation, papers, books, and journals containing so much theoretical material, concepts, techniques, and algorithms that they often overwhelm someone new to the field. What is the right technique to solve a problem? How does text summarization really work? Which are the best frameworks to solve multi-class text categorization? By combining mathematical and theoretical concepts with practical implementations of real-world use-cases using Python, this book tries to address this problem and help readers avoid the pressing issues I've faced in my journey so far.

This book follows a comprehensive and structured approach. First it tackles the basics of natural language understanding and Python constructs in the initial chapters. Once you're familiar with the basics, it addresses interesting problems in text analytics in each of the remaining chapters, including text classification, clustering, similarity analysis, text summarization, and topic models. In this book we will also analyze text structure, semantics, sentiment, and opinions. For each topic, I cover the basic concepts and use some real-world scenarios and data to implement techniques covering each concept. The idea of this book is to give you a flavor of the vast landscape of text analytics and NLP and arm you with the necessary tools, techniques, and knowledge to tackle your own problems and start solving them. I hope you find this book helpful and wish you the very best in your journey through the world of text analytics!

CHAPTER 1

▓ ▓ ▓

Natural Language Basics

We have ushered in the age of Big Data where organizations and businesses are having difficulty managing all the data generated by various systems, processes, and transactions. However, the term *Big Data* is misused a lot due to the nature of its popular but vague definition of "the 3 V's"—volume, variety, and velocity of data. This is because sometimes it is very difficult to exactly quantify what data is "Big." Some might think a billion records in a database would be Big Data, but that number seems really minute compared to the *petabytes* of data being generated by various sensors or even social media. There is a large volume of unstructured textual data present across all organizations, irrespective of their domain. Just to take some examples, we have vast amounts of data in the form of tweets, status updates, comments, hashtags, articles, blogs, wikis, and much more on social media. Even retail and e-commerce stores generate a lot of textual data from new product information and metadata with customer reviews and feedback.

The main challenges associated with textual data are twofold. The first challenge deals with effective storage and management of this data. Usually textual data is unstructured and does not adhere to any specific predefined data model or schema, which is usually followed by relational databases. However, based on the data semantics, you can store it in either SQL-based database management systems (DBMS) like SQL Server or even NoSQL-based systems like MongoDB. Organizations having enormous amounts of textual datasets often resort to file-based systems like Hadoop where they dump all the data in the Hadoop Distributed File System (HDFS) and access it as needed, which is one of the main principles of a *data lake*.

The second challenge is with regard to analyzing this data and trying to extract meaningful patterns and useful insights that would be beneficial to the organization. Even though we have a large number of machine learning and data analysis techniques at our disposal, most of them are tuned to work with numerical data, hence we have to resort to areas like *natural language processing* (NLP) and specialized techniques, transformations, and algorithms to analyze text data, or more specifically *natural language*, which is quite different from programming languages that are easily understood by machines. Remember that textual data, being highly unstructured, does not follow or adhere to structured or regular syntax and patterns—hence we cannot directly use mathematical or statistical models to analyze it.

Electronic supplementary material The online version of this chapter (doi:10.1007/978-1-4842-2388-8_1) contains supplementary material, which is available to authorized users.

Before we dive into specific techniques and algorithms to analyze textual data, we will be going over some of the main concepts and theoretical principles associated with the nature of text data in this chapter. The primary intent here is to get you familiarized with concepts and domains associated with *natural language understanding, processing*, and *text analytics*. We will be using the Python programming language in this book primarily for accessing and analyzing text data. The examples in this chapter will be pretty straightforward and fairly easy to follow. However, you can quickly skim over Chapter 2 in case you want to brush up on Python before going through this chapter. All the examples are available with this book and also in my GithHub repository at `https://github.com/dipanjanS/text-analytics-with-python` which includes programs, code snippets and datasets. This chapter covers concepts relevant to natural language, linguistics, text data formats, syntax, semantics, and grammars before moving on to more advanced topics like *text corpora*, NLP, and text analytics.

Natural Language

Textual data is unstructured data but it usually belongs to a specific language following specific syntax and semantics. Any piece of text data—a simple word, sentence, or document—relates back to some natural language most of the time. In this section, we will be looking at the definition of natural language, the philosophy of language, language acquisition, and the usage of language.

What Is Natural Language?

To understand text analytics and natural language processing, we need to understand what makes a language "natural." In simple terms, a *natural* language is one developed and evolved by humans through natural use and communication, rather than constructed and created artificially, like a computer programming language.

Human languages like English, Japanese, and Sanskrit are natural languages. Natural languages can be communicated in different forms, including speech, writing, or even signs. There has been a lot of scholarship and effort applied toward understanding the origins, nature, and philosophy of language. We will discuss that briefly in the following section.

The Philosophy of Language

We now know what a natural language means. But think about the following questions. What are the origins of a language? What makes the English language "English"? How did the meaning of the word *fruit* come into existence? How do humans communicate among themselves with language? These are definitely some heavy philosophical questions.

The *philosophy of language* mainly deals with the following four problems and seeks answers to solve them:

- The nature of meaning in a language

- The use of language

- Language cognition

- The relationship between language and reality

- *The nature of meaning in a language* is concerned with the semantics of a language and the nature of meaning itself. Here, philosophers of language or linguistics try to find out what it means to actually "mean" anything—that is, how the meaning of any word or sentence originated and came into being and how different words in a language can be synonyms of each other and form relations. Another thing of importance here is how structure and syntax in the language pave the way for semantics, or to be more specific, how words, which have their own meanings, are structured together to form meaningful sentences. *Linguistics* is the scientific study of language, a special field that deals with some of these problems we will be looking at in more detail later on. Syntax, semantics, grammars, and parse trees are some ways to solve these problems. The nature of meaning can be expressed in linguistics between two human beings, notably a sender and a receiver, as what the sender tries to express or communicate when they send a message to a receiver, and what the receiver ends up understanding or deducing from the context of the received message. Also from a non-linguistic standpoint, things like body language, prior experiences, and psychological effects are contributors to meaning of language, where each human being perceives or infers meaning in their own way, taking into account some of these factors.

- *The use of language* is more concerned with how language is used as an entity in various scenarios and communication between human beings. This includes analyzing speech and the usage of language when speaking, including the speaker's intent, tone, content and actions involved in expressing a message. This is often termed as a *speech act* in linguistics. More advanced concepts such as the origins of language creation and human cognitive activities such as language acquisition which is responsible for learning and usage of languages are also of prime interest.

- *Language cognition* specifically focuses on how the cognitive functions of the human brain are responsible for understanding and interpreting language. Considering the example of a typical sender and receiver, there are many actions involved from message communication to interpretation. Cognition tries to find out how the mind works in combining and relating specific words into sentences and then into a meaningful message and what is the relation of language to the thought process of the sender and receiver when they use the language to communicate messages.

- *The relationship between language and reality* explores the extent of truth of expressions originating from language. Usually, philosophers of language try to measure how factual these expressions are and how they relate to certain affairs in our world which are true. This relationship can be expressed in several ways, and we will explore some of them.

One of the most popular models is the *triangle of reference*, which is used to explain how words convey meaning and ideas in the minds of the receiver and how that meaning relates back to a real world entity or fact. The triangle of reference was proposed by Charles Ogden and Ivor Richards in their book, *The Meaning of Meaning*, first published in 1923, and is denoted in Figure 1-1.

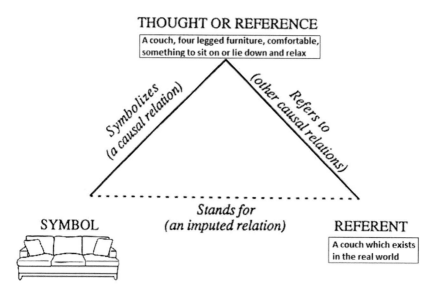

Figure 1-1. *The triangle of reference model*

The triangle of reference model is also known as the *meaning of meaning* model, and I have depicted the same in Figure 1-1 with a real example of a *couch* being perceived by a person which is present in front of him. A *symbol* is denoted as a linguistic symbol, like a word or an object that evokes thought in a person's mind. In this case, the *symbol* is the couch, and this evokes thoughts like *what is a couch, a piece of furniture that can be used for sitting on or lying down and relaxing, something that gives us comfort.* These thoughts are known as a *reference* and through this reference the person is able to relate it to something that exists in the real world, termed a *referent*. In this case the referent is the couch which the person perceives to be present in front of him.

The second way to find out relationships between language and reality is known as the *direction of fit*, and we will talk about two main directions here. The *word-to-world* direction of fit talks about instances where the usage of language can reflect reality. This indicates using words to match or relate to something that is happening or has already happened in the real world. An example would be the sentence *The Eiffel Tower is really big*, which accentuates a fact in reality. The other direction of fit, known as *world-to-word*, talks about instances where the usage of language can change reality. An example here would be the sentence *I am going to take a swim*, where the person *I* is changing reality by going to take a swim by representing the same in the sentence being communicated. Figure 1-2 shows the relationship between both the directions of fits.

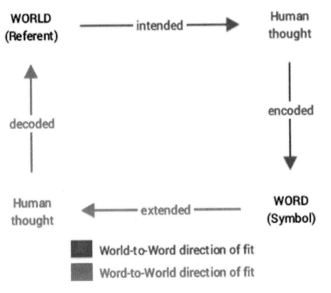

Figure 1-2. *The direction of fit representation*

It is quite clear from the preceding depiction that based on the referent that is perceived from the real world, a person can form a representation in the form of a symbol or word and consequently can communicate the same to another person, which forms a representation of the real world based on the received symbol, thus forming a cycle.

Language Acquisition and Usage

By now, we have seen what natural languages mean and the concepts behind language, its nature, meaning, and use. In this section, we will talk in further detail about how language is perceived, understood, and learned using cognitive abilities by humans, and finally we will end our discussion with the main forms of language usage, discussed in brief as *speech acts*. It is important to not only understand what natural language denotes but also how humans interpret, learn, and use the same language so that we are able to emulate some of these concepts programmatically in our algorithms and techniques when we try to extract insights from textual data.

Language Acquisition and Cognitive Learning

Language acquisition is defined as the process by which human beings utilize their cognitive abilities, knowledge, and experience to understand language based on hearing and perception and start using it in terms of words, phrases, and sentences to communicate with other human beings. In simple terms, the ability of acquiring and producing languages is language acquisition.

The history of language acquisition dates back centuries. Philosophers and scholars have tried to reason and understand the origins of language acquisition and came up with several theories, such as language being a god-gifted ability that is passed down from generation to generation. Plato indicated that a form of word-meaning mapping would have been responsible in language acquisition. Modern theories have been proposed by various scholars and philosophers, and some of the popular ones, most notably B.S. Skinner, indicated that knowledge, learning, and use of language were more of a behavioral consequent. Human beings, or to be more specific, children, when using specific words or symbols of any language, experience language based on certain stimuli which get reinforced in their memory thanks to consequent reactions to their usage repeatedly. This theory is based on *operant* or *instrumentation conditioning*, which is a type of conditional learning where the strength of a particular behavior or action is modified based on its consequences such as reward or punishment, and these consequent stimuli help in reinforcing or controlling behavior and learning. An example would be that children would learn that a specific combination of sounds made up a word from repeated usage of it by their parents or by being rewarded by appreciation when they speak it correctly or by being corrected when they make a mistake while speaking the same. This repeated conditioning would end up reinforcing the actual meaning and understanding of the word in a child's memory for the future. To sum it up, children try to learn and use language mostly behaviorally by imitating and hearing from adults.

However, this behavioral theory was challenged by renowned linguist Noam Chomsky, who proclaimed that it would be impossible for children to learn language just by imitating everything from adults. This hypothesis does stand valid in the following examples. Although words like *go* and *give* are valid, children often end up using an invalid form of the word, like *goed* or *gived* instead of *went* or *gave* in the past tense. It is assured that their parents didn't utter these words in front of them, so it would be impossible to pick these up based on the previous theory of Skinner. Consequently, Chomsky proposed that children must not only be imitating words they hear but also extracting patterns, syntax, and rules from the same language constructs, which is separate from just utilizing generic cognitive abilities based on behavior.

Considering Chomsky's view, cognitive abilities along with language-specific knowledge and abilities like syntax, semantics, concepts of parts of speech, and grammar together form what he termed a *language acquisition device* that enabled humans to have the ability of *language acquisition*. Besides cognitive abilities, what is unique and important in language learning is the syntax of the language itself, which can be emphasized in his famous sentence *Colorless green ideas sleep furiously*. If you observe the sentence and repeat it many times, it does not make sense. *Colorless* cannot be associated with green, and neither can ideas be associated with green, nor can they sleep furiously. However, the sentence has a grammatically correct syntax. This is precisely what Chomsky tried to explain—that syntax and grammar depict information that is independent from the meaning and semantics of words. Hence, he proposed that the learning and identifying of language syntax is a separate human capability compared to other cognitive abilities. This proposed hypothesis is also known as the *autonomy of syntax*. These theories are still widely debated among scholars and linguists, but it is useful to explore how the human mind tends to acquire and learn language. We will now look at the typical patterns in which language is generally used.

Language Usage

The previous section talked about speech acts and how the direction of fit model is used for relating words and symbols to reality. In this section we will cover some concepts related to speech acts that highlight different ways in which language is used in communication.

There are three main categories of speech acts: *locutionary*, *illocutionary*, and *perlocutionary* acts. *Locutionary* acts are mainly concerned with the actual delivery of the sentence when communicated from one human being to another by speaking it. *Illocutionary* acts focus further on the actual semantics and significance of the sentence which was communicated. *Perlocutionary* acts refer to the actual effect the communication had on its receiver, which is more psychological or behavioral.

A simple example would be the phrase *Get me the book from the table* spoken by a father to his child. The phrase when spoken by the father forms the locutionary act. This significance of this sentence is a directive, which directs the child to get the book from the table and forms an illocutionary act. The action the child takes after hearing this, that is, if he brings the book from the table to his father, forms the perlocutionary act.

The illocutionary act was a directive in this case. According to the philosopher John Searle, there are a total of five different classes of illocutionary speech acts, as follows:

- *Assertives* are speech acts that communicate how things are already existent in the world. They are spoken by the sender when he tries to assert a proposition that could be true or false in the real world. These assertions could be statements or declarations. A simple example would be *The Earth revolves round the Sun*. These messages represent the word-to-world direction of fit discussed earlier.

- *Directives* are speech acts that the sender communicates to the receiver asking or directing them to do something. This represents a voluntary act which the receiver might do in the future after receiving a directive from the sender. Directives can either be complied with or not complied with, since they are voluntary. These directives could be simple requests or even orders or commands. An example directive would be *Get me the book from the table*, discussed earlier when we talked about types of speech acts.

- *Commisives* are speech acts that commit the sender or speaker who utters them to some future voluntary act or action. Acts like promises, oaths, pledges, and vows represent commisives, and the direction of fit could be either way. An example commisive would be *I promise to be there tomorrow for the ceremony*.

- *Expressives* reveal a speaker or sender's disposition and outlook toward a particular proposition communicated through the message. These can be various forms of expression or emotion, such as congratulatory, sarcastic, and so on. An example expressive would be *Congratulations on graduating top of the class*.

- *Declarations* are powerful speech acts that have the capability to change the reality based on the declared proposition in the message communicated by the speaker\sender. The usual direction of fit is world-to-word, but it can go the other way also. An example declaration would be *I hereby declare him to be guilty of all charges.*

These speech acts are the primary ways in which language is used and communicated among human beings, and without even realizing it, you end up using hundreds of them on any given day. We will now look at linguistics and some of the main areas of research associated with it.

Linguistics

We have touched on what natural language means, how language is learned and used, and the origins of language acquisition. These kinds of things are formally researched and studied in linguistics by researchers and scholars called *linguists*. Formally, *linguistics* is defined as the scientific study of language, including form and syntax of language, meaning, and semantics depicted by the usage of language and context of use. The origins of linguistics can be dated back to the 4th century BCE, when Indian scholar and linguist Panini formalized the Sanskrit language description. The term *linguistics* was first defined to indicate the scientific study of languages in 1847, approximately before which the term *philology* was used to indicate the same. Although a detailed exploration of linguistics is not needed for text analytics, it is useful to know the different areas of linguistics because some of them are used extensively in natural language processing and text analytics algorithms. The main distinctive areas of study under linguistics are as follows:

- *Phonetics*: This is the study of the acoustic properties of sounds produced by the human vocal tract during speech. It includes studying the properties of sounds as well as how they are created and by human beings. The smallest individual unit of human speech in a specific language is called a *phoneme*. A more generic term across languages for this unit of speech is *phone.*

- *Phonology*: This is the study of sound patterns as interpreted in the human mind and used for distinguishing between different phonemes to find out which ones are significant. The structure, combination, and interpretations of phonemes are studied in detail, usually by taking into account a specific language at a time. The English language consists of around 45 phonemes. Phonology usually extends beyond just studying phonemes and includes things like accents, tone, and syllable structures.

- *Syntax*: This is usually the study of sentences, phrases, words, and their structures. It includes researching how words are combined together grammatically to form phrases and sentences. Syntactic order of words used in a phrase or a sentence matter because the order can change the meaning entirely.

- *Semantics*: This involves the study of meaning in language and can be further subdivided into lexical and compositional semantics.

  - *Lexical semantics*: The study of the meanings of words and symbols using morphology and syntax.

  - *Compositional semantics*: Studying relationships among words and combination of words and understanding the meanings of phrases and sentences and how they are related.

- *Morphology*: A *morpheme* is the smallest unit of language that has distinctive meaning. This includes things like words, prefixes, suffixes, and so on which have their own distinct meanings. Morphology is the study of the structure and meaning of these distinctive units or morphemes in a language. Specific rules and syntaxes usually govern the way morphemes can combine together.

- *Lexicon*: This is the study of properties of words and phrases used in a language and how they build the vocabulary of the language. These include what kinds of sounds are associated with meanings for words, the parts of speech words belong to, and their morphological forms.

- *Pragmatics*: This is the study of how both linguistic and non-linguistic factors like context and scenario might affect the meaning of an expression of a message or an utterance. This includes trying to infer whether there are any hidden or indirect meanings in the communication.

- *Discourse analysis*: This analyzes language and exchange of information in the form of sentences across conversations among human beings. These conversations could be spoken, written, or even signed.

- *Stylistics*: This is the study of language with a focus on the style of writing, including the tone, accent, dialogue, grammar, and type of voice.

- *Semiotics*: This is the study of signs, symbols, and sign processes and how they communicate meaning. Things like analogy, metaphors, and symbolism are covered in this area.

Although these are the main areas of study and research, linguistics is an enormous field with a much bigger scope than what is mentioned here. However, things like language syntax and semantics are some of the most important concepts that often form the foundations to natural language processing. The following section looks at them more closely.

Language Syntax and Structure

We already know what language, syntax, and structure indicate. Syntax and structure usually go hand in hand, where a set of specific rules, conventions, and principles usually govern the way words are combined into phrases, phrases get combines into clauses, and clauses get combined into sentences. We will be talking specifically about the English language syntax and structure in this section because in this book we will be dealing with textual data that belongs to the English language. But a lot of these concepts can be extended to other languages too. Knowledge about the structure and syntax of language is helpful in many areas like text processing, annotation, and parsing for further operations such as text classification or summarization.

In English, words usually combine together to form other constituent units. These constituents include words, phrases, clauses, and sentences. All these constituents exist together in any message and are related to each other in a hierarchical structure. Moreover, a sentence is a structured format of representing a collection of words provided they follow certain syntactic rules like grammar. Look at the bunch of words represented in Figure 1-3.

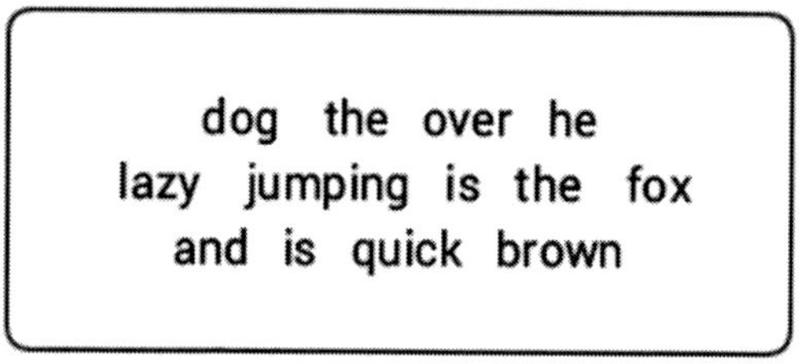

dog   the   over   he
lazy   jumping   is   the   fox
and   is   quick   brown

Figure 1-3. *A collection of words without any relation or structure*

From the collection of words in Figure 1-3, it is very difficult to ascertain what it might be trying to convey or mean. Indeed, languages are not just comprised of groups of unstructured words. Sentences with proper syntax not only help us give proper structure and relate words together but also help them convey meaning based on the order or position of the words. Considering our previous hierarchy of sentence → clause → phrase → word, we can construct the hierarchical sentence tree in Figure 1-4 using *shallow parsing*, a technique using for finding out the constituents in a sentence.

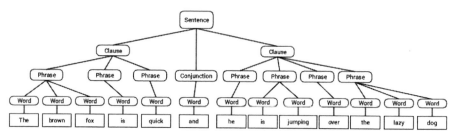

Figure 1-4. *Structured sentence following the hierarchical syntax*

From the hierarchical tree in Figure 1-4, we get the sentence *The brown fox is quick and he is jumping over the lazy dog.* We can see that the leaf nodes of the tree consist of words, which are the smallest unit here, and combinations of words form phrases, which in turn form clauses. Clauses are connected together through various filler terms or words such as conjunctions and form the final sentence. In the next section, we will look at each of these constituents in further detail and understand how to analyze them and find out what the major syntactic categories are.

Words

Words are the smallest units in a language that are independent and have a meaning of their own. Although morphemes are the smallest distinctive units, morphemes are not independent like words, and a word can be comprised of several morphemes. It is useful to annotate and tag words and analyze them into their parts of speech (POS) to see the major syntactic categories. Here, we will cover the main categories and significance of the various POS tags. Later in Chapter 3 we will examining them in further detail and looking at methods of generating POS tags programmatically.

Usually, words can fall into one of the following major categories.

- *N(oun)*: This usually denotes words that depict some object or entity which may be living or nonliving. Some examples would be *fox, dog, book,* and so on. The POS tag symbol for nouns is *N*.

- *V(erb)*: Verbs are words that are used to describe certain actions, states, or occurrences. There are a wide variety of further subcategories, such as auxiliary, reflexive, and transitive verbs (and many more). Some typical examples of verbs would be *running, jumping, read,* and *write.* The POS tag symbol for verbs is *V*.

- *Adj(ective)*: Adjectives are words used to describe or qualify other words, typically nouns and noun phrases. The phrase *beautiful flower* has the noun (N) *flower* which is described or qualified using the adjective (ADJ) *beautiful.* The POS tag symbol for adjectives is *ADJ*.

- *Adv(erb)*: Adverbs usually act as modifiers for other words including nouns, adjectives, verbs, or other adverbs. The phrase *very beautiful flower* has the adverb (ADV) *very,* which modifies the adjective (ADJ) *beautiful,* indicating the degree to which the flower is beautiful. The POS tag symbol for adverbs is *ADV*.

Besides these four major categories of parts of speech, there are other categories that occur frequently in the English language. These include pronouns, prepositions, interjections, conjunctions, determiners, and many others. Furthermore, each POS tag like the noun (N) can be further subdivided into categories like singular nouns (NN), singular proper nouns (NNP), and plural nouns (NNS). We will be looking at POS tags in further detail in Chapter 3 when we process and parse textual data and implement POS taggers to annotate text.

Considering our previous example sentence (*The brown fox is quick and he is jumping over the lazy dog*) where we built the hierarchical syntax tree, if we were to annotate it using basic POS tags, it would look like Figure 1-5.

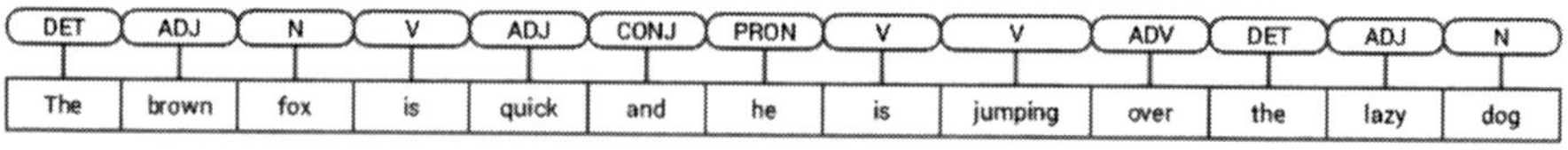

DET	ADJ	N	V	ADJ	CONJ	PRON	V	V	ADV	DET	ADJ	N
The	brown	fox	is	quick	and	he	is	jumping	over	the	lazy	dog

Figure 1-5. *Annotated words with their POS tags*

In Figure 1-5 you may notice a few unfamiliar tags. The tag DET stands for *determiner,* which is used to depict articles like *a, an, the,* and so on. The tag CONJ indicates *conjunction,* which is usually used to bind together clauses to form sentences. The PRON tag stands for *pronoun,* which represents words that are used to represent or take the place of a noun.

The tags N, V, ADJ and ADV are typical open classes and represent words belonging to an open vocabulary. *Open classes* are word classes that consist of an infinite set of words and commonly accept the addition of new words to the vocabulary which are invented by people. Words are usually added to open classes through processes like *morphological derivation,* invention based on usage, and creating *compound lexemes.* Some popular nouns added fairly recently include *Internet* and *multimedia. Closed classes* consist of a closed and finite set of words and do not accept new additions. Pronouns are a closed class.

The following section looks at the next level of the hierarchy: phrases.

Phrases

Words have their own lexical properties like parts of speech, which we saw earlier. Using these words, we can order them in ways that give meaning to the words such that each word belongs to a corresponding phrasal category and one of the words is the main or head word. In the hierarchy tree, groups of words make up *phrases,* which form the third level in the syntax tree. By principle, phrases are assumed to have at least two or more words, considering the pecking order of words ← phrases ← clauses ← sentences. However, a phrase *can* be a single word or a combination of words based on the syntax and position of the phrase in a clause or sentence. For example, the sentence *Dessert was good* has only three words, and each of them rolls up to three phrases. The word *dessert* is a noun as well as a *noun phrase, is* depicts a verb as well as a *verb phrase,* and *good* represents an adjective as well as an *adjective phrase* describing the aforementioned dessert.

There are five major categories of phrases:

- *Noun phrase (NP)*: These are phrases where a noun acts as the head word. Noun phrases act as a subject or object to a verb. Usually a noun phrases can be a set of words that can be replaced by a pronoun without rendering the sentence or clause syntactically incorrect. Some examples would be *dessert, the lazy dog,* and *the brown fox.*

- *Verb phrase (VP)*: These phrases are lexical units that have a verb acting as the head word. Usually there are two forms of verb phrases. One form has the verb components as well as other entities such as nouns, adjectives, or adverbs as parts of the object. The verb here is known as a *finite verb*. It acts as a single unit in the hierarchy tree and can function as the root in a clause. This form is prominent in *constituency grammars*. The other form is where the finite verb acts as the root of the entire clause and is prominent in *dependency grammars*. Another derivation of this includes verb phrases strictly consisting of verb components including main, auxiliary, infinitive, and participles. The sentence *He has started the engine* can be used to illustrate the two types of verb phrases that can be formed. They would be *has started the engine* and *has started*, based on the two forms just discussed.

- *Adjective phrase (ADJP)*: These are phrases with an adjective as the head word. Their main role is to describe or qualify nouns and pronouns in a sentence, and they will be either placed before or after the noun or pronoun. The sentence *The cat is too quick* has an adjective phrase, *too quick*, qualifying *cat*, which is a noun phrase.

- *Adverb phrase (ADVP)*: These phrases act like adverbs since the adverb acts as the head word in the phrase. Adverb phrases are used as modifiers for nouns, verbs, or adverbs themselves by providing further details that describe or qualify them. In the sentence *The train should be at the station pretty soon*, the adjective phrase *pretty soon* describes when the train would be arriving.

- *Prepositional phrase (PP)*: These phrases usually contain a preposition as the head word and other lexical components like nouns, pronouns, and so on. It acts like an adjective or adverb describing other words or phrases. The phrase *going up the stairs* contains a prepositional phrase *up*, describing the direction of the stairs.

These five major syntactic categories of phrases can be generated from words using several rules, some of which have been discussed, like utilizing syntax and grammars of different types. We will be exploring some of the popular grammars in a later section. *Shallow parsing* is a popular natural language processing technique to extract these constituents, including POS tags as well as phrases from a sentence. For our sentence *The brown fox is quick and he is jumping over the lazy dog*, we have obtained seven phrases from shallow parsing, as shown in Figure 1-6.

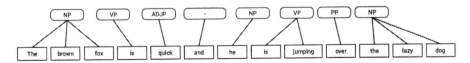

Figure 1-6. *Annotated phrases with their tags*

13

The phrase tags fall into the categories discussed earlier, although the word *and* is a conjunction and is usually used to combine clauses together. In the next section, we will be looking at clauses, their main categories, and some conventions and syntactic rules for extracting clauses from sentences.

Clauses

By nature, clauses can act as independent sentences, or several clauses can be combined together to form a sentence. A *clause* is a group of words with some relation between them that usually contains a subject and a predicate. Sometimes the subject is not present, and the predicate usually has a verb phrase or a verb with an object. By default you can classify clauses into two distinct categories: the *main clause* and the *subordinate clause*. The main clause is also known as an *independent* clause because it can form a sentence by itself and act as both sentence and clause. The subordinate or *dependent* clause cannot exist just by itself and depends on the main clause for its meaning. They are usually joined with other clauses using dependent words such as subordinating conjunctions.

With regard to syntactic properties of language, clauses can be subdivided into several categories based on syntax:

- *Declarative*: These clauses usually occur quite frequently and denote statements that do not have any specific tone associated with them. These are just standard statements, which are declared with a neutral tone and which could be factual or non-factual. An example would be *Grass is green*.

- *Imperative*: These clauses are usually in the form of a request, command, rule, or advice. The tone in this case would be a person issuing an order to one or more people to carry out an order, request, or instruction. An example would be *Please do not talk in class*.

- *Relative*: The simplest interpretation of *relative* clauses is that they are subordinate clauses and hence dependent on another part of the sentence that usually contains a word, phrase, or even a clause. This element usually acts as the antecedent to one of the words from the relative clause and relates to it. A simple example would be *John just mentioned that he wanted a soda*, having the antecedent proper noun *John*, which was referred to in the relative clause *he wanted a soda*.

- *Interrogative*: These clauses usually are in the form of questions. The type of these questions can be either affirmative or negative. Some examples would be *Did you get my mail?* and *Didn't you go to school?*

- *Exclamative*: These clauses are used to express shock, surprise, or even compliments. These expressions fall under *exclamations*, and these clauses often end with an exclamation mark. An example would be *What an amazing race!*

Usually most clauses are expressed in one of the previously mentioned syntactic forms, though this list of clause categories is not an exhaustive list and can be further categorized into several other forms. Considering our example sentence *The brown fox is quick and he is jumping over the lazy dog*, if you remember the syntax tree, the coordinating conjunction *and* divides the sentence into two clauses: *The brown fox is quick* and *he is jumping over the lazy dog*. Can you guess what categories they might fall into? (Hint: Look back at the definitions of declarative and relative clauses).

Grammar

Grammar helps in enabling both syntax and structure in language. It primarily consists of a set of rules used in determining how to position words, phrases, and clauses when constructing sentences for any natural language. Grammar is not restricted to the written word—it also operates verbally. Rules of grammar can be specific to a region, language, or dialect or be somewhat universal like the Subject-Verb-Object (SVO) model. Origins of grammar have a rich history, starting with Sanskrit in India. In the West, the study of grammar originated with the Greeks, and the earliest work was the *Art of Grammar*, written by Dionysius Thrax. Latin grammar models were developed from the Greek models, and gradually across several ages, grammars for various languages were created. It was only in the 18th century that grammar was considered as a serious candidate to be a field under linguistics.

Grammars have evolved over the course of time, leading to the birth of newer types of grammars, and various older grammars slowly lost prominence. Hence grammar is not just a fixed set of rules but also its evolution based on the usage of language over the course of time among humans. In English, there are several ways in which grammars can be classified. We will first talk about two broad classes, into which most of the popular grammatical frameworks can be grouped. Then we will further explore how these grammars represent language.

Grammar can be subdivided into two main classes—dependency grammars and constituency grammars—based on their representations for linguistic syntax and structure.

Dependency grammars

These grammars do not focus on constituents like words, phrases, and clauses but place more emphasis on words. These grammars are also known as *word-based* grammars. To understand dependency grammars, we should first know what *dependency* means in this context. Dependencies in this context are labeled word-word relations or links that are usually asymmetrical. A word has a relation or depends on another word based on the positioning of the words in the sentence. Consequently, dependency grammars assume that further constituents of phrases and clauses are derived from this dependency structure between words.

The basic principle behind a dependency grammar is that in any sentence in the language, all the words except one word has some relationship or dependency on other words in the sentence. The word that has no dependency is called the *root* of the sentence. The verb is taken as the root of the sentence in most cases. All the other words are directly or indirectly linked to the root verb using *links*, which are the dependencies. Although there are no concepts of phrases or clauses, looking at the syntax and relations between words and their dependents, one can determine the necessary constituents in the sentence.

Dependency grammars always have a one-to-one relationship correspondence for each word in the sentence. There are two aspects to this grammar representation. One is the syntax or structure of the sentence, and the other is the semantics obtained from the relationships denoted between the words. The syntax or structure of the words and their interconnections can be shown using a sentence syntax or parse tree similar to that depicted in an earlier section. Considering our sentence *The brown fox is quick and he is jumping over the lazy dog*, if we wanted to draw the dependency syntax tree for this, we would have the structure denoted in Figure 1-7.

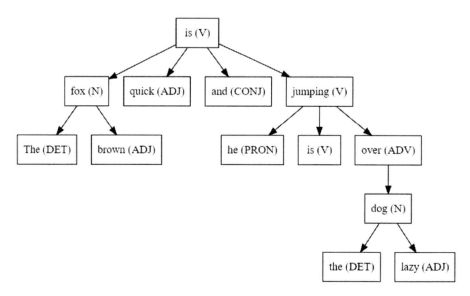

Figure 1-7. *Dependency grammar based syntax tree with POS tags*

Figure 1-7 shows that the dependencies form a tree—or to be more accurate, a *graph*—over all the words in the sentence. The graph is connected where each word has at least one directed edge going out or coming into it. The graph is also directed because each edge between two words points to one specific direction. In essence, the dependency tree is a *directed acyclic graph* (DAG). Every node in the tree has at most one incoming edge, except the root node. Because this is a directed graph, by nature dependency trees do not depict the order of the words in the sentence but emphasize more the relationship between the words in the sentence. Our sentence is annotated with the relevant POS tags discussed earlier, and the directed edges show the dependency. Now, if you remember, we just discussed earlier that there were two aspects to the representation of sentences using dependency grammar. Each directed edge represents a specific type of meaningful relationship (also known as *syntactic function*). We can annotate our sentence further showing the specific dependency relationship types between the words.

The same is depicted in Figure 1-8. An important point to remember here is that different variations of this graph might exist based on the parser you are using because it depends on how the parser was initially trained, the kind of data which was used for training it, and the kind of tag system it uses.

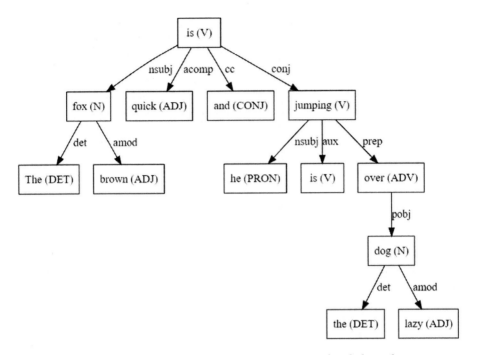

Figure 1-8. *Dependency grammar-based syntax tree annotated with dependency relationship types*

These dependency relationships each have their own meaning and are a part of a list of universal dependency types. This is discussed in an original paper, *Universal Stanford Dependencies: A Cross-Linguistic Typology* by de Marneffe et al, 2014). You can check out the exhaustive list of dependency types and their meanings at http://universaldependencies.org/u/dep/index.html. If we observe some of these dependencies, it is not too hard to understand them. Let's look in detail at some of the tags used in the dependencies for the sentence in Figure 1-8.

- The dependency tag *det* is pretty intuitive—it denotes the determiner relationship between a nominal head and the determiner. Usually the word with POS tag DET will also have the det dependency tag relation. Examples include (*fox → the*) and (*dog → the*).

- The dependency tag *amod* stands for *adjectival modifier* and stands for any adjective that modifies the meaning of a noun. Examples include (*fox → brown*) and (*dog → lazy*).

- The dependency tag *nsubj* stands for an entity that acts as a *subject* or agent in a clause. Examples include (*is → fox*) and (*jumping → he*).

- The dependencies *cc* and *conj* are more to do with linkages related to words connected by *coordinating conjunctions*. Examples include (*is → and*) and (*is → jumping*).

- The dependency tag *aux* indicates the *auxiliary* or secondary verb in the clause. Example: (*jumping → is*).

- The dependency tag *acomp* stands for *adjective complement* and acts as the complement or object to a verb in the sentence. Example: (*is → quick*).

- The dependency tag *prep* denotes a *prepositional* modifier, which usually modifies the meaning of a noun, verb, adjective, or preposition. Usually this representation is used for prepositions having a noun or noun phrase complement. Example: (jumping → over).

- The dependency tag *pobj* is used to denote the *object of a preposition*. This is usually the head of a noun phrase following a preposition in the sentence. Example: (over → dog).

The preceding tags have been extensively used in our sample sentence for annotating the various dependency relationships among the words. Now that you understand dependency relationships better, consider that often when representing a dependency grammar for sentences, instead of creating a tree with linear orders, you can also represent it with a normal graph because there is no concept of order of words in dependency grammar. Figure 1-9 depicts the same.

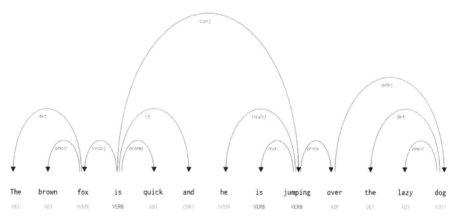

Figure 1-9. *Dependency grammar annotated graph for our sample sentence*

Figure 1-9 was created courtesy of spacy.io, which has some robust NLP modules also in a library that is open source. (When we cover constituency-based grammars next, observe that the number of nodes in dependency grammars is smaller compared to their constituency counterparts.) Currently there are various grammatical frameworks based on dependency grammar. Some popular ones include Algebraic Syntax and Operator Grammar.

Constituency Grammars

Constituency grammars are a class of grammars built upon the principle that a sentence can be represented by several constituents derived from it. These grammars can be used to model or represent the internal structure of sentences in terms of a hierarchically ordered structure of their constituents. Each and every word usually belongs to a specific lexical category in the case and forms the head word of different phrases. These phrases are formed based on rules called *phrase structure rules*. Hence, constituency grammars are also called *phrase structure grammars*. Phrase structure grammars were first introduced by Noam Chomsky in the 1950s. To understand constituency grammars we must know clearly what we mean by *constituents*. To refresh your memory, *constituents* are words or groups of words that have specific meaning and can act together as a dependent or independent unit. They can also be combined together further to form higher-order structures in a sentence, including phrases and clauses.

Phrase structure rules form the core of constituency grammars because they talk about syntax and rules that govern the hierarchy and ordering of the various constituents in the sentences. These rules cater to two things primarily. First and foremost, they determine what words are used to construct the phrases or constituents. Secondly, these rules determine how we need to order these constituents together. If we want to analyze phrase structure, we should we aware of typical schema patterns of the phrase structure rules. The generic representation of a phrase structure rule is $S{\rightarrow}AB$, which depicts that the structure S consists of constituents A and B, and the ordering is A followed by B.

There are several phrase structure rules, and we will explore them one by one to understand how exactly we extract and order constituents in a sentence. The most important rule describes how to divide a sentence or a clause. The phrase structure rule denotes a binary division for a sentence or a clause as $S{\rightarrow}NP\ VP$ where S is the *sentence* or clause, and it is divided into the subject, denoted by the *noun phrase* (NP) and the predicate, denoted by the *verb phrase* (VP).

We can apply more rules to break down each of the constituents further, but the top level of the hierarchy usually starts with a NP and VP. The rule for representing a noun phrase is $NP{\rightarrow}[DET][ADJ]N\ [PP]$, where the square brackets denote that it is optional. Usually a noun phrase consists of a noun (N) definitely as the head word and may optionally contain determinants (DET) and adjectives (ADJ) describing the noun, and a prepositional phrase (PP) at the right side in the syntax tree. Consequently, a noun phrase may contain another noun phrase as a constituent of it. Figure 1-10 shows a few examples that are governed by the aforementioned rules for noun phrases.

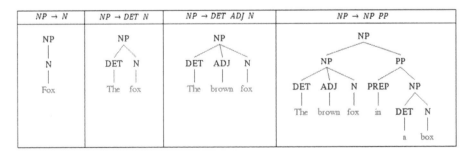

Figure 1-10. *Constituency syntax trees depicting structuring rules for noun phrases*

The syntax trees in Figure 1-10 show us the various constituents a noun phrase typically contains. As mentioned, a noun phrase denoted by NP on the left side of the production rule may also appear on the right side of the production rule, as depicted in the preceding example. This is a property called *recursion*, and we will talk about it toward the end of this section.

We will now look at rules for representing verb phrases. The rule is of the form $VP{\rightarrow}V|MD[VP][NP][PP][ADJP][ADVP]$, where the head word is usually a verb (V) or a modal (MD). A *modal* is itself an auxiliary verb, but we give it a different representation just to distinguish it from a normal verb. This is followed by optionally another verb phrase (VP) or noun phrase (NP), prepositional phrase (PP), adjective phrase (ADJP), or adverbial phrase (ADVP). The verb phrase is always the second component when we split a sentence using the binary division rule, making the noun phrase the first component. Figure 1-11 depicts a few examples for the different types of verb phrases that can be typically constructed and their representations as syntax trees.

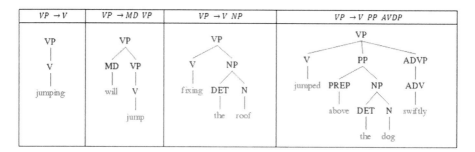

Figure 1-11. *Constituency syntax trees depicting structuring rules for verb phrases*

As depicted earlier, the syntax trees in Figure 1-11 show the representations of the various constituents in verb phrases. Using the property of recursion, a verb phrase may also contain another verb phrase inside it, as you can see in the second syntax tree. You can also see the hierarchy being maintained especially in the third and fourth syntax trees, where the NP and PP by itself are further constituents under the VP, and they can be further broken down into smaller constituents.

Since we have seen a lot of prepositional phrases being used in examples, let's look at the production rules for representing prepositional phrases. The basic rule has the form $PP{\rightarrow}PREP[NP]$, where PREP denotes a preposition, which acts as the head word, and it is optionally followed by a noun phrase (NP). Figure 1-12 depicts some representations of prepositional phrases and their corresponding syntax trees.

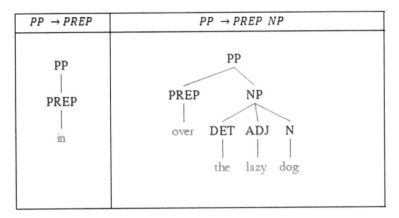

Figure 1-12. *Constituency syntax trees depicting structuring rules for prepositional phrases*

These two syntax trees show some different representations for prepositional phrases.

Recursion is an inherent property of language that allows constituents to be embedded in other constituents, which are depicted by different phrasal categories that appear on both sides of the production rules. Recursion lets us create long constituency-based syntax trees from sentences. A simple example is the representation of the sentence *The flying monkey in the circus on the trapeze by the river* depicted by the constituency parse tree in Figure 1-13.

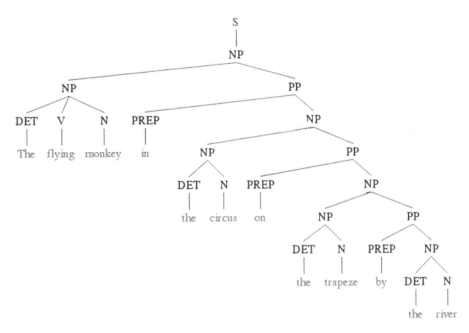

Figure 1-13. *Constituency syntax tree depicting recursive properties among constituents*

If you closely observe the syntax tree in Figure 1-13, you will notice that it is only constituted of noun phrases and prepositional phrases. However, due to the inherent recursive property that a prepositional phrase itself can consist of a noun phrase, and the noun phrase can consist of a noun phrase as well as a prepositional phrase, we notice the hierarchical structure with multiple NPs and PPs. If you go over the production rules for noun phrases and prepositional phrases, you will find the constituents shown in the tree are in adherence with the rules.

Conjunctions are used to join clauses and phrases together and form an important part of language syntax. Usually words, phrases, and even clauses can be combined together using conjunctions. The production rule can be denoted as $S{\rightarrow}S\ conj\ S\ \forall$ $S{\in}\{S,NP,VP\}$, where two constituents can be joined together by a conjunction, denoted by *conj* in the rule. A simple example for a sentence consisting of a noun phrase which, by itself, is constructed out of two noun phrases and a conjunction, would be *The brown fox and the lazy dog*. This is depicted in Figure 1-14 by the constituency syntax tree showing the adherence to the production rule.

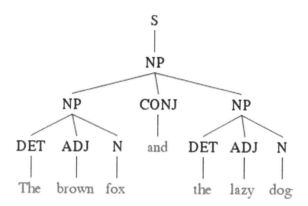

Figure 1-14. *Constituency syntax tree depicting noun phrases joined by a conjunction*

Figure 1-14 shows that the top level noun phrase is the sentence by itself and has two noun phrases as its constituents, which are joined together by a conjunction, thus satisfying our aforementioned production rule.

What if we wanted to join two sentences or clauses together with a conjunction? We can do that by putting all these rules and conventions together to generate the constituency-based syntax tree for our sample sentence *The brown fox is quick and he is jumping over the lazy dog*. This would give us the syntactic representation of our sentence as depicted in Figure 1-15.

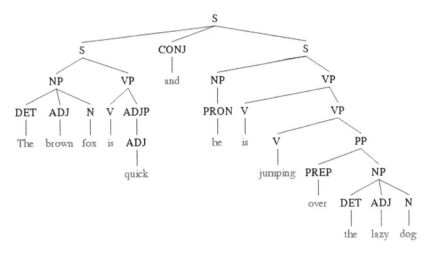

Figure 1-15. *Constituency syntax tree for our sample sentence*

From Figure 1-15, you can conclude that our sentence has two main clauses or constituents (discussed earlier), which are joined by a coordinating conjunction (*and*). Moreover, the constituency grammar–based production rules break down the top-level constituents into further constituents consisting of phrases and their words. Looking at this syntax tree, you can see that it does show the ordering of the words in the sentence and is more of a hierarchical tree–based structure with un-directed edges. Hence, this is very different compared to the dependency grammar–based syntax tree\graph with unordered words and directed edges. There are several popular grammar frameworks based on concepts derived from constituency grammar, including Phrase Structure Grammar, Arc Pair Grammar, Lexical Functional Grammar, and even the famous Context-Free Grammar, which is used extensively in describing formal language.

Word Order Typology

Typology in linguistics is a field that specifically deals with trying to classify languages based on their syntax, structure, and functionality. Languages can be classified in several ways, and one of the most common models is to classify them according to their dominant word orders, also known as *word order typology*. The primary word orders of interest occur in clauses consisting of a subject, verb, and an object. Of course, not all clauses use the subject, verb, and object, and often the subject and object are not used in certain languages. However, there exist several different classes of word orders that can be used to classify a wide variety of languages. A survey done by Russell Tomlin in 1986, summarized in Table 1-1, shows some insights derived from his analysis.

Table 1-1. *Word Order-Based Language Classification, Surveyed by Russell Tomlin, 1986*

SI No.	Word Order	Language Frequency	Example Languages
1	Subject-Object-Verb	180 (45%)	Sanskrit, Bengali, Gothic, Hindi, Latin
2	Subject-Verb-Object	168 (42%)	English, French, Mandarin, Spanish
3	Verb-Subject-Object	37 (9%)	Hebrew, Irish, Filipino, Aramaic
4	Verb-Object-Subject	12 (3%)	Baure, Malagasy, Aneityan
5	Object-Verb-Subject	5 (1%)	Apalai, Hixkaryana, Arecua
6	Object-Subject-Verb	1 (0%)	Warao

In Table 1-1, we can observe that there are six major classes of word orders, and languages like English follow the Subject-Verb-Object word order class. A simple example would be the sentence *He ate cake*, where *He* is the subject, *ate* is the verb, and *cake* is the object. The majority of languages from the table follow the Subject-Object-Verb word order. In that case, the sentence *He cake ate* would be correct if translated to those languages. This is illustrated by the English-to-Hindi translation of the same sentence in Figure 1-16.

English – detected ▾   🎤   ↹   Hindi ▾

He ate cake   उन्होंने केक खाया

                                          unhonne kek khaaya

Figure 1-16. *English-to-Hindi translation changes the word order class for the sentence He ate cake (courtesy of Google Translate)*

Even if you do not understand Hindi, you can understand by the English annotation provided by google that the word *cake* (denoted by *kek* in the text under the Hindi translation) has moved from the right end to the middle of the sentence, and the verb *ate* denoted by *khaaya* has moved from the middle to the end of the sentence, thus making the word order class become Subject-Object-Verb—the correct form for the Hindi language. This illustration gives us an indication of the importance of word order and how representation of messages can be grammatically different in various languages.

And that brings us to the end of our discussion of the syntax and structure of languages. Next we will be looking at some of the concepts around language semantics.

Language Semantics

The simplest definition of *semantics* is the study of meaning. Linguistics has its own subfield of *linguistic semantics*, which deals with the study of meaning in language, the relationships between words, phrases, and symbols, and their indication, meaning, and representation of the knowledge they signify. In simple words, semantics is more concerned with the facial expressions, signs, symbols, body language, and knowledge that are transferred when passing messages from one entity to another. There are various representations for syntax and rules for the same, including various forms of grammar we have covered in the previous sections. Representing semantics using formal rules or conventions has always been a challenge in linguistics. However, there are different ways to represent meaning and knowledge obtained from language. This section looks at relations between the lexical units of a language—predominantly words and phrases—and explores several representations and concepts around formalizing representation of knowledge and meaning.

Lexical Semantic Relations

Lexical semantics is usually concerned with identifying semantic relations between lexical units in a language and how they are correlated to the syntax and structure of the language. Lexical units are usually represented by morphemes, the smallest meaningful and syntactically correct unit of a language. Words are inherently a subset of these morphemes. Each lexical unit has its own syntax, form, and meaning. They also derive meaning from their surrounding lexical units in phrases, clauses, and sentences. A *lexicon* is a complete vocabulary of these lexical units. We will explore some concepts revolving around lexical semantics in this section.

Lemmas and Wordforms

A *lemma* is also known as the canonical or citation form for a set of words. The lemma is usually the base form of a set of words, known as a *lexeme* in this context. Lemma is the specific base form or head word that represents the lexeme. *Wordforms* are inflected forms of the lemma, which are part of the lexeme and can appear as one of the words from the lexeme in text. A simple example would the lexeme {eating, ate, eats}, which contains the wordforms, and their lemma is the word *eat*.

These words have specific meaning based on their position among other words in a sentence. This is also known as *sense* of the word, or wordsense. *Wordsense* gives a concrete representation of the different aspects of a word's meaning. Consider the word *fair* in the following sentences: *They are going to the annual fair* and *I hope the judgement is fair to all.* Even though the word *fair* is the same in both the sentences, the meaning changes based on the surrounding words and context.

Homonyms, Homographs, and Homophones

Homonyms are defined as words that share the same spelling or pronunciation but have different meanings. An alternative definition restricts the constraint on same spelling. The relationship between these words is termed as *homonymy*. Homonyms are often said to be the superset of homographs and homophones. An example of homonyms for the word *bat* can be demonstrated in the following sentences: *The bat hangs upside down from the tree* and *That baseball bat is really sturdy.*

Homographs are words that have the same written form or spelling but have different meanings. Several alternate definitions say that the pronunciation can also be different. Some examples of homographs include, the word *lead* as in *I am using a lead pencil* and *Please lead the soldiers to the camp,* and also the word *bass* in *Turn up the bass for the song* and *I just caught a bass today while I was out fishing.* Note that in both cases, the spelling stays the same but the pronunciation changes based on the context in the sentences.

Homophones are words that have the same pronunciation but different meanings, and they can have the same or different spellings. Examples would be the words *pair* (meaning couple) and *pear* (the fruit). They sound the same but have different meanings and written forms. Often these words cause problems in NLP because it is very difficult to find out the actual context and meaning using machine intelligence.

Heteronyms and Heterographs

Heteronyms are words that have the same written form or spelling but different pronunciations and meanings. By nature, they are a subset of homographs. They are also often called *heterophones*, which means "different sound." Examples of heteronyms are the words *lead* (metal, command) and *tear* (rip off something, moisture from eyes).

Heterographs are words that have the same pronunciation but different meanings and spellings. By nature they are a subset of homonyms. Their written representation might be different but they sound very similar or often exactly the same when spoken. Some examples include the words *to*, *too*, and *two*, which sound similar but have different spellings and meanings.

Polysemes

Polysemes are words that have the same written form or spelling and different but very relatable meanings. While this is very similar to homonymy, the difference is subjective and depends on the context, since these words are relatable to each other. A good example is the word *bank* which can mean (1) a financial institution, (2) the bank of the river, (3) the building that belongs to the financial institution, or (4) a verb meaning *to rely upon.* These examples use the same word *bank* and are homonyms. But only (1), (3), and (4) are polysemes representing a common theme (the financial organization representing trust and security).

Capitonyms

Capitonyms are words that have the same written form or spelling but have different meanings when capitalized. They may or may not have different pronunciations. Some examples include the words *march* (*March* indicates the month, and *march* depicts the action of walking) and *may* (*May* indicates the month, and *may* is a modal verb).

Synonyms and Antonyms

Synonyms are words that have different pronunciations and spellings but have the same meanings in some or all contexts. If two words or lexemes are synonyms, they can be substituted for each other in various contexts, and it signifies them having the same propositional meaning. Words that are synonyms are said to be *synonymous* to each other, and the state of being a synonym is called *synonymy*. Perfect synonymy is, however, almost nonexistent. The reason is that synonymy is more of a relation between senses and contextual meaning rather than just words. Consider the synonyms *big*, *huge*, and *large*. They are very relatable and make perfect sense in sentences like *That milkshake is really (big/large/huge)*. However, for the sentence *Bruce is my big brother*, it does not make sense if we substitute *big* with either *huge* or *large*. That's because the word *big* here has a context or sense depicting being grown up or older, and the other two synonyms lack this sense. Synonyms can exist for all parts of speech, including nouns, adjective, verbs, adverbs, and prepositions.

Antonyms are pairs of words that define a binary opposite relationship. These words indicate specific sense and meaning that are completely opposite to each other. The state of being an antonym is called *antonymy*. There are three types of antonyms: *graded antonyms*, *complementary antonyms*, and *relational antonyms*. Graded antonyms, as the name suggests, are antonyms with a certain grade or level when measured on a continuous scale, like the pair (*fat*, *skinny*). *Complementary antonyms* are word pairs that are opposite in their meaning but cannot be measured on any grade or scale. An example of a complementary antonym pair is (*divide*, *unite*). *Relational antonyms* are word pairs that have some relationship between them, and the antonymy is contextual, which is signified by this very relationship. An example of a relational antonym pair is (*doctor*, *patient*).

Hyponyms and Hypernyms

Hyponyms are words that are usually a subclass of another word. In this case, the hyponyms are generally words with very specific sense and context as compared to the word that is their superclass. *Hypernyms* are the words that act as the superclass to hyponyms and have a more generic sense compared to the hyponyms. An example would be the word *fruit*, which is a hypernym, and the words *mango*, *orange*, and *pear* would be possible hyponyms. The relationships depicted between these words are often termed *hyponymy* and *hypernymy*.

Semantic Networks and Models

We have seen several ways to formalize relations between words and their senses or meanings. Considering lexical semantics, there are approaches to find out the sense and meaning of each lexical unit, but what if we want to represent the meaning of some concept or theory that would involve relating these lexical units together and forming connections between them based on their meaning? *Semantic networks* aim to tackle this problem of representing knowledge and concepts using a network or a graph.

The basic unit of semantic network is an *entity* or a *concept*. A concept could be a tangible or abstract item like an idea. Sets of concepts have some relation to each other and can be represented with directed or undirected edges. Each *edge* denotes a specific type of relationship between two concepts. Let's say we are talking about the concept *fish*. We can have different concepts around fish based on their relationship to it. For instance, *fish "is-a" animal* and *fish "is-a"* part of *marine life*. These relationships are depicted as *is-a* relationships. Other similar relationships include *has-a, part-of, related-to,* and there are many more, depending on the context and semantics. These concepts and relationships together form a semantic network. There are several semantic models on the Web that have vast knowledge bases spanning different concepts. Figure 1-17 shows a possible representation for concepts related to *fish*. This model is provided courtesy of Nodebox (www.nodebox.net/perception/), where you can search for various concepts and see associated concepts to the same.

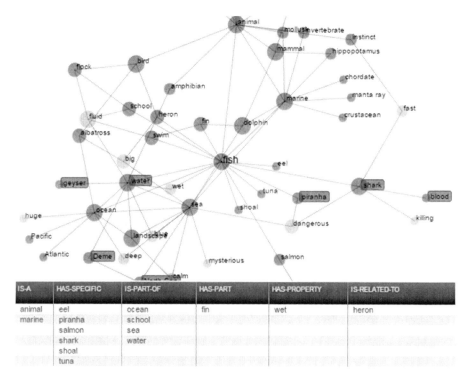

IS-A	HAS-SPECIFIC	IS-PART-OF	HAS-PART	HAS-PROPERTY	IS-RELATED-TO
animal	eel	ocean	fin	wet	heron
marine	piranha	school			
	salmon	sea			
	shark	water			
	shoal				
	tuna				

Figure 1-17. Semantic network around the concept fish

In the network in Figure 1-17, we can see some of the concepts discussed earlier around *fish* and also specific types of fish like eel, salmon, shark, and so on, which can be hyponyms to the concept *fish*. These semantic networks are formally denoted and represented by semantic data models using graph structures, where concepts or entities are the nodes and the edges denote the relationships. The Semantic Web is as extension of the World Wide Web using semantic metadata annotations and embeddings using data-modeling techniques like Resource Description Framework (RDF) and Web Ontology Language (OWL). In linguistics, we have a rich lexical corpus and database called WordNet, which has an exhaustive list of different lexical entities grouped together based on semantic similarity (for example, synonyms) into *synsets*. Semantic relationships between these synsets and consequently various words can be explored in WordNet, making it in essence a type of semantic network. We will talk about WordNet in more detail in a later section when we cover *text corpora*.

Representation of Semantics

So far we have seen how to represent semantics based on lexical units and how they can be interconnected by leveraging semantic networks. However, if we consider the normal form of communication via messages, whether written or spoken, if an entity sends a message to another entity and that entity takes some specific actions based on the message, then the second entity is said to have understood the meaning conveyed by that message. A question that might come to mind is how we formally represent the meaning or semantics conveyed by a simple sentence. Although it may be extremely easy for us to understand the meaning conveyed, representing semantics formally is not as easy as it seems.

Consider the example *Get me the book from the table*. This sentence by nature is a directive, and it directs the listener to do something. Understanding the meaning conveyed by this sentence may involve pragmatics like *which specific book?* and *which specific table?* besides the actual deed of getting the book from the table. Although the human mind is intuitive, formally representing the meanings and relationships between the various constituents is a challenge—but we can do it using techniques such as *propositional logic* (PL) and *first order logic* (FOL). Using these representations, one can represent the meaning indicated by different sentences, draw inference from them, and even discover whether one sentence entails another one based on their semantics. Representation of semantics is useful especially for carrying out our various NLP operations to make machines understand the semantics behind messages using proper representations, since machines lack the cognitive power we humans have been bestowed with.

Propositional Logic

Propositional logic (PL), also known as *sentential logic* or *statement logic*, is defined as the discipline of logic that is concerned with the study of propositions, statements, and sentences. This includes studying logical relationships and properties between propositions and statements, combining multiple propositions to form more complex propositions, and observing how the value of propositions change based on their components and logical operators. A *proposition* or *statement* is usually declarative and is capable of having a binary truth value that is either true or false. Usually a statement is more language-specific and concrete, and a proposition is more inclined toward the idea or the concepts conveyed by the statement. A simple example would be the two statements *The rocket was faster than the airship* and *The airship was slower than the rocket*, which are distinct but convey the same meaning or proposition. However, the terms statement and proposition are often used interchangeably in propositional logic.

The main focus in propositional logic is to study different propositions and how combining various propositions with logical operators change the semantics of the overall proposition. These logical operators are used more like connectors or coordinating conjunctions (if you remember them from earlier). Operators include terms like *and, or,* and *not,* which can change the meaning of a proposition by itself or when combined with several propositions. A simple example would be two propositions, *The Earth is round* and *The Earth revolves around the Sun.* These can be combined with the logical operator *and* to give us the proposition *The Earth is round and it revolves around the Sun,* which gives us the indication that the two propositions on either side of the *and* operator must be true for the combined proposition to be true.

The good part about propositional logic is that each proposition has its own *truth value,* and it is not concerned with further subdividing a proposition into smaller chunks and verifying its logical characteristics. Each proposition is considered as an indivisible, whole unit with its own truth value. Logical operators may be applied on it and several other propositions. Subdividing parts of propositions like clauses or phrases are not considered here. To represent the various building blocks of propositional logic, we use several conventions and symbols. Uppercase letters like P and Q are used to denote individual statements or propositions. The different operators used and their corresponding symbols are listed in Table 1-2, based on their order of precedence.

Table 1-2. *Logical Operators with Their Symbols and Precedence*

Sl No.	Operator Symbol	Operator Meaning	Precedence
1	¬	not	Highest
2	∧	and	
3	∨	or	
4	→	if-then	
5	↔	iff (if and only if)	Lowest

You can see that there are a total of five operators, with the *not* operator having the highest precedence, and the *iff* operator having the lowest. Logical constants are denoted as either being True or False. Constants and symbols are known as *atomic units*—all other units, more specifically the sentences and statements, are *complex units.* A *literal* is usually an atomic statement or its negation on applying the *not* operator.

Let's look at a simple example of two sentences P and Q and apply various operators on them. Consider the following representations:

P: He is hungry

Q: He will eat a sandwich

The expression P ∧ Q translates to *He is hungry and he will eat a sandwich*. This expresses that the outcome of this operation is itself also a sentence or proposition. This is the *conjunction* operation where P and Q are the *conjuncts*. The outcome of this sentence is True only if both P and Q are True.

The expression P ∨ Q translates to *He is hungry or he will eat a sandwich*. This expresses that the outcome of this operation is also another proposition formed from the *disjunction* operation where P and Q are the *disjuncts*. The outcome of this sentence is True if either P or Q or both of them are True.

The expression P → Q translates to *If he is hungry, then he will eat a sandwich*. This is the *implication* operation which determines that P is the *premise* or *antecedent* and Q is the *consequent*. It is just like a rule stating that Q will occur only if P has already occurred or is True.

The expression P ↔ Q translates to *He will eat a sandwich if and only if he is hungry* which is basically a combination of the expressions *If he is hungry then he will eat a sandwich* (P → Q) and *If he will eat a sandwich, he is hungry* (Q → P). This is the *biconditional* or *equivalence* operation that will evaluate to True if and only if the two implication operations described evaluate to True.

The expression ¬P translates to *He is not hungry*, which depicts the negation operation and will evaluate to True if and only if P evaluates to False.

This gives us an idea of the basic operations between propositions and more complex operations, which can be carried out with multiple logical connectives and by adding more propositions. A simple example: The statements P: *We will play football*, Q: *The stadium is open*, and R: *It will rain today* can be combined and represented as Q ∧ ¬R → P to depict the complex proposition *If the stadium is open and it does not rain today, then we will play football*. The semantics of the truth value or outcome of the final proposition can be evaluated based on the truth value of the individual propositions and the operators. The various outcomes of the truth values for the different operators are depicted in Figure 1-18.

P	*Q*	*¬P*	*P ∧ Q*	*P ∨ Q*	*P → Q*	*P ↔ Q*
False	*False*	*True*	*False*	*False*	*True*	*True*
False	*True*	*True*	*False*	*True*	*True*	*False*
True	*False*	*False*	*False*	*True*	*False*	*False*
True	*True*	*False*	*True*	*True*	*True*	*True*

Figure 1-18. *Truth values for various logical connectors*

Thus, using the table in Figure 1-18, we can evaluate even more complex propositions by breaking them down into simpler binary operations, evaluating the truth value for them, and combining them step by step.

Besides these outcomes, other properties like *associativity*, *commutativity*, and *distributivity* aid in evaluating complex proposition outcomes. The act of checking the validity of each operation and proposition and finally evaluating the outcome is also known as *inference*. However, besides evaluating extensive truth tables all the time, we can also make use of several inference rules to arrive at the final outcome or conclusion. The main reason for doing so would be that the size of these truth tables with the various operations starts increasing exponentially with the number of propositions increasing.

Moreover, rules of inference are easier to understand and well tested, and at the heart of them, the same truth value tables are actually applied—but we do not have to bother ourselves with the internals. Usually, a sequence of inference rules, when applied, leads to a conclusion that is often termed as a *logical proof*. The usual form of an inference rule is $P \vdash Q$, which indicates that Q can be derived by some inference operations from the set of statements represented by P. The turnstile symbol ($\vdash$) indicates that Q is some logical consequence of P. The most popular inference rules are as follows:

- *Modus Ponens*: Perhaps the most popular inference rule, it's also known as the *Implication Elimination* rule. It can be represented as $\{P \rightarrow Q, \ P\} \vdash Q$, which indicates that if P implies Q and P is asserted to be True, then it is inferred that Q is True. You can also represent this using the representation $((P \rightarrow Q) \wedge P) \rightarrow Q$, which can be evaluated easily using truth tables. A simple example would be the statement *If it is sunny, we will play football*, represented by $P \rightarrow Q$. Now if we say that *It is sunny*, this indicates that P is True, hence Q automatically is inferred as True, indicating *We will play football*.

- *Modus Tollens*: This is quite similar to the previous rule and is represented formally as $\{P \rightarrow Q, \ \neg Q\} \vdash \neg P$, which indicates that if P implies Q and Q is actually asserted to be False, then it is inferred that P is False. You can also represent this using the representation $((P \rightarrow Q) \wedge \neg Q) \rightarrow \neg P$, which can be evaluated easily using truth tables. An example proposition would be *If he is a bachelor, he is not married*, indicated by $P \rightarrow Q$. Now if we propose that *He is married*, represented by $\neg Q$, then we can infer $\neg P$, which translates to *He is not a bachelor*.

- *Disjunctive Syllogism*: This is also known as *Disjunction Elimination* and is formally represented as $\{P \vee Q, \ \neg P\} \vdash Q$, which indicates that if either P or Q is True and P is False, then Q is True. A simple example would be the statement *He is a miracle worker or a fraud* represented by $P \vee Q$ and the statement *He is not a miracle worker* represented by $\neg P$. We can then infer *He is a fraud*, depicted by Q.

- *Hypothetical Syllogism*: This is often known as the *Chain Rule of Deduction* and is formally represented as $\{P \rightarrow Q, \ Q \rightarrow R\} \vdash P \rightarrow R$, which tells us that if P implies Q, and Q implies R, we can infer that P implies R. A really interesting example to understand this would be the statement *If I am sick, I can't go to work* represented by $P \rightarrow Q$ and *If I can't go to work, the building construction will not be complete* represented by $Q \rightarrow R$. Then we can infer *If I am sick, the building construction will not be complete*, which can be represented by $P \rightarrow R$.

- *Constructive Dilemma*: This inference rule is the disjunctive version of Modus Ponens and can be formally represented as $\{(P \rightarrow Q) \land (R \rightarrow S), P \lor R\} \vdash Q \lor S$, which indicates that if P implies Q, and R implies S, and either P or R is True, then it can be inferred that either Q or S is True. Consider the following propositions: *If I work hard, I will be successful* represented by $P \rightarrow Q$, and *If I win the lottery, I will be rich* represented by $R \rightarrow S$. Now we propose that *I work hard or I win the lottery* is True, which is represented by $P \lor R$. We can then infer that *I will be successful or I will be rich*, represented by $Q \lor S$. The complement of this rule is *Destructive Dilemma* the disjunctive version of Modus Tollens.

This should give you a clear idea of how intuitive inference rules can be, and using them is much easier than going over multiple truth tables trying to find out the outcome of complex propositions. The interpretation we derive from inference gives us the semantics of the statement or proposition. A valid statement is one which would be True under all interpretations irrespective of the logical operations or various statements inside it. This is often termed as a *tautology*. The complement of a tautology is a *contradiction* or an inconsistent statement which is False under all interpretations. Note that the preceding list is just an indicative list of the most popular inference rules and is by no way an exhaustive list. Interested readers can read up more on inference and propositional calculus to get an idea of several other rules and axioms which are used besides the ones covered here.

Next we will be looking at first order logic, which tries to solve some of the shortcomings in propositional logic.

First Order Logic

First order logic (FOL), also known popularly as *predicate logic* and *first order predicate calculus*, is defined as a collection of well-defined formal systems which is used extensively in deduction, inference, and representation of knowledge. FOL allows us to use quantifiers and variables in sentences, which enable us to overcome some of the limitations with propositional logic. If we are to consider the pros and cons of propositional logic (PL), considering the points in its favor, PL is declarative and allows us to easily represent facts using a well-formed syntax. PL also allows complex representations like conjunctive, disjunctive, and negated knowledge representations. This by nature makes PL compositional wherein a composite or complex proposition is built from the simple propositions that are its components along with logical connectives. However, there are several areas where PL is lacking. It is definitely not easy to represent facts in PL because for each possible atomic fact, we will need a unique symbolic representation. Hence, due to this limitation, PL has very limited expressive power. Hence, the basic idea behind FOL is to not treat propositions as atomic entities.

FOL has a much richer syntax and necessary components for the same compared to PL. The basic components in FOL are as follows:

- *Objects*: These are specific entities or terms with individual unique identities like people, animals, and so on.

- *Relations*: These are also known as predicates and usually hold among objects or sets of objects and express some form of relationship or connection, like is_man, is_brother, is_mortal. Relations typically correspond to verbs.

- *Functions*: These are a subset of relations where there is always only one output value or object for some given input. Examples would be height, weight, age_of.

- *Properties*: These are specific attributes of objects that help in distinguishing them from other objects, like round, huge, and so on.

- *Connectives*: These are the logical connectives that are similar to the ones in PL, which include not ($\neg$), and ($\wedge$), or ($\vee$), implies ($\rightarrow$), and iff (if and only if $\leftrightarrow$).

- *Quantifiers*: These include two types of quantifiers: *universal* ($\forall$), which stands for "for all" or "all," and *existential* ($\exists$), which stands for "there exists" or "exists." They are used for quantifying entities in a logical or mathematical expression.

- *Constant symbols*: These are used to represent concrete entities or objects in the world. Examples would be *John*, *King*, *Red*, and *7*.

- *Variable symbols*: These are used to represent variables like *x*, *y*, and *z*.

- *Function symbols*: These are used to map functions to outcomes. Examples would be, age_of(John) = 25 or color_of(Tree) = Green.

- *Predicate symbols*: These map specific entities and a relation or function between them to a truth value based on the outcome. Examples would be color(sky, blue) = True.

These are the main components that go into logical representations and syntax for FOL. Usually, objects are represented by various *terms*, which could be either a *function*, *variable*, or *constant* based on the different components depicted previously. These terms do not need to be defined and do not return values. Various propositions are usually constructed using predicates and terms with the help of predicate symbols. An *n-ary predicate* is constructed from a function over n-terms which have either a True or False outcome. An *atomic sentence* can be represented by an n-ary predicate, and the outcome is True or False depending on the semantics of the sentence—that is, if the objects represented by the terms have the correct relation among themselves as specified by the predicate. A *complex sentence* or statement is formed using several atomic sentences and logical connectives. A *quantified sentence* adds the quantifiers mentioned earlier to sentences.

Quantifiers are one advantage FOL has over PL, since they enable us to represent statements about entire sets of objects without needing to represent and enumerate each object by a different name. The *universal quantifier* ($\forall$) asserts that a specific relation or predicate is True for all values associated with a specific variable. The representation $\forall x$ F(x) indicates that F holds *for all* values of *x* in the domain associated with *x*. An example would be $\forall x$ cat(x) $\rightarrow$ animal(x), which indicates that all cats are animals.

Universal quantifiers are usually used with the *implies* ($\rightarrow$) connective to form rules and statements. An important thing to remember is that universal quantifiers are almost never used in statements to indicate some relation for every entity in the world using the conjunction ($\land$) connective. An example would be the representation $\forall x$ dog(x) $\land$ eats_meat(x), which actually means that every entity in the world is a dog and they eat meat, which sounds kind of absurd! The *existential quantifier* ($\exists$) asserts that a specific relation or predicate holds True for at least some value associated with a specific variable. The representation, $\exists x$ F(x) indicates that F holds *for some* value of *x* in the domain associated with *x*. An example would be $\exists x$ student(x) $\land$ pass_exam(x), which indicates that there is at least one student who has passed the exam. This quantifier gives FOL a lot of power since we can make statements about objects or entities without specifically naming them. Existential quantifiers are usually used with the conjunction ($\land$) connective to form rules and statements. You should remember that existential quantifiers are almost never used with the implies ($\rightarrow$) connective in statements because the semantics indicated by it are usually wrong. An example would be $\exists x$ student(x) $\rightarrow$ knowledgeable(x), which tells us if you are a student you are knowledgeable—but the real problem happens if you ask what about those who are not students, are they not knowledgeable?

Considering the scope for nesting of quantifiers, ordering of multiple quantifiers may or may not matter depending on the type of quantifiers used. For multiple universal quantifiers, switching the order does not change the meaning of the statement. This can be depicted by ($\forall x$)($\forall y$) brother(x,y) $\leftrightarrow$ ($\forall y$)($\forall x$) brother(x,y), where *x* and *y* are used as variable symbols to indicate two people are brothers to each other irrespective of the order. Similarly, you can also switch the order of existential quantifiers like ($\exists x$)($\exists y$) F(x,y) $\leftrightarrow$ ($\exists y$)($\exists x$) F(x,y). Switching the order for mixed quantifiers in a sentence does matter and changes the interpretation of that sentence. This can be explained more clearly in the following examples, which are very popular in FOL:

- ($\forall x$)($\exists y$) loves(x, y) means that everyone in the world loves at least someone.

- ($\exists y$)($\forall x$) loves(x, y) means that someone is the world is loved by everyone.

- ($\forall y$)($\exists x$) loves(x, y) means that everyone in the world has at least someone who loves them.

- ($\exists x$)($\forall y$) loves(x, y) means that there is at least someone in the world who loves everyone.

From the preceding examples, you can see how the statements almost look the same but the ordering of quantifiers change the meanings significantly. There are also several other properties showing the relationship between the quantifiers. Some of the popular quantifier identities and properties are as follows:

- $(\forall x) \neg F(x) \leftrightarrow \neg(\exists x) \, F(x)$

- $\neg(\forall x) \, F(x) \leftrightarrow (\exists x) \, \neg F(x)$

- $(\forall x) \, F(x) \leftrightarrow \neg (\exists x) \, \neg F(x)$

- $(\exists x) \, F(x) \leftrightarrow \neg(\forall x) \, \neg F(x)$

- $(\forall x) \, (P(x) \wedge Q(x)) \leftrightarrow \forall x \, P(x) \wedge \forall x \, Q(x)$

- $(\exists x) \, (P(x) \vee Q(x)) \leftrightarrow \exists x \, P(x) \vee \exists x \, Q(x)$

There are a couple of other important concepts for transformation rules in predicate logic. These include *instantiation* and *generalization. Universal instantiation,* also known as *universal elimination,* is a rule of inference involving the universal quantifier. It tells us that if $(\forall x) \, F(x)$ is True, then $F(C)$ is True where C is any constant term that is present in the domain of x. The variable symbol here can be replaced by any ground term. An example depicting this would be $(\forall x)$ drinks(John, x) $\rightarrow$ drinks(John, Water).

Universal generalization, also known as *universal introduction,* is the inference rule that tells us that if $F(A) \wedge F(B) \wedge F(C) \wedge \ldots$ so on hold True, then we can infer that $(\forall x) \, F(x)$ holds True. *Existential instantiation,* also known as *existential elimination,* is an inference rule involving the existential quantifier. It tells us that if the given representation $(\exists x) \, F(x)$ exists, we can infer $F(C)$ for a new constant or variable symbol C. This is assuming that the constant or variable term C introduced in this rule should be a brand new constant that has not occurred previously in this proof or in our complete existing knowledge base. This process is also known as *skolemization,* and the constant C is known as the *skolem constant. Existential generalization,* also known as *existential introduction,* is the inference rule that tells us that assuming $F(C)$ to be True where C is a constant term, we can then infer $(\exists x) \, F(x)$ from it. This can be depicted by the representation eats_fish(Cat) $\rightarrow (\exists x)$ eats_fish(x), which can be translated as *Cats eat fish, therefore there exists something or someone at least who eats fish.*

We will now look at some examples of how FOL is used to represent natural language statements and vice versa. The examples in Table 1-3 depict some of the typical usage of FOL for representing natural language statements.

Table 1-3. *Representation of Natural Language Statements Using First Order Logic*

Sl No.	FOL Representation	Natural Language Statement
1	¬ eats(John, fish)	John does not eat fish
2	is_hot(pie) ∧ is_delicious(pie)	The pie is hot and delicious
3	is_hot(pie) ∨ is_delicious(pie)	The pie is either hot or delicious
4	study(John, exam) → pass(John, exam)	If John studies for the exam, he will pass the exam
5	∀x student(x) → pass(x, exam)	All students passed the exam
6	∃x student(x) ∧ fail(x, exam)	There is at least one student who failed the exam
7	(∃x student(x) ∧ fail(x, exam) ∧ (∀y fail(y, exam) → x=y))	There was exactly one student who failed the exam
8	∀x (spider(x) ∧ black_widow(x)) → poisonous(x)	All black widow spiders are poisonous

This gives us a good idea about the various components of FOL and the utility and advantages it gives us over PL. But FOL has its own limitation also. By nature, it allows us to quantify over variables and objects but not properties or relations. Higher order logic (HOL) allows us to quantify over relations, predicates, and functions. More specifically, second order logic enables us to quantify over predicates and functions and third order logic enables us to quantify over predicates of predicates. While they are more expressive, it is extremely difficult to determine the validity of all sentences in HOL.

Text Corpora

Text corpora is the plural form of *text corpus*. Text corpora are large and structured collection of texts or textual data, usually consisting of bodies of written or spoken text, often stored in electronic form. This includes converting old historic text corpora from physical to electronic form so that it can be analyzed and processed with ease. The primary purpose of text corpora is to leverage them for linguistic as well as statistical analysis and to use them as data for building NLP tools. *Monolingual corpora* consist of textual data in only one language, and *multilingual corpora* consist of textual data in multiple languages.

To understand the significance of text corpora, it helps to understand the origins of corpora and the reason behind it. It all started with the emergence of linguistics and people collecting data related to language to study its properties and structure. During the 1950s, statistical and quantitative methods were used to analyze collected data. But this endeavor soon reached a dead end due to the lack of large amounts of textual data over which statistical methods could be effectively applied. Besides that, cognitive learning and behavioral sciences gained a lot of focus. This empowered eminent linguist Noam Chomsky to build and formulate a sophisticated rule-based language model that formed the basis for building, annotating, and analyzing large scale text corpora.

Corpora Annotation and Utilities

Text corpora are annotated with rich metadata, which is extremely useful for getting valuable insights when utilizing the corpora for NLP and text analytics. Popular annotations for text corpora include tagging parts of speech (POS) tags, word stems, lemmas, and many more. Here are some of the most used methods and techniques for annotating text corpora:

- *POS tagging*: This is mainly used to annotate each word with a POS tag indicating the part of speech associated with it.

- *Word stems*: A *stem* for a word is a part of the word to which various affixes can be attached.

- *Word lemmas*: A *lemma* is the canonical or base form for a set of words and is also known as the *head word*.

- *Dependency grammar*: This includes finding out the various relationships among the components in sentences and annotating the dependencies.

- *Constituency grammar*: This is used to add syntactic annotation to sentences based on their constituents including phrases and clauses.

- *Semantic types and roles*: The various constituents of sentences including words and phrases are annotated with specific semantic types and roles, often obtained from an ontology, which indicates what they do. These include things like place, person, time, organization, agent, recipient, theme, and so forth.

Advanced forms of annotations include adding syntactic and semantic structure for text. These are dependency and constituency grammar–based parse trees. These specialized corpora, also known as *treebanks*, are extensively used in building POS taggers, syntax, and semantic parsers. Corpora are also used extensively by linguists for creating new dictionaries and grammars. Properties like *concordance, collocations*, and *frequency counts* enable them to find out lexical information, patterns, morphosyntactic information, and language learning. Besides linguistics, corpora are widely used in developing NLP tools like text taggers, speech recognition, machine translation, spelling and grammar checkers, text-to-speech and speech-to-text synthesizers, information retrieval, entity recognition, and knowledge extraction.

Popular Corpora

Several popular resources for text corpora have been built and have evolved over time. This section lists some of the most famous and popular corpora to whet your appetite. You can research and find out more details about the text corpora that catch your eye. Here are some popular text corpora built over time:

- *Key Word in Context*: KWIC was a methodology invented in the 1860s but used extensively around the 1950s by linguists to index documents and create corpora of concordances.

- *Brown Corpus*: This was the first million-word corpus for the English language, published by Kucera and Francis in 1961, also known as "A Standard Corpus of Present-Day American English." This corpus consists of text from a wide variety of sources and categories.

- *LOB Corpus*: The Lancaster-Oslo-Bergen (LOB) corpus was compiled in the 1970s as a result of collaboration between the University of Lancaster, the University of Oslo, and the Norwegian Computing Centre for the Humanities, Bergen. The main motivation of this project was to provide a British counterpart to the Brown corpus. This corpus is also a million-word corpus consisting of text from a wide variety of sources and categories.

- *Collins Corpus*: The Collins Birmingham University International Language Database (COBUILD), set up in 1980 at the University of Birmingham and funded by the Collins publishers, built a large electronic corpus of contemporary text in the English language that also paved the way for future corpora like the Bank of English and the Collins COBUILD English Language Dictionary.

- *CHILDES*: The Child Language Data Exchange System (CHILDES) is a corpus that was created by Brian and Catherine in 1984 that serves as a repository for language acquisition data, including transcripts, audio and video in 26 languages from over 130 different corpora. This has been merged with a larger corpus Talkbank recently. It is used extensively for analyzing the language and speech of young children.

- *WordNet*: This corpus is a semantic-oriented lexical database for the English language. It was created at Princeton University in 1985 under the supervision of George Armitage. The corpus consists of words and synonym sets (synsets). Besides these, it consists of word definitions, relationships, and examples of using words and synsets. Overall, it is a combination of a dictionary and a thesaurus.

- *Penn Treebank*: This corpus consists of tagged and parsed English sentences including annotations like POS tags and grammar-based parse trees typically found in treebanks. It can be also defined as a bank of linguistic trees and was created in the University of Pennsylvania, hence the name Penn Treebank.

- *BNC*: The British National Corpus (BNC) is one of the largest English corpora, consisting of over 100 million words of both written and spoken text samples from a wide variety of sources. This corpus is a representative sample of written and spoken British English of the late 20th century.

- *ANC*: The American National Corpus (ANC) is a large text corpus in American English that consists of over 22 million words of both spoken and written text samples since the 1990s. It includes data from a wide variety of sources, including emerging sources like email, tweets, and web information not present in the BNC.

- *COCA*: The Corpus of Contemporary American English (COCA) is the largest text corpus in American English and consists of over 450 million words, including spoken transcripts and written text from various categories and sources.

- *Google N-gram Corpus*: The Google N-gram Corpus consists of over a trillion words from various sources including books, web pages, and so on. The corpus consists of n-gram files up to 5-grams for each language.

- *Reuters Corpus*: This corpus is a collection of Reuters news articles and stories released in 2000 specifically for carrying out research in NLP and machine learning.

- *Web, chat, email, tweets*: These are entirely new forms of text corpora that have sprung up into prominence with the rise of social media. They are obtainable on the Web from various sources including Twitter, Facebook, chat rooms, and so on.

This gives us an idea of some of the most popular text corpora and also how they have evolved over time. The next section talks about how to access some of these text corpora with the help of Python and the Natural Language Toolkit (nltk) platform.

Accessing Text Corpora

We already have an idea about what constitutes a text corpus and have looked at a list of several popular text corpora that exist today. In this section, we will be leveraging Python and the Natural Language Toolkit NLTK to interface and access some of these text corpora. The next chapter talks more about Python and NLTK, so don't worry if some of the syntax or code seems overwhelming right now. The main intent of this section is to give an idea of how you can access and utilize text corpora easily for your NLP and analytics needs.

I will be using the ipython shell (https://ipython.org) for running Python code which provides a powerful interactive shell for running code as well as viewing charts and plots. We will also be using the NLTK library. You can find out more details about this project at www.nltk.org, which is all about NLTK being a complete platform and framework for accessing text resources, including corpora and libraries for various NLP and machine learning capabilities.

To start with, make sure you have Python installed. You can install Python separately or download the popular Anaconda Python distribution from Continuum Analytics from `www.continuum.io/downloads`. That version comes with a complete suite of analytics packages, including NLTK. If you want to know more about Python and what distribution would be best suited for you, Chapter 2 covers these topics in more detail.

Assuming you have Python installed now, if you installed the Anaconda distribution, you will already have NLTK installed. Note that we will be using Python 2.7 in this book, but you are welcome to use the latest version of Python—barring a few syntax changes, most of the code should be reproducible in the latest edition of Python. If you did not install the Anaconda distribution but have Python installed, you can open your terminal or command prompt and run the following command to install NLTK.

```
$ pip install nltk
```

This will install the NLTK library, and you will be ready to use it. However, the default installation of NLTK does not include all the components required in this book. To install all the components and resources of NLTK, you can start your Python shell and type the following commands—you will see the various dependencies for nltk being downloaded; a part of the output is shown in the following code snippet:

```
In [1]: import nltk

In [2]: nltk.download('all')
[nltk_data] Downloading collection u'all'
[nltk_data]    |
[nltk_data]    | Downloading package abc to
[nltk_data]    |     C:\Users\DIP.DIPSLAPTOP\AppData\Roaming\nltk_data
[nltk_data]    |     ...
[nltk_data]    |   Package abc is already up-to-date!
[nltk_data]    | Downloading package alpino to
[nltk_data]    |     C:\Users\DIP.DIPSLAPTOP\AppData\Roaming\nltk_data
[nltk_data]    |     ...
```

The preceding command will download all the necessary resources required by NLTK. If you don't want to download everything, you can also select the necessary components from a graphical user interface (GUI) using the command `nltk.download()`. Once the necessary dependencies are downloaded, you are now ready to start accessing text corpora!

Accessing the Brown Corpus

We have already talked a bit about the Brown Corpus, developed in 1961 at Brown University. This corpus consists of texts from 500 sources and has been grouped into various categories. The following code snippet loads the Brown Corpus into the system memory and shows the various available categories:

```
In [8]: # load the Brown Corpus
In [9]: from nltk.corpus import brown
```

```
In [10]: print 'Total Categories:', len(brown.categories())
Total Categories: 15

In [11]: print brown.categories()
[u'adventure', u'belles_lettres', u'editorial', u'fiction', u'government',
u'hobbies', u'humor', u'learned', u'lore', u'mystery', u'news', u'religion',
u'reviews', u'romance', u'science_fiction']
```

The preceding output tells us that there are a total of 15 categories in the corpus, like news, mystery, lore, and so on. The following code snippet digs a little deeper into the mystery category of the Brown Corpus:

```
In [19]: # tokenized sentences
In [20]: brown.sents(categories='mystery')
Out[20]: [[u'There', u'were', u'thirty-eight', u'patients', u'on', u'the',
u'bus', u'the', u'morning', u'I', u'left', u'for', u'Hanover', u',',
u'most', u'of', u'them', u'disturbed', u'and', u'hallucinating', u'.'],
[u'An', u'interne', u',', u'a', u'nurse', u'and', u'two', u'attendants',
u'were', u'in', u'charge', u'of', u'us', u'.'], ...]

In [21]: # POS tagged sentences
In [22]: brown.tagged_sents(categories='mystery')
Out[22]: [[(u'There', u'EX'), (u'were', u'BED'), (u'thirty-eight', u'CD'),
(u'patients', u'NNS'), (u'on', u'IN'), (u'the', u'AT'), (u'bus', u'NN'),
(u'the', u'AT'), (u'morning', u'NN'), (u'I', u'PPSS'), (u'left', u'VBD'),
(u'for', u'IN'), (u'Hanover', u'NP'), (u',', u','), (u'most', u'AP'),
(u'of', u'IN'), (u'them', u'PPO'), (u'disturbed', u'VBN'), (u'and', u'CC'),
(u'hallucinating', u'VBG'), (u'.', u'.')], [(u'An', u'AT'), (u'interne',
u'NN'), (u',', u','), (u'a', u'AT'), (u'nurse', u'NN'), (u'and', u'CC'),
(u'two', u'CD'), (u'attendants', u'NNS'), (u'were', u'BED'), (u'in', u'IN'),
(u'charge', u'NN'), (u'of', u'IN'), (u'us', u'PPO'), (u'.', u'.')], ...]

In [28]: # get sentences in natural form
In [29]: sentences = brown.sents(categories='mystery')
In [30]: sentences = [' '.join(sentence_token) for sentence_token in
sentences]
In [31]: print sentences[0:5] # printing first 5 sentences
[u'There were thirty-eight patients on the bus the morning I left for
Hanover , most of them disturbed and hallucinating .', u'An interne , a
nurse and two attendants were in charge of us .', u"I felt lonely and
depressed as I stared out the bus window at Chicago's grim , dirty West Side
.", u'It seemed incredible , as I listened to the monotonous drone of voices
and smelled the fetid odors coming from the patients , that technically I
was a ward of the state of Illinois , going to a hospital for the mentally
ill .', u'I suddenly thought of Mary Jane Brennan , the way her pretty eyes
could flash with anger , her quiet competence , the gentleness and sweetness
that lay just beneath the surface of her defenses .']
```

From the preceding snippet, we can see the written contents of the mystery genre and how the sentences are available in tokenized as well as annotated formats. Suppose we want to see the top nouns in the `mystery` genre? We can use the next code snippet for obtaining them. Remember that nouns have either an NN or NP in their POS tag to indicate the various forms. Chapter 3 covers POS tags in further detail:

```
In [81]: # get tagged words
In [82]: tagged_words = brown.tagged_words(categories='mystery')

In [83]: # get nouns from tagged words
In [84]: nouns = [(word, tag) for word, tag in tagged_words if any(noun_tag
in tag for noun_tag in ['NP', 'NN'])]

In [85]: print nouns[0:10] # prints the first 10 nouns
[(u'patients', u'NNS'), (u'bus', u'NN'), (u'morning', u'NN'), (u'Hanover',
u'NP'), (u'interne', u'NN'), (u'nurse', u'NN'), (u'attendants', u'NNS'),
(u'charge', u'NN'), (u'bus', u'NN'), (u'window', u'NN')]

In [85]: # build frequency distribution for nouns
In [86]: nouns_freq = nltk.FreqDist([word for word, tag in nouns])

In [87]: # print top 10 occuring nouns
In [88]: print nouns_freq.most_common(10)
[(u'man', 106), (u'time', 82), (u'door', 80), (u'car', 69), (u'room', 65),
(u'Mr.', 63), (u'way', 61), (u'office', 50), (u'eyes', 48), (u'hand', 46)]
```

That snippet prints the top ten nouns that occur the most and includes terms like *man, time, room,* and so on. We have used some advanced constructs and techniques like list comprehensions, iterables, and tuples. The next chapter covers them in further detail, including how they work and their main functionality. For now, all you need to know is we filter out the nouns from all other words based on their POS tags and then compute their frequency to get the top occurring nouns in the corpus.

Accessing the Reuters Corpus

The Reuters Corpus consists of 10,788 Reuters news documents from around 90 different categories and has been grouped into train and test sets. In machine learning terminology, *train* sets are usually used to train a model, and *test* sets are used to test the performance of that model. The following code snippet shows how to access the data for the Reuters Corpus:

```
In [94]: # load the Reuters Corpus
In [95]: from nltk.corpus import reuters

In [96]: print 'Total Categories:', len(reuters.categories())
Total Categories: 90
```

```
In [97]: print reuters.categories()
[u'acq', u'alum', u'barley', u'bop', u'carcass', u'castor-oil', u'cocoa',
u'coconut', u'coconut-oil', u'coffee', u'copper', u'copra-cake', u'corn',
u'cotton', u'cotton-oil', u'cpi', u'cpu', u'crude', u'dfl', u'dlr', u'dmk',
u'earn', u'fuel', u'gas', ...]

In [104]: # get sentences in housing and income categories
In [105]: sentences = reuters.sents(categories=['housing', 'income'])
In [106]: sentences = [' '.join(sentence_tokens) for sentence_tokens in
sentences]
In [107]: print sentences[0:5]  # prints the first 5 sentences
[u"YUGOSLAV ECONOMY WORSENED IN 1986 , BANK DATA SHOWS National Bank
economic data for 1986 shows that Yugoslavia ' s trade deficit grew , the
inflation rate rose , wages were sharply higher , the money supply expanded
and the value of the dinar fell .", u'The trade deficit for 1986 was 2 .
012 billion dlrs , 25 . 7 pct higher than in 1985 .', u'The trend continued
in the first three months of this year as exports dropped by 17 . 8 pct ,
in hard currency terms , to 2 . 124 billion dlrs .', u'Yugoslavia this year
started quoting trade figures in dinars based on current exchange rates ,
instead of dollars based on a fixed exchange rate of 264 . 53 dinars per
dollar .', u"Yugoslavia ' s balance of payments surplus with the convertible
currency area fell to 245 mln dlrs in 1986 from 344 mln in 1985 ."]

In [109]: # fileid based access
In [110]: print reuters.fileids(categories=['housing', 'income'])
[u'test/16118', u'test/18534', u'test/18540', u'test/18664', u'test/18665',
u'test/18672', u'test/18911', u'test/19875', u'test/20106', u'test/20116',
u'training/1035', u'training/1036', u'training/10602', ...]

In [111]: print reuters.sents(fileids=[u'test/16118', u'test/18534'])
[[u'YUGOSLAV', u'ECONOMY', u'WORSENED', u'IN', u'1986', u',', u'BANK',
u'DATA', u'SHOWS', u'National', u'Bank', u'economic', u'data', u'for',
u'1986', u'shows', u'that', u'Yugoslavia', u"'", u's', u'trade', u'deficit',
u'grew', u',', u'the', u'inflation', u'rate', u'rose', u',', u'wages',
u'were', u'sharply', u'higher', u',', u'the', u'money', u'supply',
u'expanded', u'and', u'the', u'value', u'of', u'the', u'dinar', u'fell',
u'.'], [u'The', u'trade', u'deficit', u'for', u'1986', u'was', u'2', u'.',
u'012', u'billion', u'dlrs', u',', u'25', u'.', u'7', u'pct', u'higher',
u'than', u'in', u'1985', u'.'], ...]
```

This gives us an idea of how to access corpora data using both categories as well as file identifiers.

Accessing the WordNet Corpus

The WordNet corpus is perhaps one of the most used corpora out there because it consists of a vast corpus of words and semantically linked synsets for each word. We will explore some of the basic features of the WordNet Corpus here, including synsets and methods of accessing the corpus data. For more advanced analysis and coverage of WordNet capabilities, see Chapter 7, which covers synsets, lemmas, hyponyms, hypernyms, and several other concepts covered in the semantics section earlier. The following code snippet should give you an idea about how to access the WordNet corpus data and synsets:

```
In [113]: # load the Wordnet Corpus
In [114]: from nltk.corpus import wordnet as wn

In [127]: word = 'hike' # taking hike as our word of interest

In [128]: # get word synsets
In [129]: word_synsets = wn.synsets(word)
In [130]: print word_synsets
[Synset('hike.n.01'), Synset('rise.n.09'), Synset('raise.n.01'),
Synset('hike.v.01'), Synset('hike.v.02')]

In [132]: # get details for each synonym in synset
     ...: for synset in word_synsets:
     ...:     print 'Synset Name:', synset.name()
     ...:     print 'POS Tag:', synset.pos()
     ...:     print 'Definition:', synset.definition()
     ...:     print 'Examples:', synset.examples()
     ...:     print
     ...:
Synset Name: hike.n.01
POS Tag: n
Definition: a long walk usually for exercise or pleasure
Examples: [u'she enjoys a hike in her spare time']

Synset Name: rise.n.09
POS Tag: n
Definition: an increase in cost
Examples: [u'they asked for a 10% rise in rates']

Synset Name: raise.n.01
POS Tag: n
Definition: the amount a salary is increased
Examples: [u'he got a 3% raise', u'he got a wage hike']

Synset Name: hike.v.01
POS Tag: v
Definition: increase
Examples: [u'The landlord hiked up the rents']

Synset Name: hike.v.02
POS Tag: v
Definition: walk a long way, as for pleasure or physical exercise
Examples: [u'We were hiking in Colorado', u'hike the Rockies']
```

The preceding code snippet depicts an interesting example with the word *hike* and its synsets, which include synonyms that are nouns as well as verbs having distinct meanings. WordNet makes it easy to semantically link words together with their synonyms as well as easily retrieve meanings and examples for various words. The preceding example tells us that *hike* can mean a long walk as well as an increase in price for salary or rent. Feel free to experiment with different words and find out their synsets, definitions, examples, and relationships.

Besides these popular corpora, there are a vast number of text corpora available that you can check and access with the `nltk.corpus` module. Thus, you can see how easy it is to access and use data from any text corpus with the help of Python and NLTK.

This brings us to the end of our discussion about text corpora. The following sections cover some ground regarding NLP and text analytics.

Natural Language Processing

I've mentioned the term *natural language processing* (NLP) several times in this chapter. By now, you may have formed some idea about what NLP means. NLP is defined as a specialized field of computer science and engineering and artificial intelligence with roots in computational linguistics. It is primarily concerned with designing and building applications and systems that enable interaction between machines and natural languages evolved for use by humans. This also makes NLP related to the area of Human-Computer Interaction (HCI). NLP techniques enable computers to process and understand natural human language and utilize it further to provide useful output. Next, we will be talking about some of the main applications of NLP.

Machine Translation

Machine translation is perhaps one of the most coveted and sought-after applications for NLP. It is defined as the technique that helps in providing syntactic, grammatical, and semantically correct translation between any two pair of languages. It was perhaps the first major area of research and development in NLP. On a simple level, machine translation is the translation of natural language carried out by a machine. By default, the basic building blocks for the machine translation process involve simple substitution of words from one language to another, but in that case we ignore things like grammar and phrasal structure consistency. Hence, more sophisticated techniques have evolved over a period of time, including combining large resources of text corpora along with statistical and linguistic techniques. One of the most popular machine translation systems is Google Translate. Figure 1-19 shows a successful machine translation operation executed by Google Translate for the sentence *What is the fare to the airport?* from English to Italian.

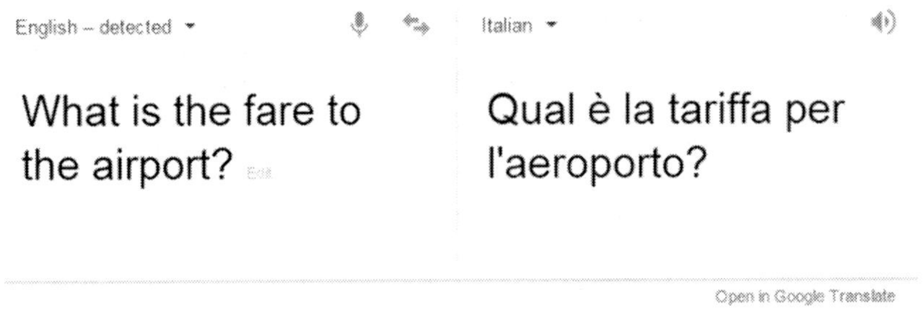

English – detected ▾   🎤   ⇄   Italian ▾   ◀))

What is the fare to the airport?

Qual è la tariffa per l'aeroporto?

Open in Google Translate

Figure 1-19. *Machine translation performed by Google Translate*

Over time, machine translation systems are getting better providing translations in real time as you speak or write into the application.

Speech Recognition Systems

This is perhaps the most difficult application for NLP. Perhaps the most difficult test of intelligence in artificial intelligence systems is the Turing Test. This test is defined as a test of intelligence for a computer. A question is posed to a computer and a human, and the test is passed if it is impossible to say which of the answers given was given by the human. Over time, a lot of progress has been made in this area by using techniques like speech synthesis, analysis, syntactic parsing, and contextual reasoning. But one chief limitation for speech recognition systems still remains: They are very domain specific and will not work if the user strays even a little bit from the expected scripted inputs needed by the system. Speech-recognition systems are now found in many places, from desktop computers to mobile phones to virtual assistance systems.

Question Answering Systems

Question Answering Systems (QAS) are built upon the principle of Question Answering, based on using techniques from NLP and information retrieval (IR). QAS is primarily concerned with building robust and scalable systems that provide answers to questions given by users in natural language form. Imagine being in a foreign country, asking a question to your personalized assistant in your phone in pure natural language, and getting a similar response from it. This is the ideal state toward which researchers and technologists are working. Some success in this field has been achieved with personalized assistants like Siri and Cortana, but their scope is still limited because they understand only a subset of key clauses and phrases in the entire human natural language.

To build a successful QAS, you need a huge knowledgebase consisting of data about various domains. Efficient querying systems into this knowledgebase would be leveraged by the QAS to provide answers to questions in natural language form. Creating and maintaining a queryable vast knowledgebase is extremely difficult—hence, you find the rise of QAS in niche domains like food, healthcare, e-commerce, and so on. Chatbots are one emerging trend that makes extensive use of QAS.

Contextual Recognition and Resolution

This covers a wide area in understanding natural language and includes both syntactic and semantic-based reasoning. *Word sense disambiguation* is a popular application, where we want to find out the contextual sense of a word in a given sentence. Consider the word *book*. It can mean *an object containing knowledge and information* when used as a noun, and it can also mean *to reserve a seat or a table* when used as a verb. Detecting these differences in sentences based on context is the main premise of word sense disambiguation—a daunting task covered in Chapter 7.

Coreference resolution is another problem in linguistics NLP is trying to address. By definition, coreference is said to occur when two or more terms or expressions in a body of text refer to the same entity. Then they are said to have the same *referent*. Consider *John just told me that he is going to the exam hall.* In this sentence, the pronoun *he* has the referent *John*. Resolving such pronouns is a part of coreference resolution, and it becomes challenging once we have multiple referents in a body of text. For example, *John just talked with Jim. He told me we have a surprise test tomorrow.* In this body of text, the pronoun *he* could refer to either *John* or *Jim*, thus making pinpointing the exact referent difficult.

Text Summarization

The main aim of *text summarization* is to take a corpus of text documents—which could be a collection of texts, paragraphs, or sentences—and reducing the content appropriately to create a summary that retains the key points of the collection. Summarization can be carried out by looking at the various documents and trying to find out the keywords, phrases, and sentences that have an important prominence in the whole collection. Two main types of techniques for text summarization include *extraction-based summarization* and *abstraction-based summarization*. With the advent of huge amounts of text and unstructured data, the need for text summarization in getting to valuable insights quickly is in great demand.

Text-summarization systems usually perform two main types of operations. The first is *generic summarization*, which tries to provide a generic summary of the collection of documents under analysis. The second type of operation is *query-based summarization*, which provides query-relevant text summaries where the corpus is filtered further based on specific queries, relevant keywords and phrases are extracted relevant to the query, and the summary is constructed. Chapter 5 covers this in detail.

Text Categorization

The main aim of *text categorization* is identifying to which category or class a specific document should be placed based on the contents of the document. This is one of the most popular applications of NLP and machine learning because with the right data, it is extremely simple to understand the principles behind its internals and implement a working text categorization system. Both supervised and unsupervised machine learning techniques can be used in solving this problem, and sometimes a combination of both is used. This has helped build a lot of successful and practical applications, including spam filters and news article categorization. We will be building our own text categorization system in Chapter 4.

Text Analytics

As mentioned before, with the advent of huge amounts of computing power, unstructured data, and success with machine learning and statistical analysis techniques, it wasn't long before text analytics started garnering a lot of attention. However, text analytics poses some challenges compared to regular analytical methods. Free-flowing text is highly unstructured and rarely follows any specific pattern—like weather data or structured attributes in relational databases. Hence, standard statistical methods aren't helpful when applied out of the box on unstructured text data. This section covers some of the main concepts in text analytics and also discusses the definition and scope of text analytics, which will give you a broad idea of what you can expect in the upcoming chapters.

Text analytics, also known as *text mining*, is the methodology and process followed to derive quality and actionable information and insights from textual data. This involves using NLP, information retrieval, and machine learning techniques to parse unstructured text data into more structured forms and deriving patterns and insights from this data that would be helpful for the end user. Text analytics comprises a collection of machine learning, linguistic, and statistical techniques that are used to model and extract information from text primarily for analysis needs, including business intelligence, exploratory, descriptive, and predictive analysis. Here are some of the main techniques and operations in text analytics:.

- Text classification

- Text clustering

- Text summarization

- Sentiment analysis

- Entity extraction and recognition

- Similarity analysis and relation modeling

Doing text analytics is sometimes a more involved process than normal statistical analysis or machine learning. Before applying any learning technique or algorithm, you have to convert the unstructured text data into a format acceptable by those algorithms. By definition, a body of text under analysis is often a document, and by applying various techniques we usually convert this document to a vector of words, which is a numeric array whose values are specific weights for each word that could either be its frequency, its occurrence, or various other depictions—some of which we will explore in Chapter 3. Often the text needs to be cleaned and processed to remove noisy terms and data, called *text pre-processing*.

Once we have the data in a machine-readable and understandable format, we can apply relevant algorithms based on the problem to be solved at hand. The applications of text analytics are manifold. Some of the most popular ones include the following:

- Spam detection

- News articles categorization

- Social media analysis and monitoring

- Bio-medical

- Security intelligence

- Marketing and CRM

- Sentiment analysis

- Ad placements

- Chatbots

- Virtual assistants

Summary

Congratulations on sticking it out till the end of this long chapter! We have started on our journey of text analytics with Python by taking a trip into the world of natural language and the various concepts and domains surrounding it. You now have a good idea of what natural language means and its significance in our world. You have also seen concepts regarding the philosophy of language and language acquisition and usage. The field of linguistics was also touched on, providing a flavor of the origins of language studies and how they have been evolving over time. We covered language syntax and semantics in detail, including the essential concepts with interesting examples to easily understand them. We also talked about resources for natural language, namely text corpora, and also looked at some practical examples with code regarding how to interface and access corpora using Python and NTLK. The chapter concluded with a discussion about the various facets of NLP and text analytics. In the next chapter, we will talk about using Python for text analytics. We will touch on setting up your Python development environment, the various constructs of Python, and how to use it for text processing. We will also look at some of the popular libraries, frameworks, and platforms we will be using in this book.

CHAPTER 2

▩ ▩ ▩

Python Refresher

In the previous chapter, we took a journey into the world of natural language and explored several interesting concepts and areas associated with it. We now have a better understanding of the entire scope surrounding natural language processing (NLP), linguistics, and text analytics. If you refresh your memory, we had also got our first taste of running Python code to access and use text corpora resources with the help of the NLTK platform.

In this chapter, we will cover a lot of ground with regard to the core components and functionality of Python as well as some of the important libraries and frameworks associated with NLP and text analytics. This chapter is aimed to be a refresher for Python and for providing the initial building blocks essential to get started with text analytics. This book assumes you have some knowledge of Python or any other programming language. If you are a Python practitioner, you can skim through the chapter, since the content here starts with setting up your Python development environment and moves on to the basics of Python.

Our main focus in the chapter will be exploring how text data is handled in Python, including data types and functions associated with it. However, we will also be covering several advanced concepts in Python, including list comprehensions, generators, and decorators, which make your life easier in developing and writing quality and reusable code. This chapter follows a more hands-on approach than the previous chapter, and we will cover various concepts with practical examples.

Getting to Know Python

Before we can dive into the Python ecosystem and look at the various components associated with it, we must look back at the origins and philosophy behind Python and see how it has evolved over time to be the choice of language powering many applications, servers, and systems today. Python is a high-level open source general-purpose programming language widely used as a scripting and across different domains. The brainchild of Guido Van Rossum, Python was conceived in the late 1980s as a successor to the ABC language, and both were developed at the Centrum Wiskunde and Informatica (CWI), Netherlands. Python was originally designed to be a scripting and interpreted language, and to this day it is still one of the most popular scripting languages out there. But with object-oriented programming (OOP) and constructs, you can use it just like any other object-oriented language, such as Java. The name *Python*, coined by Guido for the language, does not refer to the snake but the hit comedy show *Monty Python's Flying Circus*, since he was a big fan.

© Dipanjan Sarkar 2016

D. Sarkar, *Text Analytics with Python*, DOI 10.1007/978-1-4842-2388-8_2

As mentioned, Python is a general-purpose programming language that supports multiple programming paradigms, including the following popular programming paradigms:

- Object-oriented programming

- Functional programming

- Procedural programming

- Aspect-oriented programming

A lot of OOP concepts are present in Python, including classes, objects, data, and methods. Principles like abstraction, encapsulation, inheritance, and polymorphism can also be implemented and exhibited using Python. There are several advanced features in Python, including iterators, generators, list comprehensions, lambda expressions, and several modules like `itertools` and `functools`, which provide the ability to write code following the functional programming paradigm.

Python was designed keeping in mind the fact that simple and beautiful code is more elegant and easy to use rather than doing premature optimization and writing hard-to-interpret code. Python's standard libraries are power-packed with a wide variety of capabilities and features ranging from low-level hardware interfacing to handling files and working with text data. Easy extensibility and integration was considered when developing Python such that it can be easily integrated with existing applications—rich *application programming interfaces* (APIs) can even be created to provide interfaces to other applications and tools.

Python offers a lot of advantages and benefits. Here are some of the major benefits:

- *Friendly and easy to learn*: The Python programming language is extremely easy to understand and learn. Schools are starting to pick up Python as the language of choice to teach kids to code. The learning curve is not very steep, and you can do a lot of fun things in Python, from building games to automating things like reading and sending email. (In fact, there is a popular book and website dedicated to "automating the boring stuff" using Python at `https://automatetheboringstuff.com`.) Python also has a thriving and helpful developer community, which makes sure there is a ton of helpful resources and documentation out there on the Internet. The community also organizes various workshops and conferences throughout the world.

- *High-level abstractions*: Python is a *high-level language* (HLL), where a lot of the heavy lifting needed by writing low level code is eliminated by high-level abstractions. Python has a sharp focus on code simplicity and extensibility, and you can perform various operations, simple or complex, in fewer lines of code than other traditional compiled languages like C++ and C.

- *Boosts productivity*: Python boosts productivity by reducing time taken to develop, run, debug, deploy, and maintain large codebases compared to other languages like Java, C++, and C. Large programs of more than a 100 lines can be reduced to 20 lines or less on average by porting them to Python. High-level abstractions help developers focus on the problem to be solved at hand rather than worry about language-specific nuances. The hindrance of compiling and linking is also bypassed with Python. Hence, Python is often the choice of language especially when rapid prototyping and development are essential for solving an important problem in little time.

- *Complete robust ecosystem*: One of the main advantages of Python is that it is a multipurpose programming language that can be used for just about anything! From web applications to intelligent systems, Python powers a wide variety of applications and systems. We will talk about some of them later in this chapter. Besides being a multipurpose language, the wide variety of frameworks, libraries, and platforms that have been developed by using Python and to be used for Python form a complete robust ecosystem around Python. These libraries make life easier by giving us a wide variety of capabilities and functionality to perform various tasks with minimal code. Some examples would be libraries for handling databases, text data, machine learning, signal processing, image processing, deep learning, artificial intelligence—and the list goes on.

- *Open source*: As open source, Python is actively developed and updated constantly with improvements, optimizations, and new features. Now the Python Software Foundation (PSF) owns all Python-related intellectual property (IP) and administers all license-related issues. Being open source has boosted the Python ecosystem with almost all of its libraries also being open source, to which anyone can share, contribute, and suggest improvements and feedback. This helps foster healthy collaboration among technologists, engineers, researchers, and developers.

- *Easy to port, integrate, and deploy*: Python is supported on
all major operating systems (OS), including Linux, Windows,
and macOS. Code written in one OS can easily be ported into
another OS by simply copying the code files, and they will work
seamlessly. Python can also be easily integrated and extended
with existing applications and can interface with various APIs
and devices using sockets, networks, and ports. Python can be
used to invoke code for other languages, and there are Python
bindings for invoking Python code from other languages. This
helps in easy integration of Python code wherever necessary.
The most important advantage, though, is that it is very easy to
develop Python code and deploy it no matter how complex your
codebase might be. If you follow the right *continuous integration*
(CI) processes and manage your Python codebase properly,
deployment usually involves updating your latest code and
starting the necessary processes in your production environment.
It is extremely easy to get proper working code in minimal time,
which is often difficult to do with other languages.

All these features coupled with rapid strides in the application of Python in various
widespread domains over the years have made Python extremely popular. Such has been
the case that if the proper Python principles of simplicity, elegance, and minimalism are
not followed when writing code, the code is said to be not "pythonic." There is a known
style and convention around writing good Python code, and lots of articles and books
teach how to write pythonic code. Active users and developers in the Python community
call themselves Pythonistas, Pythoneers, and many more interesting names. The thriving
Python community makes the language all the more exciting since Python and its entire
ecosystem is always under active improvement and development.

The Zen of Python

You may be wondering what on earth the *Zen of Python* could be, but when you become
somewhat familiar with Python, this is one of the first things you get to know. The
beauty of Python lies in its simplicity and elegance. The Zen of Python is a set of 20
guiding principles, or *aphorisms*, that have been influential in Python's design. Long-
time Pythoneer Tim Peters documented 19 of them in 1999, and they can be accessed
at https://hg.python.org/peps/file/tip/pep-0020.txt as a part of the Python
Enhancement Proposals (PEP) number 20 (PEP 20). The best part is, if you already have
Python installed, you can access the Zen of Python at any time by running the following
code in the Python or IPython shell:

```
In [5]: import this
The Zen of Python, by Tim Peters
```

```
Beautiful is better than ugly.
Explicit is better than implicit.
Simple is better than complex.
Complex is better than complicated.
Flat is better than nested.
Sparse is better than dense.
Readability counts.
Special cases aren't special enough to break the rules.
Although practicality beats purity.
Errors should never pass silently.
Unless explicitly silenced.
In the face of ambiguity, refuse the temptation to guess.
There should be one-- and preferably only one --obvious way to do it.
Although that way may not be obvious at first unless you're Dutch.
Now is better than never.
Although never is often better than *right* now.
If the implementation is hard to explain, it's a bad idea.
If the implementation is easy to explain, it may be a good idea.
Namespaces are one honking great idea -- let's do more of those!
```

The above output showing the 19 principles that form the Zen of Python is included in the Python language itself as an easter egg. The principles are written in simple English and a lot of them are pretty self-explanatory, even if you have not written code before, and many of them contain inside jokes! Python focuses on writing simple and clean code that is readable. It also intends to make sure you focus a lot on error handling and implementing code that is easy to interpret and understand. The one principle I would most like you to remember is *Simple is better than complex*, which is applicable not only for Python but for a lot of things when you are out there in the world solving problems. Sometimes a simple approach beats a more complex one, as long as you know what you are doing, because it helps you avoid overcomplicating things.

Applications: When Should You Use Python?

Python, being a general and multipurpose programming language, can be used to build applications and systems for different domains and solve diverse real-world problems. Python comes with a standard library that hosts a large number of useful libraries and modules that can be leveraged to solve various problems. Besides the standard library, thousands of third-party libraries are readily available on the Internet, encouraging open source and active development. The official repository for hosting third-party libraries and utilities for enhancing development in Python is the Python Package Index (PyPI). Access it at https://pypi.python.org and check out the various packages. Currently there are over 80,000 packages you can install and start using.

Although Python can be used for solving a lot of problems, here are some of the most popular domains:

- *Scripting*: Python is known as a scripting language. It can be used to perform many tasks, such as interfacing with networks and hardware and handling and processing files and databases, performing OS operations, and receiving and sending email. Python is also used extensively for server-side scripting and even for developing entire web servers for serving web pages. A lot of Python scripts are used in an ad-hoc fashion for automating operations like network socket communication, handling email, parsing and extracting web pages, file sharing and transfer via FTP, communicating via different protocols, and several more.

- *Web development*: There are a lot of robust and stable Python frameworks out there that are used extensively for web development, including Django, Flask, Web2Py, and Pyramid. You can use them for developing complete enterprise web applications, and Python supports various architecture styles like RESTful APIs and the MVC architecture. It also provides ORM support to interact with databases and use OOP on top of that. Python even has frameworks like Kivy, which support cross-platform development for developing apps on multiple platforms like iOS, Android, Windows, and OS X. Python is also used for developing rich internet applications (RIA) with the Silverlight framework support in IronPython, a Python version that is well integrated with the popular Microsoft .NET framework and pyjs, a RIA development framework supporting a Python-to-JavaScript compiler and an AJAX framework.

- *Graphical user interfaces (GUIs)*: A lot of desktop-based applications with GUIs can be easily built with Python. Libraries and APIs like tkinter, PyQt, PyGTK, and wxPython allow developers to develop GUI-based apps with simple as well as complex interfaces. Various frameworks enable developers to develop GUI-based apps for different OSes and platforms.

- *Systems programming*: Being a high-level language, Python has a lot of interfaces to low-level OS services and protocols, and the abstractions on top of these services enable developers to write robust and portable system monitoring and administration tools. We can use Python to perform OS operations including creating, handling, searching, deleting, and managing files and directories. The Python standard library (PSL) has OS and POSIX bindings that can be used for handling files, multi-threading, multi-processing, environment variables, controlling sockets, pipes, and processes. This also enhances writing Python scripts for performing system-level administration tasks with minimal effort and lines of code.

- *Database programming*: Python is used a lot in connecting and accessing data from different types of databases, be it SQL or NoSQL. APIs and connectors exist for these databases like MySQL, MSSQL, MongoDB, Oracle, PostgreSQL, and SQLite. In fact, SQLite, a lightweight relational database, now comes as a part of the Python standard distribution itself. Popular libraries like SQLAlchemy and SQLObject provide interfaces to access various relational databases and also have ORM components to help implement OOP-style classes and objects on top of relational tables.

- *Scientific computing*: Python really shows its flair for being multipurpose in areas like numeric and scientific computing. You can perform simple as well as complex mathematical operations with Python, including algebra and calculus. Libraries like SciPy and NumPy help researchers, scientists, and developers leverage highly optimized functions and interfaces for numeric and scientific programming. These libraries are also used as the base for developing complex algorithms in various domains like machine learning.

- *Machine learning*: Python is regarded as one of the most popular languages today for machine learning. There is a wide suite of libraries and frameworks, like `scikit-learn`, `h2o`, `tensorflow`, `theano`, and even core libraries like `numpy` and `scipy`, for not only implementing machine learning algorithms but also using them to solve real-world advanced analytics problems.

- *Text analytics*: As mentioned, Python can handle text data very well, and this has led to several popular libraries like `nltk`, `gensim`, and `pattern` for NLP, information retrieval, and text analytics. You can also apply standard machine learning algorithms to solve problems related to text analytics. This ecosystem of readily available packages in Python reduces time and efforts taken for development. We will be exploring several of these libraries in this book.

Even though the preceding list may seem a bit overwhelming, this is just scratching the surface of what is possible with Python. It is widely used in several other domains including artificial intelligence (AI), game development, robotics, Internet of Things (IoT), computer vision, media processing, and network and system monitoring, just to name a few. To read some of the widespread success stories achieved with Python in different diverse domains like arts, science, computer science, education, and others, enthusiastic programmers and researchers can check out `www.python.org/about/success/`. To find out various popular applications developed using Python, see `www.python.org/about/apps/` and `https://wiki.python.org/moin/Applications`, where you will definitely find some applications you have used—some of them are indispensable.

Drawbacks: When Should You Not Use Python?

I have been blowing the trumpet for Python till now, but you may be wondering are there any drawbacks? Well, like any tool or language, Python has advantages and disadvantages. Yes, even Python has some disadvantages, and here we will highlight some of them so that you are aware of them when developing and writing code in Python:

- *Execution speed performance*: *Performance* is a pretty heavy term and can mean several things, so I'll pinpoint the exact area to talk about and that is execution speed. Because Python is not a fully compiled language, it will always be slower than low-level fully compiled programming languages like C and C++. There are several ways you can optimize your code, including multi-threading and multi-processing. You can also use static typing and C extensions for Python (known as Cython). You can consider using PyPy also, which is much faster than normal Python since it uses a just-in-time (JIT) compiler (see http://pypy.org), but often, if you write well-optimized code, you can develop applications in Python just fine and do not need to depend on other languages. Remember that often the problem is not with the tool but the code you write—something all developers and engineers realize with time and experience.

- *Global Interpreter Lock (GIL)*: The GIL is a mutual exclusion lock used in several programming language interpreters, like Python and Ruby. Interpreters using GIL only allow one single thread to effectively execute at a time even when run on a multi-core processor and thus limit the effectively of parallelism achieved by multi-threading depending on whether the processes are I\O bound or CPU bound and how many calls it makes outside the interpreter.

- *Version incompatibility*: If you have been following Python news, you know that once Python released the 3.x version from 2.7.x, it was backward-incompatible in several aspects, and that has indeed opened a huge can of worms. Several major libraries and packages that had been built in Python 2.7.x started breaking when users unknowingly updated their Python versions. Hence, a large chunk of enterprises and the developer community still use Python 2.7.x due to legacy code and because newer versions of those packages and libraries were never built. Code deprecation and version changes are some of the most important factors in systems breaking down.

Many of these issues are not specific to Python but apply to other languages too, so you should not be discouraged from using Python just because of the preceding points— but you should definitely remember them when writing code and building systems.

Python Implementations and Versions

There are several different implementations of Python and different versions of Python which are released periodically since it is under active development. This section discusses both implementations and versions and their significance, which should give you some idea of which Python you might want to use for your development needs. Currently, there are four major production-ready, robust, and stable implementations of Python:

- *CPython* is the regular old Python, which we know as just Python. It is both a compiler and interpreter and comes with its own set of standard packages and modules which were all written in standard C. This version can be used directly in all popular modern platforms. Most of the python third-party packages and libraries are compatible with this version.

- *PyPy* is a faster alternative Python implementation that uses a JIT compiler to make the code run faster than the CPython implementation—sometimes delivering speedups in the range of 10x–100x. It is also more memory efficient, supporting greenlets and stackless for high parallelism and concurrency.

- *Jython* is a Python implementation for the Java platform supporting Java Virtual Machine (JVM) for any version of Java ideally above version 7. Using Jython you can write code leveraging all types of Java libraries, packages, and frameworks. It works best when you know more about the Java syntax and the OOP principles that are used extensively in Java, like classes, objects, and interfaces.

- *IronPython* is the Python implementation for the popular Microsoft .NET framework, also termed as the Common Language Runtime (CLR). You can use all of Microsoft's CLR libraries and frameworks in IronPython, and even though you do not essentially have to write code in C#, it is useful to know more about syntax and constructs for C# to use IronPython effectively.

To start with I would suggest you to use the default Python which is the CPython implementation, and experiment with the other versions only if you are really interested in interfacing with other languages like C# and Java and need to use them in your codebase.

There are two major versions: the 2.x series and the 3.x series, where x is a number. Python 2.7 was the last major version in the 2.x series, released in 2010. From then on, future releases have included bug fixes and performance improvements but no new features. The latest version is Python 2.7.12, released in June 2016. The 3.x series started with Python 3.0, which introduced many backward-incompatible changes compared to Python 2.x. Each version 3 release not only has bug fixes and improvements but also introduces new features, such as the AsyncIO module released recently. As of this writing, Python 3.5.2 is the latest version in the 3.x series, released in June 2016.

There are many arguments over which version of Python should be used. We will discuss some of them later on, but the best way to go about thinking about it is to consider what problem is to be solved and the entire software ecosystem you will need to use for that, starting from libraries, dependencies, and architecture to implementation and deployment—and also considering things like reusing existing legacy codebases.

Installation and Setup

Now that you have been acquainted with Python and know more about the language, its capabilities, implementations, and versions, we will be talking about which version of Python we will be using in the book and also discussing details on how to set up your development environment and handle package management and virtual environments. This section will give you a good head start on getting things ready for following along with the various hands-on examples we will be covering in this book.

Which Python Version?

The two major Python versions, as mentioned, are the 2.x series and the 3.x series. They are quite similar, although there have been several backward-incompatible changes in the 3.x version, which has led to a huge drift between people who use 2.x and people who use 3.x. Most legacy code and a large majority of Python packages on PyPI were developed in Python 2.7.x, and many package owners do not have the time or will to port all their codebases to Python 3.x, since the effort required would not be minimal. Some of the changes in 3.x are as follows:

- All text strings are Unicode by default.

- `print` and `exec` are now functions and no longer statements.

- `range()` returns a memory-efficient iterable and not a list.

- The style for classes has changed.

- Library and name changes are based on convention and style violations.

To know more about changes introduced since Python 3.0, check `https://docs.python.org/3/whatsnew/3.0.html`, the official documentation listing the changes. That link should give you a pretty good idea of what changes can break your code if you are porting it from Python 2 to Python 3.

As for the problem of selecting which version, there is no absolute answer for this. It purely depends on the problem you are trying to solve and the current code and infrastructure you have and how you will be maintaining this code in the future along with all its necessary dependencies. If you are starting a new project completely and have a fairly good idea that you do not need any external packages and libraries that are solely dependent on Python 2.x, you can go ahead with Python 3.x and start developing your system. But if you have a lot of dependencies on external packages that might break with Python 3.x or that are available for only Python 2.x, you have no choice but to stick with Python 2.x. Besides that, often you have to deal with legacy code that's been around a long time, especially in large companies and organizations that have huge codebases. In that case, porting the whole code to Python 3.x would be wasted effort—kind of re-inventing the wheel, since you are not missing out on major functionality and capabilities by using Python 2.x, and in fact you might even end up breaking the existing code and functionality without even realizing it. In the end, this is a decision left to you, the reader, which you must make carefully considering all scenarios.

We will be using Python 2.7.11 in this book just to be on the safe side, since it is a tried and tested version of Python in all major enterprises. You are most welcome to follow along even in Python 3.x—the algorithms and techniques will be the same, although you may have to take into account changes, such as the fact that the print statement is a function in Python 3.x and so on.

Which Operating System?

There are several popular OSes out there, and everybody has their own preference. The beauty of Python is that is can run seamlessly on any OS without much hassle. The three most popular OSes include the following:

- Windows
- Linux
- OS X (now known as macOS)

You can choose any OS of your choice and use it for following along with the examples in this book. We will be using Windows as the primary OS in this book. This book is aimed at working professionals and practitioners, most of whom in their enterprise environment usually use the enterprise version of Windows. Besides that, several Python external packages are really easy to install on a UNIX-based OS like Linux and macOS. However, sometimes there are major issues in installing them for Windows, so I want to highlight such instances and make sure to address them such that executing any of the code snippets and samples here becomes easy for you. But again, you are most welcome to use any OS of your choice when following the examples in this book.

Integrated Development Environments

Integrated development environments (IDEs) are software products that enable developers to be highly productive by providing a complete suite of tools and capabilities necessary for writing, managing, and executing code. The usual components of an IDE include source editor, debugger, compiler, interpreter, and refactoring and build tools. They also have other capabilities such as code-completion, syntax highlighting, error highlighting and checks, objects, and variable explorers. IDEs can be used to manage entire codebases—much better than trying to write code in a simple text editor, which takes more time. That said, experienced developers often use simple plain text editors to write code, especially if they are working in server environments. You'll find a list of IDEs used specially for Python at https://wiki.python.org/moin/IntegratedDevelopmentEnvironments.

We will be using the Spyder IDE, which comes with the Anaconda Python distribution for writing and executing our code.

Environment Setup

This section covers details regarding how to set up your Python environment with minimal effort and the main components required.

First, head over to the official Python website and download Python 2.7.11 from www.python.org/downloads/. Or download a complete Python distribution with over 700 packages, known as the Anaconda Python distribution, from Continuum Analytics, which is built specially for data science and analytics, at www.continuum.io/downloads. This package provides a lot of advantages, especially for Windows users, where installing some of the packages like numpy and scipy can sometimes cause issues. You can get more information about Anaconda and Continuum Analytics at https://docs.continuum.io/anaconda/index. Anaconda comes with conda, an open source package and environment management system, and Spyder (Scientific Python Development Environment), an IDE for writing and executing your code.

For other OS options, check out the relevant instructions on the website.

Once you have Python downloaded, start the executable and follow the instructions on the screen, clicking the Next button at each stage. But before starting the installation, remember to check the two options shown in Figure 2-1.

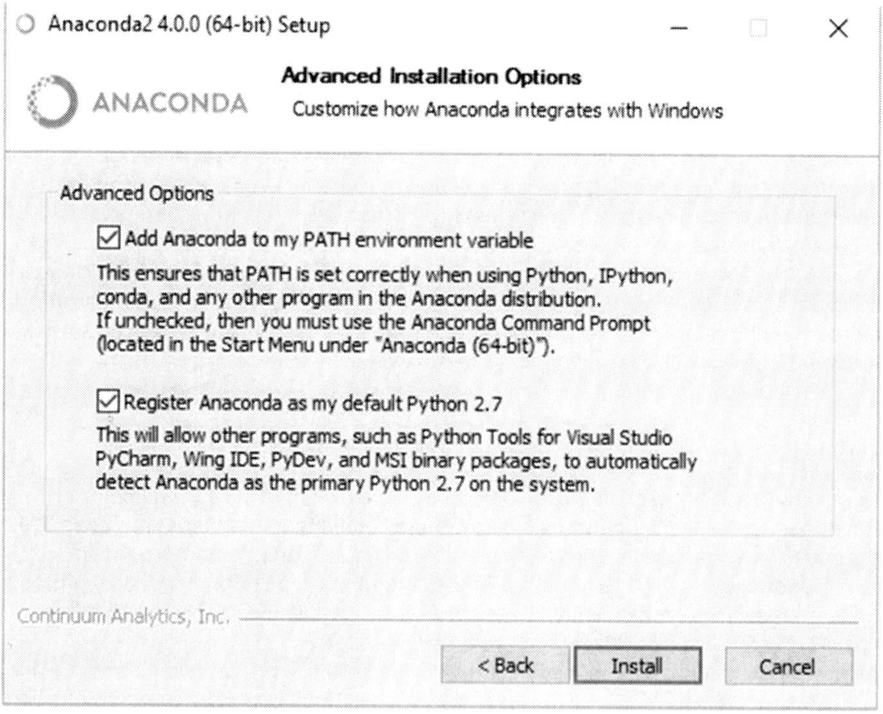

Figure 2-1. Installing the Anaconda Python distribution

Once the installation is complete, either start up Spyder by double-clicking the relevant icon or start the Python or IPython shell from the command prompt. Spyder provides a complete IDE to write and execute code in both the regular Python and IPython shell. Figure 2-2 shows how to run IPython from the command prompt.

```
Command Prompt - ipython                                              —    □    ×
(c) 2015 Microsoft Corporation. All rights reserved.

C:\Users\DIP.DIPSLAPTOP>ipython
Python 2.7.12 |Anaconda 4.0.0 (64-bit)| (default, Jun 29 2016, 11:07:13) [MSC v.1500 64 bit (AMD64)
]
Type "copyright", "credits" or "license" for more information.

IPython 4.1.2 -- An enhanced Interactive Python.
?         -> Introduction and overview of IPython's features.
%quickref -> Quick reference.
help      -> Python's own help system.
object?   -> Details about 'object', use 'object??' for extra details.

In [1]: print 'Welcome to Python!'
Welcome to Python!

In [ ]:
```

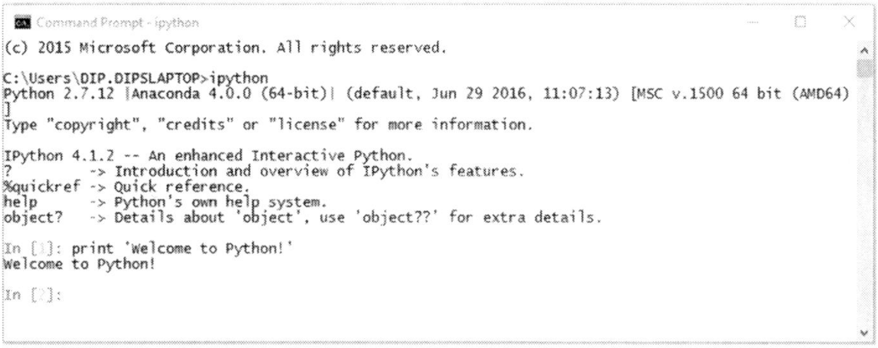

Figure 2-2. *Starting IPython from the command prompt*

Figure 2-2 depicts printing a regular sentence saying *Welcome to Python!* just to show you that Python is properly installed and working fine. The input and output execution history are kept in variables called In and Out, indicated in the figure by the prompt numbers, such as In[1]. IPython provides a lot of advantages including code completion, inline executions and plots, and running code snippets interactively. We will be running most of our snippets in the IPython shell just like the examples seen in Chapter 1.

Now that you have Anaconda installed, you are ready to start running the code samples in this book. Before we move on to the next section, I want to cover package management briefly. You can use either the pip or conda commands to install, uninstall, and upgrade packages. The shell command shown in Figure 2-3 depicts installing the pandas library via pip. Because we already have the library installed, you can use the --upgrade flag as shown in the figure.

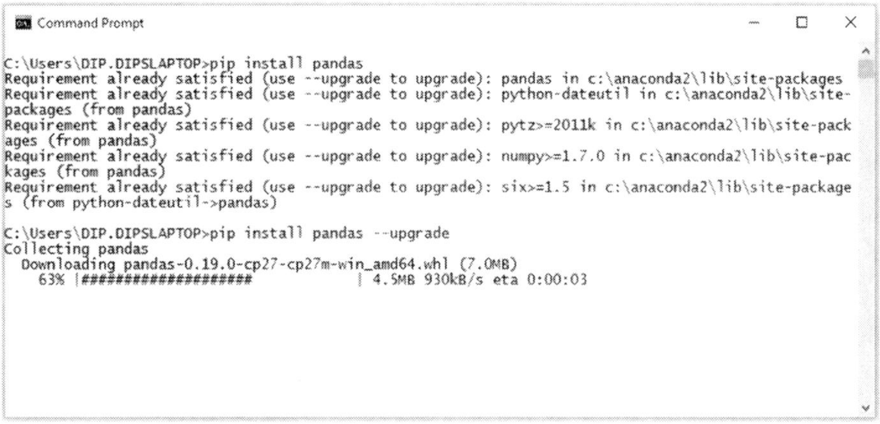

```
Command Prompt                                                        —    □    ×

C:\Users\DIP.DIPSLAPTOP>pip install pandas
Requirement already satisfied (use --upgrade to upgrade): pandas in c:\anaconda2\lib\site-packages
Requirement already satisfied (use --upgrade to upgrade): python-dateutil in c:\anaconda2\lib\site-
packages (from pandas)
Requirement already satisfied (use --upgrade to upgrade): pytz>=2011k in c:\anaconda2\lib\site-pack
ages (from pandas)
Requirement already satisfied (use --upgrade to upgrade): numpy>=1.7.0 in c:\anaconda2\lib\site-pac
kages (from pandas)
Requirement already satisfied (use --upgrade to upgrade): six>=1.5 in c:\anaconda2\lib\site-package
s (from python-dateutil->pandas)

C:\Users\DIP.DIPSLAPTOP>pip install pandas --upgrade
Collecting pandas
  Downloading pandas-0.19.0-cp27-cp27m-win_amd64.whl (7.0MB)
    63% |#####################           | 4.5MB 930kB/s eta 0:00:03
```

Figure 2-3. *Package management using pip*

The conda package manager is better than pip in several aspects because it provides a holistic view of which dependencies are going to be upgraded and the specific versions and other details during installation. Also pip often fails to install some packages in Windows, but conda has no such issues during installation. Figure 2-4 depicts how to manage packages using conda.

```
Command Prompt - conda install pandas                                —    □    ×

C:\Users\DIP.DIPSLAPTOP>conda install pandas
Fetching package metadata .........
Solving package specifications: ..........

Package plan for installation in environment C:\Anaconda2:

The following packages will be downloaded:

    package                        |            build
    ---------------------------|-----------------
    conda-env-2.6.0            |                 0          498 B
    conda-4.2.9               |             py27_0          421 KB
    pandas-0.19.0             |      np111py27_0          7.0 MB
    ---------------------------------------------------------------
                                               Total:          7.4 MB

The following packages will be UPDATED:

    conda:      4.1.12-py27_0        --> 4.2.9-py27_0
    conda-env: 2.5.2-py27_0         --> 2.6.0-0
    pandas:    0.18.0-np110py27_0 --> 0.19.0-np111py27_0

Proceed ([y]/n)?
```

Figure 2-4. *Package management using conda*

Now you have a much better idea of how to install external packages and libraries in Python. This will be useful later when we install some libraries that have been specifically built for text analytics. Your Python environment should now be set up and ready for executing code. Before we dive into the basic and advanced concepts in Python, we will conclude this section with a discussion about virtual environments.

Virtual Environments

A *virtual environment*, or *venv*, is a complete isolated Python environment with its own Python interpreter, libraries, modules, and scripts. This environment is a standalone environment isolated from other virtual environments and the default system-level Python environment. Virtual environments are extremely useful when you have multiple projects or codebases that have dependencies on different versions of the same packages or libraries. For example, if my project TextApp1 depends on nltk 2.0 and another project, TextApp2, depends on nltk 3.0, then it would be impossible to run both projects on the same system. Hence, the need for virtual environments that provide complete isolated environments that can be activated and deactivated as needed.

To set up a virtual environment, you need to install the virtualenv package as follows:

```
E:\Apress>pip install virtualenv
Collecting virtualenv
  Downloading virtualenv-15.0.2-py2.py3-none-any.whl (1.8MB)
    100% |##############################| 1.8MB 290kB/s
Installing collected packages: virtualenv
Successfully installed virtualenv-15.0.2
```

Once installed, you can create a virtual environment as follows, where we create a new project directory called test_proj and create the virtual environment inside the directory:

```
E:\Apress>mkdir test_proj && chdir test_proj
E:\Apress\test_proj>virtualenv venv
New python executable in E:\Apress\test_proj\venv\Scripts\python.exe
Installing setuptools, pip, wheel...done.
```

Once you have installed the virtual environment successfully, you can activate it using the following command:

```
E:\Apress\test_proj>venv\Scripts\activate
(venv) E:\Apress\test_proj>python --version
Python 2.7.11 :: Continuum Analytics, Inc.
```

For other OS platforms, you may need to use the command source venv/bin/activate to activate the virtual environment.

Once the virtual environment is active, you can see the (venv) notation as shown in the preceding code output, and any new packages you install will be placed in the venv folder in complete isolation from the global system Python installation. This difference is illustrated by depicting different versions for the pandas package in the global system Python and the virtual environment Python in the following code:

```
C:\Users\DIP.DIPSLAPTOP>echo 'This is Global System Python'
'This is Global System Python'
C:\Users\DIP.DIPSLAPTOP>pip freeze | grep pandas
pandas==0.18.0

(venv) E:\Apress\test_proj>echo 'This is VirtualEnv Python'
'This is VirtualEnv Python'
(venv) E:\Apress\test_proj>pip install pandas
Collecting pandas
  Downloading pandas-0.18.1-cp27-cp27m-win_amd64.whl (6.2MB)
    100% |##############################| 6.2MB 142kB/s
Installing collected packages: pandas
Successfully installed pandas-0.18.1
(venv) E:\Apress\test_proj>pip freeze | grep pandas
pandas==0.18.1
```

You can see from that code how the pandas package has different versions in the same machine: 0.18.0 for global Python and 0.18.1 for the virtual environment Python. Hence, these isolated virtual environments can run seamlessly on the same system.

Once you have finished working in the virtual environment, you can deactivate it again as follows:

```
(venv) E:\Apress\test_proj>venv\Scripts\deactivate
E:\Apress\test_proj>
```

This will bring you back to the system's default Python interpreter with all its installed libraries. This gives us a good idea about the utility and advantages of virtual environments, and once you start working on several projects, you should definitely consider using it. To find out more about virtual environments, check out http://docs.python-guide.org/en/latest/dev/virtualenvs/, the official documentation for the virtualenv package.

This brings us to the end of our installation and setup activities, and now we will be looking into Python concepts, constructs, syntax, and semantics using hands-on examples.

Python Syntax and Structure

There is a defined hierarchical syntax for Python code that you should remember when writing code. Any big Python application or system is built using several modules, which are themselves comprised of Python statements. Each statement is like a command or direction to the system directing what operations it should perform, and these statements are comprised of expressions and objects. Everything in Python is an object—including functions, data structures, types, classes and so on. This hierarchy is visualized in Figure 2-5.

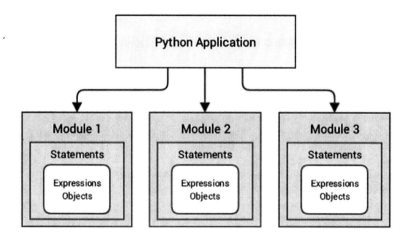

Figure 2-5. *Python program structure hierarchy*

The basic statements consist of objects, expressions which usually make use of objects and process and perform operations on them. Objects can be anything from simple data types and structures to complex objects, including functions and reserved words that have their own specific roles. Python has around 37 *keywords*, or reserved words, which have their own designated roles and functions. Table 2-1 list each keyword in detail, including examples that should be useful and handy when you are using them in your code.

Table 2-1. *Python Reserved Words*

Sl No.	Keyword	Description	Example
1	and	The logical AND operator	`(5==5 and 1==2) == False`
2	as	Used as a synonym to some object/reference	`with open('file.txt') as f`
3	assert	Asserts/checks if some expression is True	`assert 1==2, "Not Equal"`
4	async	Declares a function as asynchronous (co-routine)	`async def get_data():`
5	await	Used to invoke a co-routine	`return await get_data()`
6	break	Breaks out of an executing loop	`while True:` `break`
7	class	Create a class (OOP)	`class ClassifyText(object):`
8	continue	Continue with the next iteration of the loop	`while True:` `if a==1: continue`
9	def	Defines a function	`def add(a,b):` `return a+b`
10	del	Deletes references	`del arr`
11	elif	Else-if conditional	`if num==1: print '1'` `elif num==2: print '2'`
12	else	Else conditional	`if num==1: print '1'` `else: print 'not 1'`
13	except	Catch exceptions	`except ValueError, e: print e`
14	exec	Dynamic execution of code	`exec 'print "Hello Python"'`
15	False	Boolean False	`False == 0`
16	finally	Finally execute statements after try-except	`finally: print 'end of` `exception'`
17	for	The for loop	`for num in arr: print num`
18	from	Import specific components from modules	`from nltk.corpus import` `brown`
19	global	Declare variables as global	`global var`
20	if	If conditional	`if num==1: print '1'`

(continued)

Table 2-1. (*continued*)

SI No.	Keyword	Description	Example
21	import	Import an existing module	`import numpy`
22	in	Check or loop through some existing object	`for num in arr \ if x in y`
23	is	Used to check for equality	`type('a') is str`
24	lambda	Create an anonymous function	`lambda a: a**a`
25	None	Represents no value or null	`num = None`
26	nonlocal	Modify variable values of an outer but non global scope in functions	`nonlocal var`
27	not	The logical NOT operator	`not 1 == 2`
28	or	The logical OR operator	`1 or 2 == 1`
29	pass	Used as a placeholder indicating an empty block	`if a == 1: pass`
30	print	Prints a string or other objects	`print 'Hello World!'`
31	raise	Raises an exception	`raise Exception('overflow')`
32	return	Returns object(s) from a function after exiting	`return a, b`
33	try	Tries a code block and goes to except if exception occurs	`try: read_file()` `except Exception, e: print e`
34	while	The while loop	`while True: print value`
35	with	With an object in an expression perform some operation	`with open('file.txt') as f:` `data = f.read()`
36	yield	Generator functionality, pause and return to the caller	`def generate_func(arr):` `for num in arr: yield num+1`

Table 2-1 shows us all of Python's keywords that are used in statements. However, there are a few caveats to remember. The `async` and `await` keywords are only available in Python 3.5.x onwards. The `exec` and `print` keywords are statements only in Python 2.x—starting from Python 3.x they are functions. The keywords `False`, `True`, and `nonlocal` were introduced starting with Python 3.x in the keywords list.

Python statements usually direct the interpreter as to what they should do when executing the statements. A bunch of statements usually forms a logical block of code. Various constructs including functions and loops and conditionals help in segregating and executing blocks of code using logic and design based on user decisions. Python also focuses a lot on readability—hence, indentation is an important part of Python code. By default, Python does not use punctuation like semicolons to indicate end of statements. It also uses tabs or whitespaces to indicate and delimit specific blocks of code instead of the traditional braces or keywords as used in languages like C, C++, Java, and so on. Python accepts both spaces and tabs as indentation, with the usual norm being one tab or four spaces to indicate each specific block of code. Unindented code will always throw syntax errors, so anyone writing Python code must be extra careful with code formatting and indentation.

Python programs are usually structured around the hierarchy mentioned earlier. Each module is usually a directory with a __init__.py file, which makes the directory a package, and it may have multiple modules, each of which is an individual Python (.py) file. Each module usually has classes and objects like functions that are invoked by other modules and code. All interconnected modules finally make up a complete Python program, application, or system. Usually you start any project by writing necessary code in Python (.py) files and making it modular as it gets bigger by adding more components.

Data Structures and Types

Python has several data types and many are used as data structures for handling data. All data types are derived from the default object data type in Python. This object data type is an abstraction used by Python for managing and handling data. Code and data are all stored and handled by objects and relations among objects. Each object has three things or properties that distinguish it from other objects:

- *Identity*: This is unique and never changes once the object is created and is usually represented by the object's memory address.

- *Type*: This determines the type of object (usually the data type, which is again a child of the base object type).

- *Value*: The actual value stored by the object.

Let's say a variable is holding a string that is one of the data types. To see the three properties in action, you can use the functions depicted in the following code snippet:

```
In [46]: new_string = "This is a String"  # storing a string

In [47]: id(new_string)  # shows the object identifier (address)
Out[47]: 243047144L

In [48]: type(new_string)  # shows the object type
Out[48]: str

In [49]: new_string  # shows the object value
Out[49]: 'This is a String'
```

Python has several data types, including several core data types and complex ones including functions and classes. In this section we will talk about the core data types of Python, including some that are used extensively as data structures to handle data. These core data types are as follows:

- Numeric
- Strings
- Lists
- Sets
- Dictionaries
- Tuples
- Files
- Miscellaneous

Although that's not an exhaustive list, more than 90 percent of your time will be spent writing Python statements that make use of these objects. Let's discuss each of them in more detail to understand their properties and behavior better.

Numeric Types

The numeric data type is perhaps the most common and basic data type in Python. All kinds of applications end up processing and using numbers in some form or the other. There are mainly three numeric types: integers, floats, and complex numbers. Integers are numbers that do not have a fractional part or mantissa after the decimal point. Integers can be represented and operated upon as follows:

```
In [52]: # representing integers and operations on them
In [53]: num = 123

In [54]: type(num)
Out[54]: int

In [55]: num + 1000   # addition
Out[55]: 1123

In [56]: num * 2   # multiplication
Out[56]: 246

In [59]: num /  2   # integer division
Out[59]: 61
```

There are also various types of integers, depending on their radix or base. These include decimal, binary, octal, and hexadecimal integers. Normal nonzero leading sequences of numbers are decimal integers. Integers that start with a 0, or often 0o to prevent making mistakes, are octal integers. Numbers that start with 0x are hexadecimal, and those starting with 0b are binary integers. You can also make use of the bin(), hex(), and oct() functions for converting decimal integers to the respective base form.

The following code snippet illustrates the various forms of integers:

```
In [94]: # decimal
In [95]: 1 + 1
Out[95]: 2

In [96]: # binary
In [97]: bin(2)
Out[97]: '0b10'
In [98]: 0b1 + 0b1
Out[98]: 2
In [99]: bin(0b1 + 0b1)
Out[99]: '0b10'

In [100]: # octal
In [101]: oct(8)
Out[101]: '010'
In [102]: oct(07 + 01)
Out[102]: '010'
In [103]: 0o10
Out[103]: 8

In [104]: # hexadecimal
In [105]: hex(16)
Out[105]: '0x10'
In [106]: 0x10
Out[106]: 16
In [116]: hex(0x16 + 0x5)
Out[116]: '0x1b'
```

Floating point numbers, or floats, are represented as a sequence of numbers that include a decimal point and some numbers following it (the mantissa), an exponent part (e or E followed by a +/- sign followed by digits), or sometimes both of them. Here are some examples of floating point numbers:

```
In [126]: 1.5 + 2.6
Out[126]: 4.1

In [127]: 1e2 + 1.5e3 + 0.5
Out[127]: 1600.5

In [128]: 2.5e4
Out[128]: 25000.0

In [129]: 2.5e-2
Out[129]: 0.025
```

The floating point numbers have a range and precision similar to the double data type in the C language.

Complex numbers have two components, a real and an imaginary component represented by floating point numbers. The imaginary literal consists of the number followed by the letter j, and this symbol j at the end of the literal indicates the square root of –1. The following code snippet shows some representations and operations of complex numbers:

```
In [132]: cnum = 5 + 7j

In [133]: type(cnum)
Out[133]: complex

In [134]: cnum.real
Out[134]: 5.0

In [135]: cnum.imag
Out[135]: 7.0

In [136]: cnum + (1 - 0.5j)
Out[136]: (6+6.5j)
```

Strings

Strings are sequences or collections of characters used to store and represent textual data—which will be our data type of choice in most examples in the book. Strings can be used to store both textual as well as bytes as information. Strings have a wide variety of methods that can be used for handling and manipulating strings, which we will see in detail later in this chapter. An important point to remember is that strings are *immutable*, and any operations performed on strings always creates a new string object (remember the three properties of an object?) rather than just mutating and changing the value of the existing string object.

The following code snippet shows some string representations and some basic operations on strings:

```
In [147]: s1 = 'this is a string'
In [148]: s2 = 'this is "another" string'
In [149]: s3 = 'this is the \'third\' string'
In [150]: s4 = """this is a
     ...: multiline
     ...: string"""

In [151]: print s1, s2, s3, s4
this is a string this is "another" string this is the 'third'
string this is a
multiline
string
```

```
In [152]: print s3 + '\n' + s4
this is the 'third' string
this is a
multiline
string

In [153]: ' '.join([s1, s2])
Out[153]: 'this is a string this is "another" string'

In [154]: s1[::-1]  # reverses the string
Out[154]: 'gnirts a si siht'
```

Lists

Lists are collections of arbitrary heterogeneous or homogenous typed objects. Lists also follow a sequence based on the order in which the objects are present in the list, and each object has its own index with which it can be accessed. Lists are similar to *arrays* in other languages, with the distinction that unlike arrays, which hold homogenous items of the same type, lists can contain different types of objects. A simple example would be a list containing numbers, strings, and even sublists. If a list contains objects that are lists themselves, these are often called *nested* lists.

The following code snippet shows some examples of lists:

```
In [161]: l1 = ['eggs', 'flour', 'butter']
In [162]: l2 = list([1, 'drink', 10, 'sandwiches', 0.45e-2])
In [163]: l3 = [1, 2, 3, ['a', 'b', 'c'], ['Hello', 'Python']]

In [164]: print l1, l2, l3
['eggs', 'flour', 'butter'] [1, 'drink', 10, 'sandwiches', 0.0045] [1, 2, 3,
['a', 'b', 'c'], ['Hello', 'Python']]
```

You can also perform numerous operations on lists, including indexing, slicing, appending, popping, and many more. Some typical operations on lists are depicted in the following code snippet:

```
In [167]: # indexing lists
In [168]: l1
Out[168]: ['eggs', 'flour', 'butter']
In [169]: l1[0]
Out[169]: 'eggs'
In [170]: l1[1]
Out[170]: 'flour'
In [171]: l1[0] +' '+ l1[1]
Out[171]: 'eggs flour'

In [171]: # slicing lists
In [172]: l2[1:3]
Out[172]: ['drink', 10]
```

```
In [173]: numbers = range(10)
In [174]: numbers
Out[174]: [0, 1, 2, 3, 4, 5, 6, 7, 8, 9]
In [175]: numbers[2:5]
Out[175]: [2, 3, 4]
In [180]: numbers[:]
Out[180]: [0, 1, 2, 3, 4, 5, 6, 7, 8, 9]
In [181]: numbers[::2]
Out[181]: [0, 2, 4, 6, 8]

In [181]: # concatenating and mutating lists
In [182]: numbers * 2
Out[182]: [0, 1, 2, 3, 4, 5, 6, 7, 8, 9, 0, 1, 2, 3, 4, 5, 6, 7, 8, 9]
In [183]: numbers + 12
Out[183]: [0, 1, 2, 3, 4, 5, 6, 7, 8, 9, 1, 'drink', 10, 'sandwiches',
          0.0045]

In [184]: # handling nested lists
In [184]: l3
Out[184]: [1, 2, 3, ['a', 'b', 'c'], ['Hello', 'Python']]
In [185]: l3[3]
Out[185]: ['a', 'b', 'c']
In [186]: l3[4]
Out[186]: ['Hello', 'Python']

In [187]: l3.append(' '.join(l3[4]))  # append operation
In [188]: l3
Out[188]: [1, 2, 3, ['a', 'b', 'c'], ['Hello', 'Python'], 'Hello Python']

In [189]: l3.pop(3)  # pop operation
Out[189]: ['a', 'b', 'c']
In [190]: l3
Out[190]: [1, 2, 3, ['Hello', 'Python'], 'Hello Python']
```

Sets

Sets are unordered collections of unique and immutable objects. You can use the set() function or the curly braces {...} to create a new set. Sets are typically used to remove duplicates from a list, test memberships, and perform mathematical set operations, including union, intersection, difference, and symmetric difference.

Some set representations and operations are shown in the following code snippet:

```
In [196]: l1 = [1,1,2,3,5,5,7,9,1]

In [197]: set(l1)  # makes the list as a set
Out[197]: {1, 2, 3, 5, 7, 9}
```

```
In [198]: s1 = set(l1)

# membership testing
In [199]: 1 in s1
Out[199]: True
In [200]: 100 in s1
Out[200]: False

# initialize a second set
In [201]: s2 = {5, 7, 11}

# testing various set operations
In [202]: s1 - s2  # set difference
Out[202]: {1, 2, 3, 9}

In [203]: s1 | s2  # set union
Out[203]: {1, 2, 3, 5, 7, 9, 11}

In [204]: s1 & s2  # set intersection
Out[204]: {5, 7}

In [205]: s1 ^ s2  # elements which do not appear in both sets
Out[205]: {1, 2, 3, 9, 11}
```

Dictionaries

Dictionaries in Python are key-value mappings that are unordered and mutable. They are often known as *hashmaps, associative arrays,* and *associative memories.* Dictionaries are indexed using *keys,* which can be any immutable object type, like numeric types or strings, or even tuples, which we will see later on. Remember that keys should always be some immutable data type. Dictionary values can be immutable or mutable objects, including lists and dictionaries themselves which would lead to nested dictionaries. Dictionaries have a lot of similarity with JSON objects, if you have worked with them previously. Dictionaries are often called dicts in Python, and the dict() function is also used to create new dictionaries.

The following code snippets show some representations and operations on dictionaries:

```
In [207]: d1 = {'eggs': 2, 'milk': 3, 'spam': 10, 'ham': 15}
In [208]: d1
Out[208]: {'eggs': 2, 'ham': 15, 'milk': 3, 'spam': 10}

# retrieving items based on key
In [209]: d1.get('eggs')
Out[209]: 2
In [210]: d1['eggs']
Out[210]: 2
```

```
# get is better than direct indexing since it does not throw errors
In [211]: d1.get('orange')
In [212]: d1['orange']
Traceback (most recent call last):
  File "<ipython-input-212-ebecbf415243>", line 1, in <module>
    d1['orange']
KeyError: 'orange'

# setting items with a specific key
In [213]: d1['orange'] = 25
In [214]: d1
Out[214]: {'eggs': 2, 'ham': 15, 'milk': 3, 'orange': 25, 'spam': 10}

# viewing keys and values
In [215]: d1.keys()
Out[215]: ['orange', 'eggs', 'ham', 'milk', 'spam']
In [216]: d1.values()
Out[216]: [25, 2, 15, 3, 10]

# create a new dictionary using dict function
In [219]: d2 = dict({'orange': 5, 'melon': 17, 'milk': 10})
In [220]: d2
Out[220]: {'melon': 17, 'milk': 10, 'orange': 5}

# update dictionary d1 based on new key-values in d2
In [221]: d1.update(d2)
In [222]: d1
Out[222]: {'eggs': 2, 'ham': 15, 'melon': 17, 'milk': 10, 'orange': 5,
           'spam': 10}

# complex and nested dictionary
In [223]: d3 = {'k1': 5, 'k2': [1,2,3,4,5], 'k3': {'a': 1, 'b': 2, 'c':
          [1,2,3]}}
In [225]: d3
Out[225]: {'k1': 5, 'k2': [1, 2, 3, 4, 5], 'k3': {'a': 1, 'b': 2, 'c':
          [1, 2, 3]}}
In [226]: d3.get('k3')
Out[226]: {'a': 1, 'b': 2, 'c': [1, 2, 3]}
In [227]: d3.get('k3').get('c')
Out[227]: [1, 2, 3]
```

Tuples

Tuples are also sequences like lists, but they are immutable. Typically, tuples are used to represent fixed collections of objects or values. Tuples are created using a comma-separated sequence of values enclosed by parentheses, and optionally the tuple() function can also be used.

The following code snippet shows some representations and operations on tuples:

```
# creating a tuple with a single element
In [234]: single_tuple = (1,)
In [235]: single_tuple
Out[235]: (1,)

# original address of the tuple
In [239]: id(single_tuple)
Out[239]: 176216328L

# modifying contents of the tuple but its location changes (new tuple is
created)
In [240]: single_tuple = single_tuple + (2, 3, 4, 5)
In [241]: single_tuple
Out[241]: (1, 2, 3, 4, 5)
In [242]: id(single_tuple) # different address indicating new tuple with
          same name
Out[242]: 201211312L

# tuples are immutable hence assignment is not supported like lists
In [243]: single_tuple[3] = 100
Traceback (most recent call last):
  File "<ipython-input-247-37d1946d4128>", line 1, in <module>
    single_tuple[3] = 100
TypeError: 'tuple' object does not support item assignment

# accessing and unpacking tuples
In [243]: tup = (['this', 'is', 'list', '1'], ['this', 'is', 'list', '2'])
In [244]: tup[0]
Out[244]: ['this', 'is', 'list', '1']
In [245]: l1, l2 = tup
In [246]: print l1, l2
['this', 'is', 'list', '1'] ['this', 'is', 'list', '2']
```

Files

Files are special types of objects in Python that are used mainly for interfacing with external objects in the filesystem, including text, binary, audio, and video files, plus documents, images, and many more. Some might disagree about it being a data type in Python, but it actually is a special data type, and the name of the type, file, suits its role perfectly for handling all types of external files. You usually use the open() function to open a file, and there are various modes like read and write that are specified using a processing mode character in the function.

Some examples of file handling are show in the following code snippet:

```
In [253]: f = open('text_file.txt', 'w')    # open in write mode
In [254]: f.write("This is some text\n")  # write some text
In [255]: f.write("Hello world!")
In [256]: f.close()  # closes the file

# lists files in current directory
In [260]: import os
In [262]: os.listdir(os.getcwd())
Out[262]: ['text_file.txt']

In [263]: f = open('text_file.txt', 'r')  # opens file in read mode
In [264]: data = f.readlines()  # reads in all lines from file
In [265]: print data  # prints the text data
['This is some text\n', 'Hello world!']
```

Miscellaneous

Besides the already mentioned data types and structures, there are several other Python data types:

- The None type indicates no value/no data or null object.

- Boolean types include True and False.

- Decimal and Fraction types handle numbers in a better way.

This completes the list for Python's core data types and data structures that you will be using most of the time in your code and implementations. We will now discuss some constructs typically used for controlling the flow of code.

Controlling Code Flow

Flow of code is extremely important. A lot of it is based on business logic and rules. It also depends on the type of implementation decisions developers take when building systems and applications. Python provides several control flow tools and utilities that can be used to control the flow of your code. Here are the most popular ones:

- if-elif-else conditionals

- for loop

- while loop

- break, continue, and else in loops

- try-except

These constructs will help you understand several concepts including conditional code flow, looping, and handling exceptions.

Conditional Constructs

The concept of conditional code flow involves executing different blocks of code conditionally based on some user-defined logic implemented in the code itself. It is extremely useful when you do not want to execute a block of statements sequentially one after the other but execute a part of them based on fulfilling or not fulfilling certain conditions. The if-elif-else statements help in achieving this. The general syntax for it is as follows:

```
if <conditional check 1 is True>:    # the if conditional (mandatory)
    <code block 1>   # executed only when check 1 evaluates to True
        ...
    <code block 1>
elif <conditional check 2 is True>:  # the elif conditional (optional)
    <code block 2>   # executed only when check 1 is False and 2 is True
        ...
    <code block 2>
else:                                # the else conditional (optional)
    <code block 3>   # executed only when check 1 and 2 are False
        ...
    <code block 3>
```

An important point to remember from the preceding syntax is that the corresponding code blocks only execute based on satisfying the necessary conditions. Also, only the if statement is mandatory, and the elif and else statements do not need to be mentioned unless there is a need based on conditional logic.

The following examples depict conditional code flow:

```
In [270]: var = 'spam'
In [271]: if var == 'spam':
     ...:         print 'Spam'
     ...:
Spam

In [272]: var = 'ham'
In [273]: if var == 'spam':
     ...:         print 'Spam'
     ...: elif var == 'ham':
     ...:         print 'Ham'
     ...:
Ham
```

```
In [274]: var = 'foo'
In [275]: if var == 'spam':
     ...:     print 'Spam'
     ...: elif var == 'ham':
     ...:     print 'Ham'
     ...: else:
     ...:     print 'Neither Spam or Ham'
     ...:
Neither Spam or Ham
```

Looping Constructs

There are two main types of loops in Python: for and while loops. These looping constructs are used to execute blocks of code repeatedly until some condition is satisfied or the loop exits based on some other statements or conditionals.

The for statement is generally used to loop through items in sequence and usually loops through one or many iterables sequentially, executing the same block of code in each turn. The while statement is used more as a conditional general loop, which stops the loop once some condition is satisfied or runs the loop till some condition is satisfied. Interestingly, there is an optional else statement at the end of the loops that is executed only if the loop exits normally without any break statements. The break statement is often used with a conditional to stop executing all statements in the loop immediately and exit the closest enclosing loop. The continue statement stops executing all statements below it in the loop and brings back control to the beginning of the loop for the next iteration. The pass statement is just used as an empty placeholder—it does not do anything and is often used to indicate an empty code block. These statements constitute the core looping constructs.

The following snippets show the typical syntax normally used when constructing for and while loops:

```
# the for loop
for item in iterable:  # loop through each item in the iterable
    <code block>    # Code block executed repeatedly
else:                   # Optional else
    <code block>    # code block executes only if loop exits normally
                    without 'break'

# the while loop
while <condition>:  # loop till condition is satisfied
    <code block>    # Code block executed repeatedly
else:                   # Optional else
    <code block>    # code block executes only if loop exits normally
                    without 'break'
```

The following examples show how loops work along with the other looping constructs including pass, break, and continue:

```
# illustrating for loops
In [280]: numbers = range(0,5)
In [281]: for number in numbers:
     ...:     print number
     ...:
```

```
0
1
2
3
4
In [282]: sum = 0
In [283]: for number in numbers:
     ...:         sum += number
     ...:
In [284]: print sum
10

# role of the trailing else and break constructs
In [285]: for number in numbers:
     ...:         print number
     ...: else:
     ...:         print 'loop exited normally'
     ...:
0
1
2
3
4
loop exited normally
In [286]: for number in numbers:
     ...:         if number < 3:
     ...:             print number
     ...:         else:
     ...:             break
     ...: else:
     ...:         print 'loop exited normally'
     ...:
0
1
2

# illustrating while loops
In [290]: number = 5
In [291]: while number > 0:
     ...:         print number
     ...:         number -= 1  # important! else loop will keep running
     ...:
5
4
3
2
1
```

```
# role of continue construct
In [295]: number = 10
In [296]: while number > 0:
    ...:        if number % 2 != 0:
    ...:               number -=1 # decrement but do not print odd numbers
    ...:               continue  # go back to beginning of loop for next
iteration
    ...:        print number  # print even numbers and decrement count
    ...:        number -= 1
    ...:
10
8
6
4
2
```

```
# role of the pass construct
In [297]: number = 10
In [298]: while number > 0:
    ...:        if number % 2 != 0:
    ...:               pass # don't print odds
    ...:        else:
    ...:               print number
    ...:        number -= 1
    ...:
10
8
6
4
2
```

Handling Exceptions

Exceptions are specific events that are either triggered when some unnatural error occurs or manually. They are used extensively for error handling, event notifications, and controlling code flow. Using constructs like try-except-finally, you can make Python raise exceptions when executing code whenever any error occurs at runtime. This would also enable you to catch these exceptions and handle them as needed or ignore them altogether. In Python versions prior to 2.5.x, there were generally two versions of exception handling using the try construct. One would be try-finally, and the other would involve try-except and optionally an else clause at the end for catching exceptions. Now we have a construct that includes them all, the try-except-else-finally construct, which can be used for exception handling. The syntax is depicted as follows:

```
try:                        # The try statement
    <main code block>       # Checks for errors in this block
except <ExceptionType1>:        # Catch different exceptions
```

```
    <exception handler 1>
except <ExceptionType2>:
    <exception handler 2>
...
else:                              # Optional else statement
    <optional else block>  # Executes only if there were no exceptions
finally:                           # The finally statement
    <finally block>        # Always executes in the end
```

The flow of code in the preceding code snippet starts from the try statement and the main code block in it, which is executed first and checked for any exceptions. If any exceptions occur, they are matched based on the exception types as depicted in the preceding snippet. Assuming ExceptionType1 matches, the exception handler for ExceptionType1 is executed, which is exception handler 1. In case no exceptions were raised, only then the optional else block is executed. The finally block is always executed irrespective of any exceptions being raised or not.

The following examples depict the use of the try-except-else-finally construct:

```
In [311]: shopping_list = ['eggs', 'ham', 'bacon']
# trying to access a non-existent item in the list
In [312]: try:
    ...:        print shopping_list[3]
    ...: except IndexError as e:
    ...:        print 'Exception: '+str(e)+' has occurred'
    ...: else:
    ...:        print 'No exceptions occurred'
    ...: finally:
    ...:        print 'I will always execute no matter what!'
    ...:
Exception: list index out of range has occurred
I will always execute no matter what!
# smooth code execution without any errors
In [313]: try:
    ...:        print shopping_list[2]
    ...: except IndexError as e:
    ...:        print 'Exception: '+str(e)+' has occurred'
    ...: else:
    ...:        print 'No exceptions occurred'
    ...: finally:
    ...:        print 'I will always execute no matter what!'
    ...:
bacon
No exceptions occurred
I will always execute no matter what!
```

This brings us to the end of our discussion on the core constructs for controlling flow of code in Python. The next section covers some core concepts and constructs that are parts of the functional programming paradigm in Python.

Functional Programming

The functional programming paradigm is a style of programming with origins in lambda calculus. It treats any form of computation purely on the basis of executing and evaluating functions. Python is not a pure functional programming language but does have several constructs that can be used for functional programming. In this section we will talk about several of these constructs, including functions and some advanced concepts like generators, iterators, and comprehensions. We will also look at modules like itertools and functools that contain implementation of functional tools based on concepts from Haskell and Standard ML.

Functions

A *function* can be defined as a block of code that is executed only on request by invoking it. Functions consist of a function definition that has the function signature (function name, parameters) and a group of statements inside the function that are executed when the function is called. The Python standard library provides a huge suite of functions to choose from to perform different types of operations. Besides this, users can define their own functions using the def keyword.

Functions usually return some value always, and even when they do not return a value, by default they return the None type. One important thing to remember is that often you may see methods and functions being used interchangeably, but the distinction between functions and methods is that methods are functions that are defined within class statements. Functions are also objects, since each and every type and construct in Python is derived from the base object type. This opens up a whole new dimension where you can even pass functions as parameters or arguments to other functions. Moreover, functions can be bound to variables and even returned as results from other functions. Hence functions are often known as first-class objects in Python.

The following code snippet shows the basic structure of a function definition in Python:

```
def function(params):  # params are the input parameters
    <code block>       # code block consists of a group of statements
    return value(s)    # optional return statement
```

The params indicate the list of input parameters, which are not mandatory, and in many functions there are actually no input parameters. You can even pass functions themselves as parameters. Some logic executes in the code block, which may or may not modify the input parameters, and finally you may return some output values or not return anything entirely.

The following code snippets demonstrate some basic examples of functions with fixed arguments, variable arguments, and built-in functions:

```
# function with single argument
In [319]: def square(number):
    ...:       return number*number
    ...:
```

```
In [320]: square(5)
Out[320]: 25

# built-in function from the numpy library
In [321]: import numpy as np
In [322]: np.square(5)
Out[322]: 25

# a more complex function with variable number of arguments
In [323]: def squares(*args):
     ...:     squared_args = []
     ...:     for item in args:
     ...:         squared_args.append(item*item)
     ...:     return squared_args
     ...:
In [324]: squares(1,2,3,4,5)
Out[324]: [1, 4, 9, 16, 25]
```

The preceding example shows how to introduce variable number of arguments in a function dynamically. You can also introduce keyword arguments, where each argument has its own variable name and value, as illustrated in the following code snippet:

```
# assign specific keyword based arguments dynamically
In [325]: def person_details(**kwargs):
     ...:     for key, value in kwargs.items():
     ...:         print key, '->', value
     ...:
In [326]: person_details(name='James Bond', alias='007', job='Secret Service
          Agent')
alias -> 007
job -> Secret Service Agent
name -> James Bond
```

Recursive Functions

Recursive functions use the concept of *recursion*, wherein the function calls itself inside its code block. Care should be taken to make sure there is a stopping condition that ultimately terminates the recursive calls—otherwise the function will run into an endless loop of execution where it goes on calling itself. Recursion makes use of the call stack at each recursive call, hence they are often not very efficient compared to regular functions; nevertheless, they are extremely powerful.

The following example depicts our squares function using recursion:

```
# using recursion to square numbers
In [331]: def recursive_squares(numbers):
     ...:     if not numbers:
     ...:         return []
```

```
    ...:       else:
    ...:              return [numbers[0]*numbers[0]] + recursive_
                      squares(numbers[1:])
    ...:
In [332]: recursive_squares([1, 2, 3, 4, 5])
Out[332]: [1, 4, 9, 16, 25]
```

Anonymous Functions

Anonymous functions are functions that do not have any name and usually consist of a one-line expression that denotes a function using the lambda construct. The lambda keyword is used to define inline function objects that can be used just like regular functions, with a few differences. The general syntax for a lambda function is shown in the following code snippet:

```
lambda arg, arg2,... arg_n : <inline expression using args>
```

This expression can actually be even assigned to variables and then executed as a normal function call similar to functions created with def. However, lambda functions are expressions and never statements like the code block inside a def, and so it is extremely difficult to put complex logic inside a lambda function because it is always a single-lined inline expression. However, lambda functions are very powerful and are even used inside lists, functions, and function arguments. Besides lambda functions, Python also provides functions like map(), reduce(), and filter(), which make extensive use of lambda functions and apply them to iterables usually to transform, reduce, or filter respectively.

The following code snippet depicts some examples of lambda functions used with the constructs we just talked about:

```
# simple lambda function to square a number
In [340]: lambda_square = lambda n: n*n
In [341]: lambda_square(5)
Out[341]: 25

# map function to square numbers using lambda
In [342]: map(lambda_square, [1, 2, 3, 4, 5])
Out[342]: [1, 4, 9, 16, 25]

# lambda function to find even numbers used for filtering
In [343]: lambda_evens = lambda n: n%2 == 0
In [344]: filter(lambda_evens, [1, 2, 3, 4, 5, 6, 7, 8, 9, 10])
Out[344]: [2, 4, 6, 8, 10]

# lambda function to add numbers used for adding numbers in reduce function
In [345]: lambda_sum = lambda x, y: x + y
In [346]: reduce(lambda_sum, [1, 2, 3, 4, 5])
Out[346]: 15
```

```
# lambda function to make a sentence from word tokens with reduce function
In [347]: lambda_sentence_maker = lambda word1, word2: ' '.join([word1,
          word2])
In [348]: reduce(lambda_sentence_maker, ['I', 'am', 'making', 'a',
          'sentence', 'from', 'words!'])
Out[348]: 'I am making a sentence from words!'
```

The preceding examples should give you a pretty good idea about how lambda functions work and how powerful they are. Using a one-line construct you can create free-flowing sentences from word tokens and calculate a sum of numbers in a list! The possibilities of using lambda functions are endless, and you can use them to solve even the most complex of problems.

Iterators

Iterators are constructs used to iterate through iterables. *Iterables* are objects that are basically sequences of other objects and data. A good example would be a for loop, which is actually an iterable that iterates through a list or sequence. Iterators are objects or constructs that can be used to iterate through iterables using the next()function, which returns the next item from the iterable at each call. Once it has iterated through the entire iterable, it returns a StopIteration exception. We have seen how a for loop works in general, however behind the abstraction, the for loop actually calls the iter() function on the iterable to create an iterator object and then traverses through it using the next() function.

The following example illustrates how iterators work:

```
# typical for loop
In [350]: numbers = range(6)
In [351]: for number in numbers:
     ...:     print number
0
1
2
3
4
5

# illustrating how iterators work behind the scenes
In [352]: iterator_obj = iter(numbers)
In [353]: while True:
     ...:     try:
     ...:         print iterator_obj.next()
     ...:     except StopIteration:
     ...:         print 'Reached end of sequence'
     ...:         break
0
1
2
```

```
3
4
5
Reached end of sequence

# calling next now would throw the StopIteration exception as expected
In [354]: iterator_obj.next()
Traceback (most recent call last):
  File "<ipython-input-354-491178c4f97a>", line 1, in <module>
    iterator_obj.next()
StopIteration
```

Comprehensions

Comprehensions are interesting constructs that are similar to for loops but more efficient. They fall rightly into the functional programming paradigm following the set builder notation. Originally, the idea for list comprehensions came from Haskell, and after a series of lengthy discussions comprehensions were finally added and have been one of the most used constructs ever since. There are various types of comprehensions that can be applied on existing data types, including list, set, and dict comprehensions. The following code snippet shows the syntax of comprehensions using the very common list comprehensions and for loops, a core component in comprehensions:

```
# typical comprehension syntax
[ expression for item in iterable ]

# equivalent for loop statement
for item in iterable:
    expression

# complex and nested iterations
[ expression for item1 in iterable1 if condition1
             for item2 in iterable2 if condition2 ...
             for itemN in iterableN if conditionN ]

# equivalent for loop statement
for item1 in iterable1:
    if condition1:
        for item2 in iterable2:
            if condition2:
                ...
                    for itemN in iterableN:
                        if conditionN:
                            expression
```

This gives us an idea of how similar comprehensions are to looping constructs. The benefit we get is that they are more efficient and perform better than loops. Some caveats include that you cannot use assignment statements in comprehensions because, if you remember the syntax from earlier, they support only expressions and not statements. The same syntax is used by set and dictionary comprehensions too.

The following examples illustrate the use of different comprehensions:

```
In [355]: numbers = range(6)
In [356]: numbers
Out[356]: [0, 1, 2, 3, 4, 5]

# simple list comprehension to compute squares
In [357]: [num*num for num in numbers]
Out[357]: [0, 1, 4, 9, 16, 25]

# list comprehension to check if number is divisible by 2
In [358]: [num%2 for num in numbers]
Out[358]: [0, 1, 0, 1, 0, 1]

# set comprehension returns distinct values of the above operation
In [359]: set(num%2 for num in numbers)
Out[359]: {0, 1}

# dictionary comprehension where key:value is number: square(number)
In [361]: {num: num*num for num in numbers}
Out[361]: {0: 0, 1: 1, 2: 4, 3: 9, 4: 16, 5: 25}

# a more complex comprehension showcasing above operations in a single
comprehension
In [362]: [{'number': num,
            'square': num*num,
            'type': 'even' if num%2 == 0 else 'odd'} for num in numbers]
Out[362]:
[{'number': 0, 'square': 0, 'type': 'even'},
 {'number': 1, 'square': 1, 'type': 'odd'},
 {'number': 2, 'square': 4, 'type': 'even'},
 {'number': 3, 'square': 9, 'type': 'odd'},
 {'number': 4, 'square': 16, 'type': 'even'},
 {'number': 5, 'square': 25, 'type': 'odd'}]

# nested list comprehension - flattening a list of lists
In [364]: list_of_lists = [[1, 2, 3, 4], [5, 6, 7, 8], [9, 10, 11, 12]]
In [365]: list_of_lists
Out[365]: [[1, 2, 3, 4], [5, 6, 7, 8], [9, 10, 11, 12]]
In [367]: [item for each_list in list_of_lists for item in each_list]
Out[367]: [1, 2, 3, 4, 5, 6, 7, 8, 9, 10, 11, 12]
```

Generators

Generators are powerful, memory-efficient constructs for creating and consuming iterators. They exist in two variants: functions and expressions. Generators work on a concept known as *lazy evaluation*—hence, they are more memory efficient and perform better in most cases because they do not require the entire object to be evaluated and loaded in one go, as in list comprehensions. However, the caveat is that because generators yield one item at a time in an ad hoc fashion, there is a chance that they may perform worse in terms of execution time compared to list comprehensions, unless you are dealing with large objects with many elements.

Generator functions are implemented as regular functions using the def statement. However, they use the concept of lazy evaluation and return one object at a time using the yield statement. Unlike regular functions that have a return statement, which once executed ends the execution of the code block inside the function, generators use the yield statement, which suspends and resumes execution and the state after generating and returning each value or object. To be more precise, generator functions yield values at each step rather than returning them. This ensures that the current state including information about the local code block scope it retained and enables the generator to resume from where it left off.

The following snippet shows some examples for generator functions:

```
In [369]: numbers = [1, 2, 3, 4, 5]

In [370]: def generate_squares(numbers):
     ...:     for number in numbers:
     ...:         yield number*number

In [371]: gen_obj = generate_squares(numbers)
In [372]: gen_obj
Out[372]: <generator object generate_squares at 0x000000000F2FC2D0>
In [373]: for item in gen_obj:
     ...:     print item
     ...:
1
4
9
16
25
```

The advantages of these generators are both memory efficiency and execution time, especially when iterables and objects are large in size and occupy substantial memory. You also do not need to load whole objects into the main memory for performing various operations on them. They often work very well on streaming data where you cannot keep all the data in memory at all times. The same applies for generator expressions, which are very similar to comprehensions except they are enclosed in parentheses.

The following example illustrates:

```
In [381]: csv_string = 'The,fox,jumps,over,the,dog'

# making a sentence using list comprehension
In [382]: list_cmp_obj = [item for item in csv_string.split(',')]
In [383]: list_cmp_obj
Out[383]: ['The', 'fox', 'jumps', 'over', 'the', 'dog']
In [384]: ' '.join(list_cmp_obj)
Out[384]: 'The fox jumps over the dog'

# making a sentence using generator expression
In [385]: gen_obj = (item for item in csv_string.split(','))
In [386]: gen_obj
Out[386]: <generator object <genexpr> at 0x000000000F2FC3F0>
In [387]: ' '.join(gen_obj)
Out[387]: 'The fox jumps over the dog'
```

Both generator functions and expressions create generator objects that use the same construct as iterators and starts, stops, and resumes the function or loop at each stage, and once it is completed it raises the StopIteration exception.

The itertools and functools Modules

Various modules which are available in the Python standard library. Some of the popular ones include collections, itertools, and functools, which have various constructs and functions that can be used to boost productivity and reduce time spent writing extra code to solve problems. The itertools module is a complete module dedicated to building and operating on iterators. It has various functions that support different operations including slicing, chaining, grouping, and splitting iterators. The most comprehensive source of information for itertools is available in the official Python documentation at https://docs.python.org/2/library/itertools.html. The documentation lists each function and its role with examples. The functools module provides with functions, which enable concepts from functional programming, including wrappers and partials. These functions usually act on other functions, which it takes as input parameters and often returns a function as the result itself. The official documentation at https://docs.python.org/2/library/functools.html provides extensive information on each function.

Classes

Python classes are constructs that enable us to write code following the OOP paradigm. Concepts like objects, encapsulation, methods, inheritance, and polymorphism are heavily used in this paradigm. If you have worked on any OOP language before, like C++ or Java, chances are you will find using Python classes relatively similar to using classes in other languages. Discussing each concept would be beyond the scope of this book, but I will briefly cover the basic concepts of classes and touch up on different types of objects and inheritance.

91

Classes are basically a software model or abstraction of real-world entities that are objects. This abstraction leads to classes being called as a user-defined type, and once you define a class, you can instantiate and create instances or objects of that class. Each object has its own instance variables and methods that define the properties and behavior of that object. All classes inherit from the base object type, and you can create your own classes and inherit further classes from these user-defined classes. Classes are also ultimately objects on their own and can be bound to variables and other constructs.

The following snippet gives the basic syntax for a class:

```
class ClassName(BaseClass):
    class_variable  # shared by all instances\objects

    def __init__(self, ...): # the constructor
        # instance variables unique to each instance\object
        self.instance_variables = ...

    def __str__(self):  # string representation of the instance\object
        return repr(self)

    def methods(self, ...):  # instance methods
        <code block>
```

The preceding snippet tells us that the class named ClassName inherits from its parent class BaseClass. There can be more than one parent or base class in the parameters separated by commas. The __init__() method acts as a constructor that instantiates and creates an object of the class using the call ClassName(...), which automatically invokes the __init__() method—which may optionally take parameters based on its definition. The __str__() method is optional. It prints the string representation of the object. You can modify the default method with your own definition, and it is often used to print the current state of the object variables. The class_variable indicates class variables that are defined in the block just enclosing the class definition, and these class variables are shared by all objects or instances of the class. The instance_variables are variables that are specific to each object or instance. The methods denote instance methods that define specific behavior of the objects. The self parameter is usually used as the first parameter in methods, which is more of a convention that refers to the instance or object of ClassName on which you call the method.

The following example depicts a simple class and how it works:

```
# class definition
In [401]: class Animal(object):
     ...:         species = 'Animal'
     ...:
     ...:         def __init__(self, name):
     ...:             self.name = name
     ...:             self.attributes = []
     ...:
     ...:         def add_attributes(self, attributes):
     ...:             self.attributes.extend(attributes) \
```

```
        ...:                    if type(attributes) == list \
        ...:                    else self.attributes.append(attributes)
        ...:
        ...:        def __str__(self):
        ...:            return self.name+" is of type "+self.species+" and has
                       attributes:"+str(self.attributes)
        ...:
```

```
# instantiating the class
In [402]: a1 = Animal('Rover')
# invoking instance method
In [403]: a1.add_attributes(['runs', 'eats', 'dog'])
# user defined string representation of the Animal class
In [404]: str(a1)
Out[404]: "Rover is of type Animal and has attributes:['runs', 'eats',
          'dog']"
```

This gives us an idea of how classes work. But what if we want to target specific animals like *dogs* and *foxes*? We can apply the concept of inheritance and use the super() method to access the constructor of the base Animal class in each definition. The following examples illustrate the concept of inheritance:

```
# deriving class Dog from base class Animal
In [413]: class Dog(Animal):
     ...:        species = 'Dog'
     ...:
     ...:        def __init__(self, *args):
     ...:            super(Dog, self).__init__(*args)
```

```
# deriving class Fox from base class Animal
In [414]: class Fox(Animal):
     ...:        species = 'Fox'
     ...:
     ...:        def __init__(self, *args):
     ...:            super(Fox, self).__init__(*args)
```

```
# creating instance of class Dog
In [415]: d1 = Dog('Rover')
In [416]: d1.add_attributes(['lazy', 'beige', 'sleeps', 'eats'])
In [417]: str(d1)
Out[417]: "Rover is of type Dog and has attributes:['lazy', 'beige',
          'sleeps', 'eats']"
```

```
# creating instance of class Fox
In [418]: f1 = Fox('Silver')
In [419]: f1.add_attributes(['quick', 'brown', 'jumps', 'runs'])
In [420]: str(f1)
Out[420]: "Silver is of type Fox and has attributes:['quick', 'brown',
          'jumps', 'runs']"
```

Working with Text

We have seen most of the constructs, data types, structures, concepts, and programming paradigms associated with Python in the previous sections. This section briefly covers specific data types tailored to handle text data and shows how these data types and their associated utilities will be useful for us in the future chapters. The main data types used to handle text data in Python are strings, which can be normal strings, bytes storing binary information, or Unicode. By default, all strings are Unicode in Python 3.x, but they are not so in Python 2.x, and this is something you should definitely keep in mind when dealing with text in different Python distributions. Strings are a sequence of characters in Python similar to arrays and code with a set of attributes and methods that can be leveraged to manipulate and operate on text data easily, which makes Python the language of choice for text analytics in many scenarios. We will discuss various types of strings with several examples in the next section.

String Literals

There are various types of strings, as mentioned earlier, and you saw a few examples in one of the previous sections regarding data types. The following BNF (Backus-Naur Form) gives us the general lexical definitions for producing strings as seen in the official Python docs:

```
stringliteral   ::=  [stringprefix](shortstring | longstring)
stringprefix    ::=  "r" | "u" | "ur" | "R" | "U" | "UR" | "Ur" | "uR"
                     | "b" | "B" | "br" | "Br" | "bR" | "BR"
shortstring     ::=  "'" shortstringitem* "'" | '"' shortstringitem* '"'
longstring      ::=  "'''" longstringitem* "'''" | '"""' longstringitem*
'"""'
shortstringitem ::=  shortstringchar | escapeseq
longstringitem  ::=  longstringchar | escapeseq
shortstringchar ::=  <any source character except "\" or newline or the
quote>
longstringchar  ::=  <any source character except "\">
escapeseq       ::=  "\" <any ASCII character>
```

The preceding rules tell us that different types of string prefixes exist that can be used with different string types to produce string literals. In simple terms, the following types of string literals are used the most:

- *Short strings*: These strings are usually enclosed with single (') or double quotes (") around the characters. Some examples would be, 'Hello' and "Hello".

- *Long strings*: These strings are usually enclosed with three single (''') or double quotes (""") around the characters. Some examples would be, """Hello, I'm a long string""" or '''Hello I\'m a long string '''. Note the (\'), indicates an escape sequence discussed in the next bullet.

- *Escape sequences in strings*: These strings often have escape sequences embedded in them, where the rule for escape sequences starts with a backslash (\) followed by any ASCII character. Hence, they perform backspace interpolation. Popular escape sequences include (\n), indicating a new line character, and (\t), indicating a tab.

- *Bytes*: These are used to represent bytestrings, which create objects of the bytes data type. These strings can be created as bytes('...') or using the b'...' notation. Examples would be bytes('hello') and b'hello'.

- *Raw strings*: These strings were originally created specifically for regular expressions (regex) and creating regex patterns. These strings can be created using the r'...' notation and keep the string in its raw or native form. Hence, it does not perform any backspace interpolation and turns off the escape sequences. An example would be r'Hello'.

- *Unicode*: These strings support Unicode characters in text and are usually non-ASCII character sequences. These strings are denoted with the u'...' notation. Besides the string notation, there are several specific ways to represent special Unicode characters in the string. The usual include the hex byte value escape sequence of the format '\xVV'. Besides this, we also have Unicode escape sequences of the form '\uVVVV' and '\uVVVVVVVV', where the first form uses 4 hex-digits for encoding a 16-bit character, and the second uses 8 hex digits for encoding a 32-bit character. Some examples would be u 'H\xe8llo' and u 'H\u00e8llo' which represents the string 'Hèllo'.

The following code snippet depicts these different types of string literals and their output:

```
# simple string
In [422]: simple_string = 'hello' + " I'm a simple string"
In [423]: print simple_string
hello I'm a simple string

# multi-line string, note the \n (newline) escape character automatically
created
In [424]: multi_line_string = """Hello I'm
    ...: a multi-line
    ...: string!"""
In [425]: multi_line_string
Out[425]: "Hello I'm\na multi-line\nstring!"
In [426]: print multi_line_string
Hello I'm
a multi-line
string!
```

```
# Normal string with escape sequences leading to a wrong file path!
In [427]: escaped_string = "C:\the_folder\new_dir\file.txt"
In [428]: print escaped_string  # will cause errors if we try to open a file
          here
C:      he_folder
ew_dirile.txt

# raw string keeping the backslashes in its normal form
In [429]: raw_string = r'C:\the_folder\new_dir\file.txt'
In [430]: print raw_string
C:\the_folder\new_dir\file.txt

# unicode string literals
In [431]: string_with_unicode = u'H\u00e8llo!'
     ...: print string_with_unicode
Hèllo!
```

String Operations and Methods

Strings are iterable sequences, which means a lot of operations can be performed on them, useful especially when processing and parsing textual data into easy-to-consume formats. Several operations can be performed on strings. I have categorized them into the following segments:

- Basic operations

- Indexing and slicing

- Methods

- Formatting

- Regular expressions

These would cover the most frequently used techniques for working with strings and form the base of what we would need to get started in the next chapter (where we look at understanding and processing textual data based on concepts we learned in the first two chapters).

Basic Operations

You can perform several basic operations on strings, including concatenation and checking for substrings, characters, and lengths. The following code snippet illustrates these operations with some examples:

```
# Different ways of String concatenation
In [436]: 'Hello' + ' and welcome ' + 'to Python!'
Out[436]: 'Hello and welcome to Python!'
In [437]: 'Hello' ' and welcome ' 'to Python!'
Out[437]: 'Hello and welcome to Python!'
```

```
# concatenation of variables and literals
In [438]: s1 = 'Python!'
In [439]: 'Hello ' + s1
Out[439]: 'Hello Python!'
# we cannot concatenate a variable and a literal using this method
In [440]: 'Hello ' s1
  File "<ipython-input-440-2f801ddf3480>", line 1
    'Hello ' s1
             ^
SyntaxError: invalid syntax

# some more ways of concatenating strings
In [442]: s2 = '--Python--'
In [443]: s2 * 5
Out[443]: '--Python----Python----Python----Python----Python--'
In [444]: s1 + s2
Out[444]: 'Python!--Python--'
In [445]: (s1 + s2)*3
Out[445]: 'Python!--Python--Python!--Python--Python!--Python--'

# concatenating several strings together in parentheses
In [446]: s3 = ('This '
   ...:         'is another way '
   ...:         'to concatenate '
   ...:         'several strings!')
In [447]: s3
Out[447]: 'This is another way to concatenate several strings!'

# checking for substrings in a string
In [448]: 'way' in s3
Out[448]: True
In [449]: 'python' in s3
Out[449]: False
# computing total length of the string
In [450]: len(s3)
Out[450]: 51
```

Indexing and Slicing

As mentioned, strings are iterables—ordered sequences of characters. Hence they can be indexed, sliced, and iterated through similarly to other iterables such as lists. Each character has a specific position in the string, called its *index*. Using indexes, we can access specific parts of the string. Accessing a single character using a specific position or index in the string is called *indexing*, and accessing a part of a string, for example, a substring using a start and end index, is called *slicing*. Python supports two types of indexes. One starts from 0 and increases by 1 each time per character till the end of the string. The other starts from –1 at the end of the string and decreases by 1 each time for each character till the beginning of the string. Figure 2-6 shows the two types of indexes for the string 'PYTHON'.

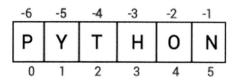

Figure 2-6. *String indexing syntax*

To access any particular character in the string, you need to use the corresponding index, and slices can be extracted using the syntax var[start:stop], which extracts all characters in the string var from index start till index stop excluding the character at the stop index.

The following examples shows how to index, slice, and iterate through strings:

```
# creating a string
In [460]: s = 'PYTHON'

# depicting string indexes
In [461]: for index, character in enumerate(s):
    ...:       print 'Character', character+':', 'has index:', index
Character P: has index: 0
Character Y: has index: 1
Character T: has index: 2
Character H: has index: 3
Character O: has index: 4
Character N: has index: 5

# string indexing
In [462]: s[0], s[1], s[2], s[3], s[4], s[5]
Out[462]: ('P', 'Y', 'T', 'H', 'O', 'N')
In [463]: s[-1], s[-2], s[-3], s[-4], s[-5], s[-6]
Out[463]: ('N', 'O', 'H', 'T', 'Y', 'P')

# string slicing
In [464]: s[:]
Out[464]: 'PYTHON'    # prints whole string when no indexes are specified
In [465]: s[1:4]
Out[465]: 'YTH'
In [466]: s[:3]
Out[466]: 'PYT'
In [467]: s[3:]
Out[467]: 'HON'
```

```
In [468]: s[-3:]
Out[468]: 'HON'
In [469]: s[:3] + s[3:]
Out[469]: 'PYTHON'
In [470]: s[:3] + s[-3:]
Out[470]: 'PYTHON'

# string slicing with offsets
In [472]: s[::1]  # no offset
Out[472]: 'PYTHON'
In [473]: s[::2]  # print every 2nd character in string
Out[473]: 'PTO'

# strings are immutable hence assignment throws error
In [476]: s[0] = 'X'
Traceback (most recent call last):
  File "<ipython-input-476-2cd5921aae94>", line 1, in <module>
    s[0] = 'X'
TypeError: 'str' object does not support item assignment

# creates a new string
In [477]: 'X' + s[1:]
Out[477]: 'XYTHON'
```

Methods

Strings and Unicode put a huge arsenal of built-in methods at your disposal, which you can use for performing various transformations, manipulations, and operations on strings. Although discussing each method in detail would be beyond the current scope, the official Python documentation at https://docs.python.org/2/library/stdtypes. html#string-methods provides all the information you need about each and every method, along with syntax and definitions. Methods are extremely useful and increase your productivity because you do not have to spend extra time writing boilerplate code to handle and manipulate strings.

The following code snippets show some popular examples of string methods in action:

```
# case conversions
In [484]: s = 'python is great'
In [485]: s.capitalize()
Out[485]: 'Python is great'
In [486]: s.upper()
Out[486]: 'PYTHON IS GREAT'

# string replace
In [487]: s.replace('python', 'analytics')
Out[487]: 'analytics is great'
```

```
# string splitting and joining
In [488]: s = 'I,am,a,comma,separated,string'
In [489]: s.split(',')
Out[489]: ['I', 'am', 'a', 'comma', 'separated', 'string']
In [490]: ' '.join(s.split(','))
Out[490]: 'I am a comma separated string'

# stripping whitespace characters
In [497]: s = '   I am surrounded by spaces      '
In [498]: s
Out[498]: '   I am surrounded by spaces      '
In [499]: s.strip()
Out[499]: 'I am surrounded by spaces'

# coverting to title case
In [500]: s = 'this is in lower case'
In [501]: s.title()
Out[501]: 'This Is In Lower Case'
```

The preceding examples just scratch the surface of the numerous manipulations and operations possible on strings. Feel free to try out other operations using different methods mentioned in the docs. We will use several of them in subsequent chapters.

Formatting

String formatting is used to substitute specific data objects and types in a string. This is mostly used when displaying text to the user. There are mainly two different types of formatting used for strings:

- *Formatting expressions*: These expressions are typically of the syntax '...%s...%s...' %(values), where the %s denotes a placeholder for substituting a string from the list of strings depicted in values. This is quite similar to the C style printf model and has been there in Python since the beginning. You can substitute values of other types with the respective alphabet following the % symbol, like %d for integers and %f for floating point numbers.

- *Formatting methods*: These strings take the form of '...{}...{}...'.format(values), which makes use of the braces {} for placeholders to place strings from values using the format method. These have been present in Python since version 2.6.x.

The following code snippets depict both types of string formatting using several examples:

```
# simple string formatting expressions
In [506]: 'Hello %s' %('Python!')
Out[506]: 'Hello Python!'
```

```
In [507]: 'Hello %s' %('World!')
Out[507]: 'Hello World!'

# formatting expressions with different data types
In [508]: 'We have %d %s containing %.2f gallons of %s' %(2, 'bottles', 2.5,
          'milk')
Out[508]: 'We have 2 bottles containing 2.50 gallons of milk'
In [509]: 'We have %d %s containing %.2f gallons of %s' %(5, 'jugs', 10.867,
          'juice')
Out[509]: 'We have 5 jugs containing 10.87 gallons of juice'

# formatting using the format method
In [511]: 'Hello {} {}, it is a great {} to meet you'.format('Mr.', 'Jones',
          'pleasure')
Out[511]: 'Hello Mr. Jones, it is a great pleasure to meet you'
In [512]: 'Hello {} {}, it is a great {} to meet you'.format('Sir',
          'Arthur', 'honor')
Out[512]: 'Hello Sir Arthur, it is a great honor to meet you'

# alternative ways of using format
In [513]: 'I have a {food_item} and a {drink_item} with me'.format(drink_
          item='soda', food_item='sandwich')
Out[513]: 'I have a sandwich and a soda with me'
In [514]: 'The {animal} has the following attributes: {attributes}'.
          format(animal='dog', attributes=['lazy', 'loyal'])
Out[514]: "The dog has the following attributes: ['lazy', 'loyal']"
```

From the preceding examples, you can see that there is no hard-and-fast rule for formatting strings, so go ahead and experiment with different formats and use the one best suited for your task.

Regular Expressions (Regexes)

Regular expressions, also called *regexes*, allow you to create string patterns and use them for searching and substituting specific pattern matches in textual data. Python offers a rich module named re for creating and using regular expressions. Entire books have been written on this topic because it is easy to use but difficult to master. Discussing every aspect of regular expressions would not be possible in these pages, but I will cover the main areas with sufficient examples.

Regular expressions or regexes are specific patterns often denoted using the raw string notation. These patterns match a specific set of strings based on the rules expressed by the patterns. These patterns then are usually compiled into bytecode that is then executed for matching strings using a matching engine. The re module also provides several flags that can change the way the pattern matches are executed. Some important flags include the following:

- re.I or re.IGNORECASE is used to match patterns ignoring case sensitivity.

- re.S or re.DOTALL causes the period (.) character to match any character including new lines.

- re.U or re.UNICODE helps in matching Unicode-based characters also (deprecated in Python 3.x).

For pattern matching, various rules are used in regexes. Some popular ones include the following:

- . for matching any single character

- ^ for matching the start of the string

- $ for matching the end of the string

- * for matching zero or more cases of the previous mentioned regex before the * symbol in the pattern

- ? for matching zero or one case of the previous mentioned regex before the ? symbol in the pattern

- [...] for matching any one of the set of characters inside the square brackets

- [^ ...] for matching a character not present in the square brackets after the ^ symbol

- | denotes the OR operator for matching either the preceding or the next regex

- + for matching one or more cases of the previous mentioned regex before the + symbol in the pattern

- \d for matching decimal digits which is also depicted as [0-9]

- \D for matching non-digits, also depicted as [^0-9]

- \s for matching white space characters

- \S for matching non whitespace characters

- \w for matching alphanumeric characters also depicted as [a-zA-Z0-9_]

- \W for matching non alphanumeric characters also depicted as [^a-zA-Z0-9_]

Regular expressions can be compiled into pattern objects and then used with a variety of methods for pattern search and substitution in strings. The main methods offered by the re module for performing these operations are as follows:

- re.compile(): This method compiles a specified regular expression pattern into a regular expression object that can be used for matching and searching. Takes a pattern and optional flags as input, discussed earlier.

- re.match(): This method is used to match patterns at the beginning of strings.

- re.search(): This method is used to match patterns occurring at any position in the string.

- re.findall(): This method returns all non-overlapping matches of the specified regex pattern in the string.

- re.finditer(): This method returns all matched instances in the form of an iterator for a specific pattern in a string when scanned from left to right.

- re.sub(): This method is used to substitute a specified regex pattern in a string with a replacement string. It only substitutes the leftmost occurrence of the pattern in the string.

The following code snippets depict some of the methods just discussed and how they are typically used when dealing with strings and regular expressions:

```
# importing the re module
In [526]: import re

# dealing with unicode matching using regexes
In [527]: s = u'H\u00e8llo'
In [528]: s
Out[528]: u'H\xe8llo'
In [529]: print s
Hèllo
# does not return the special unicode character even if it is alphanumeric
In [530]: re.findall(r'\w+', s)
Out[530]: [u'H', u'llo']
# need to explicitly specify the unicode flag to detect it using regex
In [531]: re.findall(r'\w+', s, re.UNICODE)
Out[531]: [u'H\xe8llo']

# setting up a pattern we want to use as a regex
# also creating two sample strings
In [534]: pattern = 'python'
    ...: s1 = 'Python is an excellent language'
    ...: s2 = 'I love the Python language. I also use Python to build
         applications at work!'

# match only returns a match if regex match is found at the beginning of the
string
In [535]: re.match(pattern, s1)
# pattern is in lower case hence ignore case flag helps
# in matching same pattern with different cases
In [536]: re.match(pattern, s1, flags=re.IGNORECASE)
Out[536]: <_sre.SRE_Match at 0xf378308>
```

```
# printing matched string and its indices in the original string
In [537]: m = re.match(pattern, s1, flags=re.IGNORECASE)
In [538]: print 'Found match {} ranging from index {} - {} in the string
"{}"'.format(m.group(0), m.start(), m.end(), s1)
Found match Python ranging from index 0 - 6 in the string "Python is an
excellent language"

# match does not work when pattern is not there in the
beginning of string s2
In [539]: re.match(pattern, s2, re.IGNORECASE)

# illustrating find and search methods using the re module
In [540]: re.search(pattern, s2, re.IGNORECASE)
Out[540]: <_sre.SRE_Match at 0xf378920>

In [541]: re.findall(pattern, s2, re.IGNORECASE)
Out[541]: ['Python', 'Python']

In [542]: match_objs = re.finditer(pattern, s2, re.IGNORECASE)
In [543]: print "String:", s2
     ...: for m in match_objs:
     ...:     print 'Found match "{}" ranging from index {} - {}'.format(m.
             group(0), m.start(), m.end())
String: I love the Python language. I also use Python to build applications
at work!
Found match "Python" ranging from index 11 - 17
Found match "Python" ranging from index 39 - 45

# illustrating pattern substitution using sub and subn methods
In [544]: re.sub(pattern, 'Java', s2, flags=re.IGNORECASE)
Out[544]: 'I love the Java language. I also use Java to build applications
          at work!'
In [545]: re.subn(pattern, 'Java', s2, flags=re.IGNORECASE)
Out[545]: ('I love the Java language. I also use Java to build applications
          at work!', 2)
```

This concludes our discussion on the various aspects of strings and how they can be utilized for working with text data. Strings form the basis for processing text, which is an important component in text analytics. The next section briefly discusses some of the popular text analytics frameworks.

Text Analytics Frameworks

Like I've mentioned before, the Python ecosystem is very diverse and supports a wide variety of libraries, frameworks, and modules in many domains. Because we will be analyzing textual data and performing various operations on it, you need to know about dedicated frameworks and libraries for text analytics that you can just install and start using—just like any other built-in module in the Python standard library. These frameworks have been built over a long period of time and contain various methods, capabilities, and features for operating on text, getting insights, and making the data ready for further analysis, such as applying machine learning algorithms on pre-processed textual data.

Leveraging these frameworks saves a lot of effort and time that would have been otherwise spent on writing boilerplate code to handle, process, and manipulate text data. Thus, the frameworks enable developers and researchers to focus more on solving actual problems and the necessary logic and algorithms needed for doing so. We have already seen some of the NLTK library in the first chapter. The following list of libraries and frameworks are some of the most popular text analytics frameworks, and we will be utilizing several of them throughout the course of the book:

- *NLTK*: The Natural Language Toolkit is a complete platform that contains more than 50 corpora and lexical resources. It also provides the necessary tools, interfaces, and methods to process and analyze text data.

- `pattern`: The `pattern` project started out as a research project at the Computational Linguistics & Psycholinguistics research center at the University of Antwerp. It provides tools and interfaces for web mining, information retrieval, NLP, machine learning, and network analysis. The `pattern.en` module contains most of the utilities for text analytics.

- `gensim`: The `gensim` library has a rich set of capabilities for semantic analysis, including topic modeling and similarity analysis. But the best part is that it contains a Python port of Google's very popular word2vec model (originally available as a C package), a neural network model implemented to learn distributed representations of words where similar words (semantic) occur close to each other.

- `textblob`: This is another library that provides several capabilities including text processing, phrase extraction, classification, POS tagging, text translation, and sentiment analysis.

- `spacy`: This is one of the newer libraries, which claims to provide industrial-strength NLP capabilities by providing the best implementation of each technique and algorithm, making NLP tasks efficient in terms of performance and implementation.

Besides these, there are several other frameworks and libraries that are not dedicated towards text analytics but that are useful when you want to use machine learning techniques on textual data. These include the `scikit-learn`, `numpy`, and `scipy` stack. Besides these, deep learning and tensor-based libraries like `theano`, `tensorflow`, and `keras` also come in handy if you want to build advanced deep learning models based on deep neural nets, convnets, and LSTM-based models. You can install most of these libraries using the `pip install <library>` command from the command prompt or terminal. We will talk about any caveats if present in the upcoming chapters when we use these libraries.

Summary

This chapter provides a birds-eye yet detailed view of the entire Python ecosystem and what the language offers in terms of capabilities. You read about the origins of the Python language and saw how it has evolved overtime. The language has benefits of being open source, which has resulted in an active developer community constantly striving to improve the language and add new features. By now, you also know when you should use Python and the drawbacks associated with the language—which every developer should keep in mind while building systems and applications. This chapter also discussed how to set up your own Python environment and deal with multiple virtual environments.

Starting from the very basics, we have taken a deep dive into the various structures and constructs in the Python language, including data types and controlling code flow using loops and conditionals. We also explored concepts in various programming paradigms including OOP and functional programming. Constructs like classes, functions, lambdas, iterators, generators, and comprehensions are tools that will come in handy in a lot of scenarios when writing quality Python code. You also saw how to work with text data using the `string` data type and its various syntaxes, methods, operations, and formats. We also talked about the power of regular expressions and how useful they can be in pattern matching and substitutions. To conclude our discussion, we looked at various popular text analytics frameworks, which are useful in solving problems and tasks dealing with NLP and analyzing and extracting insights from text data.

This should all get you started with programming in Python. The next chapter builds on the foundations of this chapter as we start to understand, process, and parse text data in usable formats.

CHAPTER 3

■ ■ ■

Processing and Understanding Text

So far, we have reviewed the main concepts and areas surrounding natural language processing (NLP) and text analytics. We also got a good grip on the Python programming language in the last chapter, especially on the different constructs and syntax and how to work with strings to manage textual data. To carry out different operations and analyze text, you will need to process and parse textual data into more easy-to-interpret formats.

All machine learning (ML) algorithms, be they supervised or unsupervised techniques, usually work with input features that are numeric in nature. Although this is a separate topic under feature engineering, which we shall explore in detail, to get to that, you need to clean, normalize, and pre-process the initial textual data. Usually text corpora and other textual data in their native raw format are not well formatted and standardized, and of course, we should expect this—after all, text data is highly unstructured! Text processing, or to be more specific, pre-processing, involves using a variety of techniques to convert raw text into well-defined sequences of linguistic components that have standard structure and notation.

Often additional metadata is also present in the form of annotations to give more meaning to the text components like tags. The following list gives us an idea of some of the most popular text pre-processing techniques that we will be exploring in this chapter:

- Tokenization
- Tagging
- Chunking
- Stemming
- Lemmatization

Besides these techniques, you also need to perform some basic operations much of the time, such as dealing with misspelled text, removing stopwords, and handling other irrelevant components based on the problem to be solved. An important thing to remember always is that a robust text pre-processing system is always an essential part of any application on NLP and text analytics. The primary reason for that is because all the textual components that are obtained after pre-processing—be they words, phrases, sentences, or any other tokens—form the basic building blocks of input that are fed into the further stages of the application that perform more complex analyses, including

© Dipanjan Sarkar 2016

D. Sarkar, *Text Analytics with Python*, DOI 10.1007/978-1-4842-2388-8_3

learning patterns and extracting information. Hence, the popular saying "garbage in, garbage out" is very relevant here because if we do not process the text properly, we will end up getting unwanted and irrelevant results from our applications and systems.

Text processing also helps in cleaning and standardization of the text, which helps in analytical systems, like increasing the accuracy of classifiers. We also get additional information and metadata in the form of annotations, which are also very useful in giving more information about the text. We will touch upon normalizing text using various techniques including cleaning, removing unnecessary tokens, stems, and lemmas in this chapter.

Another important aspect is to understand textual data after processing and normalizing it. This will involve revisiting some of the concepts of language syntax and structure from Chapter 1, where we talked about sentences, phrases, parts of speech, shallow parsing, and grammars. In this chapter we will look at ways to implement these concepts and use them on real data. We will follow a structured and definite path in this chapter, starting from text processing and gradually exploring the various concepts and techniques associated with it, and move on to understanding text structure and syntax. Because this book is specifically aimed towards practitioners, various code snippets and practical examples will also enable and equip you with the right tools and frameworks for implementing the concepts under discussion in solving practical problems.

Text Tokenization

Chapter 1 talked about textual structure, its components, and tokens. To be more specific, *tokens* are independent and minimal textual components that have some definite syntax and semantics. A paragraph of text or a text document has several components including sentences that can be further broken down into clauses, phrases, and words. The most popular tokenization techniques include sentence and word tokenization, which are used to break down a text corpus into sentences, and each sentence into words. Thus, tokenization can be defined as the process of breaking down or splitting textual data into smaller meaningful components called tokens. In the following section, we will look at some ways to tokenize text into sentences.

Sentence Tokenization

Sentence tokenization is the process of splitting a text corpus into sentences that act as the first level of tokens which the corpus is comprised of. This is also known as *sentence segmentation*, because we try to segment the text into meaningful sentences. Any text corpus is a body of text where each paragraph comprises several sentences.

There are various ways of performing sentence tokenization. Basic techniques include looking for specific delimiters between sentences, such as a period (.) or a newline character (\n), and sometimes even a semi-colon (;). We will use the NLTK framework, which provides various interfaces for performing sentence tokenization. We will primarily focus on the following sentence tokenizers:

- `sent_tokenize`
- `PunktSentenceTokenizer`

- RegexpTokenizer

- Pre-trained sentence tokenization models

Before we can tokenize sentences, we need some text on which we can try out these operations. We will load some sample text and also a part of the Gutenberg corpus available in NLTK itself. We load the necessary dependencies using the following snippet:

```
import nltk
from nltk.corpus import gutenberg
from pprint import pprint

alice = gutenberg.raw(fileids='carroll-alice.txt')
sample_text = 'We will discuss briefly about the basic syntax, structure and
design philosophies. There is a defined hierarchical syntax for Python code
which you should remember when writing code! Python is a really powerful
programming language!'
```

We can check the length of the *Alice in Wonderland* corpus and also the first few lines in it using the following snippet:

```
In [124]: # Total characters in Alice in Wonderland
     ...: print len(alice)
144395

In [125]: # First 100 characters in the corpus
     ...: print alice[0:100]
[Alice's Adventures in Wonderland by Lewis Carroll 1865]

CHAPTER I. Down the Rabbit-Hole

Alice was
```

The nltk.sent_tokenize function is the default sentence tokenization function that nltk recommends. It uses an instance of the PunktSentenceTokenizer class internally. However, this is not just a normal object or instance of that class—it has been pre-trained on several language models and works really well on many popular languages besides just English.

The following snippet shows the basic usage of this function on our text samples:

```
default_st = nltk.sent_tokenize
alice_sentences = default_st(text=alice)
sample_sentences = default_st(text=sample_text)

print 'Total sentences in sample_text:', len(sample_sentences)
print 'Sample text sentences :-'
pprint(sample_sentences)
print '\nTotal sentences in alice:', len(alice_sentences)
print 'First 5 sentences in alice:-'
pprint(alice_sentences[0:5])
```

109

On running the preceding snippet, you get the following output depicting the total number of sentences and what those sentences look like in the text corpora:

```
Total sentences in sample_text: 3
Sample text sentences :-
['We will discuss briefly about the basic syntax, structure and design
philosophies.',
 'There is a defined hierarchical syntax for Python code which you should
remember when writing code!',
 'Python is a really powerful programming language!']


Total sentences in alice: 1625
First 5 sentences in alice:-
[u"[Alice's Adventures in Wonderland by Lewis Carroll 1865]\n\nCHAPTER I.",
 u"Down the Rabbit-Hole\n\nAlice was beginning to get very tired of sitting
by her sister on the\nbank, and of having nothing to do: once or twice she
had peeped into the\nbook her sister was reading, but it had no pictures
or conversations in\nit, 'and what is the use of a book,' thought Alice
'without pictures or\nconversation?'",
 u'So she was considering in her own mind (as well as she could, for the\nhot
day made her feel very sleepy and stupid), whether the pleasure\nof making
a daisy-chain would be worth the trouble of getting up and\npicking the
daisies, when suddenly a White Rabbit with pink eyes ran\nclose by her.',
 u"There was nothing so VERY remarkable in that; nor did Alice think it so\
nVERY much out of the way to hear the Rabbit say to itself, 'Oh dear!",
 u'Oh dear!']
```

Now, as you can see, the tokenizer is quite intelligent and doesn't just use periods to delimit sentences. It also considers other punctuation and the capitalization of words.

We can also tokenize text of other languages. If we are dealing with German text, we can use sent_tokenize, which is already trained, or load a pre-trained tokenization model on German text into a PunktSentenceTokenizer instance and perform the same operation. The following snippet shows the same. We start with loading a German text corpus and inspecting it:

```
In [4]: from nltk.corpus import europarl_raw
   ...:
   ...: german_text = europarl_raw.german.raw(fileids='ep-00-01-17.de')
   ...: # Total characters in the corpus
   ...: print len(german_text)
   ...: # First 100 characters in the corpus
   ...: print german_text[0:100]
157171

Wiederaufnahme der Sitzungsperiode Ich erkläre die am Freitag , dem 17.
Dezember unterbrochene Sit
```

Next, we tokenize the text corpus into sentences using both the default sent_ tokenize tokenizer and also a pre-trained German language tokenizer by loading it from the nltk resources:

```
In [5]: german_sentences_def = default_st(text=german_text,
language='german')
    ...:
    ...: # loading german text tokenizer into a PunktSentenceTokenizer
          instance
    ...: german_tokenizer = nltk.data.load(resource_url='tokenizers/punkt/
          german.pickle')
    ...: german_sentences = german_tokenizer.tokenize(german_text)
    ...:
    ...: # verify the type of german_tokenizer
    ...: # should be PunktSentenceTokenizer
    ...: print type(german_tokenizer)
<class 'nltk.tokenize.punkt.PunktSentenceTokenizer'>
```

Thus we see that indeed the german_tokenizer is an instance of PunktSentenceTokenizer, which is specialized in dealing with the German language.

Next we check whether the sentences obtained from the default tokenizer are the same as the sentences obtained by this pre-trained tokenizer, and ideally it should be True. We also print some sample tokenized sentences from the output after that:

```
In [9]: print german_sentences_def == german_sentences
    ...: # print first 5 sentences of the corpus
    ...: for sent in german_sentences[0:5]:
    ...:     print sent
True

Wiederaufnahme der Sitzungsperiode Ich erkläre die am Freitag , dem 17.
Dezember unterbrochene Sitzungsperiode des Europäischen Parlaments für
wiederaufgenommen , wünsche Ihnen nochmals alles Gute zum Jahreswechsel und
hoffe , daß Sie schöne Ferien hatten .
Wie Sie feststellen konnten , ist der gefürchtete " Millenium-Bug " nicht
eingetreten .
Doch sind Bürger einiger unserer Mitgliedstaaten Opfer von schrecklichen
Naturkatastrophen geworden .
Im Parlament besteht der Wunsch nach einer Aussprache im Verlauf dieser
Sitzungsperiode in den nächsten Tagen .
Heute möchte ich Sie bitten - das ist auch der Wunsch einiger Kolleginnen
und Kollegen - , allen Opfern der Stürme , insbesondere in den verschiedenen
Ländern der Europäischen Union , in einer Schweigeminute zu gedenken .
```

Thus we see that our assumption was indeed correct, and you can tokenize sentences belonging to different languages in two different ways. Using the default PunktSentenceTokenizer class is also pretty straightforward. The following snippet shows how to use it:

```
In [11]: punkt_st = nltk.tokenize.PunktSentenceTokenizer()
    ...: sample_sentences = punkt_st.tokenize(sample_text)
    ...: pprint(sample_sentences)
['We will discuss briefly about the basic syntax, structure and design
philosophies.',
 'There is a defined hierarchical syntax for Python code which you should
remember when writing code!',
 'Python is a really powerful programming language!']
```

You can see we get a similar output, which is expected from this tokenization. The last tokenizer we will cover in sentence tokenization is using an instance of the RegexpTokenizer class to tokenize text into sentences where we will use specific regular expression-based patterns to segment sentences. Recall the regular expressions (regex) from the previous chapter, in case you want to refresh your memory. The following snippet shows how to use a regex pattern to tokenize sentences:

```
In [29]: SENTENCE_TOKENS_PATTERN = r'(?<!\w\.\w.)(?<![A-Z][a-z]\.)
(?<![A-Z]\.)(?<=\.|\?|\!)\s'
    ...: regex_st = nltk.tokenize.RegexpTokenizer(
    ...:             pattern=SENTENCE_TOKENS_PATTERN,
    ...:             gaps=True)
    ...: sample_sentences = regex_st.tokenize(sample_text)
    ...: pprint(sample_sentences)
['We will discuss briefly about the basic syntax, structure and design
philosophies.',
 ' There is a defined hierarchical syntax for Python code which you should
remember  when writing code!',
 'Python is a really powerful programming language!']
```

That output shows that we obtained the same sentences as we had obtained using the other tokenizers. This gives us an idea of tokenizing text into sentences using different nltk interfaces. In the next section we will look at tokenizing these sentences into words using several techniques.

Word Tokenization

Word tokenization is the process of splitting or segmenting sentences into their constituent words. A *sentence* is a collection of words, and with tokenization we essentially split a sentence into a list of words that can be used to reconstruct the sentence. Word tokenization is very important in many processes, especially in cleaning and normalizing text where operations like stemming and lemmatization work on each individual word based on its respective stems and lemma. Similar to sentence tokenization, nltk provides various useful interfaces for word tokenization, and we will touch up on the following main interfaces:

- word_tokenize
- TreebankWordTokenizer

- RegexpTokenizer

- Inherited tokenizers from RegexpTokenizer

For the hands-on examples, we will use the sample sentence *The brown fox wasn't that quick and he couldn't win the race* as our input to the various tokenizers. The nltk. word_tokenize function is the default and recommended word tokenizer as specified by nltk. This tokenizer is actually an instance or object of the TreebankWordTokenizer class in its internal implementation and acts as a wrapper to that core class. The following snippet illustrates its usage:

```
In [114]: sentence = "The brown fox wasn't that quick and he couldn't win
the race"
    ...:
    ...: default_wt = nltk.word_tokenize
    ...: words = default_wt(sentence)
    ...: print words
['The', 'brown', 'fox', 'was', "n't", 'that', 'quick', 'and', 'he', 'could',
"n't", 'win', 'the', 'race']
```

The TreebankWordTokenizer is based on the Penn Treebank and uses various regular expressions to tokenize the text. Of course, one primary assumption here is that we have already performed sentence tokenization beforehand. The original tokenizer used in the Penn Treebank is available as a sed script, and you can check it out at www.cis. upenn.edu/~treebank/tokenizer.sed to get an idea of the patterns used to tokenize the sentences into words. Some of the main features of this tokenizer include the following:

- Splits and separates out periods that appear at the end of a sentence

- Splits and separates commas and single quotes when followed by whitespaces

- Most punctuation characters are split and separated into independent tokens

- Splits words with standard contractions—examples would be *don't* to *do* and *n't*

The following snippet shows the usage of the TreebankWordTokenizer for word tokenization:

```
In [117]: treebank_wt = nltk.TreebankWordTokenizer()
    ...: words = treebank_wt.tokenize(sentence)
    ...: print words
['The', 'brown', 'fox', 'was', "n't", 'that', 'quick', 'and', 'he', 'could',
"n't", 'win', 'the', 'race']
```

From the preceding output, as expected, the output is similar to word_tokenize() because both use the same tokenizing mechanism.

113

We will now look at how to use regular expressions and the RegexpTokenizer class to tokenize sentences into words. Remember, there are two main parameters that are useful in tokenization: the regex pattern for building the tokenizer and the gaps parameter, which, if set to True, is used to find the gaps between the tokens. Otherwise, it is used to find the tokens themselves.

The following code snippet shows some examples of using regular expressions to perform word tokenization:

```
# pattern to identify tokens themselves
In [127]: TOKEN_PATTERN = r'\w+'
     ...: regex_wt = nltk.RegexpTokenizer(pattern=TOKEN_PATTERN,
     ...:                                 gaps=False)
     ...: words = regex_wt.tokenize(sentence)
     ...: print words
['The', 'brown', 'fox', 'wasn', 't', 'that', 'quick', 'and', 'he', 'couldn',
't', 'win', 'the', 'race']
# pattern to identify gaps in tokens
In [128]: GAP_PATTERN = r'\s+'
     ...: regex_wt = nltk.RegexpTokenizer(pattern=GAP_PATTERN,
     ...:                                 gaps=True)
     ...: words = regex_wt.tokenize(sentence)
     ...: print words
['The', 'brown', 'fox', "wasn't", 'that', 'quick', 'and', 'he', "couldn't",
'win', 'the', 'race']
# get start and end indices of each token and then print them
In [131]: word_indices = list(regex_wt.span_tokenize(sentence))
     ...: print word_indices
     ...: print [sentence[start:end] for start, end in word_indices]
[(0, 3), (4, 9), (10, 13), (14, 20), (21, 25), (26, 31), (32, 35), (36, 38),
(39, 47), (48, 51), (52, 55), (56, 60)]
['The', 'brown', 'fox', "wasn't", 'that', 'quick', 'and', 'he', "couldn't",
'win', 'the', 'race']
```

Besides the base RegexpTokenizer class, there are several derived classes that perform different types of word tokenization. The WordPunctTokenizer uses the pattern r'\w+|[^\w\s]+' to tokenize sentences into independent alphabetic and non-alphabetic tokens. The WhitespaceTokenizer tokenizes sentences into words based on whitespaces like tabs, newlines, and spaces.

The following snippet demonstrates:

```
In [132]: wordpunkt_wt = nltk.WordPunctTokenizer()
     ...: words = wordpunkt_wt.tokenize(sentence)
     ...: print words
['The', 'brown', 'fox', 'wasn', "'", 't', 'that', 'quick', 'and', 'he',
'couldn', "'", 't', 'win', 'the', 'race']
```

```
In [133]: whitespace_wt = nltk.WhitespaceTokenizer()
     ...: words = whitespace_wt.tokenize(sentence)
     ...: print words
['The', 'brown', 'fox', "wasn't", 'that', 'quick', 'and', 'he', "couldn't",
'win', 'the', 'race']
```

This concludes our discussion on tokenization. Now that we know how to separate out raw text into sentences and words, we will build upon that in the next section, where we will normalize these tokens to get clean and standardized textual data that will be easier to understand, interpret, and use in NLP and ML.

Text Normalization

Text normalization is defined as a process that consists of a series of steps that should be followed to wrangle, clean, and standardize textual data into a form that could be consumed by other NLP and analytics systems and applications as input. Often tokenization itself also is a part of text normalization. Besides tokenization, various other techniques include cleaning text, case conversion, correcting spellings, removing stopwords and other unnecessary terms, stemming, and lemmatization. Text normalization is also often called *text cleansing* or *wrangling*.

In this section, we will discuss various techniques used in the process of text normalization. Before we can jump into implementing and exploring the various techniques, use the following code snippet to load the basic dependencies and also the corpus we will be using in this section:

```
import nltk
import re
import string
from pprint import pprint

corpus = ["The brown fox wasn't that quick and he couldn't win the race",
          "Hey that's a great deal! I just bought a phone for $199",
          "@@You'll (learn) a **lot** in the book. Python is an amazing
          language!@@"]
```

Cleaning Text

Often the textual data we want to use or analyze contains a lot of extraneous and unnecessary tokens and characters that should be removed before performing any further operations like tokenization or other normalization techniques. This includes extracting out meaningful text from data sources like HTML data, which consists of unnecessary HTML tags, or even data from XML and JSON feeds. There are many ways to parse and clean this data to remove unnecessary tags. You can use functions like clean_html() from nltk or even the BeautifulSoup library to parse HTML data. You can also use your own custom logic, including regexes, xpath, and the lxml library, to parse through XML data. And getting data from JSON is substantially easier because it has definite key-value annotations.

115

Tokenizing Text

Usually, we tokenize text before or after removing unnecessary characters and symbols from the data. This choice depends on the problem you are trying to solve and the data you are dealing with. We have already looked at various tokenization techniques in the previous section. We will define a generic tokenization function here and run the same on our corpus mentioned earlier.

The following code snippet defines the tokenization function:

```
def tokenize_text(text):
    sentences = nltk.sent_tokenize(text)
    word_tokens = [nltk.word_tokenize(sentence) for sentence in sentences]
    return word_tokens
```

This function basically takes in textual data, extracts sentences from it, and finally splits each sentence into further tokens, which could be words or special characters and punctuation. The following snippet depicts the preceding function in action:

```
In [297]: token_list = [tokenize_text(text)
     ...:                     for text in corpus]
     ...: pprint(token_list)
[[['The', 'brown', 'fox', 'was', "n't", 'that', 'quick', 'and', 'he',
       'could', "n't",
   'win', 'the', 'race']],
 [['Hey', 'that', "'s", 'a', 'great', 'deal', '!'],
  ['I', 'just', 'bought', 'a', 'phone', 'for', '$', '199']],
 [['@', '@', 'You', "'ll", '(', 'learn', ')', 'a', '**lot**', 'in', 'the',
       'book', '.'],
  ['Python', 'is', 'an', 'amazing', 'language', '!'],
  ['@', '@']]]
```

You can now see how each text in the corpus has been tokenized using our custom defined function. Play around with more text data and see if you can make it even better!

Removing Special Characters

One important task in text normalization involves removing unnecessary and special characters. These may be special symbols or even punctuation that occurs in sentences. This step is often performed before or after tokenization. The main reason for doing so is because often punctuation or special characters do not have much significance when we analyze the text and utilize it for extracting features or information based on NLP and ML. We will implement both types of special characters removal, before and after tokenization.

The following snippet shows how to remove special characters *after* tokenization:

```
def remove_characters_after_tokenization(tokens):
    pattern = re.compile('[{}]'.format(re.escape(string.punctuation)))
    filtered_tokens = filter(None, [pattern.sub('', token) for token in tokens])
    return filtered_tokens
```

```
In [299]: filtered_list_1 =  [filter(None,[remove_characters_after_
                             tokenization(tokens)
      ...:                                   for tokens in sentence_tokens])
      ...:                         for sentence_tokens in token_list]
      ...: print filtered_list_1
[[['The', 'brown', 'fox', 'was', 'nt', 'that', 'quick', 'and', 'he',
'could', 'nt', 'win', 'the', 'race']], [['Hey', 'that', 's', 'a', 'great',
'deal'], ['I', 'just', 'bought', 'a', 'phone', 'for', '199']], [['You',
'll', 'learn', 'a', 'lot', 'in', 'the', 'book'], ['Python', 'is', 'an',
'amazing', 'language']]]
```

Essentially, what we do here is use the string.punctuation attribute, which consists of all possible special characters/symbols, and create a regex pattern from it. We use it to match tokens that are symbols and characters and remove them. The filter function helps us remove empty tokens obtained after removing the special character tokens using the regex sub method.

The following code snippet shows how to remove special characters *before* tokenization:

```
def remove_characters_before_tokenization(sentence,
                                          keep_apostrophes=False):
    sentence = sentence.strip()
    if keep_apostrophes:
        PATTERN = r'[?|$|&|*|%|@|(|)|~]' # add other characters here to
        remove them
        filtered_sentence = re.sub(PATTERN, r'', sentence)
    else:
        PATTERN = r'[^a-zA-Z0-9 ]' # only extract alpha-numeric characters
        filtered_sentence = re.sub(PATTERN, r'', sentence)
    return filtered_sentence
```

```
In [304]: filtered_list_2 = [remove_characters_before_tokenization(sentence)
      ...:                         for sentence in corpus]
      ...: print filtered_list_2
['The brown fox wasnt that quick and he couldnt win the race', 'Hey thats a
great deal I just bought a phone for 199', 'Youll learn a lot in the book
Python is an amazing language']
```

```
In [305]: cleaned_corpus = [remove_characters_before_tokenization(sentence,
                            keep_apostrophes=True)
      ...:                         for sentence in corpus]
      ...: print cleaned_corpus
["The brown fox wasn't that quick and he couldn't win the race", "Hey that's
a great deal! I just bought a phone for 199", "You'll learn a lot in the
book. Python is an amazing language!"]
```

The preceding outputs show two different ways of removing special characters before tokenization—removing all special characters versus retaining apostrophes and sentence periods—using regular expressions. By now, you must have realized how powerful regular expressions can be, as mentioned in Chapter 2. Usually after removing these characters, you can take the clean text and tokenize it or apply other normalization operations on it. Sometimes we want to preserve the apostrophes in the sentences as a way to track them and expand them if needed. We will explore that in the following section.

Expanding Contractions

Contractions are shortened version of words or syllables. They exist in either written or spoken forms. Shortened versions of existing words are created by removing specific letters and sounds. In case of English contractions, they are often created by removing one of the vowels from the word. Examples would be *is not* to *isn't* and *will not* to *won't*, where you can notice the apostrophe being used to denote the contraction and some of the vowels and other letters being removed. Usually contractions are avoided when used in formal writing, but informally, they are used quite extensively. Various forms of contractions exist that are tied down to the type of auxiliary verbs that give us normal contractions, negated contractions, and other special colloquial contractions, some of which may not involve auxiliaries.

By nature, contractions do pose a problem for NLP and text analytics because, to start with, we have a special apostrophe character in the word. Plus we have two or more words represented by a contraction, and this opens a whole new can of worms when we try to tokenize this or even standardize the words. Hence, there should be some definite process by which we can deal with contractions when processing text. Ideally, you can have a proper mapping for contractions and their corresponding expansions and then use it to expand all the contractions in your text. I have created a vocabulary for contractions and their corresponding expanded forms that you can access in the file contractions.py in a Python dictionary (available along with the code files for this chapter). Part of the contractions dictionary is shown below in the following snippet:

```
CONTRACTION_MAP = {
"isn't": "is not",
"aren't": "are not",
"can't": "cannot",
"can't've": "cannot have",
.
.
.
"you'll've": "you will have",
"you're": "you are",
"you've": "you have"
}
```

Remember, though, that some of the contractions can have multiple forms. An example would be that contracting *you'll* can indicate either *you will* or *you shall*. To simplify, I have taken one of these expanded forms for each contraction. The next step, to expand contractions, uses the following code snippet:

```
from contractions import CONTRACTION_MAP

def expand_contractions(sentence, contraction_mapping):
    contractions_pattern = re.compile('({})'.format('|'.join(contraction_
mapping.keys())),
                                        flags=re.IGNORECASE|re.DOTALL)
    def expand_match(contraction):
        match = contraction.group(0)
        first_char = match[0]
        expanded_contraction = contraction_mapping.get(match)\
                                if contraction_mapping.get(match)\
                                else contraction_mapping.get(match.lower())
        expanded_contraction = first_char+expanded_contraction[1:]
        return expanded_contraction

    expanded_sentence = contractions_pattern.sub(expand_match, sentence)
    return expanded_sentence
```

The preceding snippet uses the function expanded_match inside the main expand_ contractions function to find each contraction that matches the regex pattern we create out of all the contractions in our CONTRACTION_MAP dictionary. On matching any contraction, we substitute it with its corresponding expanded version and retain the correct case of the word.

To see it in action, we use it on the cleaned_corpus of text we obtained in the previous section:

```
In [311]: expanded_corpus = [expand_contractions(sentence, CONTRACTION_MAP)
     ...:                      for sentence in cleaned_corpus]
     ...: print expanded_corpus
['The brown fox was not that quick and he could not win the race', 'Hey that
is a great deal! I just bought a phone for 199', 'You will learn a lot in
the book. Python is an amazing language!']
```

You can see how each contraction has been correctly expanded in the output just like we expected it. Can you build a better contraction expander? It is definitely an interesting problem to solve.

Case Conversions

Often we want to modify the case of words or sentences to make things easier, like matching specific words or tokens. Usually there are two types of case conversion operations that are used a lot. These are lowercase and uppercase conversions, where a body of text is converted completely to lowercase or uppercase. There are other forms also, such as sentence case or proper case. Lowercase is a form where all the letters of the text are small letters, and in uppercase they are all capitalized.

The following snippet illustrates this concept:

```
# lower case
In [315]: print corpus[0].lower()
the brown fox wasn't that quick and he couldn't win the race
# upper case
In [316]: print corpus[0].upper()
THE BROWN FOX WASN'T THAT QUICK AND HE COULDN'T WIN THE RACE
```

Removing Stopwords

Stopwords, sometimes written *stop words*, are words that have little or no significance. They are usually removed from text during processing so as to retain words having maximum significance and context. Stopwords are usually words that end up occurring the most if you aggregated any corpus of text based on singular tokens and checked their frequencies. Words like *a, the, me,* and so on are stopwords. There is no universal or exhaustive list of stopwords. Each domain or language may have its own set of stopwords.

The following code snippet shows a method to filter out and remove stopwords for English:

```
def remove_stopwords(tokens):
    stopword_list = nltk.corpus.stopwords.words('english')
    filtered_tokens = [token for token in tokens if token not in stopword_
    list]
    return filtered_tokens
```

In the preceding function, we leverage the use of nltk, which has a list of stopwords for English, and use it to filter out all tokens that correspond to stopwords. We use our tokenize_text function to tokenize the expanded_corpus we obtained in the previous section and then remove the necessary stopwords using the preceding function:

```
In [332]: expanded_corpus_tokens = [tokenize_text(text)
     ...:                                 for text in expanded_corpus]
     ...: filtered_list_3 = [[remove_stopwords(tokens)
     ...:                         for tokens in sentence_tokens]
     ...:                         for sentence_tokens in expanded_corpus_
     ...:                         tokens]
     ...: print filtered_list_3
[[['The', 'brown', 'fox', 'quick', 'could', 'win', 'race']], [['Hey',
'great', 'deal', '!'], ['I', 'bought', 'phone', '199']], [['You', 'learn',
'lot', 'book', '.'], ['Python', 'amazing', 'language', '!']]]
```

The preceding output shows a reduced number of tokens compared to what we had earlier, and you can compare and check the tokens that were removed as stopwords. To see the list of all English stopwords in nltk's vocabulary, print the contents of nltk.corpus.stopwords.words('english'). One important thing to remember is that negations like *not* and *no* are removed in this case *(in the first sentence),* and it is often essential to preserve the same so the actual context of the sentence is not lost in applications like sentiment analysis, so you would need to make sure you do not remove such words in those scenarios.

Correcting Words

One of the main challenges faced in text normalization is the presence of incorrect words in the text. The definition of incorrect here covers words that have spelling mistakes as well as words with several letters repeated that do not contribute much to its overall significance. To illustrate some examples, the word *finally* could be mistakenly written as *fianlly*, or someone expressing intense emotion could write it as *finalllllyyyyyy*. The main objective here would be to standardize different forms of these words to the correct form so that we do not end up losing vital information from different tokens in the text. This section covers dealing with repeated characters as well as correcting spellings.

Correcting Repeating Characters

I will cover a method here of using a combination of syntax and semantics to correct incorrectly spelled words. We will first start with correcting the syntax of these words and then move on to semantics.

The first step in our algorithm would be to identify repeated characters in a word using a regex pattern and then use a substitution to remove the characters one by one. Consider the word *finalllyyy* from the earlier example. The pattern r'(\w*)(\w)\2(\w*)' can be used to identify characters that occur twice among other characters in the word, and in each step we will try to eliminate one of the repeated characters using a substitution for the match by utilizing the regex match groups (groups 1, 2, and 3) using the pattern r'\1\2\3' and then keep iterating through this process till no repeated characters remain.

The following snippet illustrates this:

```
In [361]: old_word = 'finalllyyy'
     ...: repeat_pattern = re.compile(r'(\w*)(\w)\2(\w*)')
     ...: match_substitution = r'\1\2\3'
     ...: step = 1
     ...:
     ...: while True:
     ...:     # remove one repeated character
     ...:     new_word = repeat_pattern.sub(match_substitution,
     ...:                                   old_word)
     ...:     if new_word != old_word:
     ...:         print 'Step: {} Word: {}'.format(step, new_word)
     ...:         step += 1 # update step
     ...:         # update old word to last substituted state
     ...:         old_word = new_word
     ...:         continue
     ...:     else:
     ...:         print "Final word:", new_word
```

```
    ...:             break
    ...:
Step: 1 Word: finalllyy
Step: 2 Word: finallly
Step: 3 Word: finally
Step: 4 Word: finaly
Final word: finaly
```

The preceding snippet shows how one repeated character is removed at each stage until we end up with the word *finaly* in the end. However, semantically this word is incorrect—the correct word was *finally*, which we obtained in step 3. We will now utilize the WordNet corpus to check for valid words at each stage and terminate the loop once it is obtained. This introduces the semantic correction needed for our algorithm, as illustrated in the following snippet:

```
In [363]: from nltk.corpus import wordnet
     ...: old_word = 'finalllyyy'
     ...: repeat_pattern = re.compile(r'(\w*)(\w)\2(\w*)')
     ...: match_substitution = r'\1\2\3'
     ...: step = 1
     ...:
     ...: while True:
     ...:     # check for semantically correct word
     ...:     if wordnet.synsets(old_word):
     ...:         print "Final correct word:", old_word
     ...:         break
     ...:     # remove one repeated character
     ...:     new_word = repeat_pattern.sub(match_substitution,
     ...:                                   old_word)
     ...:     if new_word != old_word:
     ...:         print 'Step: {} Word: {}'.format(step, new_word)
     ...:         step += 1 # update step
     ...:         # update old word to last substituted state
     ...:         old_word = new_word
     ...:         continue
     ...:     else:
     ...:         print "Final word:", new_word
     ...:         break
     ...:
Step: 1 Word: finalllyy
Step: 2 Word: finallly
Step: 3 Word: finally
Final correct word: finally
```

Thus we see from the preceding snippet that the code correctly terminated after the third step, and we obtained the correct word, adhering to both syntax and semantics.

We can build a better version of this code by writing the logic in a function, as shown in the following code, to make it more generic to deal with incorrect tokens from a list of tokens:

```
from nltk.corpus import wordnet

def remove_repeated_characters(tokens):
    repeat_pattern = re.compile(r'(\w*)(\w)\2(\w*)')
    match_substitution = r'\1\2\3'
    def replace(old_word):
        if wordnet.synsets(old_word):
            return old_word
        new_word = repeat_pattern.sub(match_substitution, old_word)
        return replace(new_word) if new_word != old_word else new_word

    correct_tokens = [replace(word) for word in tokens]
    return correct_tokens
```

That snippet uses the inner function replace() to basically emulate the behavior of our algorithm, illustrated earlier, and then call it repeatedly on each token in a sentence in the outer function remove_repeated_characters().

We can see the preceding code in action in the following snippet, with an actual example sentence:

```
In [369]: sample_sentence = 'My schooool is reallllllyyy amaaazingggg'
     ...: sample_sentence_tokens = tokenize_text(sample_sentence)[0]
     ...: print sample_sentence_tokens
['My', 'schooool', 'is', 'reallllllyyy', 'amaaazingggg']

In [370]: print remove_repeated_characters(sample_sentence_tokens)
['My', 'school', 'is', 'really', 'amazing']
```

We can see from the above output that our function performs as intended and replaces the repeating characters in each token, giving us correct tokens as desired.

Correcting Spellings

Another problem we face is incorrect or wrong spellings that occur due to human error, or even machine-based errors you may have seen thanks to features like auto-correcting text. There are various ways of dealing with incorrect spellings where the final objective is to have tokens of text with the correct spelling. This section will talk about one of the famous algorithms developed by Peter Norvig, the director of research at Google. You can find the complete detailed post explaining his algorithm and findings at http://norvig. com/spell-correct.html.

The main objective of this exercise is that, given a word, we need to find the most likely word that is the correct form of that word. The approach we would follow is to generate a set of candidate words that are near to our input word and select the most likely word from this set as the correct word. We use a corpus of correct English words in this context to identify the correct word based on its frequency in the corpus from our final set of candidates with the nearest distance to our input word. This distance, which measures how near or far a word is from our input word, is also called *edit distance*. The input corpus we use is a file containing several books from the Gutenberg corpus and also a list of most frequent words from Wiktionary and the British National Corpus. You can find the file under the name big.txt in this chapter's code resources or download it from http://norvig.com/big.txt and use it.

I'll use the following code snippet to generate a map of frequently occurring words in the English language and their counts:

```
import re, collections

def tokens(text):
    """
    Get all words from the corpus
    """
    return re.findall('[a-z]+', text.lower())

WORDS = tokens(file('big.txt').read())
WORD_COUNTS = collections.Counter(WORDS)

# top 10 words in the corpus
In [407]: print WORD_COUNTS.most_common(10)
[('the', 80030), ('of', 40025), ('and', 38313), ('to', 28766), ('in',
22050), ('a', 21155), ('that', 12512), ('he', 12401), ('was', 11410),
('it', 10681)]
```

Once we have our vocabulary, we define three functions that compute sets of words that are zero, one, and two edits away from our input word. These edits can be made by the means of insertions, deletions, additions, and transpositions. The following code defines the functions for doing this:

```
def edits0(word):
    """
    Return all strings that are zero edits away
    from the input word (i.e., the word itself).
    """
    return {word}

def edits1(word):
    """
    Return all strings that are one edit away
    from the input word.
    """
    alphabet = 'abcdefghijklmnopqrstuvwxyz'
    def splits(word):
        """
        Return a list of all possible (first, rest) pairs
        that the input word is made of.
        """
        return [(word[:i], word[i:])
                for i in range(len(word)+1)]
```

```
pairs      = splits(word)
deletes    = [a+b[1:]              for (a, b) in pairs if b]
transposes = [a+b[1]+b[0]+b[2:]    for (a, b) in pairs if len(b) > 1]
replaces   = [a+c+b[1:]            for (a, b) in pairs for c in alphabet
                                   if b]
inserts    = [a+c+b                for (a, b) in pairs for c in alphabet]
return set(deletes + transposes + replaces + inserts)

def edits2(word):
    """Return all strings that are two edits away
    from the input word.
    """
    return {e2 for e1 in edits1(word) for e2 in edits1(e1)}
```

We also define a function called known() that returns a subset of words from our
candidate set of words obtained from the edit functions, based on whether they occur in
our vocabulary dictionary WORD_COUNTS. This gives us a list of valid words from our set of
candidate words:

```
def known(words):
    """
    Return the subset of words that are actually
    in our WORD_COUNTS dictionary.
    """
    return {w for w in words if w in WORD_COUNTS}
```

We can see these functions in action on our test input word in the following code
snippet, which shows lists of possible candidate words based on edit distances from the
input word:

```
# input word
In [409]: word = 'fianlly'

# zero edit distance from input word
In [410]: edits0(word)
Out[410]: {'fianlly'}
# returns null set since it is not a valid word
In [411]: known(edits0(word))
Out[411]: set()

# one edit distance from input word
In [412]: edits1(word)
Out[412]:
{'afianlly',
 'aianlly',
 .
 .
 'yianlly',
```

```
'zfianlly',
'zianlly'}
# get correct words from above set
In [413]: known(edits1(word))
Out[413]: {'finally'}

# two edit distances from input word
In [417]: edits2(word)
Out[417]:
{'fchnlly',
 'fianjlys',

   .

   .

 'fiapgnlly',
 'finanlqly'}
# get correct words from above set
In [418]: known(edits2(word))
Out[418]: {'faintly', 'finally', 'finely', 'frankly'}
```

The preceding outputs depict a set of valid candidate words that could be potential replacements for the incorrect input word. We select our candidate words from the preceding list by giving higher priority to words with the smallest edit distances from the input word. The following code snippet illustrates:

```
In [420]: candidates = (known(edits0(word)) or
     ...:               known(edits1(word)) or
     ...:               known(edits2(word)) or
     ...:               [word])

In [421]: candidates
Out[421]: {'finally'}
```

In case there is a tie in the preceding candidates, we resolve it by taking the highest occurring word from our vocabulary dictionary WORD_COUNTS using the max(candidates, key=WORD_COUNTS.get) function. Thus we now define our function to correct words using the logic discussed earlier:

```
def correct(word):
    """
    Get the best correct spelling for the input word
    """
    # Priority is for edit distance 0, then 1, then 2
    # else defaults to the input word itself.
    candidates = (known(edits0(word)) or
                  known(edits1(word)) or
                  known(edits2(word)) or
                  [word])
    return max(candidates, key=WORD_COUNTS.get)
```

We can use the preceding function on incorrect words directly to correct them, as illustrated in the following snippet:

```
In [438]: correct('fianlly')
Out[438]: 'finally'

In [439]: correct('FIANLLY')
Out[439]: 'FIANLLY'
```

We see that this function is case sensitive and fails to correct words that are not lowercase, hence we write the following functions to make this generic to the case of words and correct their spelling regardless. The logic here is to preserve the original case of the word, convert it to lowercase, correct its spelling, and finally reconvert it back to its original case using the case_of function:

```
def correct_match(match):
    """
    Spell-correct word in match,
    and preserve proper upper/lower/title case.
    """

    word = match.group()
    def case_of(text):
        """
        Return the case-function appropriate
        for text: upper, lower, title, or just str.:
        """
        return (str.upper if text.isupper() else
                str.lower if text.islower() else
                str.title if text.istitle() else
                str)
    return case_of(word)(correct(word.lower()))

def correct_text_generic(text):
    """
    Correct all the words within a text,
    returning the corrected text.
    """
    return re.sub('[a-zA-Z]+', correct_match, text)
```

We can now use the preceding function to correct words irrespective of their case, as illustrated in the following snippet:

```
In [441]: correct_text_generic('fianlly')
Out[441]: 'finally'
```

```
In [442]: correct_text_generic('FIANLLY')
Out[442]: 'FINALLY'
```

Of course, this method is not always completely accurate, and there may be words that might not be corrected if they do not occur in our vocabulary dictionary. Using more data would help in this case, as long as we cover different words having correct spellings in our vocabulary. This same algorithm is available to be used out of the box in the pattern library, as is done in the following snippet:

```
from pattern.en import suggest

# test on wrongly spelt words
In [184]: print suggest('fianlly')
 [('finally', 1.0)]

In [185]: print suggest('flaot')
 [('flat', 0.85), ('float', 0.15)]
```

Besides this, there are several robust libraries available in Python, including PyEnchant, based on the enchant library (http://pythonhosted.org/pyenchant/), and aspell-python, which is a Python wrapper around the popular GNU Aspell. Feel free to check them out and use them for correcting word spellings!

Stemming

Understanding the process of stemming requires understanding what word stems represent. Chapter 1 talked about morphemes, the smallest independent unit in any natural language. Morphemes consist of units that are stems and affixes. Affixes are units like prefixes, suffixes, and so on, which are attached to a word stem to change its meaning or create a new word altogether. Word stems are also often known as the *base form* of a word, and we can create new words by attaching affixes to them in a process known as *inflection*. The reverse of this is obtaining the base form of a word from its inflected form, and this is known as *stemming*.

Consider the word *JUMP*. You can add affixes to it and form new words like *JUMPS*, *JUMPED*, and *JUMPING*. In this case, the base word JUMP is the word stem. If we were to carry out stemming on any of its three inflected forms, we would get back the base form. This is illustrated in Figure 3-1.

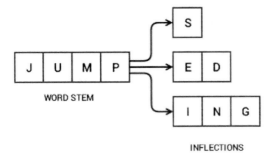

Figure 3-1. *Word stem and inflections*

The figure shows how the word stem is present in all its inflections since it forms the base on which each inflection is built upon using affixes. Stemming helps us in standardizing words to their base stem irrespective of their inflections, which helps many applications like classifying or clustering text, and even in information retrieval. Search engines make use of such techniques extensively to give better and more accurate results irrespective of the word form.

The nltk package has several implementations for stemmers. These stemmers are implemented in the stem module, which inherits the StemmerI interface in the nltk.stem. api module. You can even create your own stemmer using this class (technically it is an *interface*) as your base class. One of the most popular stemmers is the Porter stemmer, which is based on the algorithm developed by its inventor, Dr. Martin Porter. Originally, the algorithm is said to have had a total of five different phases for reduction of inflections to their stems, where each phase has its own set of rules. There also exists a Porter2 algorithm, which was the original stemming algorithm with some improvements suggested by Dr. Porter. You can see the Porter stemmer in action in the following code snippet:

```
# Porter Stemmer
In [458]: from nltk.stem import PorterStemmer
     ...: ps = PorterStemmer()

In [459]: print ps.stem('jumping'), ps.stem('jumps'), ps.stem('jumped')
jump jump jump

In [460]: print ps.stem('lying')
lie

In [461]: print ps.stem('strange')
strang
```

The Lancaster stemmer is based on the Lancaster stemming algorithm, also often known as the Paice/Husk stemmer, invented by Chris D. Paice. This stemmer is an iterative stemmer that has over 120 rules specifying specific removal or replacement for affixes to obtain the word stems. The following snippet shows the Lancaster stemmer in action:

```
# Lancaster Stemmer
In [465]: from nltk.stem import LancasterStemmer
     ...: ls = LancasterStemmer()

In [466]: print ls.stem('jumping'), ls.stem('jumps'), ls.stem('jumped')
jump jump jump

In [467]: print ls.stem('lying')
lying

In [468]: print ls.stem('strange')
strange
```

You can see that the behavior of this stemmer is different from the Porter stemmer.

There are several other stemmers, including RegexpStemmer, where you can build your own stemmer based on user-defined rules, and SnowballStemmer, which supports stemming in 13 different languages besides English.

The following code snippet shows some ways of using them for performing stemming. The RegexpStemmer uses regular expressions to identify the morphological affixes in words, and any part of the string matching the same is removed:

```
# Regex based stemmer
In [471]: from nltk.stem import RegexpStemmer
     ...: rs = RegexpStemmer('ing$|s$|ed$', min=4)

In [472]: print rs.stem('jumping'), rs.stem('jumps'), rs.stem('jumped')
jump jump jump

In [473]: print rs.stem('lying')
ly

In [474]: print rs.stem('strange')
strange
```

You can see how the stemming results are different from the previous stemmers and are based completely on our custom-defined rules based on regular expressions. The following snippet shows how to use the SnowballStemmer to stem words in other languages (you can find more details about the Snowball Project at http://snowballstem.org):

```
# Snowball Stemmer
In [486]: from nltk.stem import SnowballStemmer
     ...: ss = SnowballStemmer("german")
```

```
In [487]: print 'Supported Languages:', SnowballStemmer.languages
Supported Languages: (u'danish', u'dutch', u'english', u'finnish',
u'french', u'german', u'hungarian', u'italian', u'norwegian', u'porter',
u'portuguese', u'romanian', u'russian', u'spanish', u'swedish')

# stemming on German words
# autobahnen -> cars
# autobahn -> car
In [488]: ss.stem('autobahnen')
Out[488]: u'autobahn'

# springen -> jumping
# spring -> jump
In [489]: ss.stem('springen')
Out[489]: u'spring'
```

The Porter stemmer is used most frequently—but you should choose your stemmer based on your problem and after trial and error. If needed, you can even build your own stemmer with your own defined rules.

Lemmatization

The process of *lemmatization* is very similar to stemming—you remove word affixes to get to a base form of the word. But in this case, this base form is also known as the *root word*, but not the *root stem*. The difference is that the root stem may not always be a lexicographically correct word; that is, it may not be present in the dictionary. The root word, also known as the *lemma*, will always be present in the dictionary.

The lemmatization process is considerably slower than stemming because an additional step is involved where the root form or lemma is formed by removing the affix from the word if and only if the lemma is present in the dictionary. The nltk package has a robust lemmatization module that uses WordNet and the word's syntax and semantics, like part of speech and context, to get the root word or lemma. Remember parts of speech from Chapter 1? There were mainly three entities—nouns, verbs, and adjectives—that occur most frequently in natural language.

The following code snippet shows how to use lemmatization for words belonging to each of those types:

```
In [514]: from nltk.stem import WordNetLemmatizer
     ...:
     ...: wnl = WordNetLemmatizer()

# lemmatize nouns
In [515]: print wnl.lemmatize('cars', 'n')
     ...: print wnl.lemmatize('men', 'n')
car
men
```

```
# lemmatize verbs
In [516]: print wnl.lemmatize('running', 'v')
     ...: print wnl.lemmatize('ate', 'v')
run
eat

# lemmatize adjectives
In [517]: print wnl.lemmatize('saddest', 'a')
     ...: print wnl.lemmatize('fancier', 'a')
sad
fancy
```

The preceding snippet shows how each word is converted back to its base form using lemmatization. This helps us in standardizing words. The preceding code leverages the WordNetLemmatizer class, which internally uses the morphy() function belonging to the WordNetCorpusReader class. This function basically finds the base form or lemma for a given word using the word and its part of speech by checking the Wordnet corpus and uses a recursive technique for removing affixes from the word until a match is found in WordNet. If no match is found, the input word itself is returned unchanged.

The part of speech is extremely important here because if that is wrong, the lemmatization will not be effective, as you can see in the following snippet:

```
# ineffective lemmatization
In [518]: print wnl.lemmatize('ate', 'n')
     ...: print wnl.lemmatize('fancier', 'v')
ate
fancier
```

This brings us to the end of our discussion on various techniques for processing and normalizing text. By now, you have learned a great deal about how to process, normalize, and standardize text. In the next section, we will look at ways of analyzing and understanding various facets of textual data with regard to its syntactic properties and structure.

Understanding Text Syntax and Structure

Chapter 1 talked about language syntax and structure in detail. If you don't remember, head over to the "Language Syntax and Structure" section and skim through it quickly to get an idea of the various ways of analyzing and understanding the syntax and structure of textual data. In this section, we will look and implement some of the concepts and techniques that are used for understanding text syntax and structure. This is extremely useful in NLP and is usually done after text processing and normalization. We will focus on implementing the following techniques:

- Parts of speech (POS) tagging

- Shallow parsing

- Dependency-based parsing

- Constituency-based parsing

This book is aimed at practitioners and enforces and emphasizes the best approaches to implementing and using techniques and algorithms in real-world problems. Therefore, the following sections look at the best possible ways of leveraging existing libraries like nltk and spacy to implement and execute some of these techniques. Also, because many readers may be interested in the internals and implementing some of these techniques on your own, we will also look at ways to do that. Remember, our primary focus is always to look at ways implementing the concepts in action with practical examples—and not re-invent the wheel. Before going further, we will look at the necessary dependencies and installation details for the required libraries, because some of them are not very straightforward.

Installing Necessary Dependencies

We will be leveraging several libraries and dependencies:

- The nltk library, preferably version 3.1 or 3.2.1

- The spacy library

- The pattern library

- The Stanford parser

- Graphviz and necessary libraries for the same

We touched on installing nltk in Chapter 1. You can install it directly by going to your terminal or command prompt and typing pip install nltk, which will download and install it. Remember to install the library having a version preferably other than 3.2.0, because there are some issues with several functions in that distribution, like pos_tag().

After downloading and installing nltk, remember to download the corpora also discussed in Chapter 1. For more on downloading and installing nltk, see www.nltk.org/install.html and www.nltk.org/data.html, which describe how to install the data dependencies. You can do the same by starting the Python interpreter and using the following snippet:

```
import nltk
# download all dependencies and corpora
nltk.download('all', halt_on_error=False)
# OR use a GUI based downloader and select dependencies
nltk.download()
```

To install pattern, typing pip install pattern should pretty much download and install the library and its necessary dependencies. The link www.clips.ua.ac.be/pages/pattern-en offers more information about pattern. For spacy, you need to first install the package and then separately install its dependencies, also called a *language model*. To install spacy, type pip install spacy from the terminal. Once done, download the English language model using the command python -m spacy.en.download from the terminal, which will download around 500 MB of data in the directory of the spacy package itself. For more details, refer to https://spacy.io/docs/#getting-started, which tells you how to get started with using spacy. We will use spacy for tagging and depicting dependency-based parsing.

The Stanford Parser is a Java-based implementation for a language parser developed at Stanford, which helps in parsing sentences to understand their underlying structure. We will perform both dependency and constituency grammar–based parsing using the Stanford Parser and `nltk`, which provides an excellent wrapper to leverage and use the parser from Python itself without the need to write code in Java. You can refer to the official installation guide at `https://github.com/nltk/nltk/wiki/Installing-Third-Party-Software`, which describes how to download and install the Stanford Parser and integrate it with `nltk`. Personally, I have faced several issues, especially in Windows-based systems, so I will provide one of the best-known methods for installation of the Stanford Parser and its necessary dependencies.

To start with, make sure you first download and install the Java Development Kit (not just JRE, also known as Java Runtime Environment) by going to `www.oracle.com/technetwork/java/javase/downloads/index.html?ssSourceSiteId=otnjp`. That is the official website. Java SE 8u101 / 8u102 are the latest versions at the time of writing this book—I have used 8u102. After installing, make sure to set the "Path" for Java by adding it to the `Path` system environment variable. You can also create a `JAVA_HOME` environment variable pointing to the `java.exe` file belonging to the JDK. In my experience, neither worked for me when running the code from Python, and I had to explicitly use the Python `os` library to set the environment variable, which I will show when we dive into the implementation details. Once Java is installed, download the official Stanford Parser from `http://nlp.stanford.edu/software/stanford-parser-full-2015-04-20.zip`, which seems to work quite well. You can try out a later version by going to `http://nlp.stanford.edu/software/lex-parser.shtml#Download` and checking the Release History section. After downloading, unzip it to a known location in your filesystem. Once done, you are now ready to use the parser from `nltk`, which we will be exploring soon.

Graphviz is not really a necessity, and we will only be using it to view the dependency parse tree generated by the Stanford Parser. You can download Graphviz from its official website at `www.graphviz.org/Download_windows.php` and install it. Next, install `pygraphviz`, which you can get by downloading the wheel file from `www.lfd.uci.edu/~gohlke/pythonlibs/#pygraphviz`, based on your system architecture and python version. Then install it using the command `pip install pygraphviz-1.3.1-cp27-none-win_amd64.whl` for a 64-bit system running Python 2.7.x. Once installed, `pygraphviz` should be ready to work. Some have reported running into additional issues, though, and you may need to install `pydot-ng` and `graphviz` in the same order using the following snippet in the terminal:

```
pip install pydot-ng
pip install graphviz
```

With this, we are done installing necessary dependencies and can start implementing and looking at practical examples to understand text. However, we are not ready just yet. We still need to go through a few basic concepts of ML before we dive into code and examples.

Important Machine Learning Concepts

We will be implementing and training some of our own taggers in the following section using corpora and also leverage existing pre-built taggers. There are some important concepts related to analytics and ML that you must know in order to better understand the implementations:

- *Data preparation*: Usually consists of pre-processing the data before extracting features and training

- *Feature extraction*: The process of extracting useful features from raw data that are used to train machine learning models

- *Features*: Various useful attributes of the data (examples could be age, weight, and so on for personal data)

- *Training data*: A set of data points used to train a model

- *Testing/validation data*: A set of data points on which a pre-trained model is tested and evaluated to see how well it performs

- *Model*: Built using a combination of data/features and a machine learning algorithm that could be supervised or unsupervised

- *Accuracy*: How well the model predicts something (also has other detailed evaluation metrics like precision, recall, and F1-score)

These terms should be enough to get you started. Going into further detail is beyond the scope of this book, but you will find a lot of resources on the web about ML, in case you are interested in exploring machine learning further. Later chapters cover both supervised and unsupervised learning with regard to textual data.

Parts of Speech (POS) Tagging

Parts of speech (POS) are specific lexical categories to which words are assigned based on their syntactic context and role. Chapter 1 covered some ground on POS and mentioned the main POS being noun, verb, adjective, and adverb. The process of classifying and labeling POS tags for words called *parts of speech tagging* or *POS tagging*. POS tags are used to annotate words and depict their POS, which is really helpful when we need to use the same annotated text later in NLP-based applications because we can filter by specific parts of speech and utilize that information to perform specific analysis, such as narrowing down upon nouns and seeing which ones are the most prominent, word sense disambiguation, and grammar analysis.

We will be using the Penn Treebank notation for POS tagging. You can find more information about various POS tags and their notation at `www.cis.uni-muenchen.de/~schmid/tools/TreeTagger/data/Penn-Treebank-Tagset.pdf`, which contains detailed documentation explaining each tag with examples. The Penn Treebank project is part of the University of Pennsylvania. Its web site at `www.cis.upenn.edu/~treebank/` offers more information about the project. Remember there are various tags, such as POS tags for parts of speech assigned to words, chunk tags, which are usually assigned to phrases, and some tags are secondary tags used to depict relations. Table 3-1 gives a detailed overview of different tags with examples, in case you do not want to go through the detailed documentation for Penn Treebank tags. You can use this as a reference anytime to understand POS tags and parse trees in a better way.

Table 3-1. *Parts of Speech Tags*

SI No.	TAG	DESCRIPTION	EXAMPLE(S)
1	CC	Coordinating Conjunction	*and, or*
2	CD	Cardinal Number	*five, one, 2*
3	DT	Determiner	*a, the*
4	EX	Existential *there*	*there were two cars*
5	FW	Foreign Word	*d'hoevre, mais*
6	IN	Preposition/ Subordinating Conjunction	*of, in, on, that*
7	JJ	Adjective	*quick, lazy*
8	JJR	Adjective, comparative	*quicker, lazier*
9	JJS	Adjective, superlative	*quickest, laziest*
10	LS	List item marker	*2)*
11	MD	Verb, modal	*could, should*
12	NN	Noun, singular or mass	*fox, dog*
13	NNS	Noun, plural	*foxes, dogs*
14	NNP	Noun, proper singular	*John, Alice*
15	NNPS	Noun, proper plural	*Vikings, Indians, Germans*
16	PDT	Predeterminer	*both the cats*
17	POS	Possessive ending	*boss's*
18	PRP	Pronoun, personal	*me, you*
19	PRP$	Pronoun, possessive	*our, my, your*
20	RB	Adverb	*naturally, extremely, hardly*
21	RBR	Adverb, comparative	*better*
22	RBS	Adverb, superlative	*best*
23	RP	Adverb, particle	*about, up*
24	SYM	Symbol	*%, $*
25	TO	Infinitival to	*how to, what to do*
26	UH	Interjection	*oh, gosh, wow*

(*continued*)

Table 3-1. (*continued*)

SI No.	TAG	DESCRIPTION	EXAMPLE(S)
27	VB	Verb, base form	*run, give*
28	VBD	Verb, past tense	*ran, gave*
29	VBG	Verb, gerund/ present participle	*running, giving*
30	VBN	Verb, past participle	*given*
31	VBP	Verb, non-3rd person singular present	*I think, I take*
32	VBZ	Verb, 3rd person singular present	*he thinks, he takes*
33	WDT	Wh-determiner	*which, whatever*
34	WP	Wh-pronoun, personal	*who, what*
35	WP$	Wh-pronoun, possessive	*whose*
36	WRB	Wh-adverb	*where, when*
37	NP	Noun Phrase	*the brown fox*
38	PP	Prepositional Phrase	*in between, over the dog*
39	VP	Verb Phrase	*was jumping*
40	ADJP	Adjective Phrase	*warm and snug*
41	ADVP	Adverb Phrase	*also*
42	SBAR	Subordinating Conjunction	*whether or not*
43	PRT	Particle	*up*
44	INTJ	Interjection	*hello*
45	PNP	Prepositional Noun Phrase	*over the dog, as of today*
46	-SBJ	Sentence Subject	*the fox jumped over the dog*
47	-OBJ	Sentence Object	*the fox jumped over the dog*

The table shows the main POS tag set used in the Penn Treebank and is the most widely used POS tag set in various text analytics and NLP applications. In the following sections, we will look at some recommended POS taggers and also see how we can build our own tagger.

Recommended POS Taggers

We will discuss some recommended ways for tagging sentences here. The first method is using nltk's recommended pos_tag() function, which is actually based on the Penn Treebank. We will reuse our interesting sentence from Chapter 1 here. The following code snippet depicts how to get the POS tags of a sentence using nltk:

```
sentence = 'The brown fox is quick and he is jumping over the lazy dog'

import nltk
tokens = nltk.word_tokenize(sentence)
tagged_sent = nltk.pos_tag(tokens, tagset='universal')
In [13]: print tagged_sent
[('The', u'DET'), ('brown', u'ADJ'), ('fox', u'NOUN'), ('is', u'VERB'),
('quick', u'ADJ'), ('and', u'CONJ'), ('he', u'PRON'), ('is', u'VERB'),
('jumping', u'VERB'), ('over', u'ADP'), ('the', u'DET'), ('lazy', u'ADJ'),
('dog', u'NOUN')]
```

The preceding output shows us the POS tag for each word in the sentence. You will find the tags quite similar to the ones shown in Table 3.1. Some of them were also mentioned in Chapter 1 as general/universal tags. You can also use the pattern module to get POS tags of a sentence using the following code snippet:

```
from pattern.en import tag
tagged_sent = tag(sentence)
In [15]: print tagged_sent
 [(u'The', u'DT'), (u'brown', u'JJ'), (u'fox', u'NN'), (u'is', u'VBZ'),
(u'quick', u'JJ'), (u'and', u'CC'), (u'he', u'PRP'), (u'is', u'VBZ'),
(u'jumping', u'VBG'), (u'over', u'IN'), (u'the', u'DT'), (u'lazy', u'JJ'),
(u'dog', u'NN')]
```

That output gives us tags that purely follow the Penn Treebank format, specifying the form of adjective, noun, or verb in more detail.

Building Your Own POS Taggers

In this section, we will explore some techniques by which we can build our own POS taggers and will be leveraging some classes provided by nltk for doing so. For evaluating the performance of our taggers, we will be using some test data from the treebank corpus in nltk. We will also be using some training data for training some of our taggers. To start, we will get the necessary data for training and evaluating the taggers by reading in the tagged treebank corpus:

```
from nltk.corpus import treebank
data = treebank.tagged_sents()
train_data = data[:3500]
test_data = data[3500:]
```

```
# get a look at what each data point looks like
In [17]: print train_data[0]
 [(u'Pierre', u'NNP'), (u'Vinken', u'NNP'), (u',', u','), (u'61', u'CD'),
(u'years', u'NNS'), (u'old', u'JJ'), (u',', u','), (u'will', u'MD'),
(u'join', u'VB'), (u'the', u'DT'), (u'board', u'NN'), (u'as', u'IN'), (u'a',
u'DT'), (u'nonexecutive', u'JJ'), (u'director', u'NN'), (u'Nov.', u'NNP'),
(u'29', u'CD'), (u'.', u'.')]
```

```
# remember tokens is obtained after tokenizing our sentence
tokens = nltk.word_tokenize(sentence)
In [18]: print tokens
['The', 'brown', 'fox', 'is', 'quick', 'and', 'he', 'is', 'jumping', 'over',
'the', 'lazy', 'dog']
```

We will use the test data to evaluate our taggers and see how they work on our sample sentence by using its tokens as input. All the taggers we will be leveraging from nltk are part of the nltk.tag package. Each tagger is a child class of the base TaggerI class, and each tagger implements a tag() function that takes a list of sentence tokens as input and returns the same list of words with their POS tags as output. Besides tagging, there is an evaluate() function that is used to evaluate the performance of the tagger. This is done by tagging each input test sentence and then comparing the result with the actual tags of the sentence. We will be using the very same function to test the performance of our taggers on test_data.

We will first look at the DefaultTagger, which inherits from the SequentialBackoffTagger base class and assigns the same user input POS tag to each word. This may seem really naïve, but it is an excellent way to form a baseline POS tagger and improve upon it:

```
from nltk.tag import DefaultTagger
dt = DefaultTagger('NN')
```

```
# accuracy on test data
In [24]: print dt.evaluate(test_data)
0.145415819537
# tagging our sample sentence
In [25]: print dt.tag(tokens)
 [('The', 'NN'), ('brown', 'NN'), ('fox', 'NN'), ('is', 'NN'), ('quick',
'NN'), ('and', 'NN'), ('he', 'NN'), ('is', 'NN'), ('jumping', 'NN'),
('over', 'NN'), ('the', 'NN'), ('lazy', 'NN'), ('dog', 'NN')]
```

We can see from the preceding output we have obtained 14 percent accuracy in correctly tagging words from the treebank test dataset—which is not that great, and the output tags on our sample sentence are all nouns, just as we expected because we fed the tagger with the same tag.

We will now use regular expressions and the RegexpTagger to see if we can build a better performing tagger:

```
from nltk.tag import RegexpTagger
# define regex tag patterns
patterns = [
        (r'.*ing$', 'VBG'),            # gerunds
        (r'.*ed$', 'VBD'),             # simple past
        (r'.*es$', 'VBZ'),             # 3rd singular present
        (r'.*ould$', 'MD'),            # modals
        (r'.*\'s$', 'NN$'),            # possessive nouns
        (r'.*s$', 'NNS'),             # plural nouns
        (r'^-?[0-9]+(.[0-9]+)?$', 'CD'),  # cardinal numbers
        (r'.*', 'NN')                 # nouns (default) ... ]
rt = RegexpTagger(patterns)


# accuracy on test data
In [27]: print rt.evaluate(test_data)
0.240391131765


# tagging our sample sentence

In [28]: print rt.tag(tokens)
 [('The', 'NN'), ('brown', 'NN'), ('fox', 'NN'), ('is', 'NNS'), ('quick',
'NN'), ('and', 'NN'), ('he', 'NN'), ('is', 'NNS'), ('jumping', 'VBG'),
('over', 'NN'), ('the', 'NN'), ('lazy', 'NN'), ('dog', 'NN')]
```

That output shows that the accuracy has now increased to 24 percent. But can we do better? We will now train some n-gram taggers. *n-grams* are contiguous sequences of *n* items from a sequence of text or speech. These items could consist of words, phonemes, letters, characters, or syllables. *Shingles* are n-grams where the items only consist of words. We will use n-grams of size 1, 2, and 3, which are also known as *unigram*, *bigram*, and *trigram* respectively. The UnigramTagger, BigramTagger, and TrigramTagger are classes that inherit from the base class NGramTagger, which itself inherits from the ContextTagger class, which inherits from the SequentialBackoffTagger class. We will use train_data as training data to train the n-gram taggers based on sentence tokens and their POS tags. Then we will evaluate the trained taggers on test_data and see the result on tagging our sample sentence:

```
from nltk.tag import UnigramTagger
from nltk.tag import BigramTagger
from nltk.tag import TrigramTagger

ut = UnigramTagger(train_data)
bt = BigramTagger(train_data)
tt = TrigramTagger(train_data)

# testing performance of unigram tagger
In [31]: print ut.evaluate(test_data)
0.861361215994
In [32]: print ut.tag(tokens)
```

```
[('The', u'DT'), ('brown', None), ('fox', None), ('is', u'VBZ'), ('quick',
u'JJ'), ('and', u'CC'), ('he', u'PRP'), ('is', u'VBZ'), ('jumping', u'VBG'),
('over', u'IN'), ('the', u'DT'), ('lazy', None), ('dog', None)]

# testing performance of bigram tagger
In [33]: print bt.evaluate(test_data)
0.134669377481
In [34]: print bt.tag(tokens)
 [('The', u'DT'), ('brown', None), ('fox', None), ('is', None), ('quick',
None), ('and', None), ('he', None), ('is', None), ('jumping', None),
('over', None), ('the', None), ('lazy', None), ('dog', None)]

# testing performance of trigram tagger
In [35]: print tt.evaluate(test_data)
0.0806467228192
In [36]: print tt.tag(tokens)
 [('The', u'DT'), ('brown', None), ('fox', None), ('is', None), ('quick',
None), ('and', None), ('he', None), ('is', None), ('jumping', None),
('over', None), ('the', None), ('lazy', None), ('dog', None)]
```

The preceding output clearly shows that we obtain 86 percent accuracy on the test set using UnigramTagger tagger alone, which is really good compared to our last tagger. The None tag indicates the tagger was unable to tag that word, the reason being that it was unable to get a similar token in the training data. Accuracies of the bigram and trigram models are far less because it is not always the case that the same bigrams and trigrams it had observed in the training data will also be present in the same way in the testing data.

We will now look at an approach to combine all the taggers by creating a combined tagger with a list of taggers and use a backoff tagger. Essentially we would create a chain of taggers, and each tagger would fall back on a backoff tagger if it cannot tag the input tokens:

```
def combined_tagger(train_data, taggers, backoff=None):
    for tagger in taggers:
        backoff = tagger(train_data, backoff=backoff)
    return backoff

ct = combined_tagger(train_data=train_data,
                     taggers=[UnigramTagger, BigramTagger, TrigramTagger],
                     backoff=rt)

# evaluating the new combined tagger with backoff taggers
In [38]: print ct.evaluate(test_data)
0.910155871817
In [39]: print ct.tag(tokens)
 [('The', u'DT'), ('brown', 'NN'), ('fox', 'NN'), ('is', u'VBZ'), ('quick',
u'JJ'), ('and', u'CC'), ('he', u'PRP'), ('is', u'VBZ'), ('jumping', 'VBG'),
('over', u'IN'), ('the', u'DT'), ('lazy', 'NN'), ('dog', 'NN')]
```

We now obtain an accuracy of 91 percent on the test data, which is excellent. Also we see that this new tagger is able to successfully tag all the tokens in our sample sentence (even though a couple of them are not correct, like brown should be an adjective).

For our final tagger, we will use a supervised classification algorithm to train our tagger. The ClassifierBasedPOSTagger class lets us train a tagger by using a supervised learning algorithm in the classifier_builder parameter. This class is inherited from the ClassifierBasedTagger and has a feature_detector() function that forms the core of the training process. This function is used to generate various features from the training data, like word, previous word, tag, previous tag, case, and so on. In fact, you can even build your own feature detector function and pass it to the feature_detector parameter when instantiating an object of the ClassifierBasedPOSTagger class. The classifier we will be using is the NaiveBayesClassifier, which uses the Bayes' theorem to build a probabilistic classifier, assuming the features are independent. Read more about it at https://en.wikipedia.org/wiki/Naive_Bayes_classifier if you like (since going into more detail about the algorithm is out of our current scope).

The following code snippet shows a classification-based approach to building and evaluating a POS tagger:

```
from nltk.classify import NaiveBayesClassifier
from nltk.tag.sequential import ClassifierBasedPOSTagger

nbt = ClassifierBasedPOSTagger(train=train_data,
                               classifier_builder=NaiveBayesClassifier.
                               train)

# evaluate tagger on test data and sample sentence
In [41]: print nbt.evaluate(test_data)
0.930680607997
In [42]: print nbt.tag(tokens)
 [('The', u'DT'), ('brown', u'JJ'), ('fox', u'NN'), ('is', u'VBZ'),
('quick', u'JJ'), ('and', u'CC'), ('he', u'PRP'), ('is', u'VBZ'),
('jumping', u'VBG'), ('over', u'IN'), ('the', u'DT'), ('lazy', u'JJ'),
('dog', u'VBG')]
```

Using the preceding tagger, we get an accuracy of 93 percent on our test data—the highest out of all our taggers. Also if you observe the output tags for our sample sentence, you will see they are correct and make perfect sense. This gives us an idea of how powerful and effective classifier-based POS taggers can be. Feel free to use a different classifier, like MaxentClassifier, and compare the performance with this tagger. There are also several other ways to build and use POS taggers using nltk and other packages. Even though it is not really necessary, and this should be enough to cover your POS tagging needs, you can go ahead and explore other methods to compare with these methods and satisfy your curiosity.

Shallow Parsing

Shallow parsing, also known as *light parsing* or *chunking,* is a technique of analyzing the structure of a sentence to break it down into its smallest constituents (which are tokens such as words) and group them together into higher-level phrases. In shallow parsing, there is more focus on identifying these phrases or chunks rather than diving into further details of the internal syntax and relations inside each chunk, like we see in grammar-based parse trees obtained from deep parsing. The main objective of shallow parsing is to obtain semantically meaningful phrases and observe relations among them.

Refer to the "Language Syntax and Structure" section from Chapter 1 to refresh your memory regarding how words and phrases give structure to a sentence consisting of a bunch of words. A shallow parsed tree is also depicted there for our sample sentence. We will look at various ways of performing shallow parsing by starting with some recommended out-of-the-box shallow parsers. We will also implement some of our own shallow parsers using techniques like regular expressions, chunking, chinking, and tag-based training.

Recommended Shallow Parsers

We will be leveraging the `pattern` package here to create a shallow parser to extract meaningful chunks out of sentences. The following code snippet shows how to perform shallow parsing on our sample sentence:

```
sentence = 'The brown fox is quick and he is jumping over the lazy dog'

from pattern.en import parsetree
tree = parsetree(sentence)

# print the shallow parsed sentence tree
In [5]: print tree
   ...:
[Sentence('The/DT/B-NP/O brown/JJ/I-NP/O fox/NN/I-NP/O is/VBZ/B-VP/O quick/
JJ/B-ADJP/O and/CC/O/O he/PRP/B-NP/O is/VBZ/B-VP/O jumping/VBG/I-VP/O over/
IN/B-PP/B-PNP the/DT/B-NP/I-PNP lazy/JJ/I-NP/I-PNP dog/NN/I-NP/I-PNP')]
```

The preceding output is the raw shallow-parsed sentence tree for our sample sentence. Many of the tags will be quite familiar if you compare them to the earlier POS tags table. You will notice some new notations with I, O, and B prefixes, the popular IOB notation used in chunking, that represent Inside, Outside, and Beginning. The B- prefix before a tag indicates it is the beginning of a chunk, and I- prefix indicates that it is inside a chunk. The O tag indicates that the token does not belong to any chunk. The B- tag is always used when there are subsequent tags following it of the same type without the presence of O tags between them.

The following snippet shows how to get chunks in an easier-to-understand format:

```
# print all chunks
In [6]: for sentence_tree in tree:
   ...:     print sentence_tree.chunks
[Chunk('The brown fox/NP'), Chunk('is/VP'), Chunk('quick/ADJP'), Chunk('he/
NP'), Chunk('is jumping/VP'), Chunk('over/PP'), Chunk('the lazy dog/NP')]

# Depict each phrase and its internal constituents
In [9]: for sentence_tree in tree:
   ...:     for chunk in sentence_tree.chunks:
   ...:         print chunk.type, '->', [(word.string, word.type)
   ...:                                  for word in chunk.words]
NP -> [(u'The', u'DT'), (u'brown', u'JJ'), (u'fox', u'NN')]
VP -> [(u'is', u'VBZ')]
ADJP -> [(u'quick', u'JJ')]
NP -> [(u'he', u'PRP')]
VP -> [(u'is', u'VBZ'), (u'jumping', u'VBG')]
PP -> [(u'over', u'IN')]
NP -> [(u'the', u'DT'), (u'lazy', u'JJ'), (u'dog', u'NN')]
```

The preceding outputs show an easier-to-understand result obtained from shallow parsing of our sample sentence, where each phrase and its constituents are clearly shown.

We can create some generic functions to parse and visualize shallow parsed sentence trees in a better way and also reuse them to parse any sentence in general. The following code shows how:

```
from pattern.en import parsetree, Chunk
from nltk.tree import Tree

# create a shallow parsed sentence tree
def create_sentence_tree(sentence, lemmatize=False):
    sentence_tree = parsetree(sentence,
                              relations=True,
                              lemmata=lemmatize) # if you want to lemmatize
                              the tokens
    return sentence_tree[0]

# get various constituents of the parse tree
def get_sentence_tree_constituents(sentence_tree):
    return sentence_tree.constituents()

# process the shallow parsed tree into an easy to understand format
def process_sentence_tree(sentence_tree):

    tree_constituents = get_sentence_tree_constituents(sentence_tree)
    processed_tree = [
```

```
                        (item.type,
                          [
                              (w.string, w.type)
                              for w in item.words
                          ]
                         )
                         if type(item) == Chunk
                         else ('-',
                                [
                                    (item.string, item.type)
                                ]
                               )
                               for item in tree_constituents
                    ]

    return processed_tree

# print the sentence tree using nltk's Tree syntax
def print_sentence_tree(sentence_tree):

    processed_tree = process_sentence_tree(sentence_tree)
    processed_tree = [
                         Tree( item[0],
                            [
                                Tree(x[1], [x[0]])
                                for x in item[1]
                            ]
                            )
                            for item in processed_tree
                      ]

    tree = Tree('S', processed_tree )
    print tree
# visualize the sentence tree using nltk's Tree syntax
def visualize_sentence_tree(sentence_tree):

    processed_tree = process_sentence_tree(sentence_tree)
    processed_tree = [
                         Tree( item[0],
                            [
                                Tree(x[1], [x[0]])
                                for x in item[1]
                            ]
                            )
                            for item in processed_tree
                      ]
    tree = Tree('S', processed_tree )
    tree.draw()
```

We can see the preceding functions in action on our sample sentence in the following code snippet when we execute them:

```
# raw shallow parsed tree
In [11]: t = create_sentence_tree(sentence)
   ...: print t
Sentence('The/DT/B-NP/O/NP-SBJ-1 brown/JJ/I-NP/O/NP-SBJ-1 fox/NN/I-NP/O/NP-
SBJ-1 is/VBZ/B-VP/O/VP-1 quick/JJ/B-ADJP/O/O and/CC/O/O/O he/PRP/B-NP/O/NP-
SBJ-2 is/VBZ/B-VP/O/VP-2 jumping/VBG/I-VP/O/VP-2 over/IN/B-PP/B-PNP/O the/
DT/B-NP/I-PNP/O lazy/JJ/I-NP/I-PNP/O dog/NN/I-NP/I-PNP/O')
```

```
# processed shallow parsed tree
In [16]: pt = process_sentence_tree(t)
   ...: pt
Out[16]:
[(u'NP', [(u'The', u'DT'), (u'brown', u'JJ'), (u'fox', u'NN')]),
 (u'VP', [(u'is', u'VBZ')]),
 (u'ADJP', [(u'quick', u'JJ')]),
 ('-', [(u'and', u'CC')]),
 (u'NP', [(u'he', u'PRP')]),
 (u'VP', [(u'is', u'VBZ'), (u'jumping', u'VBG')]),
 (u'PP', [(u'over', u'IN')]),
 (u'NP', [(u'the', u'DT'), (u'lazy', u'JJ'), (u'dog', u'NN')])]
```

```
# print shallow parsed tree in an easy to understand format using nltk's
Tree syntax
In [17]: print_sentence_tree(t)
(S
  (NP (DT The) (JJ brown) (NN fox))
  (VP (VBZ is))
  (ADJP (JJ quick))
  (- (CC and))
  (NP (PRP he))
  (VP (VBZ is) (VBG jumping))
  (PP (IN over))
  (NP (DT the) (JJ lazy) (NN dog)))
```

```
# visualize the shallow parsed tree
In [18]: visualize_sentence_tree(t)
```

Figure 3-2. *Visual representation of a shallow parsed tree for our sample sentence*

The preceding outputs show some ways of creating, representing, and visualizing shallow parse trees from sentences. The visual representation shown in Figure 3-2 is very similar to the tree shown in Chapter 1 for the same sentence. The lowest level indicates the values of the actual tokens; the next level indicates the POS tags for each token; and the next higher level indicates the chunk phrasal tags. Go ahead and try out these functions on some other sentences and compare their results. In the following sections we will implement some of our own shallow parsers.

Building Your Own Shallow Parsers

We will use several techniques like regular expressions and tagging-based learners to build our own shallow parsers. As with POS tagging, we will use some training data to train our parsers if needed and evaluate all our parsers on some test data and also on our sample sentence. The treebank corpus is available in nltk with chunk annotations. We will load it first and prepare our training and testing datasets using the following code snippet:

```
from nltk.corpus import treebank_chunk
data = treebank_chunk.chunked_sents()
train_data = data[:4000]
test_data = data[4000:]

# view what a sample data point looks like
In [21]: print train_data[7]
 (S
  (NP A/DT Lorillard/NNP spokewoman/NN)
  said/VBD
  ,/,
  ``/``
  (NP This/DT)
  is/VBZ
  (NP an/DT old/JJ story/NN)
  ./.)
```

From the preceding output, you can see that our data points are sentences that are already annotated with phrase and POS tags metadata that will be useful in training shallow parsers. We will start with using regular expressions for shallow parsing using concepts of chunking and chinking. Using the process of *chunking*, we can use and specify specific patterns to identify what we would want to chunk or segment in a sentence, like phrases based on specific metadata like POS tags for each token. *Chinking* is the reverse of chunking, where we specify which specific tokens we do not want to be a part of any chunk and then form the necessary chunks excluding these tokens. Let us consider a simple sentence and use regular expressions by leveraging the RegexpParser class to create shallow parsers to illustrate both chunking and chinking for noun phrases:

```
simple_sentence = 'the quick fox jumped over the lazy dog'

from nltk.chunk import RegexpParser
from pattern.en import tag
```

```
# get POS tagged sentence
tagged_simple_sent = tag(simple_sentence)
In [83]: print tagged_simple_sent
[(u'the', u'DT'), (u'quick', u'JJ'), (u'fox', u'NN'), (u'jumped', u'VBD'),
(u'over', u'IN'), (u'the', u'DT'), (u'lazy', u'JJ'), (u'dog', u'NN')]

# illustrate NP chunking based on explicit chunk patterns
chunk_grammar = """
NP: {<DT>?<JJ>*<NN.*>}
"""
rc = RegexpParser(chunk_grammar)
c = rc.parse(tagged_simple_sent)

# view NP chunked sentence using chunking
In [86]: print c
(S
  (NP the/DT quick/JJ fox/NN)
  jumped/VBD
  over/IN
  (NP the/DT lazy/JJ dog/NN))

# illustrate NP chunking based on explicit chink patterns
chink_grammar = """
NP: {<.*>+} # chunk everything as NP
}<VBD|IN>+{
"""
rc = RegexpParser(chink_grammar)
c = rc.parse(tagged_simple_sent)

# view NP chunked sentence using chinking
In [89]: print c
(S
  (NP the/DT quick/JJ fox/NN)
  jumped/VBD
  over/IN
  (NP the/DT lazy/JJ dog/NN))
```

Thus we can see from the preceding outputs that we obtained similar results on a toy NP shallow parser using chunking as well as chinking. Remember that *chunks* are sequences of tokens that are included in a collective group (chunk), and *chinks* are tokens or sequences of tokens that are excluded from chunks.

We will now train a more generic regular expression-based shallow parser and test its performance on our test treebank data. Internally, several steps are executed to perform this parsing. The Tree structures used to represent parsed sentences in nltk get converted to ChunkString objects. We create an object of RegexpParser using defined chunking and chinking rules. Objects of classes ChunkRule and ChinkRule help in creating the complete shallow-parsed tree with the necessary chunks based on specified patterns. The following code snippet represents a shallow parser using regular expression-based patterns:

```
# create POS tagged tokens for sample sentence
tagged_sentence = tag(sentence)
In [90]: print tagged_sentence
[(u'The', u'DT'), (u'brown', u'JJ'), (u'fox', u'NN'), (u'is', u'VBZ'),
(u'quick', u'JJ'), (u'and', u'CC'), (u'he', u'PRP'), (u'is', u'VBZ'),
(u'jumping', u'VBG'), (u'over', u'IN'), (u'the', u'DT'), (u'lazy', u'JJ'),
(u'dog', u'NN')]

# create the shallow parser
grammar = """
NP: {<DT>?<JJ>?<NN.*>}
ADJP: {<JJ>}
ADVP: {<RB.*>}
PP: {<IN>}
VP: {<MD>?<VB.*>+}

"""
rc = RegexpParser(grammar)
c = rc.parse(tagged_sentence)

# view shallow parsed sample sentence
In [99]: print c
(S
  (NP The/DT brown/JJ fox/NN)
  (VP is/VBZ)
  quick/JJ
  and/CC
  he/PRP
  (VP is/VBZ jumping/VBG)
  (PP over/IN)
  (NP the/DT lazy/JJ dog/NN))

# evaluate parser performance on test data
In [100]: print rc.evaluate(test_data)
ChunkParse score:
    IOB Accuracy:   54.5%
    Precision:      25.0%
    Recall:         52.5%
    F-Measure:      33.9%
```

From the preceding output, we can see that the parse tree for our sample sentence is very similar to the one we obtained from the out-of-the-box parser in the previous section. Also, the accuracy on the overall test data is 54.5 percent, which is quite decent for a start. For more details on what each performance metric signifies, refer to the "Evaluating Classification Models" section in Chapter 4.

Remember when I said annotated tagged metadata for text is useful in many ways? We will use the chunked and tagged treebank training data now to build a shallow parser. We will leverage two chunking utility functions, tree2conlltags, to get triples of word, tag, and chunk tags for each token, and conlltags2tree to generate a parse tree from these token triples. We will be using these functions to train our parser later. First let us see how these two functions work. Remember, the chunk tags use the IOB format mentioned earlier:

```
from nltk.chunk.util import tree2conlltags, conlltags2tree

# look at a sample training tagged sentence
In [104]: train_sent = train_data[7]
     ...: print train_sent
(S
  (NP A/DT Lorillard/NNP spokeswoman/NN)
  said/VBD
  ,/,
  ``/``
  (NP This/DT)
  is/VBZ
  (NP an/DT old/JJ story/NN)
  ./.)

# get the (word, POS tag, Chunk tag) triples for each token
In [106]: wtc = tree2conlltags(train_sent)
     ...: wtc
Out[106]:
[(u'A', u'DT', u'B-NP'),
 (u'Lorillard', u'NNP', u'I-NP'),
 (u'spokeswoman', u'NN', u'I-NP'),
 (u'said', u'VBD', u'O'),
 (u',', u',', u'O'),
 (u'``', u'``', u'O'),
 (u'This', u'DT', u'B-NP'),
 (u'is', u'VBZ', u'O'),
 (u'an', u'DT', u'B-NP'),
 (u'old', u'JJ', u'I-NP'),
 (u'story', u'NN', u'I-NP'),
 (u'.', u'.', u'O')]

# get shallow parsed tree back from the WTC triples
In [107]: tree = conlltags2tree(wtc)
     ...: print tree
(S
  (NP A/DT Lorillard/NNP spokeswoman/NN)
  said/VBD
  ,/,
  ``/``
  (NP This/DT)
  is/VBZ
  (NP an/DT old/JJ story/NN)
  ./.)
```

Now that we know how these functions work, we will define a function `conll_tag_chunks()` to extract POS and chunk tags from sentences with chunked annotations and also reuse our `combined_taggers()` function from POS tagging to train multiple taggers with backoff taggers, as shown in the following code snippet:

```
def conll_tag_chunks(chunk_sents):
    tagged_sents = [tree2conlltags(tree) for tree in chunk_sents]
    return [[(t, c) for (w, t, c) in sent] for sent in tagged_sents]

def combined_tagger(train_data, taggers, backoff=None):
    for tagger in taggers:
        backoff = tagger(train_data, backoff=backoff)
    return backoff
```

We will now define a class `NGramTagChunker` that will take in tagged sentences as training input, get their (word, POS tag, Chunk tag) WTC triples, and train a `BigramTagger` with a `UnigramTagger` as the backoff tagger. We will also define a `parse()` function to perform shallow parsing on new sentences:

```
from nltk.tag import UnigramTagger, BigramTagger
from nltk.chunk import ChunkParserI

class NGramTagChunker(ChunkParserI):

    def __init__(self, train_sentences,
                    tagger_classes=[UnigramTagger, BigramTagger]):
        train_sent_tags = conll_tag_chunks(train_sentences)
        self.chunk_tagger = combined_tagger(train_sent_tags, tagger_classes)

    def parse(self, tagged_sentence):
        if not tagged_sentence:
            return None
        pos_tags = [tag for word, tag in tagged_sentence]
        chunk_pos_tags = self.chunk_tagger.tag(pos_tags)
        chunk_tags = [chunk_tag for (pos_tag, chunk_tag) in chunk_pos_tags]
        wpc_tags = [(word, pos_tag, chunk_tag) for ((word, pos_tag), chunk_tag)
                        in zip(tagged_sentence, chunk_tags)]
        return conlltags2tree(wpc_tags)
```

In the preceding class, the constructor `__init__()` function is used to train the shallow parser using n-gram tagging based on the WTC triples for each sentence. Internally, it takes a list of training sentences as input, which is annotated with chunked parse tree metadata. It uses the `conll_tag_chunks()` function that we defined earlier to get a list of WTC triples for each chunked parse tree. Finally, it trains a `Bigram` tagger with a `Unigram` tagger as a backoff tagger using these triples and stores the training model in `self.chunk_tagger`. Remember you can parse other n-gram-based taggers for training by using the `tagger_classes` parameter. Once trained, the `parse()` function can be used to evaluate the tagger on test data and also shallow parse new sentences. Internally, it takes a POS tagged sentence as input, separates out the POS tags from the sentence, and uses our trained self.chunk_tagger to get the IOB chunk tags for the sentence. This is then combined with the original sentence tokens, and we use the conlltags2tree() function to get our final shallow parsed tree.

The following snippet shows our parser in action:

```
# train the shallow parser
ntc = NGramTagChunker(train_data)

# test parser performance on test data
In [114]: print ntc.evaluate(test_data)
ChunkParse score:
    IOB Accuracy:   99.6%
    Precision:      98.4%
    Recall:        100.0%
    F-Measure:      99.2%

# parse our sample sentence
In [115]: tree = ntc.parse(tagged_sentence)
     ...: print tree
(S
  (NP The/DT brown/JJ fox/NN)
  is/VBZ
  (NP quick/JJ)
  and/CC
  (NP he/PRP)
  is/VBZ
  jumping/VBG
  over/IN
  (NP the/DT lazy/JJ dog/NN))
```

That output shows that our parser performance on the treebank test set data has an overall accuracy of 99.6 percent—which is really excellent!

Let us train and evaluate our parser on the conll2000 corpus, which contains excerpts from the *Wall Street Journal* and is a much larger corpus. We will train our parser on the first 7,500 sentences and test its performance on the remaining 3,448 sentences. The following snippet shows this:

```
from nltk.corpus import conll2000
wsj_data = conll2000.chunked_sents()
train_wsj_data = wsj_data[:7500]
test_wsj_data = wsj_data[7500:]
```

```
# look at a sample sentence in the corpus
In [125]: print train_wsj_data[10]
(S
  (NP He/PRP)
  (VP reckons/VBZ)
  (NP the/DT current/JJ account/NN deficit/NN)
  (VP will/MD narrow/VB)
  (PP to/TO)
  (NP only/RB #/# 1.8/CD billion/CD)
  (PP in/IN)
  (NP September/NNP)
  ./.)

# train the shallow parser
tc = NGramTagChunker(train_wsj_data)

# test performance on the test data
In [126]: print tc.evaluate(test_wsj_data)
ChunkParse score:
    IOB Accuracy:   66.8%
    Precision:      77.7%
    Recall:         45.4%
    F-Measure:      57.3%
```

The preceding output shows that our parser achieved an overall accuracy of around 67 percent, because this corpus is much larger than the treebank corpus. You can also look at implementing shallow parsers using other techniques, like supervised classifiers, by leveraging the ClassifierBasedTagger class.

Dependency-based Parsing

In dependency-based parsing, we try to use dependency-based grammars to analyze and infer both structure and semantic dependencies and relationships between tokens in a sentence. (Refer to the "Dependency Grammars" subsection under "Grammar" in the "Language Syntax and Structure" section from Chapter 1 if you need to refresh your memory.) Dependency-based grammars help us in annotating sentences with dependency tags that are one-to-one mappings between tokens signifying dependencies between them. A dependency grammar-based parse tree representation is a labelled and directed tree or graph, to be more precise. The nodes are always the lexical tokens, and the labelled edges show dependency relationships between the heads and their dependents. The labels on the edges indicate the grammatical role of the dependent. If you remember our sample sentence *The brown fox is quick and he is jumping over the lazy dog*, Figure 3-3 from Chapter 1 is one of the many ways of depicting the dependency relationships.

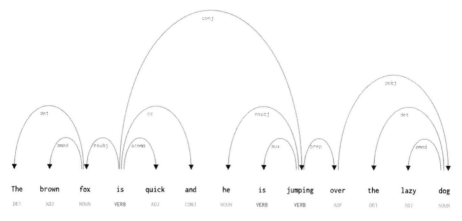

Figure 3-3. *Dependency grammar annotated graph for our sample sentence*

In this section we will look at some ways in which we can further understand the syntax and semantics between textual tokens using dependency grammar-based parsing.

Recommended Dependency Parsers

We will be using a couple of libraries to generate dependency-based parse trees and test them on our sample sentence. To start with, we will use spacy to analyze our sample sentence and generate each token and its dependencies. Figure 3-3 was generated using spacy's output and putting some beautiful CSS to make the dependencies look clear and easy to understand.

The following code snippet show how to get dependencies for each token in our sample sentence:

```
sentence = 'The brown fox is quick and he is jumping over the lazy dog'

# load dependencies
from spacy.en import English
parser = English()
parsed_sent = parser(unicode(sentence))

# generate dependency parser output
In [131]: dependency_pattern = '{left}<---{word}[{w_type}]---
>{right}\n--------'
     ...: for token in parsed_sent:
     ...:     print dependency_pattern.format(word=token.orth_,
     ...:                                      w_type=token.dep_,
     ...:                                      left=[t.orth_
     ...:                                            for t
     ...:                                            in token.lefts],
```

```
    ...:                               right=[t.orth_
    ...:                                       for t
    ...:                                   in token.rights])
[]<---The[det]--->[]
--------
[]<---brown[amod]--->[]
--------
[u'The', u'brown']<---fox[nsubj]--->[]
--------
[u'fox']<---is[ROOT]--->[u'quick', u'and', u'jumping']
--------
[]<---quick[acomp]--->[]
--------
[]<---and[cc]--->[]
--------
[]<---he[nsubj]--->[]
--------
[]<---is[aux]--->[]
--------
[u'he', u'is']<---jumping[conj]--->[u'over']
--------
[]<---over[prep]--->[u'dog']
--------
[]<---the[det]--->[]
--------
[]<---lazy[amod]--->[]
--------
[u'the', u'lazy']<---dog[pobj]--->[]
--------
```

The preceding output gives us each token and its dependency type, the left arrow points to the dependencies on its left, and the right arrow points to the dependencies on its right. You will find a lot of similarity if you match each line of the output with the previous figure showing the dependency tree. You can quickly look back at Chapter 1 in case you have forgotten what each of the dependency tags indicates.

Next, we will be using nltk and the Stanford Parser to generate the dependency tree for our sample sentence using the following code snippet:

```
# set java path
import os
java_path = r'C:\Program Files\Java\jdk1.8.0_102\bin\java.exe'
os.environ['JAVAHOME'] = java_path

# perform dependency parsing
from nltk.parse.stanford import StanfordDependencyParser
sdp = StanfordDependencyParser(path_to_jar='E:/stanford/stanford-parser-
full-2015-04-20/stanford-parser.jar',
                              path_to_models_jar='E:/stanford/stanford-
parser-full-2015-04-20/stanford-parser-3.5.2-models.jar')
```

```
result = list(sdp.raw_parse(sentence))

# generate annotated dependency parse tree
In [134]: result[0]
Out[134]:
```

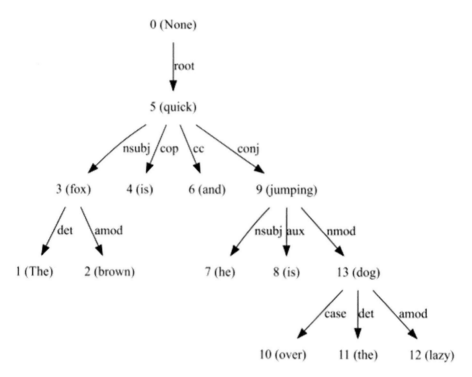

Figure 3-4. *Annotated dependency parse tree for our sample sentence*

```
# generate dependency triples
Out[136]:
[((u'quick', u'JJ'), u'nsubj', (u'fox', u'NN')),
 ((u'fox', u'NN'), u'det', (u'The', u'DT')),
 ((u'fox', u'NN'), u'amod', (u'brown', u'JJ')),
 ((u'quick', u'JJ'), u'cop', (u'is', u'VBZ')),
 ((u'quick', u'JJ'), u'cc', (u'and', u'CC')),
 ((u'quick', u'JJ'), u'conj', (u'jumping', u'VBG')),
 ((u'jumping', u'VBG'), u'nsubj', (u'he', u'PRP')),
 ((u'jumping', u'VBG'), u'aux', (u'is', u'VBZ')),
 ((u'jumping', u'VBG'), u'nmod', (u'dog', u'NN')),
 ((u'dog', u'NN'), u'case', (u'over', u'IN')),
 ((u'dog', u'NN'), u'det', (u'the', u'DT')),
 ((u'dog', u'NN'), u'amod', (u'lazy', u'JJ'))]
```

```
# print simple dependency parse tree
In [137]: dep_tree = [parse.tree() for parse in result][0]
    ...: print dep_tree
(quick (fox The brown) is and (jumping he is (dog over the lazy)))

# visualize simple dependency parse tree
In [140]: dep_tree.draw()
Out [140]:
```

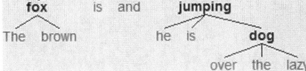

Figure 3-5. *Simple dependency parse tree for our sample sentence*

The preceding outputs shows how easily we can generate dependency parse trees for sentences and analyze and understand relationships and dependencies amongst the tokens. The Stanford Parser is quite stable and robust and integrates well with nltk. A side note would be that you will need graphviz installed to generate the annotated dependency tree shown in Figure 3-4.

Building Your Own Dependency Parsers

It is not very easy to build your own dependency grammar-based parsers from scratch because you need sufficient data, and just checking based on grammar production rules would not always scale well. The following example snippet shows how to build your own dependency parser. To do this, we first leverage nltk's DependencyGrammar class to generate production rules from a user input grammar. Once this is done, we use ProjectiveDependencyParser, a projective, production rule-based dependency parser to perform the dependency based parsing:

```
import nltk
tokens = nltk.word_tokenize(sentence)

dependency_rules = """
'fox' -> 'The' | 'brown'
'quick' -> 'fox' | 'is' | 'and' | 'jumping'
'jumping' -> 'he' | 'is' | 'dog'
'dog' -> 'over' | 'the' | 'lazy'
"""

dependency_grammar = nltk.grammar.DependencyGrammar.fromstring(dependency_rules)
```

157

```
# print production rules
In [143]: print dependency_grammar
Dependency grammar with 12 productions
  'fox' -> 'The'
  'fox' -> 'brown'
  'quick' -> 'fox'
  'quick' -> 'is'
  'quick' -> 'and'
  'quick' -> 'jumping'
  'jumping' -> 'he'
  'jumping' -> 'is'
  'jumping' -> 'dog'
  'dog' -> 'over'
  'dog' -> 'the'
  'dog' -> 'lazy'

# build dependency parser
dp = nltk.ProjectiveDependencyParser(dependency_grammar)

# parse our sample sentence
res = [item for item in dp.parse(tokens)]
tree = res[0]

# print dependency parse tree
In [145]: print tree
 (quick (fox The brown) is and (jumping he is (dog over the lazy)))
```

You can see that the preceding dependency parse tree is the same one as the one generated by the Stanford Parser. In fact, you can use tree.draw() to visualize the tree and compare it with the previous tree. Scaling these is always a challenge, and a lot of work is being done in large projects to generate these systems for rule-based dependency grammars. Some examples include the Lexical Functional Grammar (LFG) Pargram project and the Lexicalized Tree Adjoining Grammar XTAG project.

Constituency-based Parsing

Constituent-based grammars are used to analyze and determine the constituents a sentence is usually composed of. Besides determining the constituents, another important objective is to find out the internal structure of these constituents and see how they link to each other. There are usually several rules for different types of phrases based on the type of components they can contain, and we can use them to build parse trees. Refer to the "Constituency Grammars" subsection under "Grammar" in the "Language Syntax and Structure" section from Chapter 1 if you need to refresh your memory and look at some examples of sample parse trees.

In general, a constituency-based grammar helps specify how we can break a sentence into various constituents. Once that is done, it further helps in breaking down those constituents into further subdivisions, and this process repeats till we reach the level of individual tokens or words. These grammars have various production rules and usually a context-free grammar (CFG) or phrase structured grammar is sufficient for this.

Once we have a set of grammar rules, a constituency parser can be built that will process input sentences according to these rules and help in building a parse tree. The parser is what brings the grammar to life and can be said to be a procedural interpretation of the grammar. There are various types of parsing algorithms, including the following:

- Recursive Descent parsing

- Shift Reduce parsing

- Chart parsing

- Bottom-up parsing

- Top-down parsing

- PCFG parsing

Going through these in detail would be impossible given the constraints of this book. However, nltk provides some excellent information on them in its official book, available at http://www.nltk.org/book/ch08.html. I will describe some of these parsers briefly and look at PCFG parsing in detail when we implement our own parser later. *Recursive Descent parsing* usually follows a top-down parsing approach and it reads in tokens from the input sentence and tries to match them with the terminals from the grammar production rules. It keeps looking ahead by one token and advances the input read pointer each time it gets a match.

Shift Reduce parsing follows a bottom-up parsing approach where it finds sequences of tokens (words/phrases) that correspond to the righthand side of grammar productions and then replaces it with the lefthand side for that rule. This process continues until the whole sentence is reduced to give us a parse tree.

Chart parsing uses dynamic programming, which stores intermediate results and reuses them when needed to get significant efficiency gains. In this case, chart parsers store partial solutions and look them up when needed to get to the complete solution.

Recommended Constituency Parsers

We will be using nltk and the StanfordParser here to generate parse trees. We will need to set the Java path before we run our code to parse our sample sentence. We will print and also visualize the parse tree, which will be quite similar to some of the parse trees from Chapter 1, based on constituency grammars.

The following code snippet illustrates:

```
# set java path
import os
java_path = r'C:\Program Files\Java\jdk1.8.0_102\bin\java.exe'
os.environ['JAVAHOME'] = java_path

sentence = 'The brown fox is quick and he is jumping over the lazy dog'

from nltk.parse.stanford import StanfordParser
```

```
# create parser object
scp = StanfordParser(path_to_jar='E:/stanford/stanford-parser-
full-2015-04-20/stanford-parser.jar', path_to_models_jar='E:/stanford/
stanford-parser-full-2015-04-20/stanford-parser-3.5.2-models.jar')

# get parse tree
result = list(scp.raw_parse(sentence))

# print the constituency parse tree
In [150]: print result[0]
    ...:
(ROOT
  (NP
    (S
      (S
        (NP (DT The) (JJ brown) (NN fox))
        (VP (VBZ is) (ADJP (JJ quick))))
      (CC and)
      (S
        (NP (PRP he))
        (VP
          (VBZ is)
          (VP
            (VBG jumping)
            (PP (IN over) (NP (DT the) (JJ lazy) (NN dog)))))))))

# visualize constituency parse tree
In [151]: result[0].draw()
Out [151]:
```

The preceding output shows how to build constituency grammar–based parse trees for sentences. Notice the parse tree depicted in Figure 3-6 being significantly different from dependency parse trees and matching the constituency parse trees illustrated in Chapter 1. Note the nested and hierarchical constituents shown in the tree above which are some of the typical characteristics of constituency parse trees.

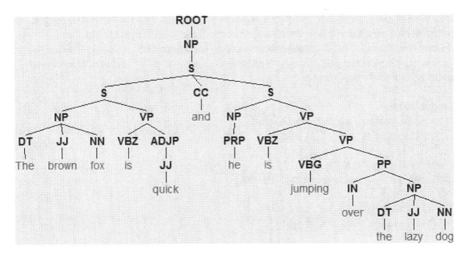

Figure 3-6. *Constituency parse tree for our sample sentence*

Building Your Own Constituency Parsers

There are various ways of building your own constituency parsers, including creating your own CFG production rules and then using a parser to use that grammar. To build your own CFG, you can use the nltk.CFG.fromstring function to feed in your own production rules and then use parsers like ChartParser or RecursiveDescentParser, both of which belong to the nltk package. Feel free to build some toy grammars and play around with these parsers.

We will look at a way to build a constituency parser that scales well and is efficient. The problem with regular CFG parsers, like chart and Recursive Descent parsers, is that they can get easily overwhelmed by the sheer number of total possible parses when parsing sentences and can become extremely slow. This is where weighted grammars like PCFG (Probabilistic Context Free Grammar) and probabilistic parsers like the Viterbi parser prove to be more effective. A PCFG is a context-free grammar that associates a probability with each of its production rules. The probability of a parse tree generated from a PCFG is simply the production of the individual probabilities of the productions used to generate it.

We will use nltk's ViterbiParser here to train a parser on the treebank corpus that provides annotated parse trees for each sentence in the corpus. This parser is a bottom-up PCFG parser that uses dynamic programming to find the most likely parse at each step. We will start our process of building our own parser by loading the necessary training data and dependencies:

```
import nltk
from nltk.grammar import Nonterminal
from nltk.corpus import treebank

# get training data
training_set = treebank.parsed_sents()

# view a sample training sentence
In [161]: print training_set[1]
(S
  (NP-SBJ (NNP Mr.) (NNP Vinken))
  (VP
    (VBZ is)
    (NP-PRD
      (NP (NN chairman))
      (PP
        (IN of)
        (NP
          (NP (NNP Elsevier) (NNP N.V.))
          (, ,)
          (NP (DT the) (NNP Dutch) (VBG publishing) (NN group))))))
  (. .))
```

Now we will build the production rules for our grammar by extracting the productions from the tagged and annotated training sentences and adding them:

```
# extract the productions for all annotated training sentences
treebank_productions = list(
                        set(production
                            for sent in training_set
                            for production in sent.productions()
                        )
                    )

# view sample productions
In [166]: treebank_productions[0:10]
Out[166]:
[VBZ -> 'cites',
 VBD -> 'spurned',
 PRN -> , ADVP-TMP ,,
 NNP -> 'ACCOUNT',
 JJ -> '36-day',
```

```
NP-SBJ-2 -> NN,
JJ -> 'unpublished',
NP-SBJ-1 -> NNP,
JJ -> 'elusive',
NNS -> 'Lids']

# add productions for each word, POS tag
for word, tag in treebank.tagged_words():
        t = nltk.Tree.fromstring("("+ tag + " " + word  +")")
        for production in t.productions():
                treebank_productions.append(production)

# build the PCFG based grammar
treebank_grammar = nltk.grammar.induce_pcfg(Nonterminal('S'),
                                   treebank_productions)
```

Now that we have our necessary grammar with production rules, we will create our parser using the following snippet by training it on the grammar and then trying to evaluate it on our sample sentence:

```
# build the parser
viterbi_parser = nltk.ViterbiParser(treebank_grammar)

# get sample sentence tokens
tokens = nltk.word_tokenize(sentence)

# get parse tree
In [170]: result = list(viterbi_parser.parse(tokens))
Traceback (most recent call last):
  File "<ipython-input-170-c2cdab3cd56c>", line 1, in <module>
    result = list(viterbi_parser.parse(tokens))
  File "C:\Anaconda2\lib\site-packages\nltk\parse\viterbi.py", line 112, in parse
    self._grammar.check_coverage(tokens)
ValueError: Grammar does not cover some of the input words: u"'brown',
'fox', 'lazy', 'dog'".
```

Unfortunately, we get an error when we try to parse our sample sentence tokens with our newly built parser. The reason is quite clear from the error: Some of the words in our sample sentence are not covered by the treebank-based grammar because they are not present in our treebank corpus. Now, because this constituency-based grammar uses POS tags and phrase tags to build the tree based on the training data, we will add the token and POS tags for our sample sentence in our grammar and rebuild the parser:

```
# get tokens and their POS tags
from pattern.en import tag as pos_tagger
tagged_sent = pos_tagger(sentence)
```

```
# check the tokens and their POS tags
In [172]: print tagged_sent
    ...:
[(u'The', u'DT'), (u'brown', u'JJ'), (u'fox', u'NN'), (u'is', u'VBZ'),
(u'quick', u'JJ'), (u'and', u'CC'), (u'he', u'PRP'), (u'is', u'VBZ'),
(u'jumping', u'VBG'), (u'over', u'IN'), (u'the', u'DT'), (u'lazy', u'JJ'),
(u'dog', u'NN')]

# extend productions for sample sentence tokens
for word, tag in tagged_sent:
    t = nltk.Tree.fromstring("("+ tag + " " + word  +")")
    for production in t.productions():
                treebank_productions.append(production)

# rebuild grammar
treebank_grammar = nltk.grammar.induce_pcfg(Nonterminal('S'),
                                    treebank_productions)
# rebuild parser
viterbi_parser = nltk.ViterbiParser(tbank_grammar)

# get parse tree for sample sentence
result = list(viterbi_parser.parse(tokens))

# print the constituency parse tree
In [178]: print result[0]
(S
  (NP-SBJ-163 (DT The) (JJ brown) (NN fox))
  (VP
    (VBZ is)
    (PRT (JJ quick))
    (S
      (CC and)
      (NP-SBJ (PRP he))
      (VP
        (VBZ is)
        (PP-1
          (VBG jumping)
          (NP (IN over) (DT the) (JJ lazy) (NN dog)))))))) (p=2.02604e-48)

# visualize the constituency parse tree
In [179]: result[0].draw()
Out [179]:
```

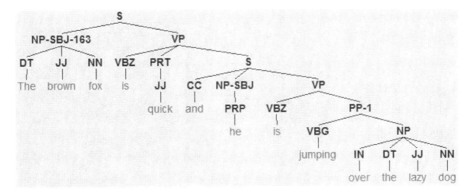

Figure 3-7. *Constituency parse tree for our sample sentence based on Treebank annotations*

We are now able to successfully generate the parse tree for our sample sentence. You can see the visual representation of the tree in Figure 3-7. Remember that this is a probabilistic PCFG parser, and you can see the overall probability of this tree mentioned in the output earlier when we printed our parse tree. The notations of the tags followed here are all based on the Treebank annotations we discussed earlier. Thus this shows how to build our own constituency-based parser.

Summary

Congratulations on reaching the end of this chapter. We have covered a major chunk of concepts, techniques, and implementations with regard to text processing, syntactic analysis, and understanding. A lot of the concepts from Chapter 1 should seem more relevant and clearer now that we have actually implemented them on real examples.

The content covered in this chapter is two-fold. We looked at concepts related to text processing and normalization. You now know the importance of processing and normalizing text, and as we move on to future chapters, you will see why it becomes more and more important to have well-processed and standardized textual data. We have covered various concepts and implemented techniques for text tokenization and normalization. These include cleaning and correcting text entities like spelling and contractions. We also built our own spelling corrector and contraction expander in the same context. We found out a way to leverage WordNet and correct words with repeated characters. Finally, we looked at various stemming and lemmatization concepts and techniques. The next part of our chapter was dedicated to analyzing and understanding text syntax and structure, where we revisited concepts from Chapter 1 including POS tagging, shallow parsing, dependency parsing, and constituency parsing.

You now know how to use taggers and parsers on real-world textual data and ways to implement your own taggers and parsers. We will be diving more into analyzing and deriving insights from text in the future chapters using various ML techniques, including classification, clustering, and summarization.

CHAPTER 4

▨ ▨ ▨

Text Classification

Learning to process and understand text is one of the first steps on the journey to getting meaningful insights from textual data. Though it is important to understand how language is structured and specific text syntax patterns, that alone is not sufficient to be of much use to businesses and organizations who want to derive useful patterns and insights and get maximum use out of their vast volumes of text data. Knowledge of language processing coupled with concepts from analytics and machine learning (ML) help in building systems that can leverage text data and help solve real-world practical problems which benefit businesses.

Various aspects of ML include supervised learning, unsupervised learning, reinforcement learning, and more recently deep learning. Each of these concepts involves several techniques and algorithms that can be leveraged on text data and to build self-learning systems that do not need too much manual supervision. An ML model is a combination of data and algorithms—you got a taste of that in Chapter 3 was we built our own parsers and taggers. The benefit of ML is that once a model is trained, we can directly use it on new and previously unseen data to start seeing useful insights and desired results.

One of the most relevant and challenging problems is *text classification* or *categorization*, which involves trying to organize text documents into various categories based on inherent properties or attributes of each text document. This is used in various domains, including email spam identification and news categorization. The concept may seem simple, and if you have a small number of documents, you can look at each document and gain some idea about what it is trying to indicate. Based on this knowledge, you can group similar documents into categories or classes. It's more challenging when the number of text documents to be classified increases to several hundred thousands or millions. This is where techniques like feature extraction and supervised or unsupervised ML come in handy. Document classification is a generic problem not limited to text alone but also can be extended for other items like music, images, video, and other media.

To formalize our problem more clearly, we will have a given set of classes or categories and several text documents. Remember that documents are basically sentences or paragraphs of text. This forms a corpus. Our task would be to determine which class or classes each document belongs to. This entire process involves several steps which we will be discussing in detail later in this chapter. Briefly, for a supervised classification problem, we need to have some labelled data that we could use for training a text classification model. This data would essentially be curated documents that are already assigned to some specific class or category beforehand. Using this, we would essentially

© Dipanjan Sarkar 2016
D. Sarkar, *Text Analytics with Python*, DOI 10.1007/978-1-4842-2388-8_4

extract features and attributes from each document and make our model learn these attributes corresponding to each particular document and its class/category by feeding it to a supervised ML algorithm. Of course, the data would need to be pre-processed and normalized before building the model. Once done, we would follow the same process of normalization and feature extraction and then feed it to the model to predict the class or category for new documents. However, for an unsupervised classification problem, we would essentially not have any pre-labelled training documents. We would use techniques like clustering and document similarity measures to cluster documents together based on their inherent properties and assign labels to them.

In this chapter, we will discuss the concept of text classification and how it can be formulated as a supervised ML problem. We will also talk about the various forms of classification and what they indicate. A clear depiction for the essential steps necessary to complete a text classification workflow will also be presented, and we will be covering some of the essential steps from the same workflow, which have not been discussed before, including feature extraction, classifiers, model evaluation, and finally we will put them all together in building a text classification system on real-world data.

What Is Text Classification?

Before we define text classification, we need to understand the scope of textual data and what we really mean by *classification*. The textual data involved here can be anything ranging from a phrase, sentence, or a complete document with paragraphs of text, which can be obtained from corpora, blogs, or anywhere from the Web. Text classification is also often called *document classification* just to cover all forms of textual content under the word *document*. The word *document* could be defined as some form of concrete representation of thoughts or events that could be in the form of writing, recorded speech, drawings, or presentations. I use the term *document* here to represent textual data such as sentences or paragraphs belonging to the English language.

Text classification is also often called *text categorization*, although I explicitly use the word *classification* here for two reasons. First, it depicts the same essence as text categorization, where we want to classify documents. The second reason is to also show that we would be using classification or a supervised ML approach here to classify or categorize the text. Text categorization can be done in many ways, as mentioned. We will be focusing explicitly on a supervised approach using classification. The process of classification is not restricted to text alone. It is used quite frequently in other domains including science, healthcare, weather forecasting, and technology.

Text or document classification is the process of assigning text documents into one or more classes or categories, assuming that we have a predefined set of classes. Documents here are textual documents, and each document can contain a sentence or even a paragraph of words. A text classification system would successfully be able to classify each document to its correct class(es) based on inherent properties of the document. Mathematically, we can define it like this: given some description and attributes d for a document D, where $d \in D$, and we have a set of predefined classes or

categories, $C = \{c_1, c_2, c_3, \dots, c_n\}$. The actual document D can have many inherent

properties and attributes that lead it to being an entity in a high-dimensional space. Using a subset of that space with a limit set of descriptions and features depicted by d, we should be able to successfully assign the original document D to its correct class C_x using a text classification system T. This can be represented by $T : D \rightarrow C_x$.

We will talk more about the text classification system in detail later in the chapter. Figure 4-1 shows a high-level conceptual representation of the text classification process.

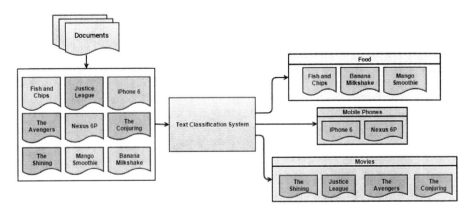

Figure 4-1. *Conceptual overview of text classification*

In Figure 4-1, we can see there are several documents representing products which can be assigned to various categories of food, mobile phones, and movies. Initially, these documents are all present together, just as a text corpus has various documents in it. Once it goes through a text classification system, represented as a black box here, we can see that each document is assigned to one specific class or category we had defined previously. Here the documents are just represented by their names, but in real data, they can contain much more, including descriptions of each product, specific attributes such as movie genre, product specifications, constituents, and many more properties that can be used as features in the text classification system to make document identification and classification easier.

There are various types of text classification. This chapter focuses on two major types, which are based on the type of content that makes up the documents:

- Content-based classification

- Request-based classification

Both types are more like different philosophies or ideals behind approaches to classifying text documents rather than specific technical algorithms or processes. *Content-based classification* is the type of text classification where priorities or weights are given to specific subjects or topics in the text content that would help determine the class of the document. A conceptual example would be that a book with more than 30 percent of its content about food preparations can be classified under cooking/recipes. *Request-based classification* is influenced by user requests and is targeted towards specific user groups and audiences. This type of classification is governed by specific policies and ideals.

Automated Text Classification

We now have an idea of the definition and scope of text classification. We have also formally defined text classification both conceptually and mathematically, where we talked about a "text classification system" being able to classify text documents to their respective categories or classes. Consider several humans doing the task of going through each document and classifying it. They would then be a part of the text classification system we are talking about. However, that would not scale very well once there were millions of text documents to be classified quickly. To make the process more efficient and faster, we can consider automating the task of text classification, which brings us to *automated text classification*.

To automate text classification, we can make use of several ML techniques and concepts. There are mainly two types of ML techniques that are relevant to solving this problem:

- Supervised machine learning

- Unsupervised machine learning

Besides these two techniques, there are also other families of learning algorithms, such as *reinforcement learning* and *semi-supervised learning*. Let us look at both supervised and unsupervised learning algorithms in more detail, from both an ML perspective how it can be leveraged in classifying text documents.

Unsupervised learning refers to specific ML techniques or algorithms that do not require any pre-labelled training data samples to build a model. We usually have a collection of data points, which could be text or numeric, depending on the problem we are trying to solve. We extract features from each of the data points using a process known as *feature extraction* and then feed the feature set for each data point into our algorithm. We are trying to extract meaningful patterns from the data, such as trying to group together similar data points using techniques like clustering or summarizing documents based on topic models. This is extremely useful in text document categorization and is also called document clustering, where we cluster documents into groups purely based on their features, similarity, and attributes, without training any model on previously labelled data. Later chapters further discuss unsupervised learning, covering topic models, document summarization, similarity analysis, and clustering.

Supervised learning refers to specific ML techniques or algorithms that are trained on pre-labelled data samples known as *training data*. Features or attributes are extracted from this data using feature extraction, and for each data point we will have its own feature set and corresponding class/label. The algorithm learns various patterns for each type of class from the training data. Once this process is complete, we have a *trained model*. This model can then be used to predict the class for future test data samples once we feed their features to the model. Thus the machine has actually learned, based on previous training data samples, how to predict the class for new unseen data samples.

There are two major types of supervised learning algorithms:

- *Classification*: The process of supervised learning is referred to as *classification* when the outcomes to be predicted are distinct categories, thus the outcome variable is a categorical variable in this case. Examples would be news categories or movie genres.

- *Regression*: Supervised learning algorithms are known as *regression* algorithms when the outcome we want to predict is a continuous numeric variable. Examples would be house prices or people's weights.

We will be specifically focusing on classification for our problem (hence the name of the chapter—we are trying to classify or categorize text documents into distinct classes or categories. We will be following a supervised learning approach in our implementations later on.

Now we are ready to define the process of automated or ML-based text classification mathematically. Say we have a training set of documents labelled with their corresponding class or category. This can be represented by *TS*, which is a set of paired documents and labels, $TS = \{(d_1, c_1), (d_2, c_2), ..., (d_n, c_n)\}$ where $d_1, d_2, ..., d_n$ is the list of text documents,

and their corresponding labels are $c_1, c_2, ..., c_n$ such that $c_x \in C = \{c1, c2, ..., cn\}$ where c_x

denotes the class label for document x and C denotes the set of all possible distinct classes, any of which can be the class or classes for each document. Assuming we have our training set, we can define a supervised learning algorithm F such that when it is trained on our training dataset *TS*, we build a classification model or classifier γ such that we can say that $F(TS) = \gamma$. Thus the supervised learning algorithm F takes the input set of (*document, class*) pairs *TS* and gives us the trained classifier γ, which is our model. This process is known as the *training process*.

This model can then take a new, previously unseen document *ND* and predict its class c_{ND} such that $c_{ND} \in C$. This process is known as the *prediction process* and can be represented by $\gamma : TD \rightarrow c_{ND}$. Thus we can see that there are two main processes in the supervised text classification process:

- Training

- Prediction

An important point to remember is that some manually labelled training data is necessary for supervised text classification, so even though we are talking about automated text classification, to kick start the process we need some manual efforts. Of course, the benefits of this are manifold because once we have a trained classifier, we can keep using it to predict and classify new documents with minimal efforts and manual supervision.

There are various learning methods or algorithms that we will be discussing in a future section. These learning algorithms are not specific to text data but are generic ML algorithms that can be applied toward various types of data after due pre-processing and feature extraction. I will touch upon a couple of supervised ML algorithms and use them in solving a real-world text classification problem. These algorithms are usually trained on the training data set and often an optional validation set such that the model that is trained does not overfit to the training data, which basically means it would then not be able to generalize well and predict properly for new instances of text documents. Often the model is tuned on several of its internal parameters based on the learning algorithm and by evaluating various performance metrics like accuracy on the validation set or by using cross-validation where we split the training dataset itself into training and validation sets by random sampling. This comprises the training process, the outcome of which yields a fully trained model that is ready to predict. In the prediction stage, we usually have new data points from the test dataset. We can use them to feed into the model after normalization and feature extraction and see how well the model is performing by evaluating its prediction performance.

There are a few types of text classification based on the number of classes to predict and the nature of predictions. These types of classification are based on the dataset, the number of classes/categories pertaining to that dataset, and the number of classes that can be predicted on any data point:

- *Binary classification* is when the total number of distinct classes or categories is two in number and any prediction can contain either one of those classes.

- *Multi-class classification,* also known as *multinomial classification,* refers to a problem where the total number of classes is more than two, and each prediction gives one class or category that can belong to any of those classes. This is an extension of the binary classification problem where the total number of classes is more than two.

- *Multi-label classification* refers to problems where each prediction can yield more than one outcome/predicted class for any data point.

Text Classification Blueprint

Now that we know the basic scope of automated text classification, this section will look at a blueprint for a complete workflow of building an automated text classifier system. This will consist of a series of steps that must be followed in both the training and testing phases mentioned in the earlier section. For building a text classification system, we need to make sure we have our source of data and retrieve that data so that we can start feeding it to our system. The following main steps outline a typical workflow for a text classification system, assuming we have our dataset already downloaded and ready to be used:

1. Prepare train and test datasets

2. Text normalization

3. Feature extraction

4. Model training

5. Model prediction and evaluation

6. Model deployment

These steps are carried out in that order for building a text classifier. Figure 4-2 shows a detailed workflow for a text classification system with the main processes highlighted in training and prediction.

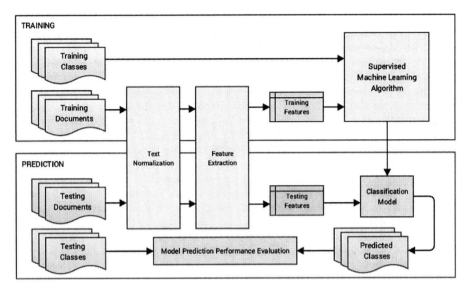

Figure 4-2. *Blueprint for building an automated text classification system*

Notice that there are two main boxes for Training and Prediction, which are the two main processes involved in building a text classifier. In general, the dataset we have is usually divided into two or three splits called the *training, validation* (optional), and *testing datasets*, respectively. You can see an overlap of the Text Normalization and Feature Extraction modules in Figure 4-2 for both processes, indicating that no matter which document we want to classify and predict its class, it must go through the same series of transformations in both the training and prediction process. Each document is first pre-processed and normalized, and then specific features pertaining to the document are extracted. These processes are always uniform in both the training and prediction processes to make sure that our classification model performs consistently in its predictions.

In the Training process, each document has its own corresponding class/category that was manually labeled or curated beforehand. These training text documents are processed and normalized in the Text Normalization module, giving us clean and standardized training text documents. They are then passed to the Feature Extraction module where different types of feature-extraction techniques are used to extract meaningful features from the processed text documents. We will cover some popular feature extraction techniques in a future section. These features are usually numeric arrays or vectors because standard ML algorithms work on numeric vectors. Once we have our features, we select a supervised ML algorithm and train our model.

Training the model involves feeding the feature vectors for the documents and the corresponding labels such that the algorithm is able to learn various patterns corresponding to each class/category and can reuse this learned knowledge to predict classes for future new documents. Often an optional validation dataset is used to evaluate the performance of the classification algorithm to make sure it generalizes well with the data during training. A combination of these features and the ML algorithm yields a Classification Model, which is the end stage of the Training process. Often this model is tuned using various model parameters with a process called *hyperparameter tuning* to build a better performing optimal model.

The Prediction process shown in the figure involves trying to either predict classes for new documents or evaluating how predictions are working on testing data. The test dataset documents go through the same process of normalization and feature extraction, and the test document features are passed to the trained Classification Model, which predicts the possible class for each of the documents based on previously learned patterns. If you have the true class labels for the documents that were manually labelled, you can evaluate the prediction performance of the model by comparing the true labels and the predicted labels using various metrics like accuracy. This would give an idea of how well the model performs its predictions for new documents.

Once we have a stable and working model, the last step is usually deploying the model, which normally involves saving the model and its necessary dependencies and deploying it as a service or as a running program that predicts categories for new documents as a batch job, or based on serving user requests if accessed as a web service. There are various ways to deploy ML models, and this usually depends on how you want to access it later on.

We will now discuss some of the main modules from the preceding blueprint and implement these modules so that we can integrate them all together to build a real-world text classifier.

Text Normalization

Chapter 3 covered text processing and normalization in detail—refer it to see the various methods and techniques available. In this section, we will define a normalizer module to normalize text documents and will be using it later when we build our classifier. Although various techniques are available, we will keep it fairly simple and straightforward here so that is it not too hard to follow our implementations step by step. We will implement and use the following normalization techniques in our module:

- Expanding contractions

- Text standardization through lemmatization

- Removing special characters and symbols

- Removing stopwords

We are not focusing too much on correcting spellings and other advanced techniques, but you can integrate the functions from the previous chapter implementation if you are interested. Our normalization module is implemented and available in `normalization.py`, available in the code files for this chapter. I will also be explaining each function here for your convenience. We will first start with loading the necessary dependencies. Remember that you will need our custom-defined contractions mapping file from Chapter 3, named `contractions.py`, for expanding contractions.

The following snippet shows the necessary imports and dependencies:

```
from contractions import CONTRACTION_MAP
import re
import nltk
import string
from nltk.stem import WordNetLemmatizer
```

```
stopword_list = nltk.corpus.stopwords.words('english')
wnl = WordNetLemmatizer()
```

We load all the English stopwords, the contraction mappings in CONTRACTION_MAP, and an instance of WordNetLemmatizer for carrying our lemmatization. We now define a function to tokenize text into tokens that will be used by our other normalization functions. The following function tokenizes and removes any extraneous whitespace from the tokens:

```
def tokenize_text(text):
    tokens = nltk.word_tokenize(text)
    tokens = [token.strip() for token in tokens]
    return tokens
```

Now we define a function for expanding contractions. This function is similar to our implementation from Chapter 3—it takes in a body of text and returns the same with its contractions expanded if there is a match. The following snippet helps us achieve this:

```
def expand_contractions(text, contraction_mapping):

    contractions_pattern = re.compile('({})'.format('|'.join(contraction_
    mapping.keys())),
                                        flags=re.IGNORECASE|re.DOTALL)
    def expand_match(contraction):
        match = contraction.group(0)
        first_char = match[0]
        expanded_contraction = contraction_mapping.get(match)\
                            if contraction_mapping.get(match)\
                            else contraction_mapping.get(match.lower())
        expanded_contraction = first_char+expanded_contraction[1:]
        return expanded_contraction

    expanded_text = contractions_pattern.sub(expand_match, text)
    expanded_text = re.sub("'", "", expanded_text)
    return expanded_text
```

Now that we have a function for expanding contractions, we implement a function for standardizing our text data by bringing word tokens to their base or root form using lemmatization. The following functions will help us in achieving that:

```
from pattern.en import tag
from nltk.corpus import wordnet as wn

# Annotate text tokens with POS tags
def pos_tag_text(text):
    # convert Penn treebank tag to wordnet tag
```

```
    def penn_to_wn_tags(pos_tag):
        if pos_tag.startswith('J'):
            return wn.ADJ
        elif pos_tag.startswith('V'):
            return wn.VERB
        elif pos_tag.startswith('N'):
            return wn.NOUN
        elif pos_tag.startswith('R'):
            return wn.ADV
        else:
            return None

    tagged_text = tag(text)
    tagged_lower_text = [(word.lower(), penn_to_wn_tags(pos_tag))
                            for word, pos_tag in
                            tagged_text]
    return tagged_lower_text

# lemmatize text based on POS tags
def lemmatize_text(text):

    pos_tagged_text = pos_tag_text(text)
    lemmatized_tokens = [wnl.lemmatize(word, pos_tag) if pos_tag
                            else word
                            for word, pos_tag in pos_tagged_text]
    lemmatized_text = ' '.join(lemmatized_tokens)
    return lemmatized_text
```

The preceding snippet depicts two functions implemented for lemmatization. The main function is lemmatize_text, which takes in a body of text data and lemmatizes each word of the text based on its POS tag if it is present and then returns the lemmatized text back to the user. For this, we need to annotate the text tokens with their POS tags. We use the tag function from pattern to annotate POS tags for each token and then further convert the POS tags from the Penn treebank syntax to WordNet syntax, since the WordNetLemmatizer checks for POS tag annotations based on WordNet formats. We convert each word token to lowercase, annotate it with its correct, converted WordNet POS tag, and return these annotated tokens, which are finally fed into the lemmatize_ text function.

The following function helps us remove special symbols and characters:

```
def remove_special_characters(text):
    tokens = tokenize_text(text)
    pattern = re.compile('[{}]'.format(re.escape(string.punctuation)))
    filtered_tokens = filter(None, [pattern.sub('', token) for token in
    tokens])
    filtered_text = ' '.join(filtered_tokens)
    return filtered_text
```

We remove special characters by tokenizing the text just so we can remove some of the tokens that are actually contractions, but we may have failed to remove them in our first step, like "s" or "re". We will do this when we remove stopwords. However, you can also remove special characters without tokenizing the text. We remove all special symbols defined in string.punctuation from our text using regular expression matches. The following function helps us remove stopwords from our text data:

```
def remove_stopwords(text):
    tokens = tokenize_text(text)
    filtered_tokens = [token for token in tokens if token not in
    stopword_list]
    filtered_text = ' '.join(filtered_tokens)
    return filtered_text
```

Now that we have all our functions defined, we can build our text normalization pipeline by chaining all these functions one after another. The following function implements this, where it takes in a corpus of text documents and normalizes them and returns a normalized corpus of text documents:

```
def normalize_corpus(corpus, tokenize=False):

    normalized_corpus = []
    for text in corpus:
        text = expand_contractions(text, CONTRACTION_MAP)
        text = lemmatize_text(text)
        text = remove_special_characters(text)
        text = remove_stopwords(text)
        normalized_corpus.append(text)
        if tokenize:
            text = tokenize_text(text)
            normalized_corpus.append(text)

    return normalized_corpus
```

That brings us to the end of our discussion and implementation of necessary functions for our text normalization module. We will now look at concepts and practical implementation for feature extraction.

Feature Extraction

There are various feature-extraction techniques that can be applied on text data, but before we jump into then, let us consider what we mean by features. Why do we need them, and how they are useful? In a dataset, there are typically many data points. Usually the rows of the dataset and the columns are various features or properties of the dataset, with specific values for each row or observation. In ML terminology, *features* are unique, measurable attributes or properties for each observation or data point in a dataset. Features are usually numeric in nature and can be absolute numeric values or categorical features that can be encoded as binary features for each category in the list using a process called *one-hot encoding*. The process of extracting and selecting features is both art and science, and this process is called *feature extraction* or *feature engineering*.

Usually extracted features are fed into ML algorithms for learning patterns that can be applied on future new data points for getting insights. These algorithms usually expect features in the form of numeric vectors because each algorithm is at heart a mathematical operation of optimization and minimizing loss and error when it tries to learn patterns from data points and observations. So, with textual data there is the added challenge of figuring out how to transform textual data and extract numeric features from it.

Now we will look at some feature-extraction concepts and techniques specially aligned towards text data.

The *Vector Space Model* is a concept and model that is very useful in case we are dealing with textual data and is very popular in information retrieval and document ranking. The Vector Space Model, also known as the *Term Vector Model*, is defined as a mathematical and algebraic model for transforming and representing text documents as numeric vectors of specific terms that form the vector dimensions. Mathematically this can be defines as follows. Say we have a document D in a document vector space VS. The number of dimensions or columns for each document will be the total number of distinct terms or words for all documents in the vector space. So, the vector space can be denoted

$$VS = \{W_1, W_2, \ldots, W_n\}$$

where there are n distinct words across all documents. Now we can represent document D in this vector space as

$$D = \{w_{D1}, w_{D2}, \ldots, w_{Dn}\}$$

where w_{Dn} denotes the weight for word n in document D. This weight is a numeric value and can represent anything, ranging from the frequency of that word in the document, to the average frequency of occurrence, or even to the TF-IDF weight (discussed shortly).

We will be talking about and implementing the following feature-extraction techniques:

- Bag of Words model
- TF-IDF model
- Advanced word vectorization models

An important thing to remember for feature extraction is that once we build a feature extractor using some transformations and mathematical operations, we need to make sure we reuse the same process when extracting features from new documents to be predicted, and not rebuild the whole algorithm again based on the new documents. We will be depicting this also with an example for each technique. Do note that for implementations based on practical examples in this section, we will be making use of the nltk, gensim, and scikit-learn libraries, which you can install using pip as discussed earlier (in case you do not have them installed already).

The implementations are divided into two major modules. The file feature_extractors.py contains the generic functions we will be using later on when building the classifier, and we have used the same functions in the feature_extraction_demo.py file to show how each technique works with some practical examples. You can access them from the code files, and as always I will be presenting the same code in this chapter for ease of understanding. We will be using the following documents depicted in the CORPUS variable to extract features from and building some of the vectorization models. To illustrate how feature extraction will work for a new document (as a part of test dataset), we will also use a separate document as shown in the variable new_doc in the following snippet:

```
CORPUS = [
'the sky is blue',
'sky is blue and sky is beautiful',
'the beautiful sky is so blue',
'i love blue cheese'
]

new_doc = ['loving this blue sky today']
```

Bag of Words Model

The Bag of Words model is perhaps one of the simplest yet most powerful techniques to extract features from text documents. The essence of this model is to convert text documents into vectors such that each document is converted into a vector that represents the frequency of all the distinct words that are present in the document vector space for that specific document. Thus, considering our sample vector from the previous mathematical notation for D, the weight for each word is equal to its frequency of occurrence in that document.

An interesting thing is that we can even create the same model for individual word occurrences as well as occurrences for n-grams, which would make it an n-gram Bag of Words model such that frequency of distinct n-grams in each document would also be considered.

The following code snippet gives us a function that implements a Bag of Words–based feature-extraction model that also accepts an ngram_range parameter to take into account n-grams as features:

```
from sklearn.feature_extraction.text import CountVectorizer

def bow_extractor(corpus, ngram_range=(1,1)):

    vectorizer = CountVectorizer(min_df=1, ngram_range=ngram_range)
    features = vectorizer.fit_transform(corpus)
    return vectorizer, features
```

The preceding function uses the CountVectorizer class. You can access its detailed API (Application Programming Interface) documentation at http://scikit-learn.org/stable/modules/generated/sklearn.feature_extraction.text.CountVectorizer.

html#sklearn.feature_extraction.text.CountVectorizer, which has a whole bunch of various parameters for more fine-tuning based on the type of features you want to extract. We use its default configuration, which is enough for most scenarios, with min_df set to 1 indicating taking terms having a minimum frequency of 1 in the overall document vector space. You can set ngram_range to various parameters like (1, 3) would build feature vectors consisting of all unigrams, bigrams, and trigrams. The following snippet shows the function in action on our sample corpora of four training documents and one test document:

```
# build bow vectorizer and get features
In [371]: bow_vectorizer, bow_features = bow_extractor(CORPUS)
     ...: features = bow_features.todense()
     ...: print features
[[0 0 1 0 1 0 1 0 1]
 [1 1 1 0 2 0 2 0 0]
 [0 1 1 0 1 0 1 1 1]
 [0 0 1 1 0 1 0 0 0]]
```

```
# extract features from new document using built vectorizer
In [373]: new_doc_features = bow_vectorizer.transform(new_doc)
     ...: new_doc_features = new_doc_features.todense()
     ...: print new_doc_features
[[0 0 1 0 0 0 1 0 0]]
```

```
# print the feature names
In [374]: feature_names = bow_vectorizer.get_feature_names()
     ...: print feature_names
[u'and', u'beautiful', u'blue', u'cheese', u'is', u'love', u'sky', u'so',
u'the']
```

That output shows how each text document has been converted to vectors. Each row represents one document from our corpus, and we do the same for both our corpora. The vectorizer is built using documents from CORPUS. We extract features from it and also use this built vectorizer to extract features from a completely new document. Each column in a vector represents the words depicted in feature_names, and the value is the frequency of that word in the document represented by the vector. It may be hard to comprehend this at first glance, so I have prepared the following function, which I hope you can use to understand the feature vectors better:

```
import pandas as pd

def display_features(features, feature_names):
    df = pd.DataFrame(data=features,
                      columns=feature_names)
    print df
```

Now you can feed the feature names and vectors to this function and see the feature matrix in a much easier-to-understand structure, shown here:

```
In [379]: display_features(features, feature_names)
   and  beautiful  blue  cheese  is  love  sky  so  the
0   0          0     1       0    1    0    1   0    1
1   1          1     1       0    2    0    2   0    0
2   0          1     1       0    1    0    1   1    1
3   0          0     1       1    0    1    0   0    0

In [380]: display_features(new_doc_features, feature_names)
   and  beautiful  blue  cheese  is  love  sky  so  the
0   0          0     1       0    0    0    1   0    0
```

That makes things much clearer, right? Consider the second document of CORPUS, represented in the preceding in row 1 of the first table. You can see that 'sky is blue and sky is beautiful' has value 2 for the feature sky, 1 for beautiful, and so on. Values of 0 are assigned for words not present in the document. Note that for the new document new_doc, there is no feature for the words today, this, or loving in the sentence. The reason for this is what I mentioned before—that the feature-extraction process, model, and vocabulary are always based on the training data and will never change or get influenced on newer documents, which it will predict later as a part of testing or otherwise. You might have guessed that this is because a model is always trained on some training data and is never influenced by newer documents unless we plan on rebuilding that model. Hence, the features in this model are always limited based on the document vector space of the training corpus.

You have now started to get an idea of how to extract meaningful vector-based features from text data, which previously seemed impossible. Try out the preceding functions by setting ngram_range to (1, 3) and see the outputs.

TF-IDF Model

The Bag of Words model is good, but the vectors are completely based on absolute frequencies of word occurrences. This has some potential problems where words that may tend to occur a lot across all documents in the corpus will have higher frequencies and will tend to overshadow other words that may not occur as frequently but may be more interesting and effective as features to identify specific categories for the documents. This is where TF-IDF comes into the picture. TF-IDF stands for Term Frequency-Inverse Document Frequency, a combination of two metrics: *term frequency* and *inverse document frequency*. This technique was originally developed as a metric for ranking functions for showing search engine results based on user queries and has come to be a part of information retrieval and text feature extraction now.

Let us formally define TF-IDF now and look at the mathematical representations for it before diving into its implementation. Mathematically, TF-IDF is the product of two metrics and can be represented as $tfidf = tf \times idf$, where term frequency *(tf)* and inverse-document frequency *(idf)* represent the two metrics.

Term frequency denoted by *tf* is what we had computed in the Bag of Words model. Term frequency in any document vector is denoted by the raw frequency value of that term in a particular document. Mathematically it can be represented as $tf(w, D) = f_{w_D}$,

where f_{w_D} denotes frequency for word w in document D, which becomes the term frequency *(tf)*. There are various other representations and computations for term frequency, such as converting frequency to a binary feature where 1 means the term has occurred in the document and 0 means it has not. Sometimes you can also normalize the absolute raw frequency using logarithms or averaging the frequency. We will be using the raw frequency in our computations.

Inverse document frequency denoted by *idf* is the inverse of the document frequency for each term. It is computed by dividing the total number of documents in our corpus by the document frequency for each term and then applying logarithmic scaling on the result. In our implementation we will be adding 1 to the document frequency for each term just to indicate that we also have one more document in our corpus that essentially has every term in the vocabulary. This is to prevent potential division-by-zero errors and smoothen the inverse document frequencies. We also add 1 to the result of our *idf* computation to avoid ignoring terms completely that might have zero *idf*. Mathematically our implementation for *idf* can be represented by

$$idf(t) = 1 + \log\frac{C}{1 + df(t)}$$

where *idf*(*t*) represents the *idf* for the term *t*, *C* represents the count of the total number of documents in our corpus, and *df*(*t*) represents the frequency of the number of documents in which the term *t* is present.

Thus the term frequency-inverse document frequency can be computed by multiplying the above two measures together. The final TF-IDF metric we will be using is a normalized version of the *tfidf* matrix we get from the product of *tf* and *idf*. We will normalize the *tfidf* matrix by dividing it with the L2 norm of the matrix, also known as the *Euclidean norm,* which is the square root of the sum of the square of each term's *tfidf* weight. Mathematically we can represent the final *tfidf* feature vector as $tfidf = \frac{tfidf}{\|tfidf\|}$,

where $\|tfidf\|$ represents the Euclidean L2 norm for the *tfidf* matrix.

The following code snippet shows an implementation of getting the *tfidf*-based feature vectors, considering we have our Bag of Words feature vectors we obtained in the previous section:

```
from sklearn.feature_extraction.text import TfidfTransformer

def tfidf_transformer(bow_matrix):

    transformer = TfidfTransformer(norm='l2',
                                   smooth_idf=True,
                                   use_idf=True)
    tfidf_matrix = transformer.fit_transform(bow_matrix)
    return transformer, tfidf_matrix
```

You can see that we have used the L2 norm option in the parameters and also made sure we smoothen the *idf*s to give weightages also to terms that may have zero *idf* so that we do not ignore them. We can see this function in action in the following code snippet:

```
import numpy as np
from feature_extractors import tfidf_transformer
feature_names = bow_vectorizer.get_feature_names()

# build tfidf transformer and show train corpus tfidf features
In [388]: tfidf_trans, tdidf_features = tfidf_transformer(bow_features)
     ...: features = np.round(tdidf_features.todense(), 2)
     ...: display_features(features, feature_names)
     and  beautiful  blue  cheese    is  love   sky    so   the
0  0.00       0.00  0.40    0.00  0.49  0.00  0.49  0.00  0.60
1  0.44       0.35  0.23    0.00  0.56  0.00  0.56  0.00  0.00
2  0.00       0.43  0.29    0.00  0.35  0.00  0.35  0.55  0.43
3  0.00       0.00  0.35    0.66  0.00  0.66  0.00  0.00  0.00

# show tfidf features for new_doc using built tfidf transformer
In [389]: nd_tfidf = tfidf_trans.transform(new_doc_features)
     ...: nd_features = np.round(nd_tfidf.todense(), 2)
     ...: display_features(nd_features, feature_names)
    and  beautiful  blue  cheese   is  love   sky   so  the
0   0.0        0.0  0.63     0.0  0.0   0.0  0.77  0.0  0.0
```

Thus the preceding outputs show the *tfidf* feature vectors for all our sample documents. We use the TfidfTransformer class, which helps us in computing the *tfidf*s for each document based on the equations described earlier.

Now we will show how the internals of this class work. You will also see how to implement the mathematical equations described earlier to compute the *tfidf*-based feature vectors. This section is dedicated to ML experts (and curious readers who are interested in how things work behind the scenes). We will start with loading necessary dependencies and computing the term frequencies (*TF*) by reusing our Bag of Words-based features for our sample corpus, which can also act as the term frequencies for our training CORPUS:

```
import scipy.sparse as sp
from numpy.linalg import norm
feature_names = bow_vectorizer.get_feature_names()

# compute term frequency
tf = bow_features.todense()
tf = np.array(tf, dtype='float64')

# show term frequencies
In [391]: display_features(tf, feature_names)
    and  beautiful  blue  cheese   is  love  sky   so  the
0   0.0        0.0   1.0     0.0  1.0   0.0  1.0  0.0  1.0
1   1.0        1.0   1.0     0.0  2.0   0.0  2.0  0.0  0.0
2   0.0        1.0   1.0     0.0  1.0   0.0  1.0  1.0  1.0
3   0.0        0.0   1.0     1.0  0.0   1.0  0.0  0.0  0.0
```

We will now compute our document frequencies (*DF*) for each term based on the number of documents in which it occurs. The following snippet shows how to obtain it from our Bag of Words feature matrix:

```
# build the document frequency matrix
df = np.diff(sp.csc_matrix(bow_features, copy=True).indptr)
df = 1 + df # to smoothen idf later
```

```
# show document frequencies
In [403]: display_features([df], feature_names)
     and  beautiful  blue  cheese  is  love  sky  so  the
0     2               3     5       2   4     2    4   2   3
```

This tells us the document frequency (*DF*) for each term and you can verify it with the documents in CORPUS. Remember that we have added 1 to each frequency value to smoothen the *idf* values later and prevent division-by-zero errors by assuming we have a document (imaginary) that has all the terms once. Thus, if you check in the CORPUS, you will see that blue occurs 4(+1) times, sky occurs 3(+1) times, and so on, considering (+1) for our smoothening.

Now that we have the document frequencies, we will compute the inverse document frequency (*idf*) using our formula defined earlier. Remember to add 1 to the total count of documents in the corpus to add the document that we had assumed earlier to contain all the terms at least once for smoothening the *idf*s:

```
# compute inverse document frequencies
total_docs = 1 + len(CORPUS)
idf = 1.0 + np.log(float(total_docs) / df)
```

```
# show inverse document frequencies
In [406]: display_features([np.round(idf, 2)], feature_names)
     and  beautiful  blue  cheese   is   love   sky    so    the
0   1.92             1.51  1.0     1.92 1.22  1.92 1.22  1.92  1.51
```

```
# compute idf diagonal matrix
total_features = bow_features.shape[1]
idf_diag = sp.spdiags(idf, diags=0, m=total_features, n=total_features)
idf = idf_diag.todense()
```

```
# print the idf diagonal matrix
In [407]: print np.round(idf, 2)
[[ 1.92  0.    0.    0.    0.    0.    0.    0.    0.   ]
 [ 0.    1.51  0.    0.    0.    0.    0.    0.    0.   ]
 [ 0.    0.    1.    0.    0.    0.    0.    0.    0.   ]
 [ 0.    0.    0.    1.92  0.    0.    0.    0.    0.   ]
 [ 0.    0.    0.    0.    1.22  0.    0.    0.    0.   ]
 [ 0.    0.    0.    0.    0.    1.92  0.    0.    0.   ]
 [ 0.    0.    0.    0.    0.    0.    1.22  0.    0.   ]
 [ 0.    0.    0.    0.    0.    0.    0.    1.92  0.   ]
 [ 0.    0.    0.    0.    0.    0.    0.    0.    1.51]]
```

You can now see the *idf* matrix that we created based on our mathematical equation, and we also convert it to a diagonal matrix, which will be helpful later on when we want to compute the product with term frequency.

Now that we have our *tf*s and *idf*s, we can compute the *tfidf* feature matrix using matrix multiplication, as shown in the following snippet:

```
# compute tfidf feature matrix
tfidf = tf * idf
```

```
# show tfidf feature matrix
In [410]: display_features(np.round(tfidf, 2), feature_names)
    and  beautiful  blue  cheese    is  love   sky    so   the
0  0.00       0.00   1.0    0.00  1.22  0.00  1.22  0.00  1.51
1  1.92       1.51   1.0    0.00  2.45  0.00  2.45  0.00  0.00
2  0.00       1.51   1.0    0.00  1.22  0.00  1.22  1.92  1.51
3  0.00       0.00   1.0    1.92  0.00  1.92  0.00  0.00  0.00
```

We now have our *tfidf* feature matrix, but wait! It is not yet over. We have to divide it with the L2 norm, if you remember from our equations depicted earlier. The following snippet computes the *tfidf* norms for each document and then divides the *tfidf* weights with the norm to give us the final desired *tfidf* matrix:

```
# compute L2 norms
norms = norm(tfidf, axis=1)
```

```
# print norms for each document
In [412]: print np.round(norms, 2)
[ 2.5   4.35  3.5   2.89]
```

```
# compute normalized tfidf
norm_tfidf = tfidf / norms[:, None]
```

```
# show final tfidf feature matrix
In [415]: display_features(np.round(norm_tfidf, 2), feature_names)
    and  beautiful  blue  cheese    is  love   sky    so   the
0  0.00       0.00  0.40    0.00  0.49  0.00  0.49  0.00  0.60
1  0.44       0.35  0.23    0.00  0.56  0.00  0.56  0.00  0.00
2  0.00       0.43  0.29    0.00  0.35  0.00  0.35  0.55  0.43
3  0.00       0.00  0.35    0.66  0.00  0.66  0.00  0.00  0.00
```

Compare the preceding obtained *tfidf* feature matrix for the documents in CORPUS to the feature matrix obtained using TfidfTransformer earlier. Note they are exactly the same, thus verifying that our mathematical implementation was correct—and in fact this very same implementation is adopted by scikit-learn's TfidfTransformer behind the scenes using some more optimizations. Now, suppose we want to compute the *tfidf*-based feature matrix for our new document new_doc. We can do it using the following snippet. We reuse the new_doc_features Bag of Words vector from before for the term frequencies:

```
# compute new doc term freqs from bow freqs
nd_tf = new_doc_features
nd_tf = np.array(nd_tf, dtype='float64')

# compute tfidf using idf matrix from train corpus
nd_tfidf = nd_tf*idf
nd_norms = norm(nd_tfidf, axis=1)
norm_nd_tfidf = nd_tfidf / nd_norms[:, None]

# show new_doc tfidf feature vector
In [418]: display_features(np.round(norm_nd_tfidf, 2), feature_names)
    and  beautiful  blue  cheese   is  love   sky    so   the
0   0.0             0.0   0.63     0.0  0.0   0.0  0.77  0.0  0.0
```

The preceding output depicts the *tfidf*-based feature vector for new_doc, and you can see it is the same as the one obtained by TfidfTransformer.

Now that we know how the internals work, we are going to implement a generic function that can directly compute the *tfidf*-based feature vectors for documents from the raw documents themselves. The following snippet depicts the same:

```
from sklearn.feature_extraction.text import TfidfVectorizer

def tfidf_extractor(corpus, ngram_range=(1,1)):

    vectorizer = TfidfVectorizer(min_df=1,
                                 norm='l2',
                                 smooth_idf=True,
                                 use_idf=True,
                                 ngram_range=ngram_range)
    features = vectorizer.fit_transform(corpus)
    return vectorizer, features
```

The preceding function makes use of the TfidfVectorizer, which directly computes the *tfidf* vectors by taking the raw documents themselves as input and internally computing the term frequencies as well as the inverse document frequencies, eliminating the need to use the CountVectorizer for computing the term frequencies based on the Bag of Words model. Support is also present for adding n-grams to the feature vectors. We can see the function in action in the following snippet:

```
# build tfidf vectorizer and get training corpus feature vectors
In [425]: tfidf_vectorizer, tdidf_features = tfidf_extractor(CORPUS)
    ...: display_features(np.round(tdidf_features.todense(), 2), feature_
        names)
    and  beautiful  blue  cheese   is   love   sky    so   the
0   0.00            0.00  0.40     0.00  0.49  0.00  0.49  0.00  0.60
1   0.44            0.35  0.23     0.00  0.56  0.00  0.56  0.00  0.00
2   0.00            0.43  0.29     0.00  0.35  0.00  0.35  0.55  0.43
3   0.00            0.00  0.35     0.66  0.00  0.66  0.00  0.00  0.00
```

```
# get tfidf feature vector for the new document
In [426]: nd_tfidf = tfidf_vectorizer.transform(new_doc)
    ...: display_features(np.round(nd_tfidf.todense(), 2), feature_names)
   and  beautiful  blue  cheese  is  love  sky  so  the
0  0.0         0.0  0.63     0.0  0.0  0.0  0.77  0.0  0.0
```

You can see from the preceding outputs that the *tfidf* feature vectors match to the ones we obtained previously. This brings us to the end of our discussion on feature extraction using *tfidf*. Now we will look at some advanced word vectorization techniques.

Advanced Word Vectorization Models

There are various approaches to creating more advanced word vectorization models for extracting features from text data. Here we will discuss a couple of them that use Google's popular word2vec algorithm. The word2vec model, released in 2013 by Google, is a neural network–based implementation that learns distributed vector representations of words based on continuous Bag of Words and skip-gram–based architectures. The word2vec framework is much faster than other neural network–based implementations and does not require manual labels to create meaningful representations among words. You can find more details on Google's word2vec project at https://code.google.com/archive/p/word2vec/. You can even try out some of the implementations yourself if you are interested.

We will be using the gensim library in our implementation, which is Python implementation for word2vec that provides several high-level interfaces for easily building these models. The basic idea is to provide a corpus of documents as input and get feature vectors for them as output. Internally, it constructs a vocabulary based on the input text documents and learns vector representations for words based on various techniques mentioned earlier, and once this is complete, it builds a model that can be used to extract word vectors for each word in a document. Using various techniques like average weighting or *tfidf* weighting, we can compute the averaged vector representation of a document using its word vectors. You can get more details about the interface for gensim's word2vec implementation at http://radimrehurek.com/gensim/models/word2vec.html.

We will be mainly focusing on the following parameters when we build our model from our sample training corpus:

- size: This parameter is used to set the size or dimension for the word vectors and can range from tens to thousands. You can try out various dimensions to see which gives the best result.

- window: This parameter is used to set the context or window size. which specifies the length of the window of words that should be considered for the algorithm to take into account as context when training.

- min_count: This parameter specifies the minimum word count needed across the corpus for the word to be considered in the vocabulary. This helps in removing very specific words that may not have much significance because they occur very rarely in the documents.

- **sample**: This parameter is used to downsample effects of occurrence of frequent words. Values between 0.01 and 0.0001 are usually ideal.

Once we build a model, we will define and implement two techniques of combining word vectors together in text documents based on certain weighing schemes. We will implement two techniques mentioned as follows.

- Averaged word vectors

- TF-IDF weighted word vectors

Let us start the feature-extraction process by building our word2vec model on our sample training corpus before going into further implementations. The following code snippet shows how:

```
import gensim
import nltk

# tokenize corpora
TOKENIZED_CORPUS = [nltk.word_tokenize(sentence)
                    for sentence in CORPUS]
tokenized_new_doc = [nltk.word_tokenize(sentence)
                     for sentence in new_doc]

# build the word2vec model on our training corpus
model = gensim.models.Word2Vec(TOKENIZED_CORPUS, size=10, window=10,
                               min_count=2, sample=1e-3)
```

As you can see, we have built the model using the parameters described earlier; you can play around with these and also look at other parameters from the documentation to change the architecture type, number of workers, and so on. Now that we have our model ready, we can start implementing our feature extraction techniques.

Averaged Word Vectors

The preceding model creates a vector representation for each word in the vocabulary. We can access them by just typing in the following code:

```
In [430]: print model['sky']
[ 0.01608407 -0.04819566  0.04227461 -0.03011346  0.0254148   0.01728328
  0.0155535   0.00774884 -0.02752112  0.01646519]

In [431]: print model['blue']
[-0.0472235   0.01662185 -0.01221706 -0.04724348 -0.04384995  0.00193343
 -0.03163504 -0.03423524  0.02661656  0.03033725]
```

Each word vector is of length 10 based on the size parameter specified earlier. But when we deal with sentences and text documents, they are of unequal length, and we must carry out some form of combining and aggregation operations to make sure the number of dimensions of the final feature vectors are the same, regardless of the length of the text document, number of words, and so on. In this technique, we will use an average weighted word vectorization scheme, where for each text document we will extract all the tokens of the text document, and for each token in the document we will capture the subsequent word vector if present in the vocabulary. We will sum up all the word vectors and divide the result by the total number of words matched in the vocabulary to get a final resulting averaged word vector representation for the text document. This can be mathematically represented using the equation

$$AWV(D) = \frac{\sum\limits_{1}^{n} wv(w)}{n}$$

where $AVW(D)$ is the averaged word vector representation for document D, containing words $w_1, w_2, ..., w_n$, and $wv(w)$ is the word vector representation for the word w.

The following snippet shows the pseudocode for the algorithm just described:

```
model := the word2vec model we built
vocabulary := unique_words(model)
document := [words]
matched_word_count := 0
vector := []

for word in words:
        if word in vocabulary:
                vector := vector + model[word]
                matched_word_count :=  matched_word_count + 1

averaged_word_vector := vector / matched_word_count
```

That snippet shows the flow of operations in a better way that is easier to understand. We will now implement our algorithm in Python using the following code snippet:

```python
import numpy as np

# define function to average word vectors for a text document
def average_word_vectors(words, model, vocabulary, num_features):

    feature_vector = np.zeros((num_features,),dtype="float64")
    nwords = 0.

    for word in words:
        if word in vocabulary:
            nwords = nwords + 1.
            feature_vector = np.add(feature_vector, model[word])
```

```
    if nwords:
        feature_vector = np.divide(feature_vector, nwords)

    return feature_vector

# generalize above function for a corpus of documents
def averaged_word_vectorizer(corpus, model, num_features):
    vocabulary = set(model.index2word)
    features = [average_word_vectors(tokenized_sentence, model, vocabulary,
    num_features)
                    for tokenized_sentence in corpus]
    return np.array(features)
```

The average_word_vectors() function must seem familiar to you—it is the concrete implementation of our algorithm shown using our pseudocode earlier. We also create a generic function averaged_word_vectorizer() to perform averaging of word vectors for a corpus of documents. The following snippet shows our function in action on our sample corpora:

```
# get averaged word vectors for our training CORPUS
In [445]: avg_word_vec_features = averaged_word_vectorizer(corpus=TOKENIZED_
CORPUS,
    ...:                                                   model=model,
    ...:                                                   num_features=10)
    ...: print np.round(avg_word_vec_features, 3)
[[ 0.006 -0.01   0.015 -0.014  0.004 -0.006 -0.024 -0.007 -0.001  0.   ]
 [-0.008 -0.01   0.021 -0.019 -0.002 -0.002 -0.011  0.002  0.003 -0.001]
 [-0.003 -0.007  0.008 -0.02  -0.001 -0.004 -0.014 -0.015  0.002 -0.01 ]
 [-0.047  0.017 -0.012 -0.047 -0.044  0.002 -0.032 -0.034  0.027  0.03 ]]

# get averaged word vectors for our test new_doc
In [447]: nd_avg_word_vec_features = averaged_word_
vectorizer(corpus=tokenized_new_doc,
    ...:                                                   model=model,
    ...:                                                   num_
                                                          features=10)
    ...: print np.round(nd_avg_word_vec_features, 3)
[[-0.016 -0.016  0.015 -0.039 -0.009  0.01  -0.008 -0.013  0.     0.023]]
```

From the preceding outputs, you can see that we have uniformly sized averaged word vectors for each document in the corpus, and these feature vectors can be used later for classification by feeding it to the ML algorithms.

TF-IDF Weighted Averaged Word Vectors

Our previous vectorizer simply sums up all the word vectors pertaining to any document based on the words in the model vocabulary and calculates a simple average by dividing with the count of matched words. This section introduces a new and novel technique of weighing each matched word vector with the word TF-TDF score and summing up all the word vectors for a document and dividing it by the sum of all the TF-IDF weights of the matched words in the document. This would basically give us a TF-IDF weighted averaged word vector for each document.

This can be mathematically represented using the equation

$$TWA(D) = \frac{\sum_{1}^{n} wv(w) \times \mathit{tfidf}(w)}{n}$$

where $TWA(D)$ is the TF-IDF weighted averaged word vector representation for document D, containing words $w_1, w_2, ..., w_n$, where $wv(w)$ is the word vector representation and $\mathit{tfidf}(w)$ is the TF-IDF weight for the word w. The following snippet shows the pseudocode for this algorithm:

```
model := the word2vec model we built
vocabulary := unique_words(model)
document := [words]
tfidfs := [tfidf(word) for each word in words]
matched_word_wts := 0
vector := []

for word in words:
        if word in vocabulary:
                word_vector := model[word]
                weighted_word_vector := tfidfs[word] x word_vector
                vector := vector + weighted_word_vector
                matched_word_wts :=  matched_word_wts + tfidfs[word]

tfidf_wtd_avgd_word_vector := vector / matched_word_wts
```

That pseudocode gives structure to our algorithm and shows how to implement the algorithm from the mathematical formula we defined earlier.

The following code snippet implements this algorithm in Python so we can use it for feature extraction:

```
# define function to compute tfidf weighted averaged word vector for a document
def tfidf_wtd_avg_word_vectors(words, tfidf_vector, tfidf_vocabulary, model,
num_features):

    word_tfidfs = [tfidf_vector[0, tfidf_vocabulary.get(word)]
                    if tfidf_vocabulary.get(word)
                    else 0 for word in words]
    word_tfidf_map = {word:tfidf_val for word, tfidf_val in zip(words, word_
    tfidfs)}

    feature_vector = np.zeros((num_features,),dtype="float64")
```

```
    vocabulary = set(model.index2word)
    wts = 0.
    for word in words:
        if word in vocabulary:
            word_vector = model[word]
            weighted_word_vector = word_tfidf_map[word] * word_vector
            wts = wts + word_tfidf_map[word]
            feature_vector = np.add(feature_vector, weighted_word_vector)
    if wts:
        feature_vector = np.divide(feature_vector, wts)

    return feature_vector

# generalize above function for a corpus of documents
def tfidf_weighted_averaged_word_vectorizer(corpus, tfidf_vectors,
                                    tfidf_vocabulary, model, num_features):

    docs_tfidfs = [(doc, doc_tfidf)
                    for doc, doc_tfidf
                    in zip(corpus, tfidf_vectors)]
    features = [tfidf_wtd_avg_word_vectors(tokenized_sentence, tfidf, tfidf_
    vocabulary,
                                    model, num_features)
                    for tokenized_sentence, tfidf in docs_tfidfs]
    return np.array(features)
```

The tfidf_wtd_avg_word_vectors() function helps us in getting the TF-IDF weighted averaged word vector representation for a document. We also create a corresponding generic function tfidf_weighted_averaged_word_vectorizer() to perform TF-IDF weighted averaging of word vectors for a corpus of documents. We can see our implemented function in action on our sample corpora using the following snippet:

```
# get tfidf weights and vocabulary from earlier results and compute result
In [453]: corpus_tfidf = tdidf_features
    ...: vocab = tfidf_vectorizer.vocabulary_
    ...: wt_tfidf_word_vec_features = tfidf_weighted_averaged_word_
vectorizer(corpus=TOKENIZED_CORPUS, tfidf_vectors=corpus_tfidf,
    ...:                             tfidf_vocabulary=vocab, model=model,
                                    num_features=10)
```

```
    ...: print np.round(wt_tfidf_word_vec_features, 3)
[[ 0.011 -0.011  0.014 -0.011  0.007 -0.007 -0.024 -0.008 -0.004 -0.004]
 [ 0.    -0.014  0.028 -0.014  0.004 -0.003 -0.012  0.011 -0.001 -0.002]
 [-0.001 -0.008  0.007 -0.019  0.001 -0.004 -0.012 -0.018  0.001 -0.014]
 [-0.047  0.017 -0.012 -0.047 -0.044  0.002 -0.032 -0.034  0.027  0.03 ]]

# compute avgd word vector for test new_doc
In [454]: nd_wt_tfidf_word_vec_features = tfidf_weighted_averaged_word_
vectorizer(corpus=tokenized_new_doc, tfidf_vectors=nd_tfidf, tfidf_
vocabulary=vocab, model=model, num_features=10)
    ...: print np.round(nd_wt_tfidf_word_vec_features, 3)
[[-0.012 -0.019  0.018 -0.038 -0.006  0.01  -0.006 -0.011 -0.003  0.023]]
```

From the preceding results, you can see how we can converted each document into TF-IDF weighted averaged numeric vectors. We also used our TF-IDF weights and vocabulary, obtained earlier when we implemented TF-IDF–based feature vector extraction from documents.

Now you have a good grasp on how to extract features from text data that can be used for training a classifier.

Classification Algorithms

Classification algorithms are supervised ML algorithms that are used to classify, categorize, or label data points based on what it has observed in the past. Each classification algorithm, being a supervised learning algorithm, requires training data. This training data consists of a set of training observations where each observation is a pair consisting of an input data point, usually a feature vector like we observed earlier, and a corresponding output outcome for that input observation. There are mainly three processes classification algorithms go through:

- *Training* is the process where the supervised learning algorithm analyzes and tries to infer patterns out of training data such that it can identify which patterns lead to a specific outcome. These outcomes are often known as the class labels/class variables/ response variables. We usually carry out the process of feature extraction or feature engineering to derive meaningful features from the raw data before training. These feature sets are fed to an algorithm of our choice, which then tries to identify and learn patterns from them and their corresponding outcomes. The result is an inferred function known as a model or a classification model. This model is expected to be generalized enough from learning patterns in the training set such that it can predict the classes or outcomes for new data points in the future.

- *Evaluation* involves trying to test the prediction performance of our model to see how well it has trained and learned on the training dataset. For this we usually use a validation dataset and test the performance of our model by predicting on that dataset and testing our predictions against the actual class labels, also called as the *ground truth*. Often we also use cross-validation, where the data is divided into *folds* and a chunk of it is used for training, with the remainder used to validate the trained model. Note that we also tune the model based on the validation results to get to an optimal configuration that yields maximum accuracy and minimum error. We also evaluate our model against a holdout or test dataset, but we never tune our model against that dataset because that would lead to it being biased or overfit against very specific features from the dataset. The holdout or test dataset is something of a representative sample of what new, real data samples might look like for which the model will generate predictions and how it might perform on these new data samples. Later we will look at various metrics that are typically used to evaluate and measure model performance.

- *Tuning*, also known as *hyperparameter tuning* or *optimization*, is where we focus on trying to optimize a model to maximize its prediction power and reduce errors. Each model is at heart a mathematical function with several parameters that determine model complexity, learning capability, and so on. These are known as hyperparameters because they cannot be learned directly from data and must be set prior to running and training the model. Hence, the process of choosing an optimal set of model hyperparameters such that the performance of the model yields good prediction accuracy is known as *model tuning*, and we can carry it out in various ways, including randomized search and grid search. We will not be covering this in our implementations since this is more inclined towards core machine learning and is out of our current scope as the models we will be building work well with default hyperparameter configurations. But there are plenty of resources on the Web if you are interested in model tuning and optimization.

There are various types of classification algorithms, but we will not be venturing into each one in detail. Our focus remains text classification, and I do not want to bore everyone with excessive mathematical derivations for each algorithm. However, I will touch upon a couple of algorithms that are quite effective for text classification and try to explain them, keeping the mathematical formulae to the base essentials. These algorithms are the following:

- Multinomial Naïve Bayes
- Support vector machines

There are also several other algorithms besides these you can look up, including logistic regression, decision trees, and neural networks. And ensemble techniques use a collection or ensemble of models to learn and predict outcomes that include random forests and gradient boosting, but they often don't perform very well for text classification because they are very prone to overfitting. I recommend you be careful if you plan on experimenting with them. Besides these, deep learning–based techniques have also recently become popular. They use multiple hidden layers and combine several neural network models to build a complex classification model.

We will now briefly look at some of the concepts surrounding multinomial naïve Bayes and support vector machines before using them for our classification problem.

Multinomial Naïve Bayes

This algorithm is a special case of the popular naïve Bayes algorithm, which is used specifically for prediction and classification tasks where we have more than two classes. Before looking at multinomial naïve Bayes, let us look at the definition and formulation of the naïve Bayes algorithm. The naïve Bayes algorithm is a supervised learning algorithm that puts into action the very popular Bayes' theorem. However, there is a "naïve" assumption here that each feature is independent of the others. Mathematically we can formulate this as follows: Given a response class variable y and a set of n features in the form of a feature vector $\{x_1, x_2, ..., x_n\}$, using Bayes' theorem we can denote the probability of the occurrence of y given the features as

$$P(y \mid x_1, x_2, ..., x_n) = \frac{P(y) \times P(x_1, x_2, ..., x_n \mid y)}{P(x_1, x_2, ..., x_n)}$$

under the assumption that $P(x_i \mid y, x_1, x_2, ..., x_{i-1}, x_{i+1}, ..., x_n) = P(x_i \mid y)$, and for all i we can represent this as

$$P(y \mid x_1, x_2, ..., x_n) = \frac{P(y) \times \prod_{i=1}^{n} P(x_i \mid y)}{P(x_1, x_2, ..., x_n)}$$

where i ranges from 1 to n. In simple terms, this can be written as $posterior = \dfrac{prior \times likelihood}{evidence}$ and now, since $P(x_1, x_2, ..., x_n)$ is constant, the model can be expressed like this:

$$P(y \mid x_1, x_2, ..., x_n) \propto P(y) \times \prod_{i=1}^{n} P(x_i \mid y)$$

This means that under the previous assumptions of independence among the features where each feature is conditionally independent of every other feature, the conditional distribution over the class variable which is to be predicted, y can be represented using the following mathematical equation as

$$P(y \mid x_1, x_2, \ldots, x_n) = \frac{1}{Z} P(y) \times \prod_{i=1}^{n} P(x_i \mid y)$$

where the evidence measure, $Z = p(x)$ is a constant scaling factor dependent on the feature variables. From this equation, we can build the naïve Bayes classifier by combining it with a rule known as the *MAP decision rule*, which stands for *maximum a posteriori*. Going into the statistical details would be impossible in the current scope, but by using it, the classifier can be represented as a mathematical function that can assign a predicted class label $\hat{y} = C_k$ for some k using the following representation:

$$\hat{y} = \underset{k \in \{1, 2, \ldots, K\}}{argmax} P(C_k) \times \prod_{i=1}^{n} P(x_i \mid C_k)$$

This classifier is often said to be simple, quite evident from its name and also because of several assumptions we make about our data and features that might not be so in the real world. Nevertheless, this algorithm still works remarkably well in many use cases related to classification, including multi-class document classification, spam filtering, and so on. They can train really fast compared to other classifiers and also work well even when we do not have sufficient training data. Models often do not perform well when they have a lot of features, and this phenomenon is known as the *curse of dimensionality*. Naïve Bayes takes care of this problem by decoupling the class variable–related conditional feature distributions, thus leading to each distribution being independently estimated as a single dimension distribution.

Multinomial naïve Bayes is an extension of the preceding algorithm for predicting and classifying data points, where the number of distinct classes or outcomes is more than two. In this case the feature vectors are usually assumed to be word counts from the Bag of Words model, but TF-IDF–based weights will also work. One limitation is that negative weight-based features can't be fed into this algorithm. This distribution can be represented as $p_y = \{p_{y1}, p_{y2}, \ldots, p_{yn}\}$ for each class label y, and the total number of features is n, which could be represented as the total vocabulary of distinct words or terms in text analytics. From the preceding equation, $p_{yi} = P(x_i \mid y)$ represents the probability of feature i in any observation sample that has an outcome or class y. The parameter p_y can be estimated with a smoothened version of maximum likelihood estimation (with relative frequency of occurrences), and represented as

$$\hat{p}_{yi} = \frac{F_{yi} + \alpha}{F_y + \alpha n}$$

where $F_{yi} = \sum_{x \in TD} x_i$ is the frequency of occurrence for the feature i in a sample for class label y in our training dataset TD, and $F_y = \sum_{i=1}^{|TD|} F_{yi}$ is the total frequency of all features for the class label y. There is some amount of smoothening one with the help of priors $\alpha \geq 0$, which accounts for the features that are not present in the learning data points and helps in getting rid of zero-probability-related issues. Some specific settings for this parameter are used quite often. The value of $\alpha = 1$ is known as Laplace smoothing, and $\alpha < 1$ is known as Lidstone smoothing. The scikit-learn library provides an excellent implementation for multinomial naïve Bayes in the class MultinomialNB, which we will be leveraging when we build our text classifier later on.

Support Vector Machines

In machine learning, *support vector machines* (SVM) are supervised learning algorithms used for classification, regression, novelty, and anomaly or outlier detection. Considering a binary classification problem, if we have training data such that each data point or observation belongs to a specific class, the SVM algorithm can be trained based on this data such that it can assign future data points into one of the two classes. This algorithm represents the training data samples as points in space such that points belonging to either class can be separated by a wide gap between them, called a *hyperplane*, and the new data points to be predicted are assigned classes based on which side of this hyperplane they fall into. This process is for a typical linear classification process. However, SVM can also perform non-linear classification by an interesting approach known as a *kernel trick*, where kernel functions are used to operate on high-dimensional feature spaces that are non-linear separable. Usually, inner products between data points in the feature space help achieve this.

The SVM algorithm takes in a set of training data points and constructs a hyperplane of a collection of hyperplanes for a high dimensional feature space. The larger the margins of the hyperplane, the better the separation, so this leads to lower generalization errors of the classifier. Let us represent this formally and mathematically. Consider a training dataset of n data points $(\vec{x}_1, y_1), \ldots, (\vec{x}_n, y_n)$ such that the class variable $y_i \in \{-1, 1\}$ where each value indicates the class corresponding to the point $\vec{x}_i$. Each data point $\vec{x}_i$ is a feature vector. The objective of the SVM algorithm is to find the max-margin hyperplane that separates the set of data points having class label of $y_i = 1$ from the set of data points having class label $y_i = -1$ such that the distance between the hyperplane and sample data points from either class nearest to it is maximized. These sample data points are known as the support vectors. Figure 4-3, courtesy of Wikipedia, shows what the vector space with the hyperplane looks like.

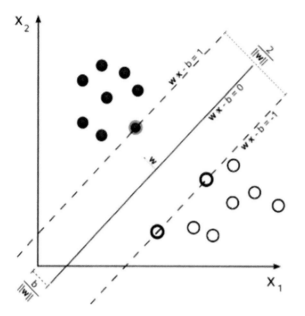

Figure 4-3. *Two-class SVM depicting hyperplane and support vectors (courtesy: Wikipedia)*

You can clearly see the hyperplane and the support vectors in the figure. The hyperplane can be defined as the set of points $\vec{x}$ which satisfy $\vec{w} \cdot \vec{x} + b = 0$ where $\vec{w}$ is the normal vector to the hyperplane, as shown in Figure 4-3, and $\dfrac{b}{\|\vec{w}\|}$ gives us the offset of the hyperplane from the origin toward the support vectors highlighted in the figure. There are two main types of margins that help in separating out the data points belonging to the different classes.

When the data is linearly separable, as in Figure 4-3, we can have hard margins that are basically represented by the two parallel hyperplanes depicted by the dotted lines, which help in separating the data points belonging to the two different classes. This is done taking into account that the distance between them is as large as possible. The region bounded by these two hyperplanes forms the margin with the max-margin hyperplane being in the middle. These hyperplanes are shown in the figure having the equations $\vec{w} \cdot \vec{x} + b = 1$ and $\vec{w} \cdot \vec{x} + b = -1$.

Often the data points are not linearly separable, for which we can use the *hinge loss* function, which can be represented as $\max\left(0, 1 - y_i\left(\vec{w} \cdot \vec{x}_i + b\right)\right)$ and in fact the scikit-learn implementation of SVM can be found in SVC, LinearSVC, or SGDClassifier where we will use the 'hinge' loss function (set by default) defined previously to optimize and build the model. This loss function helps us in getting the soft margins and is often known as a *soft-margin SVM*.

For a multi-class classification problem, if we have *n* classes, for each class a binary classifier is trained and learned that helps in separating between each class and the other *n-1* classes. During prediction, the *scores* (distances to hyperplanes) for each classifier are computed, and the maximum score is chosen for selecting the class label. Also often stochastic gradient descent is used for minimizing the loss function in SVM algorithms. Figure 4-4 shows how three classifiers are trained in total for a three-class SVM problem over the very popular iris dataset. This figure is built using a scikit-learn model and is obtained from the official documentation available at `http://scikit-learn.org`.

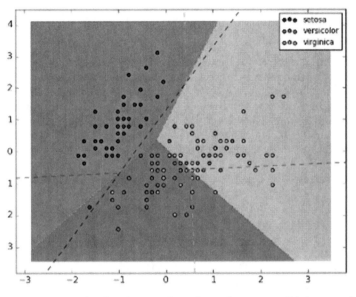

Figure 4-4. *Multi-class SVM on three classes (courtesy: scikit-learn.org)*

In Figure 4-4 you can clearly see that a total of three SVM classifiers have been trained for each of the three classes and are then combined for the final predictions so that data points belonging to each class can be labeled correctly. There are a lot of resources and books dedicated entirely towards supervised ML and classification. Interested readers should check them out to gain more in-depth knowledge on how these techniques work and how they can be applied to various problems in analytics.

Evaluating Classification Models

Training, tuning, and building models are an important part of the whole analytics lifecycle, but even more important is knowing how well these models are performing. Performance of classification models is usually based on how well they predict outcomes for new data points. Usually this performance is measured against a test or holdout dataset that consists of data points which was not used to influence or train the classifier in any way. This test dataset usually has several observations and corresponding labels.

We extract features in the same way as it was followed when training the model. These features are fed to the already trained model, and we obtain predictions for each data point. These predictions are then matched with the actual labels to see how well or how accurately the model has predicted.

Several metrics determine a model's prediction performance, but we will mainly focus on the following metrics:

- Accuracy

- Precision

- Recall

- F1 score

Let us look at a practical example to see how these metrics can be computed. Consider a binary classification problem of classifying emails as either 'spam' or 'ham'. Assuming we have a total of 20 emails, for which we already have the actual manual labels, we pass it through our built classifier to get predicted labels for each email. This gives us 20 predicted labels. Now we want to measure the classifier performance by comparing each prediction with its actual label. The following code snippet sets up the initial dependencies and the actual and predicted labels:

```
from sklearn import metrics
import numpy as np
import pandas as pd
from collections import Counter

actual_labels = ['spam', 'ham', 'spam', 'spam', 'spam',
                 'ham', 'ham', 'spam', 'ham', 'spam',
                 'spam', 'ham', 'ham', 'ham', 'spam',
                 'ham', 'ham', 'spam', 'spam', 'ham']

predicted_labels = ['spam', 'spam', 'spam', 'ham', 'spam',
                    'spam', 'ham', 'ham', 'spam', 'spam',
                    'ham', 'ham', 'spam', 'ham', 'ham',
                    'ham', 'spam', 'ham', 'spam', 'spam']

ac = Counter(actual_labels)
pc = Counter(predicted_labels)
```

Let us now see the total number of emails belonging to either 'spam' or 'ham' based on the actual labels and our predicted labels using the following snippet:

```
In [517]: print 'Actual counts:', ac.most_common()
    ...: print 'Predicted counts:', pc.most_common()
Actual counts: [('ham', 10), ('spam', 10)]
Predicted counts: [('spam', 11), ('ham', 9)]
```

Thus we see that there are a total of 10 emails that are 'spam' and 10 emails that are 'ham'. Our classifier has predicted a total of 11 emails as 'spam' and 9 as 'ham'. How do we now compare which email was actually 'spam' and what it was classified as? A confusion matrix is an excellent way to measure this performance across the two classes. A *confusion matrix* is a tabular structure that helps visualize the performance of classifiers. Each column in the matrix represents classified instances based on predictions, and each row of the matrix represents classified instances based on the actual class labels. (It can be vice-versa if needed.) We usually have a class label defined as the *positive class*, which could be typically the class of our interest. Figure 4-5 shows a typical two-class confusion matrix where (p) denotes the positive class and (n) denotes the negative class.

	p' (Predicted)	n' (Predicted)
p (Actual)	True Positive	False Negative
n (Actual)	False Positive	True Negative

Figure 4-5. *A confusion matrix from a two-class classification problem*

You can see some terms in the matrix depicted in Figure 4-5. True Positive (TP) indicates the number of correct hits or predictions for our positive class. False Negative (FN) indicates the number of instances we missed for that class by predicting it falsely as the negative class. False Positive (FP) is the number of instances we predicted wrongly as the positive class when it was actually not. True Negative (TN) is the number of instances we correctly predicted as the negative class.

The following code snippet constructs a confusion matrix with our data:

```
In [519]: cm = metrics.confusion_matrix(y_true=actual_labels,
     ...:                                y_pred=predicted_labels,
     ...:                                labels=['spam','ham'])
     ...: print pd.DataFrame(data=cm,
     ...:                 columns=pd.MultiIndex(levels=[['Predicted:'],
     ...:                                               ['spam','ham']],
     ...:                                       labels=[[0,0],[0,1]]),
     ...:                 index=pd.MultiIndex(levels=[['Actual:'],
```

```
   ...:                                              ['spam','ham']],
   ...:                                    labels=[[0,0],[0,1]]))
           Predicted:
                 spam ham
Actual: spam        5   5
        ham         6   4
```

We now get a confusion matrix similar to the figure. In our case, let us consider 'spam' to be the positive class. We can now define the preceding metrics in the following snippet:

```
positive_class = 'spam'

true_positive = 5.
false_positive = 6.
false_negative = 5.
true_negative = 4.
```

Now that we have the necessary values from the confusion matrix, we can calculate our four performance metrics one by one. We have taken the values from earlier as floats to help with computations involving divisions. We will use the metrics module from scikit-learn, which is very powerful and helps in computing these metrics with a single function. And we will define and compute these metrics manually so that you can understand them clearly and see what goes on behind the scenes of those functions from the metrics module.

Accuracy is defined as the overall accuracy or proportion of correct predictions of the model, which can be depicted by the formula

$$Accuracy = \frac{TP + TN}{TP + FP + FN + TN}$$

where we have our correct predictions in the numerator divided by all the outcomes in the denominator. The following snippet shows the computations for accuracy:

```
In [522]: accuracy = np.round(
     ...:                   metrics.accuracy_score(y_true=actual_labels,
     ...:                                 y_pred=predicted_labels),2)
     ...: accuracy_manual = np.round(
     ...:                    (true_positive + true_negative) /
     ...:                      (true_positive + true_negative +
     ...:                       false_negative + false_positive),2)
     ...: print 'Accuracy:', accuracy
     ...: print 'Manually computed accuracy:', accuracy_manual
Accuracy: 0.45
Manually computed accuracy: 0.45
```

Precision is defined as the number of predictions made that are actually correct or relevant out of all the predictions based on the positive class. This is also known as *positive predictive value* and can be depicted by the formula

$$Precision = \frac{TP}{TP+FP}$$

where we have our correct predictions in the numerator for the positive class divided by all the predictions for the positive class including the false positives. The following snippet shows the computations for precision:

```
In [523]: precision = np.round(
     ...:                 metrics.precision_score(y_true=actual_labels,
     ...:                                         y_pred=predicted_labels,
     ...:                                         pos_label=positive_
                                                  class),2)
     ...: precision_manual = np.round(
     ...:                   (true_positive) /
     ...:                   (true_positive + false_positive),2)
     ...: print 'Precision:', precision
     ...: print 'Manually computed precision:', precision_manual
Precision: 0.45
Manually computed precision: 0.45
```

Recall is defined as the number of instances of the positive class that were correctly predicted. This is also known as *hit rate, coverage,* or *sensitivity* and can be depicted by the formula

$$Recall = \frac{TP}{TP+FN}$$

where we have our correct predictions for the positive class in the numerator divided by correct and missed instances for the positive class, giving us the hit rate. The following snippet shows the computations for recall:

```
In [524]: recall = np.round(
     ...:               metrics.recall_score(y_true=actual_labels,
     ...:                                    y_pred=predicted_labels,
     ...:                                    pos_label=positive_class),2)
     ...: recall_manual = np.round(
     ...:                 (true_positive) /
     ...:                 (true_positive + false_negative),2)
     ...: print 'Recall:', recall
     ...: print 'Manually computed recall:', recall_manual
Recall: 0.5
Manually computed recall: 0.5
```

F1 score is another accuracy measure that is computed by taking the harmonic mean of the precision and recall and can be represented as follows:

$$F1\ Score = \frac{2 \times Precision \times Recall}{Precision + Recall}$$

We can compute the same using the following code snippet:

```
In [526]: f1_score = np.round(
     ...:                  metrics.f1_score(y_true=actual_labels,
     ...:                                   y_pred=predicted_labels,
     ...:                                   pos_label=positive_class),2)
     ...: f1_score_manual = np.round(
     ...:                     (2 * precision * recall) /
     ...:                     (precision + recall),2)
     ...: print 'F1 score:', f1_score
     ...: print 'Manually computed F1 score:', f1_score_manual
F1 score: 0.48
Manually computed F1 score: 0.47
```

This should give you a pretty good idea about the main metrics used most often when evaluating classification models. We will be measuring the performance of our models using the very same metrics, and you may remember seeing these metrics from Chapter 3, when we were building some of our taggers and parsers.

Building a Multi-Class Classification System

We have gone through all the steps necessary for building a classification system, from normalization to feature extraction, model building, and evaluation. In this section, we will be putting everything together and applying it on some real-world data to build a multi-class text classification system. For this, we will be using the 20 newsgroups dataset available for download using `scikit-learn`. The 20 newsgroups dataset comprises around 18,000 newsgroups posts spread across 20 different categories or topics, thus making this a 20-class classification problem! Remember the more classes, the more complex or difficult trying to build an accurate classifier gets. It is recommended that you remove the headers, footers, and quotes from the text documents to prevent the model from overfitting or not generalizing well due to certain specific headers or email addresses, so we will make sure we take care of this. We will also remove documents that are empty or have no content after removing these three items because it would be pointless to try and extract features from empty documents.

Let us start with loading the necessary dataset and defining functions for building the training and testing datasets:

```
from sklearn.datasets import fetch_20newsgroups
from sklearn.cross_validation import train_test_split
```

```
def get_data():
    data = fetch_20newsgroups(subset='all',
                              shuffle=True,
                              remove=('headers', 'footers', 'quotes'))
    return data

def prepare_datasets(corpus, labels, test_data_proportion=0.3):
    train_X, test_X, train_Y, test_Y = train_test_split(corpus, labels,
                                                        test_size=0.33,
random_state=42)
    return train_X, test_X, train_Y, test_Y

def remove_empty_docs(corpus, labels):
    filtered_corpus = []
    filtered_labels = []
    for doc, label in zip(corpus, labels):
        if doc.strip():
            filtered_corpus.append(doc)
            filtered_labels.append(label)

    return filtered_corpus, filtered_labels
```

We can now get the data, see the total number of classes in our dataset, and split our data into training and test datasets using the following snippet (in case you do not have the data downloaded, feel free to connect to the Internet and take some time to download the complete corpus):

```
# get the data
In [529]: dataset = get_data()

# print all the classes
In [530]: print dataset.target_names
['alt.atheism', 'comp.graphics', 'comp.os.ms-windows.misc', 'comp.sys.ibm.
pc.hardware', 'comp.sys.mac.hardware', 'comp.windows.x', 'misc.forsale',
'rec.autos', 'rec.motorcycles', 'rec.sport.baseball', 'rec.sport.hockey',
'sci.crypt', 'sci.electronics', 'sci.med', 'sci.space', 'soc.religion.
christian', 'talk.politics.guns', 'talk.politics.mideast', 'talk.politics.
misc', 'talk.religion.misc']

# get corpus of documents and their corresponding labels
In [531]: corpus, labels = dataset.data, dataset.target
     ...: corpus, labels = remove_empty_docs(corpus, labels)

# see sample document and its label index, name
In [548]: print 'Sample document:', corpus[10]
     ...: print 'Class label:',labels[10]
     ...: print 'Actual class label:', dataset.target_names[labels[10]]
Sample document: the blood of the lamb.
```

This will be a hard task, because most cultures used most animals for blood sacrifices. It has to be something related to our current post-modernism state. Hmm, what about used computers?

Cheers,
Kent
Class label: 19
Actual class label: talk.religion.misc

```
# prepare train and test datasets
In [549]: train_corpus, test_corpus, train_labels, test_labels = prepare_
datasets(corpus,
    ...:                                                          labels, test_
data_proportion=0.3)
```

You can see from the preceding snippet how a sample document and label looks. Each document has its own class label, which is one of the 20 topics it is categorized into. The labels obtained are numbers, but we can easily map it back to the original category name if needed using the preceding snippet. We also split our data into train and test datasets, where the test dataset is 30 percent of the total data. We will build our model on the training data and test its performance on the test data. In the following snippet, we will use the normalization module we built earlier to normalize our datasets:

```
from normalization import normalize_corpus

norm_train_corpus = normalize_corpus(train_corpus)
norm_test_corpus = normalize_corpus(test_corpus)
```

Remember, a lot of normalization steps take place that we implemented earlier for each document in the corpora, so it may take some time to complete. Once we have normalized documents, we will use our feature extractor module built earlier to start extracting features from our documents. We will build models for Bag of Words, TF-IDF, averaged word vector, and TF-IDF weighted averaged word vector features separately and compare their performances.

The following snippet extracts necessary features based on the different techniques:

```
from feature_extractors import bow_extractor, tfidf_extractor
from feature_extractors import averaged_word_vectorizer
from feature_extractors import tfidf_weighted_averaged_word_vectorizer
import nltk
import gensim

# bag of words features
bow_vectorizer, bow_train_features = bow_extractor(norm_train_corpus)
bow_test_features = bow_vectorizer.transform(norm_test_corpus)
```

```
# tfidf features
tfidf_vectorizer, tfidf_train_features = tfidf_extractor(norm_train_corpus)
tfidf_test_features = tfidf_vectorizer.transform(norm_test_corpus)

# tokenize documents
tokenized_train = [nltk.word_tokenize(text)
                    for text in norm_train_corpus]
tokenized_test = [nltk.word_tokenize(text)
                    for text in norm_test_corpus]
# build word2vec model
model = gensim.models.Word2Vec(tokenized_train,
                                size=500,
                                window=100,
                                min_count=30,
                                sample=1e-3)

# averaged word vector features
avg_wv_train_features = averaged_word_vectorizer(corpus=tokenized_train,
                                                  model=model,
                                                  num_features=500)
avg_wv_test_features = averaged_word_vectorizer(corpus=tokenized_test,
                                                 model=model,
                                                 num_features=500)

# tfidf weighted averaged word vector features
vocab = tfidf_vectorizer.vocabulary_
tfidf_wv_train_features =
tfidf_weighted_averaged_word_vectorizer(corpus=tokenized_train,

tfidf_vectors=tfidf_train_features,

tfidf_vocabulary=vocab, model=model,

num_features=500)
tfidf_wv_test_features =
tfidf_weighted_averaged_word_vectorizer(corpus=tokenized_test,

tfidf_vectors=tfidf_test_features,

tfidf_vocabulary=vocab, model=model,

num_features=500)
```

Once we extract all the necessary features from our text documents using the preceding feature extractors, we define a function that will be useful for evaluation our classification models based on the four metrics discussed earlier, as shown in the following snippet:

```
from sklearn import metrics
import numpy as np

def get_metrics(true_labels, predicted_labels):
```

```
print 'Accuracy:', np.round(
                    metrics.accuracy_score(true_labels,
                                           predicted_labels),
                    2)
print 'Precision:', np.round(
                    metrics.precision_score(true_labels,
                                            predicted_labels,
                                            average='weighted'),
                    2)
print 'Recall:', np.round(
                    metrics.recall_score(true_labels,
                                         predicted_labels,
                                         average='weighted'),
                    2)
print 'F1 Score:', np.round(
                    metrics.f1_score(true_labels,
                                     predicted_labels,
                                     average='weighted'),
                    2)
```

We now define a function that trains the model using an ML algorithm and the training data, performs predictions on the test data using the trained model, and then evaluates the predictions using the preceding function to give us the model performance:

```
def train_predict_evaluate_model(classifier,
                                 train_features, train_labels,
                                 test_features, test_labels):
    # build model
    classifier.fit(train_features, train_labels)
    # predict using model
    predictions = classifier.predict(test_features)
    # evaluate model prediction performance
    get_metrics(true_labels=test_labels,
                predicted_labels=predictions)
    return predictions
```

We now import two ML algorithms (discussed in detail earlier) so that we can start building our models with them based on our extracted features. We will be using scikit-learn as mentioned to import the necessary classification algorithms, saving us the time and effort that would have been spent otherwise reinventing the wheel:

```
from sklearn.naive_bayes import MultinomialNB
from sklearn.linear_model import SGDClassifier

mnb = MultinomialNB()
svm = SGDClassifier(loss='hinge', n_iter=100)
```

Now we will train, predict, and evaluate models for all the different types of features using both multinomial naïve Bayes and support vector machines using the following snippet:

```
# Multinomial Naive Bayes with bag of words features
In [558]: mnb_bow_predictions = train_predict_evaluate_model(classifier=mnb,
    ...:                                                 train_features=bow_
                                                         train_features,
    ...:                                                 train_labels=train_
                                                         labels,
    ...:                                                 test_features=bow_test_
                                                         features,
    ...:                                                 test_labels=test_
                                                         labels)
Accuracy: 0.67
Precision: 0.72
Recall: 0.67
F1 Score: 0.65

# Support Vector Machine with bag of words features
In [559]: svm_bow_predictions = train_predict_evaluate_model(classifier=svm,
    ...:                                                 train_features=bow_
                                                         train_features,
    ...:                                                 train_labels=train_
                                                         labels,
    ...:                                                 test_features=bow_test_
                                                         features,
    ...:                                                 test_labels=test_
                                                         labels)
Accuracy: 0.61
Precision: 0.66
Recall: 0.61
F1 Score: 0.62

# Multinomial Naive Bayes with tfidf features
In [560]: mnb_tfidf_predictions = train_predict_evaluate_
model(classifier=mnb,
    ...:                                                 train_features=tfidf_
                                                         train_features,
    ...:                                                 train_labels=train_
                                                         labels,
    ...:                                                 test_features=tfidf_
                                                         test_features,
    ...:                                                 test_labels=test_
                                                         labels)
Accuracy: 0.72
```

```
Precision: 0.78
Recall: 0.72
F1 Score: 0.7

# Support Vector Machine with tfidf features
In [561]: svm_tfidf_predictions = train_predict_evaluate_
model(classifier=svm,
    ...:                                         train_features=tfidf_
                                                 train_features,
    ...:                                         train_labels=train_
                                                 labels,
    ...:                                         test_features=tfidf_
                                                 test_features,
    ...:                                         test_labels=test_
                                                 labels)
Accuracy: 0.77
Precision: 0.77
Recall: 0.77
F1 Score: 0.77

# Support Vector Machine with averaged word vector features
In [562]: svm_avgwv_predictions = train_predict_evaluate_
model(classifier=svm,
    ...:                                         train_features=avg_wv_
                                                 train_features,
    ...:                                         train_labels=train_
                                                 labels,
    ...:                                         test_features=avg_wv_
                                                 test_features,
    ...:                                         test_labels=test_
                                                 labels)
Accuracy: 0.55
Precision: 0.55
Recall: 0.55
F1 Score: 0.52

# Support Vector Machine with tfidf weighted averaged word vector features
In [563]: svm_tfidfwv_predictions = train_predict_evaluate_model(classifier
=svm,
    ...:
train_features=tfidf_wv_train_features,
    ...:
train_labels=train_labels, test_features=tfidf_wv_test_features,
    ...:                         test_labels=test_labels)
Accuracy: 0.53
Precision: 0.55
Recall: 0.53
F1 Score: 0.52
```

We built a total of six models using various types of extracted features and evaluated the performance of the model on the test data. From the preceding results, we can see that the SVM-based model built using TF-IDF features yielded the best results of 77 percent accuracy as well as precision, recall, and F1 score. We can build the confusion matrix for our SVM TF-IDF–based model to get an idea of the classes for which our model might not be performing well:

```
In [597]: import pandas as pd
     ...: cm = metrics.confusion_matrix(test_labels, svm_tfidf_predictions)
     ...: pd.DataFrame(cm, index=range(0,20), columns=range(0,20))
Out[597]:
```

	0	1	2	3	4	5	6	7	8	9	10	11	12	13	14	15	16	17	18	19
0	157	3	0	1	1	0	2	3	4	1	4	4	1	4	5	34	3	7	7	22
1	1	225	8	7	8	14	8	0	2	1	0	2	5	4	4	1	4	0	3	0
2	1	20	219	19	9	18	8	1	0	0	0	3	5	2	3	2	1	1	2	0
3	1	11	25	223	9	5	8	2	1	1	1	2	6	3	1	0	1	0	0	0
4	0	4	7	15	228	6	5	2	3	1	0	3	9	3	3	1	1	0	1	0
5	0	21	18	1	2	272	0	1	1	0	0	0	4	3	1	0	0	1	0	0
6	0	2	7	11	12	2	269	10	3	2	1	1	10	1	4	0	2	1	1	0
7	1	5	2	2	2	3	4	247	19	1	3	2	9	3	2	0	3	3	4	1
8	3	1	0	4	2	2	5	27	252	3	4	2	1	4	1	3	2	2	4	0
9	2	1	1	0	2	3	4	3	6	277	12	2	1	1	2	4	2	0	2	0
10	0	0	0	0	0	0	1	3	2	4	282	1	2	1	4	1	0	1	1	0
11	3	5	3	3	1	2	2	2	2	3	0	259	6	2	0	1	5	2	5	0
12	1	6	6	15	7	2	13	10	8	4	4	2	211	4	5	1	1	1	0	1
13	2	4	0	1	2	4	3	0	2	1	1	1	7	268	4	2	3	0	3	0
14	0	5	3	0	2	4	2	5	4	1	2	0	8	3	264	2	4	1	3	1
15	11	1	0	0	1	1	0	0	4	1	2	2	1	7	5	291	4	4	3	5
16	4	1	0	0	0	4	2	1	7	2	2	11	3	2	4	2	227	3	13	3
17	6	0	1	0	1	3	0	2	3	2	4	6	1	3	1	6	5	259	10	2
18	10	1	2	1	0	1	2	1	5	3	3	7	0	9	6	4	33	7	164	3
19	21	5	0	1	0	2	4	3	7	2	1	1	0	11	3	57	22	7	3	63

Figure 4-6. *20-class confusion matrix for our SVM based model*

From the confusion matrix shown in Figure 4-6, we can see a large number of documents for class label 0 that got misclassified to class label 15, and similarly for class label 18, many documents got misclassified into class label 16. Many documents for class label 19 got misclassified into class label 15. On printing the class label names for them, we can observe the following output:

```
In [600]: class_names = dataset.target_names
     ...: print class_names[0], '->', class_names[15]
     ...: print class_names[18], '->', class_names[16]
     ...: print class_names[19], '->', class_names[15]
alt.atheism -> soc.religion.christian
talk.politics.misc -> talk.politics.guns
talk.religion.misc -> soc.religion.christian
```

From the preceding output we can see that the misclassified categories are not vastly different from the actual correct category. Christian, religion, and atheism are based on some concepts related to the existence of God and religion and possibly have similar features. Talks about miscellaneous issues and guns related to politics also must be having similar features. We can further analyze and look at the misclassified documents in detail using the following snippet (due to space constraints I only include the first few misclassified documents in each case):

```
In [621]: import re
     ...: num = 0
     ...: for document, label, predicted_label in zip(test_corpus, test_
labels, svm_tfidf_predictions):
     ...:     if label == 0 and predicted_label == 15:
     ...:         print 'Actual Label:', class_names[label]
     ...:         print 'Predicted Label:', class_names[predicted_label]
     ...:         print 'Document:-'
     ...:         print re.sub('\n', ' ', document)
     ...:         print
     ...:         num += 1
     ...:         if num == 4:
     ...:             break
     ...:
     ...:
Actual Label: alt.atheism
Predicted Label: soc.religion.christian
Document:-
I would like a list of Bible contadictions from those of you who dispite
being free from Christianity are well versed in the Bible.

Actual Label: alt.atheism
Predicted Label: soc.religion.christian
Document:-
  They spent quite a bit of time on the wording of the Constitution.  They
picked words whose meanings implied the intent.  We have already looked in
the dictionary to define the word.  Isn't this sufficient?    But we were
discussing it in relation to the death penalty.  And, the Constitution need
not define each of the words within.  Anyone who doesn't know what cruel is
can look in the dictionary (and we did).

Actual Label: alt.atheism
Predicted Label: soc.religion.christian
Document:-
Our Lord and Savior David Keresh has risen!      He has been seen
alive!          Spread the word!      ----------------------------
-----------------------------------------------------------------

Actual Label: alt.atheism
Predicted Label: soc.religion.christian
Document:-
  "This is your god" (from John Carpenter's "They Live," natch)

In [623]: num = 0
```

```
...: for document, label, predicted_label in zip(test_corpus, test_
labels, svm_tfidf_predictions):
...:     if label == 18 and predicted_label == 16:
...:         print 'Actual Label:', class_names[label]
...:         print 'Predicted Label:', class_names[predicted_label]
...:         print 'Document:-'
...:         print re.sub('\n', ' ', document)
...:         print
...:         num += 1
...:         if num == 4:
...:             break
...:
...:
```

Actual Label: talk.politics.misc
Predicted Label: talk.politics.guns
Document:-
After the initial gun battle was over, they had 50 days to come out
peacefully. They had their high priced lawyer, and judging by the posts here
they had some public support. Can anyone come up with a rational explanation
why the didn't come out (even after they negotiated coming out after the
radio sermon) that doesn't include the Davidians wanting to commit suicide/
murder/general mayhem?

Actual Label: talk.politics.misc
Predicted Label: talk.politics.guns
Document:-
Yesterday, the FBI was saying that at least three of the bodies had gunshot
wounds, indicating that they were shot trying to escape the fire. Today's
paper quotes the medical examiner as saying that there is no evidence of
gunshot wounds in any of the recovered bodies. At the beginning of this
siege, it was reported that while Koresh had a class III (machine gun)
license, today's paper quotes the government as saying, no, they didn't have
a license. Today's paper reports that a number of the bodies were found
with shoulder weapons next to them, as if they had been using them while
dying -- which doesn't sound like the sort of action I would expect from a
suicide. Our government lies, as it tries to cover over its incompetence
and negligence. Why should I believe the FBI's claims about anything else,
when we can see that they are LYING? This system of government is beyond
reform.

Actual Label: talk.politics.misc
Predicted Label: talk.politics.guns
Document:-
 Well, for one thing most, if not all the Dividians (depending on whether
they could show they acted in self-defense and there were no illegal
weapons), could have gone on with their life as they were living it. No one
was forcing them to give up their religion or even their legal weapons. The
Dividians had survived a change in leadership before so even if Koresch

himself would have been convicted and sent to jail, they still could have carried on.   I don't think the Dividians were insane, but I don't see a reason for mass suicide (if the fire was intentional set by some of the Dividians.) We also don't know that, if the fire was intentionally set from inside, was it a generally know plan or was this something only an inner circle knew about, or was it something two or three felt they had to do with or without Koresch's knowledge/blessing, etc.? I don't know much about Masada. Were some people throwing others over? Did mothers jump over with their babies in their arms?

```
Actual Label: talk.politics.misc
Predicted Label: talk.politics.guns
Document:-
rja@mahogany126.cray.com (Russ Anderson) writes...      The fact is that
Koresh and his followers involved themselves   in a gun battle to control
the Mt Carmel complex. That is not    in dispute. From what I remember of the
trial, the authories    couldn't reasonably establish who fired first, the
big reason    behind the aquittal. Mitchell S Todd
```

Thus you can see how to analyze and look at documents that have been misclassified and then maybe go back and tune our feature extraction methods by removing certain words or weighing words differently to reduce or give prominence.

This brings us to the end of our discussion and implementation of our text classification system. Feel free to implement more models using other innovative feature-extraction techniques or supervised learning algorithms and compare their performance.

Applications and Uses

Text classification and categorization is used in several real-world scenarios and applications, including the following:

- News articles categorization

- Spam filtering

- Music or movie genre categorization

- Sentiment analysis

- Language detection

The possibilities with text data are indeed endless, and with a little effort you can apply classification to solve various problems and automate otherwise time-consuming operations and scenarios.

Summary

Text classification is indeed a powerful tool, and we have covered almost all aspects related to it in this chapter. We started off our journey with look at the definition and scope of text classification. Next, we defined automated text classification as a supervised learning problem and looked at the various types of text classification. We also briefly covered some ML concepts related to the various types of algorithms. A typical text classification system blueprint was also defined to describe the various modules and steps involved when building an end-to-end text classifier. Each module in the blueprint was then expanded upon. Normalization was touched upon in detail in Chapter 3, and we built a normalization module here specially for text classification. Various feature-extraction techniques were explored in detail, including Bag of Words, TF-IDF, and advanced word vectorization techniques.

You should now be clear about not only the mathematical representations and concepts but also ways to implement them using our code samples. Various supervised learning methods were discussed with focus on multinomial naïve Bayes and support vector machines, which work well with text data, and we looked at ways to evaluate classification model performance and even implemented those metrics. Finally, we put everything we learned together into building a robust 20-class text classification system on real data, evaluated various models, and analyzed model performance in detail. We wrapped up our discussion by looking at some areas where text classification is used frequently.

We have just scratched the surface of text analytics here with classification. We will be looking at more ways to analyze and derive insights from textual data in future chapters.

CHAPTER 5

▦ ▦ ▦

Text Summarization

We have come a long way on our journey through the world of text analytics and natural language processing (NLP). You have seen how to process and annotate textual data to use it for various applications. We have also ventured into the world of machine learning (ML) and built our own multi-class text classification system by leveraging various feature-extraction techniques and supervised machine learning algorithms.

In this chapter, we will tackle a slightly different problem in the world of text analytics. The world is rapidly evolving with regard to technology, commerce, business, and media. Gone are the days when we would wait for newspapers to come to our home and be updated about the various events around the world. We now have the Internet and various forms of social media that we consume to stay updated about daily events and stay connected with the world as well as our friends and family. With short messages and statuses, social media websites like Facebook and Twitter have opened up a completely different dimension to sharing and consuming information. We as humans tend to have short attention spans, and this leads us to get bored when consuming or reading large text documents and articles. This brings us to *text summarization*, an extremely important concept in text analytics that is used by businesses and analytical firms to shorten and summarize huge documents of text such that they still retain their key essence or theme and present this summarized information to consumers and clients. This is analogous to an *elevator pitch*, where an executive summary can describe a process, product, service, or business while retaining the core important themes and values in the time it takes to ride an elevator.

Say you have a whole corpus of text documents that ranges from sentences to paragraphs, and you are tasked with trying to derive meaningful insights from it. At first glance, this may seem difficult because you do not even know what to do with these documents, let alone use some analytical or ML techniques on the data. A good way to start would be to use some unsupervised learning approaches specifically aimed at text summarization and information extraction. Here are a few of the things you could do with text documents:

- Extract the key influential phrases from the documents

- Extract various diverse concepts or topics present in the documents

- Summarize the documents to provide a gist that retains the important parts of the whole corpus

© Dipanjan Sarkar 2016

D. Sarkar, *Text Analytics with Python*, DOI 10.1007/978-1-4842-2388-8_5

This chapter will cover concepts, techniques, and practical implementations of ways to perform all three operations. We can describe our problem formally now, which we will try to solve in this chapter, along with some of the concepts related to it. Given a set of documents, text summarization aims to reduce a document or set of documents in a corpus to a summary of user-specified length such that it retains the key important concepts and themes from the corpus. We will also discuss other ways to summarize documents and extract information from them, including topic models and key phrase extraction.

In this chapter, we will talk about text summarization as well as information extraction from text documents, which captures and summarizes the main themes or concepts of the document corpus. We will start with a detailed discussion of the various types of summarization and information extraction techniques and discuss some concepts essential for understanding the practical implementations later. The chapter will also briefly cover some background dependencies related to text processing and feature extraction before moving on to each technique. We will discuss the three major concepts and techniques of key phrase extraction, topic models, and automated text summarization.

Text Summarization and Information Extraction

Text summarization and information extraction deal with trying to extract key important concepts and themes from a huge corpus of text, essentially reducing it in the process. Before we dive deeper into the concepts and techniques, we should first understand the need for text summarization. The concept of information overload is one of the prime reasons behind the demand for text summarization. Since print and verbal media came into prominence, there has been an abundance of books, articles, audio, and video. This began all the way back in the 3rd or 4th century B.C., when people referred to a huge quantity of books, as there seemed to be no end to the production of books, and this overload of information was often met with disapproval. The Renaissance gave us the invention of the printing press by Gutenberg around 1440 A.D., which led to the mass production of books, manuscripts, articles, and pamphlets. This greatly increased information overload, with scholars complaining about an excess of information, which was becoming extremely difficult to consume, process, and manage.

In the 20th century, advances in computers and technology ushered in the digital age, culminating in the Internet. The Internet opened up a whole window of possibilities into producing and consuming information with social media, news web sites, email, and instant messaging capabilities. This in turn has led to an explosive increase in the amount of information and to unwanted information in the form of spam, unwanted statuses, and tweets—and even to bots posting more unwanted content across the Web.

Information overload, then, is the presence of excess data or information, which consumers find difficult to process in making well-informed decisions. The overload occurs when the amount of information as input to the system starts exceeding the processing capability of the system. We as humans have limited cognitive processing capabilities and are also wired in such a way that we cannot spend a long time reading a single piece of information or data because the mind tends to wander every now and then. Thus when we get loaded with information, it leads to a reduction in making qualitative decisions.

By now you can probably guess where I am going with this concept and why we need summarization and information extraction. Businesses thrive on making key and well-informed decisions and usually they have a huge amount of data and information. Getting insights from it is no piece of cake, and automating it is tough because what to do with all that data is often unclear. Executives rarely have time to listen to long talks or go through pages and pages of important information. The idea of summarization and information extraction is to get an idea of the key important topics and themes of huge documents of information and summarize them into a few lines that can be read, understood, and interpreted easily, thus easing the process of making well-informed decisions in shorter time frames. We need efficient and scalable processes and techniques that can perform this on text data, and the most popular techniques are *keyphrase extraction, topic modeling*, and *automated document summarization*. The first two techniques are more into extracting key information in the form of concepts, topics, and themes from documents, thus reducing them, and the last technique is all about summarizing large text documents into a few lines that give the key essence or information which the document is trying to convey. We will cover each technique in detail in future sections along with practical examples but right now, we will briefly talk about what each technique entails and their scope:

- *Keyphrase extraction* is perhaps the simplest out of the three techniques. It involves extracting keywords or phrases from a text document or corpus that capture its main concepts or themes. This can be said to be a simplistic form of topic modeling. You might have seen keywords or phrases described in a research paper or even some product in an online store that describes the entity in a few words or phrases, capturing its main idea or concept.

- *Topic modeling* usually involves using statistical and mathematical modeling techniques to extract main topics, themes, or concepts from a corpus of documents. Note here the emphasis on *corpus* of documents because the more diverse set of documents you have, the more topics or concepts you can generate—unlike with a single document where you will not get too many topics or concepts if it talks about a singular concept. Topic models are also often known as *probabilistic statistical models*, which use specific statistical techniques including singular valued decomposition and latent dirichlet allocation to discover connected latent semantic structures in text data that yield topics and concepts. They are used extensively in text analytics and even bioinformatics.

- *Automated document summarization* is the process of using a computer program or algorithm based on statistical and ML techniques to summarize a document or corpus of documents such that we obtain a short summary that captures all the essential concepts and themes of the original document or corpus. A wide variety of techniques for building automated document summarizers exist, including various extraction- and abstraction-based techniques. The key concept behind all these algorithms is to find a representative subset of the original dataset such that the core essence of the dataset from the semantic and conceptual standpoints is contained in this subset. Document summarization usually involves trying to extract and construct an executive summary from a single document. But the same algorithms can be extended to multiple documents, though usually the idea is not to combine several diverse documents together, which would defeat the purpose of the algorithm. The same concept is not only applied in text analytics but also to image and video summarization.

We will discuss some important mathematical and ML concepts, text normalization, and feature extraction processes in the following sections, before moving to cover each technique in further detail.

Important Concepts

Several important mathematical and ML-based concepts will be useful later on because we will be basing several of our implementations on them. Some will be familiar to you, but I will briefly touch on them again for the sake of completeness so that you can refresh your memory. We will also cover some concepts from natural language processing in this section.

Documents

A *document* is usually an entity containing a whole body of text data with optional headers and other metadata information. A corpus usually consists of a collection of documents. These documents can be simple sentences or complete paragraphs of textual information. *Tokenized corpus* refers to a corpus where each document is tokenized or broken down into *tokens*, which are usually words.

Text Normalization

Text normalization is the process of cleaning, normalizing, and standardizing textual data with techniques like removing special symbols and characters, removing extraneous HTML tags, removing stopwords, correcting spellings, stemming, and lemmatization.

Feature Extraction

Feature extraction is a process whereby we extract meaningful features or attributes from raw textual data for feeding it into a statistical or ML algorithm. This process is also known as *vectorization* because usually the end transformation of this process is numerical vectors from raw text tokens. The reason is that conventional algorithms work on numerical vectors and cannot work directly on raw text data. There are various feature-extraction methods including Bag of Words–based binary features that tell us whether a word or group of words exist or not in the document, Bag of Words–based frequency features that tell us the frequency of occurrence of a word or group of words in a document, and term frequency and inverse document frequency or TF-IDF–weighted features that take into account the term frequency and inverse document frequency when weighing each term. Refer to Chapter 4 for more on feature extraction.

Feature Matrix

A *feature matrix* usually refers to a mapping from a collection of documents to features where each row indicates a document and each column indicates a particular feature, usually a word or a set of words. We will represent collections of documents or sentences through feature matrices after feature extraction and we will often apply statistical and ML techniques on these matrices later on in our practical examples.

Singular Value Decomposition

Singular Value Decomposition (SVD) is a technique from linear algebra that is used quite frequently in summarization algorithms. SVD is the process of factorization of a matrix that is real or complex. Formally we can define SVD as follows. Consider a matrix M that has dimensions of $m \times n$ where m denotes the number of rows and n denotes the number of columns. Mathematically the matrix M can be represented using SVD as a factorization such that

$$M_{m \times n} = U_{m \times m} S_{m \times n} V^T_{n \times n}$$

where we have the following decompositions:

- U is an $m \times m$ unitary matrix such that $U^T U = I_{m \times m}$ where I is the identity matrix. The columns of U indicate left singular vectors.

- S is a diagonal $m \times n$ matrix with positive real numbers on the diagonal of the matrix. This is also often also represented as a vector of m values that indicate the singular values.

- V^T is a $n \times n$ unitary matrix such that $V^T V = I_{n \times n}$ where I is the identity matrix. The rows of V indicate right singular vectors.

This tells us that U and V are *orthogonal*. The singular values of S are particularly important in summarization algorithms. We will be using SVD particularly for low rank matrix approximation where we approximate the original matrix M with a matrix $\hat{M}$ such that this new matrix is a truncated version of the original matrix M with a rank k and can be represented by SVD as $\hat{M} = U\hat{S}V^T$ where $\hat{S}$ is a truncated version of the original S matrix, which now consists of only the top k largest singular values, and the other singular values are represented by zero. We will be using a nice implementation from `scipy` to extract the top k singular values and also return the corresponding U, S and V matrices. The following code snippet we will be using is in the `utils.py` file:

```python
from scipy.sparse.linalg import svds

def low_rank_svd(matrix, singular_count=2):

    u, s, vt = svds(matrix, k=singular_count)
    return u, s, vt
```

We will be using this implementation in topic modeling as well as document summarization in future sections. Figure 5-1 gives a nice depiction of the preceding process, which yields k singular vectors from the original SVD decomposition, and shows how we can get the low rank matrix approximation from the same.

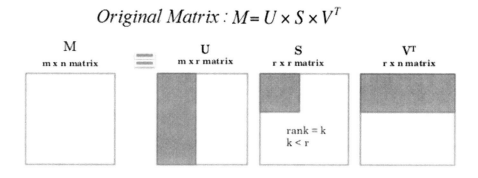

Figure 5-1. *Singular Value Decomposition with low rank matrix approximation*

You can clearly see that k singular values are retained in the low rank matrix approximation and how the original matrix M is decomposed into U, S, and V using SVD. In our computations, usually the rows of the matrix M will denote terms, and the columns will denote documents. This matrix, also known as the *term-document matrix*, is usually obtained after feature extraction by converting a document-term matrix into its transpose before applying SVD. I will try to keep the math to a minimum in the rest of the chapter unless it is absolutely essential to understand how the algorithms work. The following sections will briefly touch upon text normalization and feature extraction to highlight the techniques and methods that we will be using in this chapter.

Text Normalization

Chapter 3 covered text normalization in detail, and we built our own normalization module in Chapter 4. We will be reusing the same module in this chapter but will be adding a couple of enhancements specifically for the benefit of some of our algorithms. You can find all the text normalization–related code in the normalization.py file. The main steps performed in text normalization include the following:

1. Sentence extraction

2. Unescape HTML escape sequences

3. Expand contractions

4. Lemmatize text

5. Remove special characters

6. Remove stopwords

Steps 3–6 remain the same from Chapter 4, except step 5 where we substitute each special character with a blank space depicted by the code pattern.sub(' ', token) instead of the empty string in Chapter 4.

Step 1 is a new function where we take in a text document, remove its newlines, parse the text, converting it into ASCII format, and break it down into its sentence constituents. The function is depicted in the following snippet:

```
def parse_document(document):
    document = re.sub('\n', ' ', document)
    if isinstance(document, str):
        document = document
    elif isinstance(document, unicode):
        return unicodedata.normalize('NFKD', document).encode('ascii',
        'ignore')
    else:
        raise ValueError('Document is not string or unicode!')
    document = document.strip()
    sentences = nltk.sent_tokenize(document)
    sentences = [sentence.strip() for sentence in sentences]
    return sentences
```

Step 2 deals with unescaping special HTML characters that are escaped or encoded. The full list at www.theukwebdesigncompany.com/articles/entity-escape-characters. php basically shows how some special symbols or even regular characters are escaped into a different code, for example, & is escaped as &. So we use the following function to unescape them and bring them back to their original unescaped form so we can normalize them properly in the subsequent stages:

```
from HTMLParser import HTMLParser

html_parser = HTMLParser()
def unescape_html(parser, text):
    return parser.unescape(text)
```

We also parameterize our lemmatization operation in our final normalization function so as to make it optional because in some scenarios it works perfectly while in other scenarios we may not want to use lemmatization. The complete normalization function is depicted as follows:

```
def normalize_corpus(corpus, lemmatize=True, tokenize=False):

    normalized_corpus = []
    for text in corpus:
        text = html_parser.unescape(text)
        text = expand_contractions(text, CONTRACTION_MAP)
        if lemmatize:
            text = lemmatize_text(text)
        else:
            text = text.lower()
        text = remove_special_characters(text)
        text = remove_stopwords(text)
        if tokenize:
            text = tokenize_text(text)
            normalized_corpus.append(text)
        else:
            normalized_corpus.append(text)

    return normalized_corpus
```

We will be using this function for most of our normalization needs. Refer to the normalization.py file for all the detailed helper functions we use for normalizing text which we also discussed in Chapter 4.

Feature Extraction

We will use a generic function here to perform various types of feature extraction from text data. The types of features which we will be working with are as follows:

- Binary term occurrence–based features

- Frequency bag of words–based features

- TF-IDF–weighted features

We will use the following function in most of our practical examples in future sections for feature extraction from text documents. You can also find this function in the utils.py module in the code files associated with this chapter:

```
from sklearn.feature_extraction.text import CountVectorizer, TfidfVectorizer

def build_feature_matrix(documents, feature_type='frequency'):

    feature_type = feature_type.lower().strip()

    if feature_type == 'binary':
        vectorizer = CountVectorizer(binary=True, min_df=1,
                                     ngram_range=(1, 1))
    elif feature_type == 'frequency':
        vectorizer = CountVectorizer(binary=False, min_df=1,
                                     ngram_range=(1, 1))
    elif feature_type == 'tfidf':
        vectorizer = TfidfVectorizer(min_df=1,
                                     ngram_range=(1, 1))
    else:
        raise Exception("Wrong feature type entered. Possible values:
        'binary', 'frequency', 'tfidf'")

    feature_matrix = vectorizer.fit_transform(documents).astype(float)

    return vectorizer, feature_matrix
```

Now that we have covered the necessary background concepts and dependencies needed for this chapter, we will be deep diving into each text summarization and information extraction technique in detail.

Keyphrase Extraction

One of the simplest yet most powerful techniques of extracting important information from unstructured text documents is keyphrase extraction. *Keyphrase extraction*, also known as *terminology extraction*, is defined as the process or technique of extracting key important and relevant terms or phrases from a body of unstructured text such that the core topics or themes of the text document(s) are captured in these key phrases. This technique falls under the broad umbrella of information retrieval and extraction. Keyphrase extraction finds its uses in many areas, including the following:

- Semantic web

- Query-based search engines and crawlers

- Recommendation systems

- Tagging systems

- Document similarity

- Translation

Keyphrase extraction is often the starting point for carrying out more complex tasks in text analytics or NLP, and the output from this can itself act as features for more complex systems. There are various approaches for keyphrase extraction. We will be covering the following two techniques:

- Collocations

- Weighted tag–based phrase extraction

An important thing to remember here is that we will be extracting phrases that are usually collections of words, though sometimes that can include a single word. If you are extracting keywords, that is also known as *keyword extraction*, and it is a subset of keyphrase extraction.

Collocations

The term *collocation* is actually a concept borrowed from analyzing corpora and linguistics. A collocation is a sequence or group of words that tend to occur frequently such that this frequency tends to be more than what could be termed as a random or chance occurrence. Various types of collocations can be formed based on the parts of speech of the various terms like nouns, verbs, and so on. There are various ways to extract collocations, and one of the best is to use an n-gram grouping or segmentation approach where we construct n-grams out of a corpus, count the frequency of each n-gram, and rank them based on their frequency of occurrence to get the most frequent n-gram collocations.

The idea is to have a corpus of documents, which could be paragraphs or sentences, tokenize them to form sentences, flatten the list of sentences to form one large sentence or string, over which we slide a window of size *n* based on the n-gram range, and compute n-grams across the string. Once computed, we count each n-gram based on its frequency of occurrence and then rank them based on their frequency. This yields the most frequent collocations on the basis of frequency.

We will implement this from scratch initially so that you can understand the algorithm better and then we will use some of nltk's built-in capabilities to show the same. We will start by loading some necessary dependencies and a corpus on which we will be computing collocations. We will use the nltk Gutenberg corpus's book, Lewis Carroll's *Alice in Wonderland* as our corpus. We also normalize the corpus to standardize the text content using our normalization module specified earlier:

```
from nltk.corpus import gutenberg
from normalization import normalize_corpus
import nltk
from operator import itemgetter

# load corpus
alice = gutenberg.sents(fileids='carroll-alice.txt')
alice = [' '.join(ts) for ts in alice]
norm_alice = filter(None, normalize_corpus(alice, lemmatize=False))
```

```
# print first line
In [772]: print norm_alice[0]
alice adventures wonderland lewis carroll 1865
```

Now that we have loaded our corpus, we will define a function to flatten the corpus into one big string of text. The following function will help us do that for a corpus of documents:

```
def flatten_corpus(corpus):
    return ' '.join([document.strip()
                        for document in corpus])
```

We will define a function to compute n-grams based on some input list of tokens and the parameter *n*, which determines the degree of the n-gram like a unigram, bigram, and so on. The following code snippet computes n-grams for an input sequence:

```
def compute_ngrams(sequence, n):
    return zip(*[sequence[index:]
                    for index in range(n)])
```

This function basically takes in a sequence of tokens and computes a list of lists having sequences where each list contains all items from the previous list except the first item removed from the previous list. It constructs *n* such lists and then zips them all together to give us the necessary n-grams. We can see the function in action on a sample sequence in the following snippet:

```
In [802]: compute_ngrams([1,2,3,4], 2)
Out[802]: [(1, 2), (2, 3), (3, 4)]

In [803]: compute_ngrams([1,2,3,4], 3)
Out[803]: [(1, 2, 3), (2, 3, 4)]
```

The preceding output shows bigrams and trigrams for an input sequence. We will now utilize this function and build upon it to generate the top n-grams based on their frequency of occurrence. The following code snippet helps us in getting the top n-grams:

```
def get_top_ngrams(corpus, ngram_val=1, limit=5):

    corpus = flatten_corpus(corpus)
    tokens = nltk.word_tokenize(corpus)

    ngrams = compute_ngrams(tokens, ngram_val)
    ngrams_freq_dist = nltk.FreqDist(ngrams)
    sorted_ngrams_fd = sorted(ngrams_freq_dist.items(),
                                key=itemgetter(1), reverse=True)
    sorted_ngrams = sorted_ngrams_fd[0:limit]
    sorted_ngrams = [(' '.join(text), freq)
                        for text, freq in sorted_ngrams]

    return sorted_ngrams
```

We make use of `nltk`'s `FreqDist` class to create a counter of all the n-grams based on their frequency and then we sort them based on their frequency and return the top n-grams based on the specified user limit. We will now compute the top bigrams and trigrams on our corpus using the following code snippet:

```
# top 10 bigrams
In [805]: get_top_ngrams(corpus=norm_alice, ngram_val=2,
   ...:                     limit=10)
Out[805]:
[(u'said alice', 123),
 (u'mock turtle', 56),
 (u'march hare', 31),
 (u'said king', 29),
 (u'thought alice', 26),
 (u'said hatter', 22),
 (u'white rabbit', 22),
 (u'said mock', 20),
 (u'said gryphon', 18),
 (u'said caterpillar', 18)]

# top 10 trigrams
In [806]: get_top_ngrams(corpus=norm_alice, ngram_val=3,
   ...:                     limit=10)
Out[806]:
[(u'said mock turtle', 20),
 (u'said march hare', 10),
 (u'poor little thing', 6),
 (u'white kid gloves', 5),
 (u'little golden key', 5),
 (u'march hare said', 5),
 (u'certainly said alice', 5),
 (u'mock turtle said', 5),
 (u'mouse mouse mouse', 4),
 (u'join dance join', 4)]
```

The preceding output shows sequences of two and three words generated by n-grams along with the number of times they occur throughout the corpus. We can see most of the collocations point to people who are speaking something as *"said <person>".* We also see the people who are popular characters in *"Alice in Wonderland"* like the *mock turtle*, the *king*, the *rabbit*, the *hatter*, and of course *Alice* herself being depicted in the aforementioned collocations.

We will now look at `nltk`'s collocation finders, which enable us to find collocations using various measures like raw frequencies, pointwise mutual information, and so on. Just to explain briefly, *pointwise mutual information* can be computed for two events or terms as the logarithm of the ratio of the probability of them occurring together by the product of their individual probabilities assuming that they are independent of each other. Mathematically we can represent it like this:

$$pmi(x,y) = log \frac{p(x,y)}{p(x)p(y)}$$

This measure is symmetric. The following code snippet shows how to compute these collocations using these measures:

```
# bigrams
from nltk.collocations import BigramCollocationFinder
from nltk.collocations import BigramAssocMeasures

finder = BigramCollocationFinder.from_documents([item.split()
                                                for item
                                                in norm_alice])
bigram_measures = BigramAssocMeasures()
# raw frequencies
In [813]: finder.nbest(bigram_measures.raw_freq, 10)
Out[813]:
[(u'said', u'alice'),
 (u'mock', u'turtle'),
 (u'march', u'hare'),
 (u'said', u'king'),
 (u'thought', u'alice'),
 (u'said', u'hatter'),
 (u'white', u'rabbit'),
 (u'said', u'mock'),
 (u'said', u'caterpillar'),
 (u'said', u'gryphon')]
# pointwise mutual information
In [814]: finder.nbest(bigram_measures.pmi, 10)
Out[814]:
[(u'abide', u'figures'),
 (u'acceptance', u'elegant'),
 (u'accounting', u'tastes'),
 (u'accustomed', u'usurpation'),
 (u'act', u'crawling'),
 (u'adjourn', u'immediate'),
 (u'adoption', u'energetic'),
 (u'affair', u'trusts'),
 (u'agony', u'terror'),
 (u'alarmed', u'proposal')]

# trigrams
from nltk.collocations import TrigramCollocationFinder
from nltk.collocations import TrigramAssocMeasures

finder = TrigramCollocationFinder.from_documents([item.split()
                                                 for item
                                                 in norm_alice])
```

```
trigram_measures = TrigramAssocMeasures()
# raw frequencies
In [817]: finder.nbest(trigram_measures.raw_freq, 10)
Out[817]:
[(u'said', u'mock', u'turtle'),
 (u'said', u'march', u'hare'),
 (u'poor', u'little', u'thing'),
 (u'little', u'golden', u'key'),
 (u'march', u'hare', u'said'),
 (u'mock', u'turtle', u'said'),
 (u'white', u'kid', u'gloves'),
 (u'beau', u'ootiful', u'soo'),
 (u'certainly', u'said', u'alice'),
 (u'might', u'well', u'say')]
# pointwise mutual information
In [818]: finder.nbest(trigram_measures.pmi, 10)
Out[818]:
[(u'accustomed', u'usurpation', u'conquest'),
 (u'adjourn', u'immediate', u'adoption'),
 (u'adoption', u'energetic', u'remedies'),
 (u'ancient', u'modern', u'seaography'),
 (u'apple', u'roast', u'turkey'),
 (u'arithmetic', u'ambition', u'distraction'),
 (u'brother', u'latin', u'grammar'),
 (u'canvas', u'bag', u'tied'),
 (u'cherry', u'tart', u'custard'),
 (u'circle', u'exact', u'shape')]
```

Now you know how to compute collocations for a corpus using an n-gram generative approach. We will now look at a better way of generating key phrases based on parts of speech tagging and term weighing in the next section.

Weighted Tag–Based Phrase Extraction

Here's a slightly different approach to extracting keyphrases. This method borrows concepts from a couple of papers, namely K. Barker and N. Cornachhia's "Using Noun Phrase Heads to Extract Document Keyphrases" and "KEA: Practical Automatic Keyphrase Extraction" by Ian Witten et al., which you can refer to for further details on their experimentations and approaches. We follow a two-step process in our algorithm here:

1. Extract all noun phrases chunks using shallow parsing

2. Compute TF-IDF weights for each chunk and return the top weighted phrases

For the first step, we will use a simple pattern based on parts of speech (POS) tags to extract noun phrase chunks. You will be familiar with this from Chapter 3 where we explored chunking and shallow parsing. Before discussing our algorithm, let us define the corpus on which we will be testing our implementation. We use a sample description of elephants taken from Wikipedia as shown in the following code:

```
toy_text = """
Elephants are large mammals of the family Elephantidae
and the order Proboscidea. Two species are traditionally recognised,
the African elephant and the Asian elephant. Elephants are scattered
throughout sub-Saharan Africa, South Asia, and Southeast Asia. Male
African elephants are the largest extant terrestrial animals. All
elephants have a long trunk used for many purposes,
particularly breathing, lifting water and grasping objects. Their
incisors grow into tusks, which can serve as weapons and as tools
for moving objects and digging. Elephants' large ear flaps help
to control their body temperature. Their pillar-like legs can
carry their great weight. African elephants have larger ears
and concave backs while Asian elephants have smaller ears
and convex or level backs.
"""
```

Now that we have our corpus ready, we will use the pattern, " NP: {<DT>? <JJ>* <NN.*>+}" for extracting all possible noun phrases from our corpus of documents/sentences. You can always experiment with more sophisticated patterns later, incorporating verb, adjective, or even adverb phrases. However, I will keep things simple and concise here to focus on the core logic. Once we have our pattern, we will define a function to parse and extract these phrases using the following snippet (we also load the necessary dependencies at this point):

```
from normalization import parse_document
import itertools
import nltk
from normalization import stopword_list
from gensim import corpora, models

def get_chunks(sentences, grammar = r'NP: {<DT>? <JJ>* <NN.*>+}'):
    # build chunker based on grammar pattern
    all_chunks = []
    chunker = nltk.chunk.regexp.RegexpParser(grammar)

    for sentence in sentences:
        # POS tag sentences
        tagged_sents = nltk.pos_tag_sents(
                            [nltk.word_tokenize(sentence)])
```

```
    # extract chunks
    chunks = [chunker.parse(tagged_sent)
                for tagged_sent in tagged_sents]
    # get word, pos tag, chunk tag triples
    wtc_sents = [nltk.chunk.tree2conlltags(chunk)
                    for chunk in chunks]

    flattened_chunks = list(
                        itertools.chain.from_iterable(
                            wtc_sent for wtc_sent in wtc_sents)
                        )
    # get valid chunks based on tags
    valid_chunks_tagged = [(status, [wtc for wtc in chunk])
                    for status, chunk
                    in itertools.groupby(flattened_chunks,
                                    lambda (word,pos,chunk): chunk
                                    != 'O')]
    # append words in each chunk to make phrases
    valid_chunks = [' '.join(word.lower()
                            for word, tag, chunk
                            in wtc_group
                                if word.lower()
                                    not in stopword_list)
                            for status, wtc_group
                            in valid_chunks_tagged
                                if status]
    # append all valid chunked phrases
    all_chunks.append(valid_chunks)

return all_chunks
```

The comments in the preceding function are self-explanatory. Basically, we have a defined grammar pattern for chunking or extracting noun phrases. We define a chunker over the same pattern, and for each sentence in the document, we first annotate it with its POS tags (hence, we should not normalize the text) and then build a shallow parse tree with noun phrases as the chunks and all other POS tag–based words as chinks, which are not parts of any chunks. Once this is done, we use the tree2conlltags function to generate (w,t,c) triples, which are words, POS tags, and the IOB-formatted chunk tags discussed in Chapter 3. We remove all tags with chunk tag of 'O' since they are basically words or terms that do not belong to any chunk (if you remember our discussion of shallow parsing in Chapter 3). Finally, from these valid chunks, we combine the chunked terms to generate phrases from each chunk group. We can see this function in action on our corpus in the following snippet:

```
sentences = parse_document(toy_text)
valid_chunks = get_chunks(sentences)
# print all valid chunks
In [834]: print valid_chunks
 [['elephants', 'large mammals', 'family elephantidae', 'order
proboscidea'], ['species', 'african elephant', 'asian elephant'],
```

```
['elephants', 'sub-saharan africa', 'south asia', 'southeast asia'],
['male african elephants', 'extant terrestrial animals'], ['elephants',
'long trunk', 'many purposes', 'breathing', 'water', 'grasping objects'],
['incisors', 'tusks', 'weapons', 'tools', 'objects', 'digging'],
['elephants', 'large ear flaps', 'body temperature'], ['pillar-like legs',
'great weight'], ['african elephants', 'ears', 'backs', 'asian elephants',
'ears', 'convex', 'level backs']]
```

The preceding output shows all the valid keyphrases per sentence of our document. You can already see, since we targeted noun phrases, all phrases talk about noun based entities. We will now build on top of our get_chunks() function by implementing the necessary logic for step 2, where we will build a TF-IDF–based model on our keyphrases using gensim and then compute TF-IDF–based weights for each keyphrase based on its occurrence in the corpus. Finally, we will sort these keyphrases based on their TF-IDF weights and show the top *n* keyphrases where *n* is specified by the user:

```
def get_tfidf_weighted_keyphrases(sentences,
                                  grammar=r'NP: {<DT>? <JJ>* <NN.*>+}',
                                  top_n=10):
    # get valid chunks
    valid_chunks = get_chunks(sentences, grammar=grammar)
    # build tf-idf based model
    dictionary = corpora.Dictionary(valid_chunks)
    corpus = [dictionary.doc2bow(chunk) for chunk in valid_chunks]
    tfidf = models.TfidfModel(corpus)
    corpus_tfidf = tfidf[corpus]
    # get phrases and their tf-idf weights
    weighted_phrases = {dictionary.get(id): round(value,3)
                        for doc in corpus_tfidf
                        for id, value in doc}
    weighted_phrases = sorted(weighted_phrases.items(),
                              key=itemgetter(1), reverse=True)
    # return top weighted phrases
    return weighted_phrases[:top_n]
```

We can now test this function on our toy corpus from before by using the following code snippet to generate the top ten keyphrases:

```
# top 10 tf-idf weighted keyphrases for toy_text
In [836]: get_tfidf_weighted_keyphrases(sentences, top_n=10)
Out[836]:
[(u'pillar-like legs', 0.707),
 (u'male african elephants', 0.707),
 (u'great weight', 0.707),
 (u'extant terrestrial animals', 0.707),
 (u'large ear flaps', 0.684),
 (u'body temperature', 0.684),
 (u'ears', 0.667),
 (u'species', 0.577),
```

```
(u'african elephant', 0.577),
(u'asian elephant', 0.577)]
```

Interestingly we see various types of elephants being depicted in the keyphrases, like Asian and African elephants, and also typical attributes of elephants like "great weight", "large ear flaps", and "pillar like legs". Thus you can get an idea of how keyphrase extraction can extract key important concepts from text documents and summarize them. Try out these functions on other corpora to see interesting results!

Topic Modeling

We have seen how keyphrases can be extracted using a couple of techniques. Though these phrases point out key pivotal points from a document or corpus, it is simplistic and often does not portray the various themes or concepts in a corpus, particularly when we have different distinguishing themes or concepts in a corpus of documents. Topic models have been designed specifically for the purpose of extracting various distinguishing concepts or topics from a large corpus containing various types of documents, where each document talks about one or more concepts. These concepts can be anything from thoughts to opinions, facts, outlooks, statements, and so on. The main aim of topic modeling is to use mathematical and statistical techniques to discover hidden and latent semantic structures in a corpus.

Topic modeling involves extracting features from document terms and using mathematical structures and frameworks like matrix factorization and SVD to generate clusters or groups of terms that are distinguishable from each other, and these cluster of words form topics or concepts. These concepts can be used to interpret the main themes of a corpus and also make semantic connections among words that co-occur together frequently in various documents. There are various frameworks and algorithms to build topic models. We will cover the following three methods:

- Latent semantic indexing

- Latent Dirichlet allocation

- Non-negative matrix factorization

The first two methods are quite popular and have been around a long time. The last technique, non-negative matrix factorization, is a very recent technique that is extremely effective and gives excellent results. We will leverage gensim and scikit-learn for our practical implementations and also look at how to build our own topic model based on latent semantic indexing. This will give you an idea of how these techniques work and also how to convert mathematical frameworks into practical implementations. We will use the following toy corpus initially to test our topic models:

```
toy_corpus = ["The fox jumps over the dog",
"The fox is very clever and quick",
"The dog is slow and lazy",
"The cat is smarter than the fox and the dog",
"Python is an excellent programming language",
"Java and Ruby are other programming languages",
```

```
"Python and Java are very popular programming languages",
"Python programs are smaller than Java programs"]
```

You can see that we have eight documents in the preceding corpus: the first four talk about various animals, and the last four are about programming languages. Thus this shows that there are two distinct topics in the corpus. We generalized that using our brains, but the following sections will try to extract that same information using computational methods. Once we build some topic modeling frameworks, we will use the same to generate topics on real product reviews from Amazon.

Latent Semantic Indexing

Our first technique is latent semantic indexing (LSI), which has been around since the 1970s when it was first developed as a statistical technique to correlate and find out semantically linked terms from corpora. LSI is not just used for text summarization but also in information retrieval and search. LSI uses the very popular SVD technique discussed earlier in the "Important Concepts" section. The main principle behind LSI is that similar terms tend to be used in the same context and hence tend to co-occur more. The term *LSI* comes from the fact that this technique has the ability to uncover latent hidden terms which correlate semantically to form topics.

We will now try to implement an LSI by leveraging gensim and extract topics from the toy corpus. To start, we load the necessary dependencies and normalize the toy corpus using the following code snippet:

```
from gensim import corpora, models
from normalization import normalize_corpus
import numpy as np

norm_tokenized_corpus = normalize_corpus(toy_corpus, tokenize=True)
# view the normalized tokenized corpus
In [841]: norm_tokenized_corpus
Out[841]:
[[u'fox', u'jump', u'dog'],
 [u'fox', u'clever', u'quick'],
 [u'dog', u'slow', u'lazy'],
 [u'cat', u'smarter', u'fox', u'dog'],
 [u'python', u'excellent', u'programming', u'language'],
 [u'java', u'ruby', u'programming', u'language'],
 [u'python', u'java', u'popular', u'programming', u'language'],
 [u'python', u'program', u'small', u'java', u'program']]
```

We now build a dictionary or vocabulary, which gensim uses to map each unique term into a numeric value. Once built, we convert the preceding tokenized corpus into a numeric Bag of Words vector representation where each term and its frequency in a sentence is depicted by a tuple (term, frequency), as seen in the following snippet:

```
# build the dictionary
dictionary = corpora.Dictionary(norm_tokenized_corpus)
```

```
# view the dictionary mappings
In [846]: print dictionary.token2id
{u'program': 17, u'lazy': 5, u'clever': 4, u'java': 13, u'programming': 10,
u'language': 11, u'python': 9, u'smarter': 7, u'fox': 1, u'dog': 2, u'cat':
8, u'jump': 0, u'popular': 15, u'slow': 6, u'excellent': 12, u'quick': 3,
u'small': 16, u'ruby': 14}

# convert tokenized documents into bag of words vectors
corpus = [dictionary.doc2bow(text) for text in norm_tokenized_corpus]
# view the converted vectorized corpus
In [849]: corpus
Out[849]:
[[(0, 1), (1, 1), (2, 1)],
 [(1, 1), (3, 1), (4, 1)],
 [(2, 1), (5, 1), (6, 1)],
 [(1, 1), (2, 1), (7, 1), (8, 1)],
 [(9, 1), (10, 1), (11, 1), (12, 1)],
 [(10, 1), (11, 1), (13, 1), (14, 1)],
 [(9, 1), (10, 1), (11, 1), (13, 1), (15, 1)],
 [(9, 1), (13, 1), (16, 1), (17, 2)]]
```

We will now build a TF-IDF–weighted model over this corpus where each term in each document will contain its TF-IDF weight. This is analogous to feature extraction or vector space transformation where each document is represented by a TF-IDF vector of its terms, as we have done in the past. Once this is done, we build an LSI model on these features and take an input of the number of topics we want to generate. This number is based on intuition and trial and error, so feel free to play around with this parameter when you build topic models on corpora. We will set this parameter to 2, based on the number of topics we expect our toy corpus to contain:

```
# build tf-idf feature vectors
tfidf = models.TfidfModel(corpus)
corpus_tfidf = tfidf[corpus]

# fix the number of topics
total_topics = 2

# build the topic model
lsi = models.LsiModel(corpus_tfidf,
                      id2word=dictionary,
                      num_topics=total_topics)
```

Now that our topic modeling framework is built, we can see the generated topics in the following code snippet:

```
In [855]: for index, topic in lsi.print_topics(total_topics):
   ...:         print 'Topic #'+str(index+1)
   ...:         print topic
   ...:         print
```

```
Topic #1
-0.459*"language" + -0.459*"programming" + -0.344*"java" + -0.344*"python" +
-0.336*"popular" + -0.318*"excellent" + -0.318*"ruby" + -0.148*"program" +
-0.074*"small" + -0.000*"clever"

Topic #2
0.459*"dog" + 0.459*"fox" + 0.444*"jump" + 0.322*"smarter" + 0.322*"cat" +
0.208*"lazy" + 0.208*"slow" + 0.208*"clever" + 0.208*"quick" + -0.000*"ruby"
```

Let's take a moment to understand those results. At first, ignoring the weights,
you can see that the first topic contains terms related to programming languages and
the second topic contains terms related to animals, which is in line with the main two
concepts from our toy corpus mentioned earlier. If you now look at the weights, higher
weightage and same sign exists for the terms that contribute toward each of the topics.
The first topic has related terms with negative weights, and the second topic has related
terms with positive weights. The sign just indicates the direction of the topic, that is,
similar correlated terms in the topics will have the same sign or direction. The following
function helps display the topics in a better way with or without thresholds:

```
def print_topics_gensim(topic_model, total_topics=1,
                        weight_threshold=0.0001,
                        display_weights=False,
                        num_terms=None):

    for index in range(total_topics):
        topic = topic_model.show_topic(index)
        topic = [(word, round(wt,2))
                    for word, wt in topic
                    if abs(wt) >= weight_threshold]
        if display_weights:
            print 'Topic #'+str(index+1)+' with weights'
            print topic[:num_terms] if num_terms else topic
        else:
            print 'Topic #'+str(index+1)+' without weights'
            tw = [term for term, wt in topic]
            print tw[:num_terms] if num_terms else tw
        print
```

We can try out this function on our toy corpus topic model using the following
snippet to see how we can get the topics and play around with the parameters:

```
# print topics without weights
In [860]: print_topics_gensim(topic_model=lsi,
    ...:                       total_topics=total_topics,
    ...:                       num_terms=5,
    ...:                       display_weights=False)
Topic #1 without weights
[u'language', u'programming', u'java', u'python', u'popular']
```

```
Topic #2 without weights
[u'dog', u'fox', u'jump', u'smarter', u'cat']

# print topics with their weights
In [861]: print_topics_gensim(topic_model=lsi,
    ...:                       total_topics=total_topics,
    ...:                       num_terms=5,
    ...:                       display_weights=True)
Topic #1 with weights
[(u'language', -0.46), (u'programming', -0.46), (u'java', -0.34),
(u'python', -0.34), (u'popular', -0.34)]

Topic #2 with weights
[(u'dog', 0.46), (u'fox', 0.46), (u'jump', 0.44), (u'smarter', 0.32),
(u'cat', 0.32)]
```

We have successfully built a topic modeling framework using LSI that can distinguish and show topics from a corpus of documents. Now we will use SVD to build our own LSI topic model framework from the ground up using the mathematical concepts discussed at the beginning of this chapter. We will start by building a TF-IDF feature matrix, which is actually a document-term matrix (if you remember from our classification exercise in Chapter 4). We will transpose this to form a term-document matrix before computing SVD using the following snippet. Besides this, we also fix the number of topics we want to generate and extract the term names from the features so we can map them with their weights:

```
from utils import build_feature_matrix, low_rank_svd

# build the term document tf-idf weighted matrix
norm_corpus = normalize_corpus(toy_corpus)
vectorizer, tfidf_matrix = build_feature_matrix(norm_corpus,
                                    feature_type='tfidf')
td_matrix = tfidf_matrix.transpose()
td_matrix = td_matrix.multiply(td_matrix > 0)

# fix total topics and get the terms used in the term-document matrix
total_topics = 2
feature_names = vectorizer.get_feature_names()
```

Once this is done, we compute the SVD for our term-document matrix using our low_rank_svd() function such that we build a low ranked matrix approximation taking only the top *k* singular vectors, which will be equal to our number of topics in this case. Using the *S* and *U* components, we multiply them together to generate each term and its weightage per topic giving us the necessary weights per topic similar to what you saw earlier:

```
u, s, vt = low_rank_svd(td_matrix, singular_count=total_topics)
weights = u.transpose() * s[:, None]
```

Now that we have our term weights, we need to connect them back to our terms. We define two utility functions for generating these topics by connecting the terms with their weights and then printing these topics using a function with configurable parameters:

```
# get topics with their terms and weights
def get_topics_terms_weights(weights, feature_names):
    feature_names = np.array(feature_names)
    sorted_indices = np.array([list(row[::-1])
                               for row
                               in np.argsort(np.abs(weights))])
    sorted_weights = np.array([list(wt[index])
                                   for wt, index
                                   in zip(weights,sorted_indices)])
    sorted_terms = np.array([list(feature_names[row])
                                for row
                                in sorted_indices])

    topics = [np.vstack((terms.T,
                    term_weights.T)).T
              for terms, term_weights
              in zip(sorted_terms, sorted_weights)]

    return topics

# print all the topics from a corpus
def print_topics_udf(topics, total_topics=1,
                     weight_threshold=0.0001,
                     display_weights=False,
                     num_terms=None):

    for index in range(total_topics):
        topic = topics[index]
        topic = [(term, float(wt))
                 for term, wt in topic]
        topic = [(word, round(wt,2))
                 for word, wt in topic
                 if abs(wt) >= weight_threshold]

        if display_weights:
            print 'Topic #'+str(index+1)+' with weights'
            print topic[:num_terms] if num_terms else topic
        else:
            print 'Topic #'+str(index+1)+' without weights'
            tw = [term for term, wt in topic]
            print tw[:num_terms] if num_terms else tw
        print
```

We are now ready to see our function in action. The following snippet utilizes the previously defined functions to generate topics using our LSI implementation using SVD by connecting the terms with their weights for each topic:

```
In [871]: topics = get_topics_terms_weights(weights, feature_names)
     ...: print_topics_udf(topics=topics,
     ...:                   total_topics=total_topics,
     ...:                   weight_threshold=0,
     ...:                   display_weights=True)
Topic #1 with weights
[(u'dog', 0.72), (u'fox', 0.72), (u'jump', 0.43), (u'smarter', 0.34),
(u'cat', 0.34), (u'slow', 0.23), (u'lazy', 0.23), (u'quick', 0.23),
(u'clever', 0.23), (u'program', 0.0), (u'java', 0.0), (u'excellent', -0.0),
(u'small', 0.0), (u'popular', 0.0), (u'python', 0.0), (u'programming',
-0.0), (u'language', -0.0), (u'ruby', 0.0)]

Topic #2 with weights
[(u'programming', -0.73), (u'language', -0.73), (u'python', -0.56),
(u'java', -0.56), (u'popular', -0.34), (u'ruby', -0.33), (u'excellent',
-0.33), (u'program', -0.21), (u'small', -0.11), (u'fox', 0.0), (u'dog',
0.0), (u'jump', 0.0), (u'clever', 0.0), (u'quick', 0.0), (u'lazy', 0.0),
(u'slow', 0.0), (u'smarter', 0.0), (u'cat', 0.0)]
```

From the preceding output we see that both topics have all the terms, but notice the weights more minutely. Do you see any difference? Of course, the terms in topic one related to programming have *zero* value, indicating they do not contribute to the topic at all. Let us put a proper threshold and get only the relevant terms per topic as follows:

```
# applying a scoring threshold
In [874]: topics = get_topics_terms_weights(weights, feature_names)
     ...: print_topics_udf(topics=topics,
     ...:                   total_topics=total_topics,
     ...:                   weight_threshold=0.15,
     ...:                   display_weights=True)
Topic #1 with weights
[(u'dog', 0.72), (u'fox', 0.72), (u'jump', 0.43), (u'smarter', 0.34),
(u'cat', 0.34), (u'slow', 0.23), (u'lazy', 0.23), (u'quick', 0.23),
(u'clever', 0.23)]

Topic #2 with weights
[(u'programming', -0.73), (u'language', -0.73), (u'python', -0.56),
(u'java', -0.56), (u'popular', -0.34), (u'ruby', -0.33), (u'excellent',
-0.33), (u'program', -0.21)]

 In [875]: topics = get_topics_terms_weights(weights, feature_names)
     ...: print_topics_udf(topics=topics,
     ...:                   total_topics=total_topics,
     ...:                   weight_threshold=0.15,
```

```
    ...:                        display_weights=False)
Topic #1 without weights
[u'dog', u'fox', u'jump', u'smarter', u'cat', u'slow', u'lazy', u'quick',
u'clever']

Topic #2 without weights
[u'programming', u'language', u'python', u'java', u'popular', u'ruby',
u'excellent', u'program']
```

This gives us much better depiction of the topics, similar to the ones obtained earlier, where each topic clearly has distinguishable concepts from the other. Thus you can see how simple matrix computations helped us in implementing a powerful topic model framework! We define the following function as a generic reusable topic modeling framework using LSI:

```python
def train_lsi_model_gensim(corpus, total_topics=2):

    norm_tokenized_corpus = normalize_corpus(corpus, tokenize=True)
    dictionary = corpora.Dictionary(norm_tokenized_corpus)
    mapped_corpus = [dictionary.doc2bow(text)
                     for text in norm_tokenized_corpus]
    tfidf = models.TfidfModel(mapped_corpus)
    corpus_tfidf = tfidf[mapped_corpus]
    lsi = models.LsiModel(corpus_tfidf,
                          id2word=dictionary,
                          num_topics=total_topics)
    return lsi
```

We will use the preceding function later to extract topics from product reviews. Let us now look at the next technique to build topic models using latent Dirichlet allocation.

Latent Dirichlet Allocation

The latent Dirichlet allocation (LDA) technique is a generative probabilistic model where each document is assumed to have a combination of topics similar to a probabilistic latent semantic indexing model—but in this case, the latent topics contain a *Dirichlet prior* over them. The math behind in this technique is pretty involved, so I will try to summarize it because going it specific detail would be out of the current scope. I recommend readers to go through this excellent talk by Christine Doig available at http://chdoig.github.io/pygotham-topic-modeling/#/, from which we will be borrowing some excellent pictorial representations. The plate notation for the LDA model is depicted in Figure 5-2.

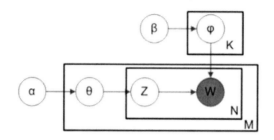

- K is the number of topics
- N is the number of words in the document
- M is the number of documents to analyse
- α is the Dirichlet-prior concentration parameter of the per-document topic distribution
- β is the same parameter of the per-topic word distribution
- φ(k) is the word distribution for topic k
- θ(i) is the topic distribution for document i
- z(i,j) is the topic assignment for w(i,j)
- w(i,j) is the j-th word in the i-th document
- φ and θ are Dirichlet distributions, z and w are multinomials.

Figure 5-2. *LDA plate notation (courtesy of C. Doig, Introduction to Topic Modeling in Python)*

Figure 5-3 shows a good representation of how each of the parameters connects back to the text documents and terms. It is assumed that we have *M* documents, *N* number of words in the documents, and *K* total number of topics we want to generate.

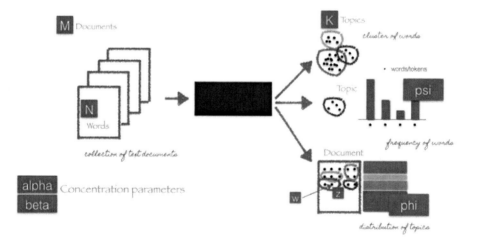

Figure 5-3. *End-to-end LDA framework (courtesy of C. Doig, Introduction to Topic Modeling in Python)*

The black box in the figure represents the core algorithm that makes use of the previously mentioned parameters to extract K topics from the documents. The following steps give a very simplistic explanation of what happens in the algorithm for everyone's benefit:

1. Initialize the necessary parameters.

2. For each document, randomly initialize each word to one of the K topics.

3. Start an iterative process as follows and repeat it several times.

4. For each document D:

    a. For each word W in document:

- For each topic T:

  - Compute $P(T|D)$, which is proportion of words in D assigned to topic T.

  - Compute $P(W|T)$, which is proportion of assignments to topic T over all documents having the word W.

- Reassign word W with topic T with probability $P(T|D) \times P(W|T)$ considering all other words and their topic assignments.

Once this runs for several iterations, we should have topic mixtures for each document and then generate the constituents of each topic from the terms that point to that topic. We use gensim in the following implementation to build an LDA-based topic model:

```
def train_lda_model_gensim(corpus, total_topics=2):

    norm_tokenized_corpus = normalize_corpus(corpus, tokenize=True)
    dictionary = corpora.Dictionary(norm_tokenized_corpus)
    mapped_corpus = [dictionary.doc2bow(text)
                        for text in norm_tokenized_corpus]
    tfidf = models.TfidfModel(mapped_corpus)
    corpus_tfidf = tfidf[mapped_corpus]
    lda = models.LdaModel(corpus_tfidf,
                            id2word=dictionary,
                            iterations=1000,
                            num_topics=total_topics)
    return lda

# use the function to generate topics on toy corpus
In [922]: lda_gensim = train_lda_model_gensim(toy_corpus,
    ...:                                       total_topics=2)
    ...:
    ...: print_topics_gensim(topic_model=lda_gensim,
```

```
      ...:                        total_topics=2,
      ...:                        num_terms=5,
      ...:                        display_weights=True)
Topic #1 with weights
[(u'fox', 0.08), (u'dog', 0.08), (u'jump', 0.07), (u'clever', 0.07),
(u'quick', 0.07)]

Topic #2 with weights
[(u'programming', 0.08), (u'language', 0.08), (u'java', 0.07), (u'python',
0.07), (u'ruby', 0.07)]
```

You can play around with various model parameters in the LdaModel class, which belongs to gensim's ldamodel module. This implementation works best with a corpus that has many documents. We see how the concepts are quite distinguishing across the two topics just as before, but note in this case the weights are positive, making it easier to interpret than LSI. Even scikit-learn has finally included an LDA-based topic model implementation in its library. The following snippet makes use of the same to build an LDA topic model:

```
from sklearn.decomposition import LatentDirichletAllocation

# get tf-idf based features
norm_corpus = normalize_corpus(toy_corpus)
vectorizer, tfidf_matrix = build_feature_matrix(norm_corpus,
                                  feature_type='tfidf')
# build LDA model
total_topics = 2
lda = LatentDirichletAllocation(n_topics=total_topics,
                                max_iter=100,
                                learning_method='online',
                                learning_offset=50.,
                                random_state=42)
lda.fit(tfidf_matrix)

# get terms and their weights
feature_names = vectorizer.get_feature_names()
weights = lda.components_

# generate topics from their terms and weights
topics = get_topics_terms_weights(weights, feature_names)
```

In that snippet, the LDA model is applied on the document-term TF-IDF feature matrix, which is decomposed into two matrices, namely a document-topic matrix and a topic-term matrix. We use the topic-term matrix stored in lda.components_ to retrieve the weights for each term per topic. Once we have these weights, we use our get_topics_terms_weights() function from our LSI modeling to build the topics based on the terms and weights per topic. We can now view the topics using our print_topics_udf() function, which we implemented earlier:

```
In [926]: topics = get_topics_terms_weights(weights, feature_names)
     ...: print_topics_udf(topics=topics,
     ...:                   total_topics=total_topics,
     ...:                   num_terms=8,
     ...:                   display_weights=True)
Topic #1 with weights
[(u'fox', 1.86), (u'dog', 1.86), (u'jump', 1.19), (u'clever', 1.12),
(u'quick', 1.12), (u'lazy', 1.12), (u'slow', 1.12), (u'cat', 1.06)]

Topic #2 with weights
[(u'programming', 1.8), (u'language', 1.8), (u'java', 1.64), (u'python',
1.64), (u'program', 1.3), (u'ruby', 1.11), (u'excellent', 1.11),
(u'popular', 1.06)]
```

We can now see similar results for the two topics with distinguishable concepts where the first topic is about the animals and their characteristics from the first four documents and the second topic is all about programming languages and their attributes from the last four documents.

Non-negative Matrix Factorization

The last technique we will look at is non-negative matrix factorization (NNMF), which is another matrix decomposition technique similar to SVD, though NNMF operates on non-negative matrices and works well for multivariate data. NNMF can be formally defined like so: Given a non-negative matrix V, the objective is to find two non-negative matrix factors W and H such that when they are multiplied, they can approximately reconstruct V. Mathematically this is represented by

$$V \approx WH$$

such that all three matrices are non-negative. To get to this approximation, we usually use a cost function like the Euclidean distance or L2 norm between two matrices, or the Frobenius norm which is a slight modification of the L2 norm. This can be represented as

$$arg\min_{W,H} \frac{1}{2} \|V - WH\|^2$$

where we have our three non-negative matrices V, W, and H. This can be further simplified as follows:

$$\frac{1}{2} \sum_{i,j} \left(V_{ij} - WH_{ij} \right)^2$$

This implementation is available in the NMF class in the scikit-learn decomposition module that we will be using in the section.

We can build an NNMF-based topic model using the following snippet on our toy corpus which gives us the feature names and their weights just like in LDA:

```
from sklearn.decomposition import NMF
# build tf-idf document-term matrix
norm_corpus = normalize_corpus(toy_corpus)
vectorizer, tfidf_matrix = build_feature_matrix(norm_corpus,
                                    feature_type='tfidf')
# build topic model
total_topics = 2
nmf = NMF(n_components=total_topics,
        random_state=42, alpha=.1, l1_ratio=.5)
nmf.fit(tfidf_matrix)
# get terms and their weights
feature_names = vectorizer.get_feature_names()
weights = nmf.components_
```

Now that we have our terms and their weights, we can use our defined functions from before to print the topics as follows:

```
In [928]: topics = get_topics_terms_weights(weights, feature_names)
    ...: print_topics_udf(topics=topics,
    ...:                     total_topics=total_topics,
    ...:                     num_terms=None,
    ...:                     display_weights=True)
Topic #1 with weights
[(u'programming', 0.55), (u'language', 0.55), (u'python', 0.4), (u'java',
0.4), (u'popular', 0.24), (u'ruby', 0.23), (u'excellent', 0.23),
(u'program', 0.09), (u'small', 0.03)]

Topic #2 with weights
[(u'dog', 0.57), (u'fox', 0.57), (u'jump', 0.35), (u'smarter', 0.26),
(u'cat', 0.26), (u'quick', 0.13), (u'slow', 0.13), (u'clever', 0.13),
(u'lazy', 0.13)]
```

What we have observed is that non-negative matrix factorization works the best even with small corpora with few documents compared to the other methods, but again, this depends on the type of data you are dealing with.

Extracting Topics from Product Reviews

We will now utilize our earlier functions and build topic models using the three techniques on some real-world data. For this, I have extracted some reviews for a particular product from Amazon. Data enthusiasts can get more information about the source of this data from http://jmcauley.ucsd.edu/data/amazon/, which contains various product reviews based on product types and categories. The product of our interest is the very popular video game *The Elder Scrolls V: Skyrim* developed by Bethesda

Softworks. It is perhaps one of the best role-playing games out there. (You can view the product information and its reviews on Amazon at www.amazon.com/dp/B004HYK956 if you are interested.) In our case, the extracted reviews are available in a CSV file named amazon_skyrim_reviews.csv, available along with the code files of this chapter. Let us first load the reviews before extracting topics:

```python
import pandas as pd
import numpy as np
# load reviews
CORPUS = pd.read_csv('amazon_skyrim_reviews.csv')
CORPUS = np.array(CORPUS['Reviews'])

# view sample review
In [946]: print CORPUS[12]
I base the value of a game on the amount of enjoyable gameplay I can get out
of it and this one was definitely worth the price!
```

Now that we have our corpus of product reviews loaded, let us set the number of topics to 5 and extract topics using all the three techniques implemented in the earlier sections. The following code snippet achieves the same:

```python
# set number of topics
total_topics = 5

# Technique 1: Latent Semantic Indexing
In [958]: lsi_gensim = train_lsi_model_gensim(CORPUS,
     ...:                                     total_topics=total_topics)
     ...: print_topics_gensim(topic_model=lsi_gensim,
     ...:                     total_topics=total_topics,
     ...:                     num_terms=10,
     ...:                     display_weights=False)
Topic #1 without weights
[u'skyrim', u'one', u'quest', u'like', u'play', u'oblivion', u'go', u'get',
u'time', u'level']

Topic #2 without weights
[u'recommend', u'love', u'ever', u'best', u'great', u'level', u'highly',
u'play', u'elder', u'scroll']

Topic #3 without weights
[u'recommend', u'highly', u'fun', u'love', u'ever', u'wonderful', u'best',
u'everyone', u'series', u'scroll']

Topic #4 without weights
[u'fun', u'scroll', u'elder', u'recommend', u'highly', u'wonderful', u'fan',
u'graphic', u'series', u'cool']

Topic #5 without weights
```

```
[u'fun', u'love', u'elder', u'scroll', u'highly', u'5', u'dont', u'hour',
u'series', u'hundred']

# Technique 2a: Latent Dirichlet Allocation (gensim)
In [959]: lda_gensim = train_lda_model_gensim(CORPUS,
     ...:                                 total_topics=total_topics)
     ...: print_topics_gensim(topic_model=lda_gensim,
     ...:                     total_topics=total_topics,
     ...:                     num_terms=10,
     ...:                     display_weights=False)
Topic #1 without weights
[u'quest', u'good', u'skyrim', u'love', u'make', u'best', u'time', u'go',
u'play', u'every']

Topic #2 without weights
[u'good', u'play', u'get', u'really', u'like', u'one', u'hour', u'buy',
u'go', u'skyrim']

Topic #3 without weights
[u'fun', u'gameplay', u'skyrim', u'best', u'want', u'time', u'one', u'play',
u'review', u'like']

Topic #4 without weights
[u'love', u'play', u'one', u'much', u'great', u'ever', u'like', u'fun',
u'recommend', u'level']

Topic #5 without weights
[u'great', u'long', u'love', u'scroll', u'elder', u'oblivion', u'play',
u'month', u'never', u'skyrim']

# Technique 2b: Latent Dirichlet Allocation (scikit-learn)
In [960]: norm_corpus = normalize_corpus(CORPUS)
     ...: vectorizer, tfidf_matrix = build_feature_matrix(norm_corpus,
     ...:                                 feature_type='tfidf')
     ...: feature_names = vectorizer.get_feature_names()
     ...:
     ...:
     ...: lda = LatentDirichletAllocation(n_topics=total_topics,
     ...:                                 max_iter=100,
     ...:                                 learning_method='online',
     ...:                                 learning_offset=50.,
     ...:                                 random_state=42)
     ...: lda.fit(tfidf_matrix)
     ...: weights = lda.components_
     ...: topics = get_topics_terms_weights(weights, feature_names)
     ...: print_topics_udf(topics=topics,
     ...:                  total_topics=total_topics,
     ...:                  num_terms=10,
     ...:                  display_weights=False)
```

Topic #1 without weights
[u'statrs', u'expression', u'demand', u'unnecessary', u'mining', u'12yr',
u'able', u'snowy', u'shopkeepers', u'arpg']

Topic #2 without weights
[u'game', u'play', u'get', u'one', u'skyrim', u'great', u'like', u'time',
u'quest', u'much']

Topic #3 without weights
[u'de', u'pagar', u'cr\xe9dito', u'momento', u'responsabilidad', u'compras',
u'para', u'futuras', u'recomiendo', u'skyrimseguridad']

Topic #4 without weights
[u'booklet', u'proudly', u'ending', u'destiny', u'estatic', u'humungous',
u'chirstmas', u'bloodthey', u'accolade', u'scaled']

Topic #5 without weights
[u'game', u'play', u'fun', u'good', u'buy', u'one', u'whatnot', u'titles',
u'haveseen', u'best']

```
# Technique 3: Non-negative Matrix Factorization
In [961]: nmf = NMF(n_components=total_topics,
     ...:                 random_state=42, alpha=.1, l1_ratio=.5)
     ...: nmf.fit(tfidf_matrix)
     ...:
     ...: feature_names = vectorizer.get_feature_names()
     ...: weights = nmf.components_
     ...:
     ...: topics = get_topics_terms_weights(weights, feature_names)
     ...: print_topics_udf(topics=topics,
     ...:                     total_topics=total_topics,
     ...:                     num_terms=10,
     ...:                     display_weights=False)
```
Topic #1 without weights
[u'game', u'get', u'skyrim', u'play', u'time', u'like', u'quest', u'one',
u'go', u'much']

Topic #2 without weights
[u'game', u'best', u'ever', u'fun', u'play', u'hour', u'great', u'rpg',
u'definitely', u'one']

Topic #3 without weights
[u'write', u'review', u'describe', u'justice', u'word', u'game', u'simply',
u'try', u'period', u'really']

Topic #4 without weights
[u'scroll', u'elder', u'series', u'always', u'love', u'pass', u'buy',
u'franchise', u'game', u'best']

Topic #5 without weights

```
[u'recommend', u'love', u'game', u'highly', u'great', u'play', u'wonderful',
u'like', u'oblivion', u'would']
```

The preceding outputs show five topics per technique. If you observe them closely, you will notice that there will always be some overlap between topics, but they bring out distinguishing concepts from the review. We can conclude a few observations:

- All topic modeling techniques bring out concepts related to people describing this game with adjectives like *wonderful, great,* and *highly recommendable.*

- They also describe the game's genre as RPG (role-playing game) or ARPG (action role-playing game).

- Game features like *gameplay* and *graphics* are associated with positive words like *good, great, fun,* and *cool.*

- The word *oblivion* comes up in many of the topic models. This is in reference to the previous game of the *Elder Scrolls* series, called *The Elder Scrolls IV: Oblivion.* This is an indication of customers comparing this game with its predecessor in the reviews.

Go ahead and play around with these functions and the data. You might even try building topic models on new data sources. Remember, topic modeling often acts as a starting point to digging deeper into the data to uncover patterns by querying with specific topic concepts or even clustering and grouping text documents and analyzing their similarity.

Automated Document Summarization

We briefly talked about document summarization at the beginning of this chapter, in trying to extract the gist from a large document or corpus such that it retains the core essence or meaning of the corpus. The idea of document summarization is a bit different from keyphrase extraction or topic modeling. The end result is still in the form of some document, but with a few sentences based on the length we might want the summary to be. This is similar to having a research paper with an abstract or an executive summary. The main objective of automated document summarization is to perform this summarization without involving human inputs except for running any computer programs. Mathematical and statistical models help in building and automating the task of summarizing documents by observing their content and context.

There are mainly two broad approaches towards document summarization using automated techniques:

- *Extraction-based techniques*: These methods use mathematical and statistical concepts like SVD to extract some key subset of content from the original document such that this subset of content contains the core information and acts as the focal point of the entire document. This content could be words, phrases, or sentences. The end result from this approach is a short executive summary of a couple of lines are taken or extracted from the original document. No new content is generated in this technique—hence the name *extraction-based*.

- *Abstraction-based techniques*: These methods are more complex and sophisticated and leverage language semantics to create representations. They also make use of NLG techniques where the machine uses knowledge bases and semantic representations to generate text on its own and creates summaries just like a human would write them.

Most research today exists for extraction-based techniques because it is comparatively harder to build abstraction-based summarizers. But some advances have been made in that area with regard to creating abstract summaries mimicking humans. Let us look at an implementation of document summarization by leveraging gensim's summarization module. We will be using our Wikipedia description of elephants as the document on which we will test all our summarization techniques. We start by loading the necessary dependencies and the corpus as follows:

```
from normalization import normalize_corpus, parse_document
from utils import build_feature_matrix, low_rank_svd
import numpy as np


toy_text = """
Elephants are large mammals of the family Elephantidae
and the order Proboscidea. Two species are traditionally recognised,
the African elephant and the Asian elephant. Elephants are scattered
throughout sub-Saharan Africa, South Asia, and Southeast Asia. Male
African elephants are the largest extant terrestrial animals. All
elephants have a long trunk used for many purposes,
particularly breathing, lifting water and grasping objects. Their
incisors grow into tusks, which can serve as weapons and as tools
for moving objects and digging. Elephants' large ear flaps help
to control their body temperature. Their pillar-like legs can
carry their great weight. African elephants have larger ears
and concave backs while Asian elephants have smaller ears
and convex or level backs.
"""
```

We now define a function to summarize an input document to a fraction of its original size, which will be taken as a user input parameter `summary_ratio` in the following function. The output will be the summarized document:

```
from gensim.summarization import summarize, keywords

def text_summarization_gensim(text, summary_ratio=0.5):

    summary = summarize(text, split=True, ratio=summary_ratio)
    for sentence in summary:
        print sentence
```

We will now parse our input document to remove the newlines and extract sentences and then pass the complete document to the preceding function where `gensim` takes care of normalization and summarizes the document, as shown in the following snippet:

```
In [978]: docs = parse_document(toy_text)
     ...: text = ' '.join(docs)
     ...: text_summarization_gensim(text, summary_ratio=0.4)
Two species are traditionally recognised,  the African elephant and the
Asian elephant.
All  elephants have a long trunk used for many purposes,  particularly
breathing, lifting water and grasping objects.
African elephants have larger ears  and concave backs while Asian elephants
have smaller ears  and convex or level backs.
```

If you observe the preceding output and compare it with the original document, we had a total of nine sentences in the original document, and it has been summarize to a total of three sentences. But if you read the summarized document, you will see the core meaning and themes of the document have been retained, which include the two species of elephants, how they are distinguishable from each other, and their common characteristics. This summarization implementation from `gensim` is based on a popular algorithm called TextRank.

Now that we have seen how interesting text summarization can be, let us look at a couple of extraction-based summarization algorithms. We will be mainly focusing on the following two techniques:

- Latent semantic analysis

- TextRank

We will first explore the concepts and math behind each technique and then implement those using Python. Finally, we will test them on our toy document from before. Before we deep dive into the techniques, let us prepare our toy document by parsing and normalizing it as follows:

```
# parse and normalize document
sentences = parse_document(toy_text)
norm_sentences = normalize_corpus(sentences,lemmatize=True)
```

```
# check total sentences in document
In [992]: total_sentences = len(norm_sentences)
     ...: print 'Total Sentences in Document:', total_sentences
Total Sentences in Document: 9
```

Once we have a working summarization algorithm, we will also construct a generic function for each technique and test it on a real product description from Wikipedia in a future section.

Latent Semantic Analysis

Here, we will be looking at summarizing text documents by utilizing document sentences, the terms in each sentence of the document, and applying SVD to them using some sort of feature weights like Bag of Words or TF-IDF weights. The core principle behind latent semantic analysis (LSA) is that in any document, there exists a latent structure among terms which are related contextually and hence should also be correlated in the same singular space. The approach we follow in our implementation is taken from the popular paper published in 2004 by J. Steinberger and K. Jezek, "Using latent semantic analysis in text summarization and summary evaluation," which proposes some improvements over some excellent work done by Y. Gong and X. Liu's "Generic Text Summarization Using Relevance Measure and Latent Semantic Analysis," published in 2001. I recommend you to read these two papers if you are interested in learning more about this technique.

The main idea in our implementation is to use SVD such that, if you remember the equation from SVD where $M = USV^T$ such that U and V are the orthogonal matrices and S was the diagonal matrix, which can also be represented as a vector of the singular values. The original matrix can be represented as a term-document matrix, where the rows will be terms and each column will be a document, that is, a sentence from our document in this case. The values can be any type of weighting, like Bag of Words model-based frequencies, TF-IDFS, or binary occurrences. We will use our low_rank_svd() function to create a low rank matrix approximation for M based on the number of concepts k, which will be our number of singular values. The same k columns from matrix U will point to the term vectors for each of the k concepts, and in case of matrix V, the k rows based on the top k singular values point to sentence vectors. Once we have U, S, and V^T from the SVD for the top k singular values based on the number of concepts k, we perform the following computations. Remember, the input parameters we need are the number of concepts k and the number of sentences n which we want the final summary to contain:

- Get the sentence vectors from the matrix V (k rows).

- Get the top k singular values from S.

- Apply a threshold-based approach to remove singular values that are less than half of the largest singular value if any exist. This is a heuristic, and you can play around with this value if you want. Mathematically, $S_i = 0$ *iff* $S_i < \frac{1}{2}\max(S)$.

- Multiply each term sentence column from V squared with its corresponding singular value from S also squared, to get sentence weights per topic.

- Compute the sum of the sentence weights across the topics and take the square root of the final score to get the salience scores for each sentence in the document.

The preceding salience score computations for each sentence can be mathematically represented as

$$SS = \sqrt{\sum_{i=1}^{k} S_i V_i^T}$$

where *SS* denotes the saliency score for each sentence by taking the dot product between the singular values and the sentence vectors from V^T. Once we have these scores, we sort them in descending order, pick the top *n* sentences corresponding to the highest scores, and combine them to form our final summary based on the order in which they were present in the original document. Let us implement the above steps in our code using the following snippet:

```
# set the number of sentences and topics for summarized document
num_sentences = 3
num_topics = 3

# build document term matrix based on bag of words features
vec, dt_matrix = build_feature_matrix(sentences,
                                       feature_type='frequency')
# convert to term document matrix
td_matrix = dt_matrix.transpose()
td_matrix = td_matrix.multiply(td_matrix > 0)

# get low rank SVD components
u, s, vt = low_rank_svd(td_matrix, singular_count=num_topics)

# remove singular values below threshold
sv_threshold = 0.5
min_sigma_value = max(s) * sv_threshold
s[s < min_sigma_value] = 0

# compute salience scores for all sentences in document
salience_scores = np.sqrt(np.dot(np.square(s), np.square(vt)))

# print salience score for each sentence
In [996]: print np.round(salience_scores, 2)
[ 2.93  3.28  1.67  1.8   2.24  4.51  0.71  1.22  5.24]

# rank sentences based on their salience scores
top_sentence_indices = salience_scores.argsort()[-num_sentences:][::-1]
top_sentence_indices.sort()
```

```
# view top sentence index positions
In [997]: print top_sentence_indices
[1 5 8]

# get document summary by combining above sentences
In [998]: for index in top_sentence_indices:
    ...:         print sentences[index]
Two species are traditionally recognised,  the African elephant and the
Asian elephant.
Their  incisors grow into tusks, which can serve as weapons and as
tools  for moving objects and digging.
African elephants have larger ears  and concave backs while Asian elephants
have smaller ears  and convex or level backs.
```

You can see how a few matrix operations give us a concise and excellent summarized document that covers the main topics from the document about elephants. Compare it with the one generated earlier using gensim. Do you see some similarity between the summaries?

We will now build a generic reusable function for LSA using the previous algorithm so that we can use it on our product description document later on and you can also use this function on your own data:

```
def lsa_text_summarizer(documents, num_sentences=2,
                        num_topics=2, feature_type='frequency',
                        sv_threshold=0.5):

    vec, dt_matrix = build_feature_matrix(documents,
                                          feature_type=feature_type)

    td_matrix = dt_matrix.transpose()
    td_matrix = td_matrix.multiply(td_matrix > 0)

    u, s, vt = low_rank_svd(td_matrix, singular_count=num_topics)
    min_sigma_value = max(s) * sv_threshold
    s[s < min_sigma_value] = 0

    salience_scores = np.sqrt(np.dot(np.square(s), np.square(vt)))
    top_sentence_indices = salience_scores.argsort()[-num_sentences:][::-1]
    top_sentence_indices.sort()

    for index in top_sentence_indices:
        print sentences[index]
```

This concludes our discussion on LSA, and we will move on to the next technique for extraction-based document summarization.

TextRank

The TextRank summarization algorithm internally uses the popular PageRank algorithm, which is used by Google for ranking web sites and pages and measures their importance. It is used by the Google search engine when providing relevant web pages based on search queries. To understand TextRank better, we need to understand some of the concepts surrounding PageRank.

The core algorithm in PageRank is a graph-based scoring or ranking algorithm, where pages are scored or ranked based on their importance. Web sites and pages contain further links embedded in them, which link to more pages with more links, and this continues across the Internet. This can be represented as a graph-based model where vertices indicate the web pages, and edges indicate links among them. This can be used to form a voting or recommendation system such that when one vertex links to another one in the graph, it is basically casting a vote. Vertex importance is decided not only on the number of votes or edges but also the importance of the vertices that are connected to it and their importance. This helps in determining the score or rank for each vertex or page. This is evident from Figure 5-4, which represents a sample of pages with their importance.

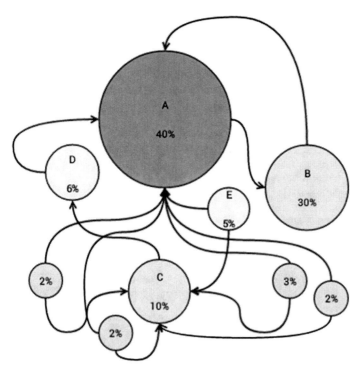

Figure 5-4. *PageRank scores for a simple network*

In Figure 5-4, we can see that vertex denoting Page B has a higher score than Page C, even if it has fewer edges compared to Page C, because Page A is an important page which is connected to Page B. Thus we can now formally define PageRank as follows.

Consider a directed graph represented as $G = (V, E)$ such that V represents the set of vertices or pages and E represents the set of edges or links, and E is a subset of $V \times V$. Assuming we have a given page V_i for which we want to compute the PageRank, we can mathematically define it as

$$PR(V_i) = (1-d) + d \times \sum_{j \in In(V_i)} \frac{PR(V_j)}{|Out(V_j)|}$$

where for the vertex/page V_i we have $PR(V_i)$, which indicates the PageRank score, $In(V_i)$ represents the set of pages which point to this vertex/page, $Out(V_i)$ represents the set of pages which the vertex/page V_i points to, and d is the damping factor usually having a value between 0 to 1—ideally it is set to 0.85.

Coming back to the TextRank algorithm, when summarizing a document, we will have sentences, keywords, or phrases as the vertices of the algorithm based on the type of summarization we are trying to do. We might have multiple links between these vertices, and the modification which we make from the original PageRank algorithm is to have a weight coefficient say w_{ij} between the edge connecting two vertices V_i and V_j such that this weight indicates the strength of this connection between them. Thus we now formally define the new function for computing TextRank of vertices as

$$TR(V_i) = (1-d) + d \times \sum_{V_j \in In(V_i)} \frac{w_{ji} \, TR(V_j)}{\sum_{V_k \in Out(V_j)} w_{jk}}$$

where TR indicates the weighted PageRank score for a vertex now defined as the TextRank for that vertex. Thus we can now formulate the algorithm and identify the main steps we will be following:

1. Tokenize and extract sentences from the document to be summarized.

2. Decide on the number of sentences k that we want in the final summary.

3. Build document term feature matrix using weights like TF-IDF or Bag of Words.

4. Compute a document similarity matrix by multiplying the matrix with its transpose.

5. Use these documents (sentences in our case) as the vertices and the similarities between each pair of documents as the weight or score coefficient mentioned earlier and feed them to the PageRank algorithm.

6. Get the score for each sentence.

7. Rank the sentences based on score and return the top k sentences.

257

The following code snippet shows how to construct the connected graph among all the sentences from our toy document by making use of the document similarity scores and the documents themselves as the vertices. We will use the `networkx` library to help us plot this graph. Remember, each document is a sentence in our case which will also be the vertices in the graph:

```
import networkx

# define number of sentences in final summary
num_sentences = 3

# construct weighted document term matrix
vec, dt_matrix = build_feature_matrix(norm_sentences,
                                       feature_type='tfidf')

# construct the document similarity matrix
similarity_matrix = (dt_matrix * dt_matrix.T)
# view the document similarity matrix
In [1011]: print np.round(similarity_matrix.todense(), 2)
[[ 1.    0.    0.03  0.05  0.03  0.    0.15  0.    0.06]
 [ 0.    1.    0.    0.07  0.    0.    0.    0.    0.11]
 [ 0.03  0.    1.    0.03  0.02  0.    0.03  0.    0.04]
 [ 0.05  0.07  0.03  1.    0.03  0.    0.04  0.    0.11]
 [ 0.03  0.    0.02  0.03  1.    0.07  0.03  0.    0.04]
 [ 0.    0.    0.    0.    0.07  1.    0.    0.    0.  ]
 [ 0.15  0.    0.03  0.04  0.03  0.    1.    0.    0.05]
 [ 0.    0.    0.    0.    0.    0.    0.    1.    0.  ]
 [ 0.06  0.11  0.04  0.11  0.04  0.    0.05  0.    1.  ]]

# build the similarity graph
similarity_graph = networkx.from_scipy_sparse_matrix(similarity_matrix)
# view the similarity graph
In [1013]: networkx.draw_networkx(similarity_graph)
Out [1013]:
```

In Figure 5-5, we can see how the sentences of our toy document are now linked to each other based on document similarities. The graph gives an idea how well connected some sentences are to other sentences.

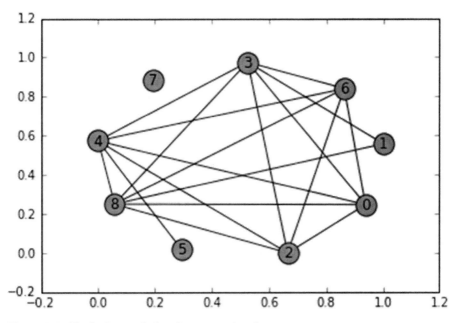

Figure 5-5. *Similarity graph showing connections between sentences*

We will now compute the PageRank scores for all the sentences, rank them, and build our summary using the top three sentences:

```
# compute pagerank scores for all the sentences
scores = networkx.pagerank(similarity_graph)

# rank sentences based on their scores
ranked_sentences = sorted(((score, index)
                           for index, score
                           in scores.items()),
                          reverse=True)
# view the ranked sentences
In [1030]: ranked_sentences
Out[1030]:
```

```
[(0.11889477617125277, 8),
 (0.11456045476451866, 3),
 (0.11285293843138654, 0),
 (0.11210156056437962, 6),
 (0.11139550507847462, 4),
 (0.1111111111111111, 7),
 (0.10709498606197024, 5),
 (0.10610242758495998, 2),
 (0.10588624023194664, 1)]
```

```python
# get the top sentence indices for our summary
top_sentence_indices = [ranked_sentences[index][1]
                        for index in range(num_sentences)]
top_sentence_indices.sort()
```

```python
# view the top sentence indices
In [1032]: print top_sentence_indices
 [0, 3, 8]
```

```python
# construct the document summary
In [1033]: for index in top_sentence_indices:
     ...:     print sentences[index]
Elephants are large mammals of the family Elephantidae  and the order
Proboscidea.
Male  African elephants are the largest extant terrestrial animals.
African elephants have larger ears  and concave backs while Asian elephants
have smaller ears  and convex or level backs.
```

We finally get our desired summary by using the TextRank algorithm. The content is also quite meaningful where it talks about elephants being mammals, their taxonomy, and how Asian and African elephants can be distinguished.

We will now define a generic function as follows to compute TextRank-based summaries on any document:

```python
def textrank_text_summarizer(documents, num_sentences=2,
                             feature_type='frequency'):

    vec, dt_matrix = build_feature_matrix(norm_sentences,
                                          feature_type='tfidf')
    similarity_matrix = (dt_matrix * dt_matrix.T)

    similarity_graph = networkx.from_scipy_sparse_matrix(similarity_matrix)
    scores = networkx.pagerank(similarity_graph)

    ranked_sentences = sorted(((score, index)
                              for index, score
                              in scores.items()),
                             reverse=True)
```

```
top_sentence_indices = [ranked_sentences[index][1]
                            for index in range(num_sentences)]
top_sentence_indices.sort()

for index in top_sentence_indices:
    print sentences[index]
```

We have covered two document-summarization techniques and also built generic reusable functions to compute automated document summaries for any text document. In the following section, we will summarize a product description from a wiki page.

Summarizing a Product Description

Building on what we talked about in the product reviews from the topic modeling section, here we will be summarizing a description for the same product—a role-playing video game named *The Elder Scrolls V: Skyrim*. We have taken several lines from the Wikipedia page containing the product's detailed description. In this section, we will perform automated document summarization on the product description utilizing our functions from the previous section. We will start with loading the product description and normalizing the content:

```
# load the document
DOCUMENT = """
The Elder Scrolls V: Skyrim is an open world action role-playing video game
developed by Bethesda Game Studios and published by Bethesda Softworks.
It is the fifth installment in The Elder Scrolls series, following
The Elder Scrolls IV: Oblivion. Skyrim's main story revolves around
the player character and their effort to defeat Alduin the World-Eater,
a dragon who is prophesied to destroy the world.
The game is set two hundred years after the events of Oblivion
and takes place in the fictional province of Skyrim. The player completes
quests
and develops the character by improving skills.
Skyrim continues the open world tradition of its predecessors by allowing the
player to travel anywhere in the game world at any time, and to
ignore or postpone the main storyline indefinitely. The player may freely roam
over the land of Skyrim, which is an open world environment consisting
of wilderness expanses, dungeons, cities, towns, fortresses and villages.
Players may navigate the game world more quickly by riding horses,
or by utilizing a fast-travel system which allows them to warp to previously
Players have the option to develop their character. At the beginning of the game,
players create their character by selecting one of several races,
including humans, orcs, elves and anthropomorphic cat or lizard-like
creatures,
```

and then customizing their character's appearance.discovered locations. Over the
course of the game, players improve their character's skills, which are
numerical
representations of their ability in certain areas. There are eighteen skills
divided evenly among the three schools of combat, magic, and stealth.
Skyrim is the first entry in The Elder Scrolls to include Dragons in the game's
wilderness. Like other creatures, Dragons are generated randomly in the world
and will engage in combat.
"""

```
# normalize the document
In [1045]: sentences = parse_document(DOCUMENT)
     ...: norm_sentences = normalize_corpus(sentences,lemmatize=True)
     ...: print "Total Sentences:", len(norm_sentences)
Total Sentences: 13
```

We can see that there are a total of 13 sentences in this description. Let us now
generate the document summaries using our functions in the following code snippet:

```
# LSA document summarization
In [1053]: lsa_text_summarizer(norm_sentences, num_sentences=3,
     ...:                        num_topics=5, feature_type='frequency',
     ...:                        sv_threshold=0.5)
The Elder Scrolls V: Skyrim is an open world action role-playing video
game  developed by Bethesda Game Studios and published by Bethesda
Softworks.
Players may navigate the game world more quickly by riding horses,  or
by utilizing a fast-travel system which allows them to warp to
previously  Players have the option to develop their character.
At the beginning of the game,  players create their character by selecting
one of several races,  including humans, orcs, elves and anthropomorphic
cat or lizard-like creatures,  and then customizing their character's
appearance.discovered locations.
```

```
# TextRank document summarization
In [1054]: textrank_text_summarizer(norm_sentences, num_sentences=3,
     ...:                             feature_type='tfidf')
The Elder Scrolls V: Skyrim is an open world action role-playing video
game  developed by Bethesda Game Studios and published by Bethesda
Softworks.
Players may navigate the game world more quickly by riding horses,  or
by utilizing a fast-travel system which allows them to warp to
previously  Players have the option to develop their character.
Skyrim is the first entry in The Elder Scrolls to include Dragons in the
game's  wilderness.
```

You can see from the preceding outputs that we were successfully able to summarize our product description from 13 to 3 lines, and this short summary depicts the core essence of the product description, like the name of the game and its various features regarding its gameplay and characters.

This concludes our discussion on automated text summarization. I encourage you to try out these techniques on more documents and test it with various different parameters like more number of topics, different feature types like TF-IDF, Bag of Words, binary occurrences, and even word vectors.

Summary

In this chapter, we covered some interesting areas in NLP and text analytics with regard to information extraction, document summarization, and topic modeling. We started with an overview of the evolution of information and learned about concepts like information overload leading to the need for text summarization and information retrieval. We talked about the various ways we can extract key information from textual data and ways of summarizing large documents. We covered important mathematical concepts like SVD and low rank matrix approximation and utilized them in several of our algorithms. We mainly covered three approaches towards reducing information overload, including keyphrase extraction, topic models, and automated document summarization. Keyphrase extraction includes methods like collocations and weighted tagged term–based approaches for getting keyphrases or terms from corpora. We built several topic modeling techniques, including latent semantic indexing, latent Dirichlet allocation, and the very recently implemented non-negative matrix factorization. Finally, we looked at two extraction-based techniques for automated document summarization: LSA and TextRank. We implemented each method and observed results on real-world data to get a good idea of how these methods worked and how effective simple mathematical operations can be in generating actionable insights.

CHAPTER 6

■ ■ ■

Text Similarity and Clustering

Previous chapters have covered several techniques of analyzing text and extracting interesting insights. We have looked at supervised machine learning (ML) techniques that are used to classify or categorize text documents into several pre-assumed categories. Unsupervised techniques like topic models and document summarization have also been also covered, which involved trying to extract and retrieve key themes and information from large text documents and corpora. In this chapter, we will be looking at several other techniques and use-cases that leverage unsupervised learning and information retrieval concepts.

If you refresh your memory of Chapter 4, text categorization is indeed an interesting problem that has several applications, most notably in the classification of news articles and email. But one constraint in text classification is that we need some training data with manually labeled categories because we use supervised learning algorithms to build our classification model. The efforts of building this dataset are definitely not easy, because to build a good model, you need a sizeable amount of training data. For this, we need to spend time and manual effort in labeling data, building a model, and then finally using it to classify new documents. Can we instead make the machine do it? Yes, as a matter of fact, we can. This chapter specifically addresses looking at the content of text documents, analyzing their similarity using various measures, and clustering similar documents together.

Text data is unstructured and highly noisy. We get the benefits of well-labeled training data and supervised learning when performing text classification. But document clustering is an unsupervised learning process, where we are trying to segment and categorize documents into separate categories by making the machine learn about the various text documents, their features, similarities, and the differences among them. This makes document clustering more challenging, albeit interesting. Consider having a corpus of documents that talk about various different concepts and ideas. Humans are wired in such a way that we use our learning from the past and apply it to distinguish documents from each other. For example, the sentence *The fox is smarter than the dog* is more similar to *The fox is faster than the dog* than it is to *Python is an excellent programming language*. We can easily spot and intuitively figure out specific keyphrases like *Python, fox, dog, programming,* and so on, which help us determine which sentences or documents are more similar. But can we do that programmatically? In this chapter, we will focus on several concepts related to text similarity, distance metrics, and unsupervised ML algorithms to answer the following questions:

© Dipanjan Sarkar 2016

D. Sarkar, *Text Analytics with Python*, DOI 10.1007/978-1-4842-2388-8_6

- How do we measure similarity between documents?

- How can we use distance measures to find the most relevant documents?

- When is a distance measure called a metric?

- How do we cluster or group similar documents?

- Can we visualize document clusters?

Although we will be focused on trying to answer these questions, we will cover essential concepts and information needed to understand various techniques for solving these problems. We will also use some practical examples to illustrate concepts related to text similarity, distance metrics, and document clustering. Also, many of these techniques can be combined with some of the techniques we learned previously and vice versa. For example, concepts of text similarity using distance metrics are also used to build document clusters. You can also use features from topic models for measuring text similarity. Besides this, clustering is often a starting point to get a feel for the possible groups or categories that your data might consist of, or to even visualize these clusters or groups of similar text documents. This can then be plugged in to other systems like supervised classification systems, or you can even combine them both and build weighted classifiers. The possibilities are indeed endless!

In this chapter, we will first cover some important concepts related to distance measures, metrics, and unsupervised learning and brush up on text normalization and feature extraction. Once the basics are covered, our objective will be to understand and analyze term similarity, document similarity, and finally document clustering.

Important Concepts

Our main objectives in this chapter are to understand text similarity and clustering. Before moving on to the actual techniques and algorithms, this section will discuss some important concepts related to information retrieval, document similarity measures, and machine learning. Even though some of these concepts might be familiar to you from the previous chapters, all of them will be useful to us as we gradually journey through this chapter. Without further ado, let's get started.

Information Retrieval (IR)

Information retrieval (IR) is the process of retrieving or fetching relevant sources of information from a corpus or set of entities that hold information based on some demand. For example, it could be a query or search that users enter in a search engine and then get relevant search items pertaining to their query. In fact, search engines are the most popular use-case or application of IR.

The relevancy of documents with information compared to the demand can be measured in several ways. It can include looking for specific keywords from the search text or using some similarity measures to see the similarity rank or score of the documents with respect to the entered query. This makes is quite different from string matching or matching regular expressions because more than often the words in a search string can have different order, context, and semantics in the collection of documents (entities), and these words can even have multiple different resolutions or possibilities based on synonyms, antonyms, and negation modifiers.

Feature Engineering

Feature engineering or *feature extraction* is something which you know quite well by now. Methods like Bag of Words, TF-IDF, and word vectorization models are typically used to represent or model documents in the form of numeric vectors so that applying mathematical or machine learning techniques become much easier. You can use various document representations using these feature-extraction techniques or even map each letter or a word to a corresponding unique numeric identifier.

Similarity Measures

Similarity measures are used frequently in text similarity analysis and clustering. Any similarity or distance measure usually measures the degree of closeness between two entities, which can be any text format like documents, sentences, or even terms. This measure of similarity can be useful in identifying similar entities and distinguishing clearly different entities from each other. Similarity measures are very effective, and sometimes choosing the right measure can make a lot of difference in the performance of your final analytics system. Various scoring or ranking algorithms have also been invented based on these distance measures. Two main factors determine the degree of similarity between entities:

- Inherent properties or features of the entities

- Measure formula and properties

There are several distance measures that measure similarity, and we will be covering several of them in future sections. However, an important thing to remember is that all distance measures of similarity are not distance metrics of similarity. The excellent paper by A. Huang, "Similarity Measures for Text Document Clustering," talks about this in detail. Consider a distance measure d and two entities (say they are documents in our context) x and y. The distance between x and y, which is used to determine the degree of similarity between them, can be represented as $d(x, y)$, but the measure d can be called as a *distance metric of similarity* if and only if it satisfies the following four conditions:

1. The distance measured between any two entities, say x and y, must be always non-negative, that is, $d(x,y) \geq 0$.

2. The distance between two entities should always be zero if and only if they are both identical, that is, $d(x,y) \geq 0 \; iff \; x = y$.

3. This distance measure should always be symmetric, which means that the distance from x to y is always the same as the distance from y to x. Mathematically this is represented as $d(x,y) = d(y,x)$.

4. This distance measure should satisfy the *triangle inequality* property, which can be mathematically represented $d(x, z) \leq d(x, y) + d(y, z)$.

This tells us important criteria and gives us a good framework we can use to check whether a distance measure can be used as a distance metric for measuring similarity. I don't have room here to go into more detail, but you may be interested in knowing that the very popular *KL-divergence* measure, also known as *Kullback-Leibler divergence*, is a distance measure that violates the third property, where this measure is asymmetric, hence it kind of does not make sense to use it as a measure of similarity for text documents—but otherwise, this is extremely useful in differentiating between various distributions and patterns.

Unsupervised Machine Learning Algorithms

Unsupervised machine learning algorithms are the family of ML algorithms that try to discover latent hidden structures and patterns in data from their various attributes and features. Besides this, several unsupervised learning algorithms are also used to reduce the feature space, which is often of a higher dimension to one with a lower dimension. The data on which these algorithms operate is essentially unlabeled data that does not have any pre-determined category or class. We apply these algorithms with the intent of finding patterns and distinguishing features that might help us in grouping various data points into groups or clusters. These algorithms are popularly known as *clustering algorithms*. Even the topic models covered in Chapter 5 belong to the unsupervised learning family of algorithms.

This concludes our discussion on the important concepts and background information necessary for this chapter. We will now move on to a brief coverage of text normalization and feature extraction, where we introduce a few things which are specific to this chapter.

Text Normalization

We will need to normalize our text documents and corpora as usual before we perform any further analyses or NLP. For this we will reuse our normalization module from Chapter 5 but with a few more additions specifically aimed toward this chapter. The complete normalization module is available in the code files for this chapter in the file `normalization.py`, but I will still be highlighting the new additions in our normalization module in this section for your benefit.

To start, we have updated our stopwords list with several new words that have been carefully selected after analyzing many corpora. The following code snippet illustrates:

```
stopword_list = nltk.corpus.stopwords.words('english')
stopword_list = stopword_list + ['mr', 'mrs', 'come', 'go', 'get', 'tell',
'listen', 'one', 'two', 'three', 'four', 'five',
'six', 'seven', 'eight',
'nine', 'zero', 'join', 'find', 'make', 'say', 'ask',
'tell', 'see', 'try', 'back', 'also']
```

You can see the new additions are words that are mostly generic verbs or nouns without a lot of significance. This will be useful to us in feature extraction during text clustering. We also add a new function in our normalization pipeline, which is to only extract text tokens from a body of text for which we use regular expressions, as depicted in the following function:

```
import re

def keep_text_characters(text):
    filtered_tokens = []
    tokens = tokenize_text(text)
    for token in tokens:
        if re.search('[a-zA-Z]', token):
            filtered_tokens.append(token)
    filtered_text = ' '.join(filtered_tokens)
    return filtered_text
```

We add this in our final normalization function along with the other functions that we have reused from previous chapters, including expanding contractions, unescaping HTML, tokenization, removing stopwords, special characters, and lemmatization. The updated normalization function is shown in the following snippet:

```
def normalize_corpus(corpus, lemmatize=True,
                     only_text_chars=False,
                     tokenize=False):

    normalized_corpus = []
    for text in corpus:
        text = html_parser.unescape(text)
        text = expand_contractions(text, CONTRACTION_MAP)
        if lemmatize:
            text = lemmatize_text(text)
        else:
            text = text.lower()
        text = remove_special_characters(text)
        text = remove_stopwords(text)
        if only_text_chars:
            text = keep_text_characters(text)

        if tokenize:
            text = tokenize_text(text)
            normalized_corpus.append(text)
        else:
            normalized_corpus.append(text)

    return normalized_corpus
```

Thus, as you can see, the preceding function is very similar to the one from Chapter 5 with only the addition of keeping text characters using the keep_text_characters() function, which can be executed by setting the only_text_chars parameter to True.

Feature Extraction

We will also be using a feature-extraction function similar to the one used in Chapter 5. The code will be very similar to our previous feature extractor, except we will be adding some new parameters in this chapter. The function can be found in the utils.py file and is also shown in the following snippet:

```
from sklearn.feature_extraction.text import CountVectorizer, TfidfVectorizer

def build_feature_matrix(documents, feature_type='frequency',
                         ngram_range=(1, 1), min_df=0.0, max_df=1.0):

    feature_type = feature_type.lower().strip()

    if feature_type == 'binary':
        vectorizer = CountVectorizer(binary=True, min_df=min_df,
                                     max_df=max_df, ngram_range=ngram_range)
    elif feature_type == 'frequency':
        vectorizer = CountVectorizer(binary=False, min_df=min_df,
                                     max_df=max_df, ngram_range=ngram_range)
    elif feature_type == 'tfidf':
        vectorizer = TfidfVectorizer(min_df=min_df, max_df=max_df,
                                     ngram_range=ngram_range)
    else:
        raise Exception("Wrong feature type entered. Possible values:
'binary', 'frequency',
                        'tfidf'")

    feature_matrix = vectorizer.fit_transform(documents).astype(float)

    return vectorizer, feature_matrix
```

You can see from the function definition that we have capabilities for Bag of Words frequency, occurrences, and also TF-IDF–based features. The new additions in this function include the addition of the min_df, max_df and ngram_range parameters and also accepting them as optional arguments. The ngram_range is useful when we want to add bigrams, trigrams, and so on as additional features. The min_df parameter can be expressed by a threshold value within a range of [0.0, 1.0] and it will ignore terms as features that will have a document frequency strictly lower than the input threshold value. The max_df parameter can also be expressed by a threshold value within a range of [0.0, 1.0] and it will ignore terms as features that will have a document frequency strictly higher than the input threshold value. The intuition behind this would be that these words, if they occur in almost all the documents, tend to have little value that would help us in distinguishing among various types of documents. We will now deep dive into the various techniques for text similarity.

Text Similarity

The main objective of *text similarity* is to analyze and measure how two entities of text are close or far apart from each other. These entities of text can be simple tokens or terms, like words, or whole documents, which may include sentences or paragraphs of text. There are various ways of analyzing text similarity, and we can classify the intent of text similarity broadly into the following two areas:

- *Lexical similarity*: This involves observing the contents of the text documents with regard to syntax, structure, and content and measuring their similarity based on these parameters.

- *Semantic similarity*: This involves trying to find out the semantics, meaning, and context of the documents and then trying to see how close they are to each other. Dependency grammars and entity recognition are handy tools that can help in this.

Note that the most popular area is *lexical similarity*, because the techniques are more straightforward, easy to implement, and you can also cover several parts of semantic similarity using simple models like the Bag of Words. Usually distance metrics will be used to measure similarity scores between text entities, and we will be mainly covering the following two broad areas of text similarity:

- *Term similarity*: Here we will measure similarity between individual tokens or words.

- *Document similarity*: Here we will be measuring similarity between entire text documents.

The idea is to implement and use several distance metrics and see how we can measure and analyze similarity among entities that are just simple words, and then how things change when we measure similarity among documents that are groups of individual words.

Analyzing Term Similarity

We will start with analyzing term similarity—or similarity between individual word tokens, to be more precise. Even though this is not used a lot in practical applications, it can be used as an excellent starting point for understanding text similarity. Of course, several applications and use-cases like autocompleters, spell check, and correctors use some of these techniques to correct misspelled terms. Here we will be taking a couple of words and measuring the similarity between then using different word representations as well as distance metrics. The word representations we will be using are as follows:

- Character vectorization
- Bag of Characters vectorization

For character vectorization, it is an extremely simple process of just mapping each character of the term to a corresponding unique number. We can do that using the function depicted in the following snippet:

```python
import numpy as np

def vectorize_terms(terms):
    terms = [term.lower() for term in terms]
    terms = [np.array(list(term)) for term in terms]
    terms = [np.array([ord(char) for char in term])
                for term in terms]
    return terms
```

The function takes input a list of words or terms and returns the corresponding character vectors for the words. Bag of Characters vectorization is very similar to the Bag of Words model except here we compute the frequency of each character in the word. Sequence or word orders are not taken into account. The following function helps in computing this:

```python
from scipy.stats import itemfreq

def boc_term_vectors(word_list):
    word_list = [word.lower() for word in word_list]
    unique_chars = np.unique(
                        np.hstack([list(word)
                        for word in word_list]))
    word_list_term_counts = [{char: count for char, count in
itemfreq(list(word))}
                            for word in word_list]

    boc_vectors = [np.array([int(word_term_counts.get(char, 0))
                        for char in unique_chars])
                    for word_term_counts in word_list_term_counts]
    return list(unique_chars), boc_vectors
```

In that function, we take in a list of words or terms and then extract the unique characters from all the words. This becomes our feature list, just like we do in Bag of Words, where instead of characters, unique words are our features. Once we have this list of unique_chars, we get the count for each of the characters in each word and build our Bag of Characters vectors.

We can now see our previous functions in action in the following snippet. We will be using a total of four example terms and computing the similarity among them later on:

```python
root = 'Believe'
term1 = 'beleive'
term2 = 'bargain'
term3 = 'Elephant'
```

```
terms = [root, term1, term2, term3]

# Character vectorization
vec_root, vec_term1, vec_term2, vec_term3 = vectorize_terms(terms)
# show vector representations
In [103]: print '''
     ...: root: {}
     ...: term1: {}
     ...: term2: {}
     ...: term3: {}
     ...: '''.format(vec_root, vec_term1, vec_term2, vec_term3)
root: [ 98 101 108 105 101 118 101]
term1: [ 98 101 108 101 105 118 101]
term2: [ 98  97 114 103  97 105 110]
term3: [101 108 101 112 104  97 110 116]

# Bag of characters vectorization
features, (boc_root, boc_term1, boc_term2, boc_term3) = boc_term_
vectors(terms)
# show features and vector representations
In [105]: print 'Features:', features
     ...: print '''
     ...: root: {}
     ...: term1: {}
     ...: term2: {}
     ...: term3: {}
     ...: '''.format(boc_root, boc_term1, boc_term2, boc_term3)
Features: ['a', 'b', 'e', 'g', 'h', 'i', 'l', 'n', 'p', 'r', 't', 'v']

root: [0 1 3 0 0 1 1 0 0 0 0 1]
term1: [0 1 3 0 0 1 1 0 0 0 0 1]
term2: [2 1 0 1 0 1 0 1 0 1 0 0]
term3: [1 0 2 0 1 0 1 1 1 0 1 0]
```

Thus you can see how we can easily transform text terms into numeric vector representations. We will now be using several distance metrics to compute similarity between the root word and the other three words mentioned in the preceding snippet. There are a lot of distance metrics out there that you can use to compute and measure similarities. We will be covering the following five metrics in this section:

- Hamming distance

- Manhattan distance

- Euclidean distance

- Levenshtein edit distance

- Cosine distance and similarity

We will be looking at the concepts for each distance metric and using the power of numpy arrays to implement the necessary computations and mathematical formulae. Once we do that, we will put them in action by measuring the similarity of our example terms. First, though, we will set up some necessary variables storing the root term, the other terms with which its similarity will be measures, and their various vector representations using the following snippet:

```
root_term = root
root_vector = vec_root
root_boc_vector = boc_root

terms = [term1, term2, term3]
vector_terms = [vec_term1, vec_term2, vec_term3]
boc_vector_terms = [boc_term1, boc_term2, boc_term3]
```

We are now ready to start computing similarity metrics and will be using the preceding terms and their vector representations to measure similarities.

Hamming Distance

The *Hamming distance* is a very popular distance metric used frequently in information theory and communication systems. It is distance measured between two strings under the assumption that they are of equal length. Formally, it is defined as the number of positions that have different characters or symbols between two strings of equal length. Considering two terms u and v of length n, we can mathematically denote Hamming distance as

$$hd(u,v) = \sum_{i=1}^{n}(u_i \neq v_i)$$

and you can also normalize it if you want by dividing the number of mismatches by the total length of the terms to give the normalized hamming distance, which is represented as

$$norm\_hd(u,v) = \frac{\sum_{i=1}^{n}(u_i \neq v_i)}{n}$$

whereas you already know n denotes the length of the terms.

The following function computes the Hamming distance between two terms and also has the capability to compute the normalized distance:

```
def hamming_distance(u, v, norm=False):
    if u.shape != v.shape:
        raise ValueError('The vectors must have equal lengths.')
    return (u != v).sum() if not norm else (u != v).mean()
```

We will now measure the Hamming distance between our root term and the other terms using the following code snippet:

```
# compute Hamming distance
In [115]: for term, vector_term in zip(terms, vector_terms):
    ...:        print 'Hamming distance between root: {} and term: {} is {}'.
format(root_term,
    ...:                                    term, hamming_distance(root_vector, vector_
term, norm=False))

Hamming distance between root: Believe and term: believe is 2
Hamming distance between root: Believe and term: bargain is 6
Traceback (most recent call last):
  File "<ipython-input-115-3391bd2c4b7e>", line 4, in <module>
    hamming_distance(root_vector, vector_term, norm=False))
ValueError: The vectors must have equal lengths.

# compute normalized Hamming distance
In [117]: for term, vector_term in zip(terms, vector_terms):
    ...:        print 'Normalized Hamming distance between root: {} and term:
{} is
    ...:                                            {}'.format(root_term,
                                                    term,
    ...:                 round(hamming_distance(root_vector, vector_term,
                         norm=True), 2))

Normalized Hamming distance between root: Believe and term: believe is 0.29
Normalized Hamming distance between root: Believe and term: bargain is 0.86
Traceback (most recent call last):
  File "<ipython-input-117-7dfc67d08c3f>", line 4, in <module>
    round(hamming_distance(root_vector, vector_term, norm=True), 2))
ValueError: The vectors must have equal lengths
```

You can see from the preceding output that terms 'Believe' and 'believe' ignoring their case are most similar to each other with the Hamming distance of 2 or 0.29, compared to the term 'bargain' giving scores of 6 or 0.86 (here, the smaller the score, the more similar are the terms). The term 'Elephant' throws an exception because the length of that term (term3) is 8 compared to length 7 of the root term 'Believe', hence Hamming distance can't be computed because the base assumption of strings being of equal length is violated.

Manhattan Distance

The *Manhattan distance* metric is similar to the Hamming distance conceptually, where instead of counting the number of mismatches, we subtract the difference between each pair of characters at each position of the two strings. Formally, Manhattan distance is also known as *city block distance, L1 norm, taxicab metric* and is defined as the distance between two points in a grid based on strictly horizontal or vertical paths instead of the diagonal distance conventionally calculated by the Euclidean distance metric. Mathematically it can be denoted as

$$md(u,v) = \|u - v\|_1 = \sum_{i=1}^{n} |u_i - v_i|$$

where u and v are the two terms of length n. The same assumption of the two terms having equal length from Hamming distance holds good here. We can also compute the normalized Manhattan distance by dividing the sum of the absolute differences by the term length. This can be denoted by

$$norm\_md(u,v) = \frac{\|u - v\|_1}{n} = \frac{\sum_{i=1}^{n} |u_i - v_i|}{n}$$

where n is the length of each of the terms u and v. The following function helps us in implementing Manhattan distance with the capability to also compute the normalized Manhattan distance:

```
def manhattan_distance(u, v, norm=False):
    if u.shape != v.shape:
        raise ValueError('The vectors must have equal lengths.')
    return abs(u - v).sum() if not norm else abs(u - v).mean()
```

We will now compute the Manhattan distance between our root term and the other terms using the previous function, as shown in the following code snippet:

```
# compute Manhattan distance
In [120]: for term, vector_term in zip(terms, vector_terms):
     ...:     print 'Manhattan distance between root: {} and term: {} is
              {}'.format(root_term,
     ...:                 term, manhattan_distance(root_vector,
                          vector_term, norm=False))

Manhattan distance between root: Believe and term: believe is 8
Manhattan distance between root: Believe and term: bargain is 38
Traceback (most recent call last):
  File "<ipython-input-120-b228f24ad6a2>", line 4, in <module>
    manhattan_distance(root_vector, vector_term, norm=False))
ValueError: The vectors must have equal lengths.

# compute normalized Manhattan distance
In [122]: for term, vector_term in zip(terms, vector_terms):
     ...:     print 'Normalized Manhattan distance between root: {} and
              term: {} is {}'.format(root_term,
```

```
    ...:                        term,
    ...:                        round(manhattan_distance(root_vector, vector_term,
                               norm=True),2))
    ...:
    ...:
Normalized Manhattan distance between root: Believe and term: believe is 1.14
Normalized Manhattan distance between root: Believe and term: bargain is 5.43
Traceback (most recent call last):
  File "<ipython-input-122-d13a48d56a22>", line 4, in <module>
    round(manhattan_distance(root_vector, vector_term, norm=True),2))
ValueError: The vectors must have equal lengths.
```

From those results you can see that as expected, the distance between 'Believe' and 'believe' ignoring their case is most similar to each other, with a score of 8 or 1.14, as compared to 'bargain', which gives a score of 38 or 5.43 (here the smaller the score, the more similar the words). The term 'Elephant' yields an error because it has a different length compared to the base term just as we noticed earlier when computing Hamming distances.

Euclidean Distance

We briefly mentioned the Euclidean distance when comparing it with the Manhattan distance in the earlier section. Formally, the *Euclidean distance* is also known as the *Euclidean norm*, *L2 norm*, or *L2 distance* and is defined as the shortest straight-line distance between two points. Mathematically this can be denoted as

$$ed(u,v) = \|u - v\|_2 = \sqrt{\sum_{i=1}^{n}(u_i - v_i)^2}$$

where the two points u and v are vectorized text terms in our scenario, each having length n. The following function helps us in computing the Euclidean distance between two terms:

```
def euclidean_distance(u, v):
    if u.shape != v.shape:
        raise ValueError('The vectors must have equal lengths.')
    distance = np.sqrt(np.sum(np.square(u - v)))
    return distance
```

We can now compare the Euclidean distance among our terms by using the preceding function as depicted in the following code snippet:

```
# compute Euclidean distance
In [132]: for term, vector_term in zip(terms, vector_terms):
    ...:     print 'Euclidean distance between root: {} and term: {} is
{}'.format(root_term,
    ...:                        term, round(euclidean_distance(root_
                               vector, vector_term),2))
```

277

```
Euclidean distance between root: Believe and term: believe is 5.66
Euclidean distance between root: Believe and term: bargain is 17.94
Traceback (most recent call last):
  File "<ipython-input-132-90a4dbe8ce60>", line 4, in <module>
    round(euclidean_distance(root_vector, vector_term),2))
ValueError: The vectors must have equal lengths.
```

From the preceding outputs you can see that the terms 'Believe' and 'believe' are the most similar with a score of 5.66 compared to 'bargain' giving us a score of 17.94, and 'Elephant' throws a ValueError because the base assumption that strings being compared should have equal lengths holds good for this distance metric also.

So far, all the distance metrics we have used work on strings or terms of the same length and fail when they are not of equal length. So how do we deal with this problem? We will now look at a couple of distance metrics that work even with strings of unequal length to measure similarity.

Levenshtein Edit Distance

The *Levenshtein edit distance*, often known as just Levenshtein distance, belongs to the family of edit distance–based metrics and is used to measure the distance between two sequence of strings based on their differences—similar to the concept behind Hamming distance. The Levenshtein edit distance between two terms can be defined as the minimum number of edits needed in the form of additions, deletions, or substitutions to change or convert one term to the other. These substitutions are character-based substitutions, where a single character can be edited in a single operation. Also, as mentioned before, the length of the two terms need not be equal here. Mathematically, we can represent the Levenshtein edit distance between two terms as $ld_{u,v}(|u|, |v|)$ such that u and v are our two terms where $|u|$ and $|v|$ are their lengths. This distance can be represented by the following formula

$$ld_{u,v}(i,j) = \begin{cases} max(i,j) & if \ min(i,j)=0 \\ min \begin{cases} ld_{u,v}(i-1,j)+1 \\ ld_{u,v}(i,j-1)+1 \\ ld_{u,v}(i-1,j-1)+C_{u_i \neq v_j} \end{cases} & otherwise \end{cases}$$

where i and j are basically indices for the terms u and v. The third equation in the minimum above has a cost function denoted by $C_{u_i \neq v_j}$ such that it has the following conditions

$$C_{u_i \neq v_j} = \begin{cases} 1 & if \ u_i \neq v_j \\ 0 & if \ u_i = v_j \end{cases}$$

and this denotes the indicator function, which depicts the cost associated with two characters being matched for the two terms (the equation represents the match or mismatch operation). The first equation in the previous minimum stands for the deletion operation, and the second equation represents the insertion operation. The function $ld_{u,v}(i,j)$ thus covers all the three operations of insertion, deletion, and addition as we mentioned earlier and it denotes the Levenshtein distance as measured between the first i characters for the term u and the first j characters of the term v. There are also several interesting boundary conditions with regard to the Levenshtein edit distance:

- The minimum value that the edit distance between two terms can take is the difference in length of the two terms.

- The maximum value of the edit distance between two terms can be the length of the term that is larger.

- If the two terms are equal, the edit distance is zero.

- Hamming distance between two terms is an upper bound for Levenshtein edit distance if and only if the two terms have equal length.

- This being a distance metric also satisfies the triangle inequality property, discussed earlier when we talked about distance metrics.

There are various ways of implementing Levenshtein distance computations for terms. Here we will start with an example of two of our terms. Considering the root term 'believe' and another term 'beleive' (we ignore case in our computations). The edit distance would be 2 because we would need the following two operations:

- 'beleive' → 'beliive' (substitution of e to i)

- 'beliive' → 'believe' (substitution of i to e)

To implement this, we build a matrix that will basically compute the Levenshtein distance between all the characters of both terms by comparing each character of the first term with the characters of the second term. For computation, we follow a dynamic programming approach to get the edit distance between the two terms based on the last computed value. For the given two terms, the Levenshtein edit distance matrix our algorithm should generate is shown in Figure 6-1.

	b	e	l	i	e	v	e
b	0	1	2	3	4	5	6
e	1	0	1	2	3	4	5
l	2	1	0	1	2	3	4
e	3	2	1	1	1	2	3
i	4	3	2	1	2	2	3
v	5	4	3	2	2	2	3
e	6	5	4	3	2	3	2

Figure 6-1. *Levenshtein edit distance matrix between terms*

You can see in Figure 6-1 that the edit distances are computed for each pair of characters in the terms, as mentioned earlier, and the final edit distance value highlighted in the figure gives us the actual edit distance between the two terms. This algorithm is also known as the Wagner-Fischer algorithm and is available in the paper by R. Wagner and M. Fischer titled "The String-to-String Correction Problem," which you can refer to if you are more interested in the details. The pseudocode for the same is shown in the snippet below, courtesy of the paper:

```
function levenshtein_distance(char u[1..m], char v[1..n]):
# for all i and j, d[i,j] will hold the Levenshtein distance between the
first i characters of
# u and the first j characters of v, note that d has (m+1)*(n+1) values
int d[0..m, 0..n]

# set each element in d to zero
d[0..m, 0..n] := 0

# source prefixes can be transformed into empty string by dropping all
characters
for i from 1 to m:
   d[i, 0] := i

# target prefixes can be reached from empty source prefix by inserting every
character
for j from 1 to n:
    d[0, j] := j

# build the edit distance matrix
for j from 1 to n:
    for i from 1 to m:
        if s[i] = t[j]:
            substitutionCost := 0
        else:
            substitutionCost := 1
            d[i, j] := minimum(d[i-1, j] + 1,              # deletion
                             d[i, j-1] + 1,                 # insertion
                             d[i-1, j-1] + substitutionCost)  # substitution

# the final value of the matrix is the edit distance between the terms
return d[m, n]
```

You can see from the preceding function definition pseudocode how we have captured the necessary formulae we used earlier to define Levenshtein edit distance.

We will now implement this pseudocode in Python. The preceding algorithm uses $O(mn)$ space because it stores the entire distance matrix, but it is enough to just store the previous and current row of distances to get to the final result. We will do the same in our code but we will also store the results in a matrix so that we can visualize it in the end. The following function implements Levenshtein edit distance as mentioned:

```python
import copy
import pandas as pd

def levenshtein_edit_distance(u, v):
    # convert to lower case
    u = u.lower()
    v = v.lower()
    # base cases
    if u == v: return 0
    elif len(u) == 0: return len(v)
    elif len(v) == 0: return len(u)
    # initialize edit distance matrix
    edit_matrix = []
    # initialize two distance matrices
    du = [0] * (len(v) + 1)
    dv = [0] * (len(v) + 1)
    # du: the previous row of edit distances
    for i in range(len(du)):
        du[i] = i
    # dv : the current row of edit distances
    for i in range(len(u)):
        dv[0] = i + 1
        # compute cost as per algorithm
        for j in range(len(v)):
            cost = 0 if u[i] == v[j] else 1
            dv[j + 1] = min(dv[j] + 1, du[j + 1] + 1, du[j] + cost)
        # assign dv to du for next iteration
        for j in range(len(du)):
            du[j] = dv[j]
        # copy dv to the edit matrix
        edit_matrix.append(copy.copy(dv))
    # compute the final edit distance and edit matrix
    distance = dv[len(v)]
    edit_matrix = np.array(edit_matrix)
    edit_matrix = edit_matrix.T
    edit_matrix = edit_matrix[1:,]
    edit_matrix = pd.DataFrame(data=edit_matrix,
                               index=list(v),
                               columns=list(u))
    return distance, edit_matrix
```

That function returns both the final Levenshtein edit distance and the complete edit matrix between the two terms u and v, which are taken as input. Remember, we need to pass the terms directly in their raw string format and not their vector representations. Also, we do not consider case of strings here and convert them to lowercase.

The following snippet computes the Levenshtein edit distance between our example terms using the preceding function:

```
In [223]: for term in terms:
     ...:     edit_d, edit_m = levenshtein_edit_distance(root_term, term)
     ...:     print 'Computing distance between root: {} and term: {}'.
             format(root_term,
     ...:                                                      term)
     ...:     print 'Levenshtein edit distance is {}'.format(edit_d)
     ...:     print 'The complete edit distance matrix is depicted below'
     ...:     print edit_m
     ...:     print '-'*30
```

```
Computing distance between root: Believe and term: beleive
Levenshtein edit distance is 2
The complete edit distance matrix is depicted below
   b  e  l  i  e  v  e
b  0  1  2  3  4  5  6
e  1  0  1  2  3  4  5
l  2  1  0  1  2  3  4
e  3  2  1  1  1  2  3
i  4  3  2  1  2  2  3
v  5  4  3  2  2  2  3
e  6  5  4  3  2  3  2
------------------------------
Computing distance between root: Believe and term: bargain
Levenshtein edit distance is 6
The complete edit distance matrix is depicted below
   b  e  l  i  e  v  e
b  0  1  2  3  4  5  6
a  1  1  2  3  4  5  6
r  2  2  2  3  4  5  6
g  3  3  3  3  4  5  6
a  4  4  4  4  4  5  6
i  5  5  5  4  5  5  6
n  6  6  6  5  5  6  6
------------------------------
Computing distance between root: Believe and term: Elephant
Levenshtein edit distance is 7
The complete edit distance matrix is depicted below
   b  e  l  i  e  v  e
e  1  1  2  3  4  5  6
l  2  2  1  2  3  4  5
e  3  2  2  2  2  3  4
p  4  3  3  3  3  3  4
h  5  4  4  4  4  4  4
a  6  5  5  5  5  5  5
n  7  6  6  6  6  6  6
t  8  7  7  7  7  7  7
------------------------------
```

You can see from the preceding outputs that `'Believe'` and `'beleive'` are the closest to each other, with an edit distance of 2 and the distances between `'Believe'`, `'bargain'`, and `'Elephant'` are 6, indicating a total of 6 edit operations needed. The edit distance matrices provide a more detailed insight into how the algorithm computes the distances per iteration.

Cosine Distance and Similarity

The *Cosine distance* is a metric that can be actually derived from the Cosine similarity and vice versa. Considering we have two terms such that they are represented in their vectorized forms, Cosine similarity gives us the measure of the cosine of the angle between them when they are represented as non-zero positive vectors in an inner product space. Thus term vectors having similar orientation will have scores closer to 1 ($\cos 0°$) indicating the vectors are very close to each other in the same direction (near to zero degree angle between them). Term vectors having a similarity score close to 0 ($\cos 90°$) indicate unrelated terms with a near orthogonal angle between then. Term vectors with a similarity score close to –1 ($\cos 180°$) indicate terms that are completely oppositely oriented to each other. Figure 6-2 illustrates this more clearly, where u and v are our term vectors in the vector space.

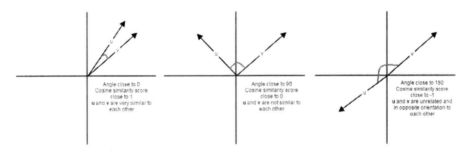

Figure 6-2. *Cosine similarity representations for term vectors*

Thus you can see from the position of the vectors, the plots show more clearly how the vectors are close or far apart from each other, and the cosine of the angle between them gives us the Cosine similarity metric. Now we can formally define Cosine similarity as the dot product of the two term vectors u and v, divided by the product of their L2 norms. Mathematically, we can represent the dot product between two vectors as

$$u \cdot v = \|u\| \; \|v\| \cos(\theta)$$

where θ is the angle between u and v and $\|u\|$ represents the L2 norm for vector u and $\|v\|$ is the L2 norm for vector v. Thus we can derive the Cosine similarity from the above formula as

$$cs(u,v) = \cos(\theta) = \frac{u \cdot v}{\|u\| \, \|v\|} = \frac{\sum\limits_{i=1}^{n} u_i \, v_i}{\sqrt{\sum\limits_{i=1}^{n} u_i^2} \, \sqrt{\sum\limits_{i=1}^{n} v_i^2}}$$

where $cs(u, v)$ is the Cosine similarity score between u and v. Here u_i and v_i are the various features or components of the two vectors, and the total number of these features or components is n. In our case, we will be using the Bag of Characters vectorization to build these term vectors, and n will be the number of unique characters across the terms under analysis. An important thing to note here is that the Cosine similarity score usually ranges from –1 to +1, but if we use the Bag of Characters–based character frequencies for terms or Bag of Words–based word frequencies for documents, the score will range from 0 to 1 because the frequency vectors can never be negative, and hence the angle between the two vectors cannot exceed 90 . The Cosine distance is complimentary to the similarity score can be computed by the formula,

$$cd(u,v) = 1 - cs(u,v) = 1 - \cos(\theta) = 1 - \frac{u \cdot v}{\|u\| \, \|v\|} = 1 - \frac{\sum\limits_{i=1}^{n} u_i \, v_i}{\sqrt{\sum\limits_{i=1}^{n} u_i^2} \, \sqrt{\sum\limits_{i=1}^{n} v_i^2}}$$

where $cd(u, v)$ denotes the Cosine distance between the term vectors u and v. The following function implements computation of Cosine distance based on the preceding formulae:

```
def cosine_distance(u, v):
    distance = 1.0 - (np.dot(u, v) /
                      (np.sqrt(sum(np.square(u))) * np.sqrt(sum(np.
                      square(v))))
                     )
    return distance
```

We will now test the similarity between our example terms using their Bag of Character representations, which we created earlier, available in the boc_root_vector and the boc_vector_terms variables, as depicted in the following code snippet:

```
In [235]: for term, boc_term in zip(terms, boc_vector_terms):
    ...:     print 'Analyzing similarity between root: {} and term: {}'.
format(root_term,
    ...:                                                          term)
    ...:     distance = round(cosine_distance(root_boc_vector, boc_term),2)
    ...:     similarity = 1 - distance
    ...:     print 'Cosine distance  is {}'.format(distance)
    ...:     print 'Cosine similarity  is {}'.format(similarity)
    ...:     print '-'*40
```

```
Analyzing similarity between root: Believe and term: believe
Cosine distance  is -0.0
Cosine similarity  is 1.0
----------------------------------------
Analyzing similarity between root: Believe and term: bargain
Cosine distance  is 0.82
Cosine similarity  is 0.18
----------------------------------------
Analyzing similarity between root: Believe and term: Elephant
Cosine distance  is 0.39
Cosine similarity  is 0.61
----------------------------------------
```

These vector representations do not take order of characters into account, hence the similarity between the terms "Believe" and "believe" is 1.0 or a perfect 100 percent because it contains the same characters with the same frequency. You can see how this can be used in combination with a semantic dictionary like WordNet to provide correct spelling suggestions by suggesting semantically and syntactically correct words from a vocabulary when users type a misspelled word, by measuring the similarity between the words. You can even try our different features here instead of single character frequencies, like taking two characters at a time and computing their frequencies to build the term vectors. This takes into account some of the sequences that characters maintain in various terms. Try out different possibilities and compare the results! This distance measure works very well when measuring similarity between large documents or sentences, and we will see that in the next section when we discuss document similarity.

Analyzing Document Similarity

We analyzed similarity between terms using various similarity and distance metrics in the previous sections. We also saw how vectorization was useful so that mathematical computations become much easier, especially when computing distances between vectors. In this section, we will try to analyze similarities between documents. By now, you must already know that a document is defined as a body of text which can be comprised of sentences or paragraphs of text. For analyzing document similarity, we will be using our utils module to extract features from document using the build_feature_matrix() function. We will vectorize documents using their TF-IDFs similarly to what we did previously when we classified text documents or summarized entire documents. Once we have the vector representations of the various documents, we will compute similarity between the documents using several distance or similarity metrics. The metrics we will cover in this section are as follows:

- Cosine similarity

- Hellinger-Bhattacharya distance

- Okapi BM25 ranking

As usual, we will cover the concepts behind each metric, look at its mathematical representations and definitions, and then implement it using Python. We will also test our metrics on a toy corpus here with nine documents and a separate corpus with three documents, which will be our *query* documents. For each of these three documents, we will try to find out the most similar documents from the corpus of nine documents, which will act as our *index*. Consider this to be a mini-simulation of what happens in a search engine when you search with a sentence and the most relevant results are returned to you from its index of web pages. In our case, the queries are in the form of three documents, and relevant documents for each of these three will be returned from the index of nine documents based on similarity metrics.

We will start with loading the necessary dependencies and the corpus of documents on which we will be testing our various metrics, as shown in the following code snippet:

```
from normalization import normalize_corpus
from utils import build_feature_matrix
import numpy as np

# load the toy corpus index
toy_corpus = ['The sky is blue',
'The sky is blue and beautiful',
'Look at the bright blue sky!',
'Python is a great Programming language',
'Python and Java are popular Programming languages',
'Among Programming languages, both Python and Java are the most used in
Analytics',
'The fox is quicker than the lazy dog',
'The dog is smarter than the fox',
'The dog, fox and cat are good friends']

# load the docs for which we will be measuring similarities
query_docs = ['The fox is definitely smarter than the dog',
              'Java is a static typed programming language unlike Python',
              'I love to relax under the beautiful blue sky!']
```

From that snippet you can see that we have various documents in our corpus index that talk about the *sky, programming languages,* and *animals.* We also have three query documents for which we want to get the most relevant documents from the toy_corpus index, based on similarity computations. Before we start looking at metrics, we will normalize the documents and vectorize them by extracting their TF-IDF features, as shown in the following snippet:

```
# normalize and extract features from the toy corpus
norm_corpus = normalize_corpus(toy_corpus, lemmatize=True)
tfidf_vectorizer, tfidf_features = build_feature_matrix(norm_corpus,
                                            feature_
                                            type='tfidf',
                                            ngram_range=(1, 1),
                                            min_df=0.0, max_
                                            df=1.0)
```

```
# normalize and extract features from the query corpus
norm_query_docs = normalize_corpus(query_docs, lemmatize=True)
query_docs_tfidf = tfidf_vectorizer.transform(norm_query_docs)
```

Now that we have our documents normalized and vectorized with TF-IDF–based vector representations, we will look at how to compute similarity for each of the metrics we specified at the beginning of this section.

Cosine Similarity

We have seen the concepts with regards to computing Cosine similarity and also implemented the same for term similarity. Here, we will reuse the same concepts to compute the Cosine similarity scores for documents instead of terms. The document vectors will be the Bag of Words model–based vectors with TF-IDF values instead of term frequencies. We have also taken only unigrams here, but you can experiment with bigrams and so on as document features during the vectorization process. For each of the three query documents, we will compute its similarity with the nine documents in toy_corpus and return the *n* most similar documents where *n* is a user input parameter.

We will define a function that will take in the vectorized corpus and the document corpus for which we want to compute similarities. We will get the similarity scores using the dot product operation as before and finally we will sort them in reverse order and get the top *n* documents with the highest similarity score. The following function implements this:

```
def compute_cosine_similarity(doc_features, corpus_features,
                              top_n=3):
    # get document vectors
    doc_features = doc_features.toarray()[0]
    corpus_features = corpus_features.toarray()
    # compute similarities
    similarity = np.dot(doc_features,
                        corpus_features.T)
    # get docs with highest similarity scores
    top_docs = similarity.argsort()[::-1][:top_n]
    top_docs_with_score = [(index, round(similarity[index], 3))
                           for index in top_docs]
    return top_docs_with_score
```

In that function, corpus_features are the vectorized documents belonging to the toy_corpus index from which we want to retrieve similar documents. These documents will be retrieved on the basis of their similarity score with doc_features, which basically represents the vectorized document belonging to each of the query_docs, as shown in the following snippet:

```
# get Cosine similarity results for our example documents
In [243]: print 'Document Similarity Analysis using Cosine Similarity'
     ...: print '='*60
     ...: for index, doc in enumerate(query_docs):
```

```
    ...:
    ...:        doc_tfidf = query_docs_tfidf[index]
    ...:        top_similar_docs = compute_cosine_similarity(doc_tfidf,
    ...:                                          tfidf_features,
    ...:                                          top_n=2)
    ...:        print 'Document',index+1 ,':', doc
    ...:        print 'Top', len(top_similar_docs), 'similar docs:'
    ...:        print '-'*40
    ...:        for doc_index, sim_score in top_similar_docs:
    ...:            print 'Doc num: {} Similarity Score: {}\nDoc: {}'.
               format(doc_index+1,
    ...:
sim_score, toy_corpus[doc_index])
    ...:            print '-'*40
    ...:        print
```

```
Document Similarity Analysis using Cosine Similarity
============================================================
Document 1 : The fox is definitely smarter than the dog
Top 2 similar docs:
----------------------------------------
Doc num: 8 Similarity Score: 1.0
Doc: The dog is smarter than the fox
----------------------------------------
Doc num: 7 Similarity Score: 0.426
Doc: The fox is quicker than the lazy dog
----------------------------------------


Document 2 : Java is a static typed programming language unlike Python
Top 2 similar docs:
----------------------------------------
Doc num: 5 Similarity Score: 0.837
Doc: Python and Java are popular Programming languages
----------------------------------------
Doc num: 6 Similarity Score: 0.661
Doc: Among Programming languages, both Python and Java are the most used in
Analytics
----------------------------------------


Document 3 : I love to relax under the beautiful blue sky!
Top 2 similar docs:
----------------------------------------
Doc num: 2 Similarity Score: 1.0
Doc: The sky is blue and beautiful
----------------------------------------
Doc num: 1 Similarity Score: 0.72
Doc: The sky is blue
----------------------------------------
```

The preceding output depicts the top two most relevant documents for each of the query documents based on Cosine similarity scores, and you can see that the outputs are quite what were expected. Documents about *animals* are similar to the document that mentions *the fox* and *the dog*; documents about *Python* and *Java* are most similar to the query document talking about them; and *the beautiful blue sky* is indeed similar to documents that talk about *the sky* being *blue* and *beautiful!*

Also note the Cosine similarity scores in the preceding outputs, where 1.0 indicates perfect similarity, 0.0 indicates no similarity, and any score between them indicates some level of similarity based on how large that score is. For instance, in the last example, the main document vectors are `['sky', 'blue', 'beautiful']` and because they all match with the first document from the toy corpus, we get a 1.0 or 100 percent similarity score, and only `['sky', 'blue']` match from the second most similar document, and we get a 0.72 or 72 percent similarity score. And you should remember our discussion from earlier where I mentioned briefly that Cosine similarity using Bag of Words–based vectors only looks at token weights and does not consider order or sequence of the terms, which is quite desirable in large documents because the same content may be depicted in different ways, and capturing sequences there might lead to loss of information due to unwanted mismatches.

We recommend using scikit-learn's `cosine_similarity()` utility function, which you can find under the `sklearn.metrics.pairwise` module. It uses similar logic as our implementation but is much more optimized and performs well on large corpora of documents. You can also use gensim's `similarities` module or the `cossim()` function directly available in the `gensim.matutils` module.

Hellinger-Bhattacharya Distance

The *Hellinger-Bhattacharya distance* (*HB-distance*) is also called the *Hellinger distance* or the *Bhattacharya distance*. The Bhattacharya distance, originally introduced by A. Bhattacharya, is used to measure the similarity between two discrete or continuous probability distributions. E. Hellinger introduced the Hellinger integral in 1909, which is used in the computation of the Hellinger distance. Overall, the Hellinger-Bhattacharya distance is an f-divergence, which in the theory of probability is defined as a function $D_f(P \| Q)$, which

can be used to measure the difference between P and Q probability distributions. There are many instances of f-divergences, including KL-divergence and HB-distance. Remember that KL-divergence is not a distance metric because it violates the symmetric condition from the four conditions necessary for a distance measure to be a metric.

HB-distance is computable for both continuous and discrete probability distributions. In our case, we will be using the TF-IDF–based vectors as our document distributions. This makes it discrete distributions because we have specific TF-IDF values for specific feature terms, unlike continuous distributions. We can define the Hellinger-Bhattacharya distance mathematically as

$$hbd(u,v) = \frac{1}{\sqrt{2}} \left\| \sqrt{u} - \sqrt{v} \right\|_2$$

where $hbd(u, v)$ denotes the Hellinger-Bhattacharya distance between the document vectors u and v, and it is equal to the Euclidean or L2 norm of the difference of the square root of the vectors divided by the square root of 2. Considering the document vectors u and v to be discrete with n number of features, we can further expand the above formula into

$$hbd(u,v) = \frac{1}{\sqrt{2}} \sqrt{\sum_{i=1}^{n} \left(\sqrt{u_i} - \sqrt{v_i} \right)^2}$$

such that $u = (u_1, u_2, ..., u_n)$ and $v = (v_1, v_2, ..., v_n)$ are the document vectors having length n indicating n features, which are the TF-IDF weights of the various terms in the documents. As with the previous computation of Cosine similarity, we will build our function on the same principles; basically we will accept as input a corpus of document vectors and a single document vector for which we want to get the n most similar documents from the corpus based on their HB-distances. The function implements the preceding concepts in Python in the following snippet:

```python
def compute_hellinger_bhattacharya_distance(doc_features, corpus_features,
                                            top_n=3):
    # get document vectors
    doc_features = doc_features.toarray()[0]
    corpus_features = corpus_features.toarray()
    # compute hb distances
    distance = np.hstack(
                    np.sqrt(0.5 *
                        np.sum(
                            np.square(np.sqrt(doc_features) -
                                    np.sqrt(corpus_features)),
                        axis=1)))
    # get docs with lowest distance scores
    top_docs = distance.argsort()[:top_n]
    top_docs_with_score = [(index, round(distance[index], 3))
                        for index in top_docs]
    return top_docs_with_score
```

From the preceding implementation, you case see that we sort the documents based on their scores in ascending order, unlike Cosine similarity, where 1.0 indicates perfect similarity—since this is a distance metric between distributions, a value of 0 indicates perfect similarity, and higher values indicate some dissimilarity being present. We can now apply this function to our example corpora, compute their HB-distances, and see the results in the following snippet:

```python
# get Hellinger-Bhattacharya distance based similarities for our example
documents
In [246]: print 'Document Similarity Analysis using Hellinger-Bhattacharya
distance'
     ...: print '='*60
     ...: for index, doc in enumerate(query_docs):
```

```
    ...:
    ...:         doc_tfidf = query_docs_tfidf[index]
    ...:         top_similar_docs = compute_hellinger_bhattacharya_
             distance(doc_tfidf,
    ...:                                         tfidf_features,
    ...:                                         top_n=2)
    ...:         print 'Document',index+1 ,':', doc
    ...:         print 'Top', len(top_similar_docs), 'similar docs:'
    ...:         print '-'*40
    ...:         for doc_index, sim_score in top_similar_docs:
    ...:             print 'Doc num: {} Distance Score: {}\nDoc: {}'.
                 format(doc_index+1,
    ...:                                     sim_score, toy_corpus[doc_
                                         index])
    ...:             print '-'*40
    ...:         print
    ...:
    ...:
Document Similarity Analysis using Hellinger-Bhattacharya distance
==================================================================
Document 1 : The fox is definitely smarter than the dog
Top 2 similar docs:
----------------------------------------
Doc num: 8 Distance Score: 0.0
Doc: The dog is smarter than the fox
----------------------------------------
Doc num: 7 Distance Score: 0.96
Doc: The fox is quicker than the lazy dog
----------------------------------------


Document 2 : Java is a static typed programming language unlike Python
Top 2 similar docs:
----------------------------------------
Doc num: 5 Distance Score: 0.53
Doc: Python and Java are popular Programming languages
----------------------------------------
Doc num: 4 Distance Score: 0.766
Doc: Python is a great Programming language
----------------------------------------


Document 3 : I love to relax under the beautiful blue sky!
Top 2 similar docs:
----------------------------------------
Doc num: 2 Distance Score: 0.0
Doc: The sky is blue and beautiful
----------------------------------------
Doc num: 1 Distance Score: 0.602
Doc: The sky is blue
----------------------------------------
```

291

You can see from the preceding outputs that documents with lower HB-distance scores are more similar to the query documents, and the result documents are quite similar to what we obtained using Cosine similarity. Compare the results and try out these functions with larger corpora! I recommend using gensim's `hellinger()` function, available in the `gensim.matutils` module (which uses the same logic as our preceding function) when building large-scale systems for analyzing similarity.

Okapi BM25 Ranking

There are several techniques that are quite popular in information retrieval and search engines, including PageRank and Okapi BM25. The acronym *BM* stands for *best matching*. This technique is also known as BM25, but for the sake of completeness I refer to it as Okapi BM25, because originally although the concepts behind the BM25 function were merely theoretical, the City University in London built the Okapi Information Retrieval system in the 1980s–90s, which implemented this technique to retrieve documents on actual real-world data. This technique can also be called a *framework* or *model* based on probabilistic relevancy and was developed by several people in the 1970s–80s, including computer scientists S. Robertson and K. Jones. There are several functions that rank documents based on different factors, and BM25 is one of them. Its newer variant is BM25F; other variants include BM15 and BM25+.

The Okapi BM25 can be formally defined as a document ranking and retrieval function based on a Bag of Words–based model for retrieving relevant documents based on a user input query. This query can be itself a document containing a sentence or collection of sentences, or it can even be a couple of words. The Okapi BM25 is actually not just a single function but is a framework consisting of a whole collection of scoring functions combined together. Say we have a query document QD such that $QD = (q_1, q_2, \ldots, q_n)$ containing n terms or keywords and we have a corpus document CD in the corpus of documents from which we want to get the most relevant documents to the query document based on similarity scores, just as we have done earlier. Assuming we have these, we can mathematically define the BM25 score between these two documents as

$$bm25(CD, QD) = \sum_{i=1}^{n} idf(q_i) \cdot \frac{f(q_i,\ CD) \cdot (k_1 + 1)}{f(q_i,\ CD) + k_1 \cdot \left(1 - b + b \cdot \dfrac{|CD|}{avgdl}\right)}$$

where the function $bm25(CD, QD)$ computes the BM25 rank or score of the document CD based on the query document QD. The function $idf(q_i)$ gives us the *inverse document frequency* (IDF) of the term q_i in the corpus that contains CD and from which we want to retrieve the relevant documents. If you remember, we computed IDFs in Chapter 4 when we implemented the TF-IDF feature extractor. Just to refresh your memory, it can represented by

$$idf(t) = 1 + log \frac{C}{1 + df(t)}$$

where $idf(t)$ represents the idf for the term t and C represents the count of the total number of documents in our corpus and $df(t)$ represents the frequency of the number of documents in which the term t is present. There are various other methods of implementing IDF, but we will be using this one, and on a side note the end outcome from the different implementations is very similar. The function $f(q_i, CD)$ gives us the frequency of the term q_i in the corpus document CD. The expression $|CD|$ indicates the total length of the document CD which is measured by its number of words, and the term $avgdl$ represents the average document length of the corpus from which we will be retrieving documents. Besides that, you will also observe there are two free parameters, k_1, which is usually in the range of $[1.2, 2.0]$, and b, which is usually taken as 0.75. We will be taking the value of k_1 to be 1.5 in our implementation.

There are several steps we must go through to successfully implement and compute BM25 scores for documents:

1. Build a function to get inverse document frequency (IDF) values for terms in corpus.

2. Build a function for computing BM25 scores for query document and corpus documents.

3. Get Bag of Words–based features for corpus documents and query documents.

4. Compute average length of corpus documents and IDFs of the terms in the corpus documents using function from point 1.

5. Compute BM25 scores, rank relevant documents, and fetch the n most relevant documents for each query document using the function in point 2.

We will start with implementing a function to extract and compute inverse document frequencies of all the terms in a corpus of documents by using its Bag of Words features, which will contain the term frequencies, and then convert them to IDFs using the formula mentioned earlier. The following function implements this:

```
import scipy.sparse as sp

def compute_corpus_term_idfs(corpus_features, norm_corpus):

    dfs = np.diff(sp.csc_matrix(corpus_features, copy=True).indptr)
    dfs = 1 + dfs # to smoothen idf later
    total_docs = 1 + len(norm_corpus)
    idfs = 1.0 + np.log(float(total_docs) / dfs)
    return idfs
```

We will now implement the main function for computing BM25 score for all the documents in our corpus based on the query document and retrieving the top n relevant documents from the corpus based on their BM25 score. The following function implements the BM25 scoring framework:

```
def compute_bm25_similarity(doc_features, corpus_features,
                            corpus_doc_lengths, avg_doc_length,
                            term_idfs, k1=1.5, b=0.75, top_n=3):
    # get corpus bag of words features
    corpus_features = corpus_features.toarray()
    # convert query document features to binary features
    # this is to keep a note of which terms exist per document
    doc_features = doc_features.toarray()[0]
    doc_features[doc_features >= 1] = 1

    # compute the document idf scores for present terms
    doc_idfs = doc_features * term_idfs
    # compute numerator expression in BM25 equation
    numerator_coeff = corpus_features * (k1 + 1)
    numerator = np.multiply(doc_idfs, numerator_coeff)
    # compute denominator expression in BM25 equation
    denominator_coeff =  k1 * (1 - b +
                                (b * (corpus_doc_lengths /
                                       avg_doc_length)))
    denominator_coeff = np.vstack(denominator_coeff)
    denominator = corpus_features + denominator_coeff
    # compute the BM25 score combining the above equations
    bm25_scores = np.sum(np.divide(numerator,
                                    denominator),
                         axis=1)
    # get top n relevant docs with highest BM25 score
    top_docs = bm25_scores.argsort()[::-1][:top_n]
    top_docs_with_score = [(index, round(bm25_scores[index], 3))
                            for index in top_docs]
    return top_docs_with_score
```

The comments in the function are self-explanatory and explain how the BM25 scoring function is implemented. In simple terms, we first compute the numerator expression in the BM25 mathematical equation we specified earlier and then compute the denominator expression. Finally, we divide the numerator by the denominator to get the BM25 scores for all the corpus documents. Then we sort them in descending order and return the top n relevant documents with the highest BM25 score. In the following snippet, we will test our function on our example corpora and see how it performs for each of the query documents:

```
# build bag of words based features first
vectorizer, corpus_features = build_feature_matrix(norm_corpus,
                                                    feature_type='frequency')
query_docs_features = vectorizer.transform(norm_query_docs)

# get average document length of the corpus (avgdl)
doc_lengths = [len(doc.split()) for doc in norm_corpus]
avg_dl = np.average(doc_lengths)
```

```
# Get the corpus term idfs
corpus_term_idfs = compute_corpus_term_idfs(corpus_features,
                                            norm_corpus)


# analyze document similarity using BM25 framework
In [253]: print 'Document Similarity Analysis using BM25'
     ...: print '='*60
     ...: for index, doc in enumerate(query_docs):
     ...:
     ...:     doc_features = query_docs_features[index]
     ...:     top_similar_docs = compute_bm25_similarity(doc_features,
     ...:                                                corpus_features,
     ...:                                                doc_lengths,
     ...:                                                avg_dl,
     ...:                                                corpus_term_idfs,
     ...:                                                k1=1.5, b=0.75,
     ...:                                                top_n=2)
     ...:     print 'Document',index+1 ,':', doc
     ...:     print 'Top', len(top_similar_docs), 'similar docs:'
     ...:     print '-'*40
     ...:     for doc_index, sim_score in top_similar_docs:
     ...:         print 'Doc num: {} BM25 Score: {}\nDoc: {}'.format(doc_
                   index+1,
     ...:                                             sim_score, toy_corpus[doc_
                                                      index])
     ...:         print '-'*40
     ...:     print
```

```
Document Similarity Analysis using BM25
============================================================
Document 1 : The fox is definitely smarter than the dog
Top 2 similar docs:
------------------------------------------
Doc num: 8 BM25 Score: 7.334
Doc: The dog is smarter than the fox
------------------------------------------
Doc num: 7 BM25 Score: 3.88
Doc: The fox is quicker than the lazy dog
------------------------------------------


Document 2 : Java is a static typed programming language unlike Python
Top 2 similar docs:
------------------------------------------
Doc num: 5 BM25 Score: 7.248
Doc: Python and Java are popular Programming languages
------------------------------------------
Doc num: 6 BM25 Score: 6.042
```

```
Doc: Among Programming languages, both Python and Java are the most used in
Analytics
----------------------------------------


Document 3 : I love to relax under the beautiful blue sky!
Top 2 similar docs:
----------------------------------------
Doc num: 2 BM25 Score: 7.334
Doc: The sky is blue and beautiful
----------------------------------------
Doc num: 1 BM25 Score: 4.984
Doc: The sky is blue
----------------------------------------
```

You can now see how for each query document, we get expected and relevant documents that have similar concepts just like the query documents. You can see that the results are quite similar to the previous methods—because, of course, they are all similarity and ranking metrics and are expected to return similar results. Notice the BM25 scores of the relevant documents. The higher the score, the more relevant is the document. Unfortunately, I was not able to find any production-ready scalable implementation of the BM25 ranking framework in `nltk` or `scikit-learn`. However, gensim seems to have a `bm25` module under the `gensim.summarization` package and if you are interested you can give it a try. But the core of the algorithm is based on what we implemented, and this should work pretty well on its own!

Try loading a bigger corpus of documents and test out these functions on some sample query strings and documents. In fact, information retrieval frameworks like Solr and Elasticsearch are built on top of Lucene, which use these types of ranking algorithms to return relevant documents from an index of stored documents—and you can build your own search engine using them! Interested readers can check out **www.elastic.co/blog/found-bm-vs-lucene-default-similarity** by elastic.co, the company behind the popular Elasticsearch product, which tells that the performance of BM25 is much better than the default similarity ranking implementation of Lucene.

Document Clustering

Document clustering or *cluster analysis* is an interesting area in NLP and text analytics that applies unsupervised ML concepts and techniques. The main premise of document clustering is similar to that of document categorization, where you start with a whole corpus of documents and are tasked with segregating them into various groups based on some distinctive properties, attributes, and features of the documents. Document classification needs pre-labeled training data to build a model and then categorize documents. Document clustering uses unsupervised ML algorithms to group the documents into various clusters. The properties of these clusters are such that documents inside one cluster are more similar and related to each other compared to documents belonging to other clusters. Figure 6-3, courtesy of `scikit-learn`, visualizes an example of clustering data points into three clusters based on its features.

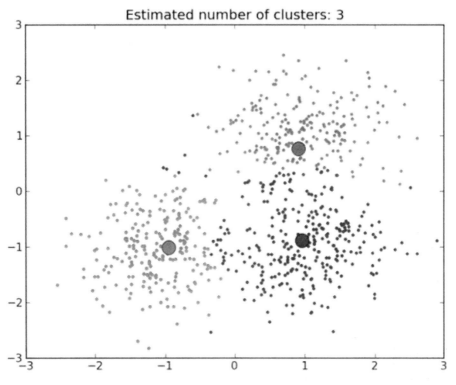

Figure 6-3. *Sample cluster analysis results (courtesy: scikit-learn)*

The cluster analysis in Figure 6-3 depicts three clusters among the data points, which are visualized using different colors. An important thing to remember here is that clustering is an unsupervised learning technique, and from Figure 6-3 it is pretty clear that there will always be some overlap among the clusters because there is no such definition of a perfect cluster. All the techniques are based on math, heuristics, and some inherent attributes toward generating clusters, and they are never a 100 percent perfect. Hence, there are several techniques or methods for finding clusters. Some popular clustering algorithms are briefly described as follows:

- *Hierarchical clustering models*: These clustering models are also known as *connectivity-based clustering methods* and are based on the concept that similar objects will be closer to related objects in the vector space than unrelated objects, which will be farther away from them. Clusters are formed by connecting objects based on their distance and they can be visualized using a *dendrogram*. The output of these models is a complete, exhaustive hierarchy of clusters. They are mainly subdivided into agglomerative and divisive clustering models.

- *Centroid-based clustering models*: These models build clusters in such a way that each cluster has a central representative member that represents each cluster and has the features that distinguish that particular cluster from the rest. There are various algorithms in this, like k-means, k-medoids, and so on, where we need to set the number of clusters 'k' in advance, and distance metrics like squares of distances from each data point to the centroid need to be minimized. The disadvantage of these models is that you need to specify the 'k' number of clusters in advance, which may lead to local minima, and you may not get a true clustered representation of your data.

- *Distribution-based clustering models*: These models make use of concepts from probability distributions when clustering data points. The idea is that objects having similar distributions can be clustered into the same group or cluster. *Gaussian mixture models* (GMM) use algorithms like the Expectation-Maximization algorithm for building these clusters. Feature and attribute correlations and dependencies can also be captured using these models, but it is prone to overfitting.

- *Density-based clustering models*: These clustering models generate clusters from data points that are grouped together at areas of high density compared to the rest of the data points, which may occur randomly across the vector space in sparsely populated areas. These sparse areas are treated as noise and are used as border points to separate clusters. Two popular algorithms in this area include DBSCAN and OPTICS.

Several other clustering models have been recently introduced, including algorithms like BIRCH and CLARANS. Entire books and journals have been written just for clustering alone—it is a very interesting topic offering a lot of value. Covering each and every method would be impossible for us in the current scope, so we will cover a total of three different clustering algorithms, illustrating them with real-world data for better understanding:

- K-means clustering

- Affinity propagation

- Ward's agglomerative hierarchical clustering

For each algorithm, we will be covering its theoretical concepts as we have done previously with other methods. We will also illustrate how each method works by applying each clustering algorithm on some real-world data pertaining to movies and their synopses. We will also look at detailed cluster statistics and focus on visualizing the clusters using tried-and-tested methods, because it is often difficult to visualize results from clustering, and practitioners often face challenges in this area.

Clustering Greatest Movies of All Time

We will be clustering a total of 100 different popular movies based on their IMDb synopses as our raw data. IMDb, also known as the Internet Movie Database (www.imdb.com), is an online database that hosts extensive detailed information about movies, video games, and television shows. It also aggregates reviews and synopses for movies and shows and has several curated lists. The list we are interested in is available at www.imdb.com/list/ls055592025/, titled Top 100 Greatest Movies of All Time (The Ultimate List). We will be clustering these movies into groups using the IMDb synopsis and description of each movie.

Before we begin our analysis, I would like to thank Brandon Rose for helping me out with getting this data, which he personally retrieved and curated, and also for giving me some excellent pointers on visualizing clusters. He has done some detailed clustering analysis with this data himself. If you are interested, you can get the raw data and also see his document clustering analysis in his repository at https://github.com/brandomr/ document_cluster, which is also described in further detail in his personal blog, which is dedicated to analytics, at http://brandonrose.org.

We have downloaded data pertaining to the top 100 movie titles and their synopses from IMDb from the repository mentioned earlier. We parsed and cleaned it up and also added the synopses for a few movies that were missing from the original data. We added these synopses and movie descriptions from Wikipedia. Once parsed, we stored them in a data frame and saved it as a .csv file called movie_data.csv, which you can find in the code files for this chapter. We will be loading and using the data from this file in our clustering analysis, starting with loading and looking at the contents of our movie data points in the following snippet:

```
import pandas as pd
import numpy as np

# load movie data
movie_data = pd.read_csv('movie_data.csv')

# view movie data
In [256]: print movie_data.head()

                     Title                                   Synopsis
0              The Godfather  In late summer 1945, guests are gathered...
1  The Shawshank Redemption  In 1947, Andy Dufresne (Tim Robbins),...
2           Schindler's List  The relocation of Polish Jews from...
3                Raging Bull  The film opens in 1964, where an older...
4                 Casablanca  In the early years of World War II...

# print sample movie and its synopsis
In [268]: print 'Movie:', movie_titles[0]
     ...: print 'Movie Synopsis:', movie_synopses[0][:1000]
     ...:
Movie: The Godfather
```

Movie Synopsis: In late summer 1945, guests are gathered for the wedding reception of Don Vito Corleone's daughter Connie (Talia Shire) and Carlo Rizzi (Gianni Russo). Vito (Marlon Brando), the head of the Corleone Mafia family, is known to friends and associates as "Godfather." He and Tom Hagen (Robert Duvall), the Corleone family lawyer, are hearing requests for favors because, according to Italian tradition, "no Sicilian can refuse a request on his daughter's wedding day." One of the men who asks the Don for a favor is Amerigo Bonasera, a successful mortician and acquaintance of the Don, whose daughter was brutally beaten by two young men because she refused their advances; the men received minimal punishment. The Don is disappointed in Bonasera, who'd avoided most contact with the Don due to Corleone's nefarious business dealings. The Don's wife is godmother to Bonasera's shamed daughter, a relationship the Don uses to extract new loyalty from the undertaker. The Don agrees to have his men punish

You can see that we have our movie titles and their corresponding synopses, which we load into a data frame and then store them in variables. A sample movie and a part of its corresponding synopsis are also depicted in the preceding output. The main idea is to cluster these movies into groups using their synopsis as raw input. We will extract features from these synopses and use unsupervised learning algorithms on them to cluster them together. The movie titles are just for representation and will be useful when we would want to visualize and display clusters and their statistics. The data to be fed to the clustering algorithms will be features extracted from the movie synopses just to make things clearer. Before we can jump into each of the clustering methods, we will follow the same process of normalization and feature extraction that we have followed in all our other processes:

```
from normalization import normalize_corpus
from utils import build_feature_matrix

# normalize corpus
norm_movie_synopses = normalize_corpus(movie_synopses,
                                       lemmatize=True,
                                       only_text_chars=True)

# extract tf-idf features
vectorizer, feature_matrix = build_feature_matrix(norm_movie_synopses,
                                                  feature_type='tfidf',
                                                  min_df=0.24, max_df=0.85,
                                                  ngram_range=(1, 2))
# view number of features
In [275]: print feature_matrix.shape
(100, 307)

# get feature names
feature_names = vectorizer.get_feature_names()
# print sample features
In [277]: print feature_names[:20]
```

[u'able', u'accept', u'across', u'act', u'agree', u'alive', u'allow',
u'alone', u'along', u'already', u'although', u'always', u'another',
u'anything', u'apartment', u'appear', u'approach', u'arm', u'army',
u'around']

We keep text tokens in our normalized text and extract TF-IDF–based features
for unigrams and bigrams such that each feature occurs in at least in 25 percent of the
documents and at most 85 percent of the documents using the terms min_df and max_df.
We can see that we have a total of 100 rows for the 100 movies and a total of 307 features
for each movie. Some sample features are also printed in the preceding snippet. We will
start our clustering analysis next, now that we have our features and documents ready.

K-means Clustering

The *k-means clustering algorithm* is a centroid-based clustering model that tries to cluster
data into groups or clusters of equal variance. The criteria or measure that this algorithm
tries to minimize is *inertia*, also known as *within-cluster sum-of-squares*. Perhaps the one
main disadvantage of this algorithm is that the number of clusters k need to be specified
in advance, as is the case with all other centroid-based clustering models. This algorithm
is perhaps the most popular clustering algorithm out there and is frequently used due to
its ease of use as well as the fact that it is scalable with large amounts of data.

We can now formally define the k-means clustering algorithm along with its
mathematical notations. Consider that we have a dataset X with N data points or samples
and we want to group them into K clusters where K is a user-specified parameter. The
k-means clustering algorithm will segregate the N data points into K disjoint separate
clusters C_i, and each of these clusters can be described by the means of the cluster
samples. These means become the cluster centroids μ_k such that these centroids are not
bound by the condition that they have to be actual data points from the N samples in
X. The algorithm chooses these centroids and builds the clusters in such a way that the
inertia or within-cluster sums of squares are minimized. Mathematically, this can be
represented as

$$min\sum_{i=1}^{K}\sum_{x_n \in C_i}\|x_n - \mu_i\|^2$$

with regard to clusters C_i and centroids μ_i such that $i \in \{1, 2, ..., k\}$. This optimization is
an NP *hard problem* for all you algorithm enthusiasts out there. Lloyd's algorithm is a
solution to this problem, which is an iterative procedure consisting of the following steps.

1. Choose initial k centroids μ_k by taking k random samples from
   the dataset X.

2. Update clusters by assigning each data point or sample to its
   nearest centroid point. Mathematically, we can represent this
   as $C_k = \{x_n : \|x_n - \mu_k\| \le all \|x_n - \mu_i\|\}$ where C_k denotes the
   clusters.

3. Recalculate and update clusters based on the new cluster data points for each cluster obtained from step 2. Mathematically, this can be represented as

$$\mu_k = \frac{1}{C_k} \sum_{x_n \in C_k} x_n$$

where μ_k denotes the centroids.

The preceding steps are repeated in an iterative fashion till the outputs of steps 2 and 3 do not change anymore. One caveat of this method is that even though the optimization is guaranteed to converge, it might lead to a local minimum, hence in reality, this algorithm is run multiple times with several epochs and iterations, and the results might be averaged from them if needed. The convergence and occurrence of local minimum are highly dependent on the initialization of the initial centroids in step 1. One way is to make multiple iterations with multiple random initializations and take the average. Another way would be to use the kmeans++ scheme as implemented in scikit-learn, which initializes the initial centroids to be far apart from each other and has proven to be effective. We will now use k-means clustering to cluster the movie data from earlier, in the following code snippet:

```
from sklearn.cluster import KMeans
# define the k-means clustering function
def k_means(feature_matrix, num_clusters=5):
    km = KMeans(n_clusters=num_clusters,
                max_iter=10000)
    km.fit(feature_matrix)
    clusters = km.labels_
    return km, clusters
# set k = 5, lets say we want 5 clusters from the 100 movies
num_clusters = 5

# get clusters and assigned the cluster labels to the movies
km_obj, clusters = k_means(feature_matrix=feature_matrix,
                           num_clusters=num_clusters)
movie_data['Cluster'] = clusters
```

That snippet uses our implemented k-means function to cluster the movies based on the TF-IDF features from the movie synopses, and we assign the cluster label for each movie from the outcome of this cluster analysis by storing it in the movie_data dataframe in the 'Cluster' column. You can see that we have taken k to be 5 in our analysis. We can now see the total number of movies for each of the 5 clusters using the following snippet:

```
In [284]: from collections import Counter
     ...: # get the total number of movies per cluster
     ...: c = Counter(clusters)
     ...: print c.items()
[(0, 29), (1, 5), (2, 21), (3, 15), (4, 30)]
```

You can see that there are five cluster labels as expected, from 0 to 5, and each of them has some movies belonging to the cluster whose counts are mentioned as the

302

second element of each tuple in the preceding list. But can we do more than just see cluster counts? Of course we can! We will now define some functions to extract detailed cluster analysis information, print them, and then visualize the clusters. We will start by defining a function to extract important information from our cluster analysis:

```
def get_cluster_data(clustering_obj, movie_data,
                     feature_names, num_clusters,
                     topn_features=10):

    cluster_details = {}
    # get cluster centroids
    ordered_centroids = clustering_obj.cluster_centers_.argsort()[:, ::-1]
    # get key features for each cluster
    # get movies belonging to each cluster
    for cluster_num in range(num_clusters):
        cluster_details[cluster_num] = {}
        cluster_details[cluster_num]['cluster_num'] = cluster_num
        key_features = [feature_names[index]
                        for index
                        in ordered_centroids[cluster_num, :topn_features]]
        cluster_details[cluster_num]['key_features'] = key_features

        movies = movie_data[movie_data['Cluster'] == cluster_num]['Title'].
        values.tolist()
        cluster_details[cluster_num]['movies'] = movies

    return cluster_details
```

The preceding function is pretty self-explanatory. What it does is basically extract the key features per cluster that were essential in defining the cluster from the centroids. It also retrieves the movie titles that belong to each cluster and stores everything in a dictionary.

We will now define a function that uses this data structure and prints the results in a clear format:

```
def print_cluster_data(cluster_data):
    # print cluster details
    for cluster_num, cluster_details in cluster_data.items():
        print 'Cluster {} details:'.format(cluster_num)
        print '-'*20
        print 'Key features:', cluster_details['key_features']
        print 'Movies in this cluster:'
        print ', '.join(cluster_details['movies'])
        print '='*40
```

Before we analyze the results of our k-means clustering algorithm, we will also define a function to visualize the clusters. If you remember, we talked earlier about challenges associated with visualizing clusters. This happens because we deal with multidimensional feature spaces and unstructured text data. Numeric feature vectors themselves may not make any sense to readers if they were visualized directly. So, there are some techniques like *principal component analysis* (PCA) or *multidimensional scaling* (MDS) to reduce the dimensionality such that we can visualize these clusters in 2- or 3-dimensional plots. We will be using MDS in our implementation for visualizing clusters.

MDS is an approach towards non-linear dimensionality reduction such that the results can be visualized better in lower dimensional systems. The main idea is having a distance matrix such that distances between various data points are captured. We will be using Cosine similarity for this. MDS tries to build a lower-dimensional representation of our data with higher numbers of features in the vector space such that the distances between the various data points obtained using Cosine similarity in the higher dimensional feature space is still similar in this lower-dimensional representation.

The scikit-learn implementation for MDS has two types of algorithms: metric and non-metric. We will be using the metric approach because we will use the Cosine similarity–based distance metric to build the input similarity matrix between the various movies. Mathematically, MDS can be defined as follows: Let S be our similarity matrix between the various data points (movies) obtained using Cosine similarity on the feature matrix and X be the coordinates of the n input data points (movies). Disparities are represented by $\hat{d}_{ij} = t(S_{ij})$, which is usually some optimal transformation of the similarity values or could even be the raw similarity values themselves. The objective function for MDS, called *stress*, is defined as $sum_{i<j} d_{ij}(X) - \hat{d}_{ij}(X)$. We implement MDS-based

visualization for clusters in the following function:

```
import matplotlib.pyplot as plt
from sklearn.manifold import MDS
from sklearn.metrics.pairwise import cosine_similarity
import random
from matplotlib.font_manager import FontProperties

def plot_clusters(num_clusters, feature_matrix,
                  cluster_data, movie_data,
                  plot_size=(16,8)):
    # generate random color for clusters
    def generate_random_color():
        color = '#%06x' % random.randint(0, 0xFFFFFF)
        return color
    # define markers for clusters
    markers = ['o', 'v', '^', '<', '>', '8', 's', 'p', '*', 'h', 'H', 'D', 'd']
    # build cosine distance matrix
    cosine_distance = 1 - cosine_similarity(feature_matrix)
    # dimensionality reduction using MDS
    mds = MDS(n_components=2, dissimilarity="precomputed",
              random_state=1)
    # get coordinates of clusters in new low-dimensional space
    plot_positions = mds.fit_transform(cosine_distance)
    x_pos, y_pos = plot_positions[:, 0], plot_positions[:, 1]
    # build cluster plotting data
```

```
cluster_color_map = {}
cluster_name_map = {}
for cluster_num, cluster_details in cluster_data.items():
    # assign cluster features to unique label
    cluster_color_map[cluster_num] = generate_random_color()
    cluster_name_map[cluster_num] = ', '.join(cluster_details['key_
    features'][:5]).strip()
# map each unique cluster label with its coordinates and movies
cluster_plot_frame = pd.DataFrame({'x': x_pos,
                                   'y': y_pos,
                                   'label': movie_data['Cluster'].
                                   values.tolist(),
                                   'title': movie_data['Title'].values.
                                   tolist()
                                   })
grouped_plot_frame = cluster_plot_frame.groupby('label')
# set plot figure size and axes
fig, ax = plt.subplots(figsize=plot_size)
ax.margins(0.05)
# plot each cluster using co-ordinates and movie titles
for cluster_num, cluster_frame in grouped_plot_frame:
    marker = markers[cluster_num] if cluster_num < len(markers) \
             else np.random.choice(markers, size=1)[0]
    ax.plot(cluster_frame['x'], cluster_frame['y'],
            marker=marker, linestyle='', ms=12,
            label=cluster_name_map[cluster_num],
            color=cluster_color_map[cluster_num], mec='none')
    ax.set_aspect('auto')
    ax.tick_params(axis= 'x', which='both', bottom='off', top='off',
                   labelbottom='off')
    ax.tick_params(axis= 'y', which='both', left='off', top='off',
                   labelleft='off')
fontP = FontProperties()
fontP.set_size('small')
ax.legend(loc='upper center', bbox_to_anchor=(0.5, -0.01),
fancybox=True,
          shadow=True, ncol=5, numpoints=1, prop=fontP)
#add labels as the film titles
for index in range(len(cluster_plot_frame)):
    ax.text(cluster_plot_frame.ix[index]['x'],
            cluster_plot_frame.ix[index]['y'],
            cluster_plot_frame.ix[index]['title'], size=8)
# show the plot
plt.show()
```

The function is quite big, but the self-explanatory comments explain each step clearly. We build our similarity matrix first using the Cosine similarity between documents, get the cosine distances, and then transform the high dimensional feature

305

space into 2 dimensions using MDS. Then we plot the clusters using `matplotlib` with a bit of necessary formatting to view the results in a nice way. This function is a generic function and will work with any clustering algorithm with a dynamic number of clusters. Each cluster will have its own color, symbol, and label in the terms of top distinguishing features in the legend. The actual plot will plot each movie with its corresponding cluster label with its own color and symbol.

We are now ready to analyze the cluster results of our k-means clustering using the preceding functions. The following code snippet depicts the detailed analysis results for k-means clustering:

```
# get clustering analysis data
cluster_data =  get_cluster_data(clustering_obj=km_obj, movie_data=movie_
data,
                                 feature_names=feature_names, num_
                                 clusters=num_clusters,
                                 topn_features=5)

# print clustering analysis results
In [294]: print_cluster_data(cluster_data)

Cluster 0 details:
--------------------
Key features: [u'car', u'police', u'house', u'father', u'room']
Movies in this cluster:
Psycho, Sunset Blvd., Vertigo, West Side Story, E.T. the Extra-Terrestrial,
2001: A Space Odyssey, The Silence of the Lambs, Singin' in the Rain, It's
a Wonderful Life, Some Like It Hot, Gandhi, To Kill a Mockingbird, Butch
Cassidy and the Sundance Kid, The Exorcist, The French Connection, It
Happened One Night, Rain Man, Fargo, Close Encounters of the Third Kind,
Nashville, The Graduate, American Graffiti, Pulp Fiction, The Maltese
Falcon, A Clockwork Orange, Rebel Without a Cause, Rear Window, The Third
Man, North by Northwest
=========================================
Cluster 1 details:
--------------------
Key features: [u'water', u'attempt', u'cross', u'death', u'officer']
Movies in this cluster:
Chinatown, Apocalypse Now, Jaws, The African Queen, Mutiny on the Bounty
=========================================
Cluster 2 details:
--------------------
Key features: [u'family', u'love', u'marry', u'war', u'child']
Movies in this cluster:
The Godfather, Gone with the Wind, The Godfather: Part II, The Sound of
Music, A Streetcar Named Desire, The Philadelphia Story, An American in
Paris, Ben-Hur, Doctor Zhivago, High Noon, The Pianist, Goodfellas, The
King's Speech, A Place in the Sun, Out of Africa, Terms of Endearment,
Giant, The Grapes of Wrath, Wuthering Heights, Double Indemnity, Yankee
Doodle Dandy
```

306

```
===========================================
Cluster 3 details:
--------------------
Key features: [u'apartment', u'new', u'woman', u'york', u'life']
Movies in this cluster:
Citizen Kane, Titanic, 12 Angry Men, Rocky, The Best Years of Our Lives, My
Fair Lady, The Apartment, City Lights, Midnight Cowboy, Mr. Smith Goes to
Washington, Annie Hall, Good Will Hunting, Tootsie, Network, Taxi Driver
===========================================
Cluster 4 details:
--------------------
Key features: [u'kill', u'soldier', u'men', u'army', u'war']
Movies in this cluster:
The Shawshank Redemption, Schindler's List, Raging Bull, Casablanca, One
Flew Over the Cuckoo's Nest, The Wizard of Oz, Lawrence of Arabia, On the
Waterfront, Forrest Gump, Star Wars, The Bridge on the River Kwai, Dr.
Strangelove or: How I Learned to Stop Worrying and Love the Bomb, Amadeus,
The Lord of the Rings: The Return of the King, Gladiator, From Here to
Eternity, Saving Private Ryan, Unforgiven, Raiders of the Lost Ark, Patton,
Braveheart, The Good, the Bad and the Ugly, The Treasure of the Sierra
Madre, Platoon, Dances with Wolves, The Deer Hunter, All Quiet on the
Western Front, Shane, The Green Mile, Stagecoach
===========================================
```

```
# visualize the clusters
In [295]: plot_clusters(num_clusters=num_clusters,
     ...:               feature_matrix=feature_matrix,
     ...:               cluster_data=cluster_data,
     ...:               movie_data=movie_data,
     ...:               plot_size=(16,8))
```

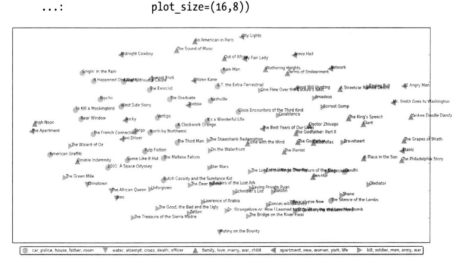

Figure 6-4. *Visualizing the output of K-means clustering on IMDb movie data*

The preceding output shows the key features for each cluster and the movies in each cluster, and you can also see the same in the visualization in Figure 6-4 (there is a lot in that figure—if the text appears too small, check out the kmeans_clustering.png file, available along with the code files for this chapter). Each cluster is depicted by the main themes that define that cluster by its top features, and you can see popular movies like *The Godfather* and *The Godfather: Part II* in the same cluster along with other movies like *Ben-Hur* and so on which talk about 'family', 'love', 'war', and so on. Movies like *Star Wars, The Lord of the Rings, The Deer Hunter, Gladiator, Forrest Gump,* and so on are clustered together associated with themes like 'kill', 'soldier', 'army', and 'war'. Definitely interesting results considering the data used for clustering was just a few paragraphs of synopsis per movie. Look more closely at the results and the visualization. Can you notice any other interesting patterns?

Affinity Propagation

The k-means algorithm, although very popular, has the drawback that the user has to pre-define the number of clusters. What if in reality there are more clusters or lesser clusters? There are some ways of checking the cluster quality and seeing what the value of the optimum *k* might be. Interested readers can check out the *elbow method* and the *silhouette coefficient*, which are popular methods of determining the optimum *k*. Here we will talk about an algorithm that tries to build clusters based on inherent properties of the data without any pre-assumptions about the number of clusters. The *affinity propagation* (AP) algorithm is based on the concept of "message passing" among the various data points to be clustered, and no pre-assumption is needed about the number of possible clusters.

AP creates these clusters from the data points by passing messages between pairs of data points until convergence is achieved. The entire dataset is then represented by a small number of *exemplars* that act as representatives for samples. These exemplars are analogous to the centroids you obtain from k-means or k-medoids. The messages that are sent between pairs represent how suitable one of the points might be in being the exemplar or representative of the other data point. This keeps getting updated in every iteration until convergence is achieved, with the final exemplars being the representatives of each cluster. Remember, one drawback of this method is that it is computationally intensive because messages are passed between each pair of data points across the entire dataset and can take substantial time to converge for large datasets.

We can now define the steps involved in the AP algorithm (courtesy of Wikipedia and scikit-learn). Consider that we have a dataset X with n data points such that $X = \{x_1, x_2, \ldots, x_n\}$, and let $sim(x, y)$ be the similarity function that quantifies the similarity between two points x and y. In our implementation, we will be using Cosine similarity again for this. The AP algorithm iteratively proceeds by executing two message-passing steps as follows:

1. Responsibility updates are sent around, which can be mathematically represented as

$$r(i, k) \leftarrow sim(i, k) - \max_{k' \neq k} \{a(i, k') + sim(i, k')\}$$

where the responsibility matrix is R and $r(i, k)$ is a measure which quantifies how well x_k can serve as being the representative or exemplar for x_i in comparison to the other candidates.

2. Availability updates are then sent around which can be mathematically represented as

$$a(i,k) \leftarrow \min\left(0, r(k,k) + \sum_{i' \notin \{i,k\}} \max(0, r(i', k))\right) \text{ for } i \neq k \text{ and}$$

availability for $i = k$ is represented as

$$a(k,k) \leftarrow \sum_{i' \neq k} \max(0, r(i', k))$$

where the availability matrix is A and $a(i, k)$ represents how appropriate it would be for x_i to pick x_k as its exemplar, considering all the other points' preference to pick x_k as an exemplar.

Those two steps keep occurring per iteration until convergence is achieved. The following function implements AP such that it takes in a feature matrix and returns the necessary clusters for each sample based on its features and the other samples:

```
from sklearn.cluster import AffinityPropagation

def affinity_propagation(feature_matrix):
    sim = feature_matrix * feature_matrix.T
    sim = sim.todense()
    ap = AffinityPropagation()
    ap.fit(sim)
    clusters = ap.labels_
    return ap, clusters
```

We will now use this function to cluster our movies based on their synopses and then we will print the number of movies in each cluster and the total number of clusters formed by this algorithm:

```
# get clusters using affinity propagation
ap_obj, clusters = affinity_propagation(feature_matrix=feature_matrix)
movie_data['Cluster'] = clusters

# get the total number of movies per cluster
In [299]: c = Counter(clusters)
     ...: print c.items()
[(0, 5), (1, 6), (2, 12), (3, 6), (4, 2), (5, 7), (6, 10), (7, 7), (8, 4),
(9, 8), (10, 3), (11, 4), (12, 5), (13, 7), (14, 4), (15, 3), (16, 7)]

# get total clusters
In [300]: total_clusters = len(c)
     ...: print 'Total Clusters:', total_clusters
Total Clusters: 17
```

From the preceding results, we can see that a total of 17 clusters have been created by AP on our movie data containing 100 movies. Each cluster has movies ranging from as low as 2 to as high as 12 movies. We shall now extract detailed cluster information, display cluster statistics, and visualize the clusters similar to what we did for k-means clustering, using our utility functions that we implemented in the K-means clustering section:

```
# get clustering analysis data
cluster_data = get_cluster_data(clustering_obj=ap_obj, movie_data=movie_
data,
                                feature_names=feature_names, num_
                                clusters=total_clusters,
                                topn_features=5)

# print clustering analysis results
In [302]: print_cluster_data(cluster_data)
    ...:
Cluster 0 details:
--------------------
Key features: [u'able', u'always', u'cover', u'end', u'charge']
Movies in this cluster:
The Godfather, The Godfather: Part II, Doctor Zhivago, The Pianist,
Goodfellas
========================================
Cluster 1 details:
--------------------
Key features: [u'alive', u'accept', u'around', u'agree', u'attack']
Movies in this cluster:
Casablanca, One Flew Over the Cuckoo's Nest, Titanic, 2001: A Space Odyssey,
The Silence of the Lambs, Good Will Hunting
========================================
Cluster 2 details:
--------------------
Key features: [u'apartment', u'film', u'final', u'fall', u'due']
Movies in this cluster:
The Shawshank Redemption, Vertigo, West Side Story, Rocky, Tootsie,
Nashville, The Graduate, The Maltese Falcon, A Clockwork Orange, Taxi
Driver, Rear Window, The Third Man
========================================
Cluster 3 details:
--------------------
Key features: [u'arrest', u'film', u'evening', u'final', u'fall']
Movies in this cluster:
The Wizard of Oz, Psycho, E.T. the Extra-Terrestrial, My Fair Lady, Ben-Hur,
Close Encounters of the Third Kind
========================================
Cluster 4 details:
--------------------
```

```
Key features: [u'become', u'film', u'city', u'army', u'die']
Movies in this cluster:
12 Angry Men, Mr. Smith Goes to Washington
========================================
Cluster 5 details:
--------------------
Key features: [u'behind', u'city', u'father', u'appear', u'allow']
Movies in this cluster:
Forrest Gump, Amadeus, Gladiator, Braveheart, The Exorcist, A Place in the
Sun, Double Indemnity
========================================
Cluster 6 details:
--------------------
Key features: [u'body', u'allow', u'although', u'city', u'break']
Movies in this cluster:
Schindler's List, Gone with the Wind, Lawrence of Arabia, Star Wars, The
Lord of the Rings: The Return of the King, From Here to Eternity, Raiders of
the Lost Ark, The Best Years of Our Lives, The Deer Hunter, Stagecoach
========================================
Cluster 7 details:
--------------------
Key features: [u'brother', u'bring', u'close', u'although', u'car']
Movies in this cluster:
Gandhi, Unforgiven, To Kill a Mockingbird, The Good, the Bad and the Ugly,
Butch Cassidy and the Sundance Kid, High Noon, Shane
========================================
Cluster 8 details:
--------------------
Key features: [u'child', u'everyone', u'attempt', u'fall', u'face']
Movies in this cluster:
Chinatown, Jaws, The African Queen, Mutiny on the Bounty
========================================
Cluster 9 details:
--------------------
Key features: [u'continue', u'bring', u'daughter', u'break', u'allow']
Movies in this cluster:
The Bridge on the River Kwai, Dr. Strangelove or: How I Learned to Stop
Worrying and Love the Bomb, Apocalypse Now, Saving Private Ryan, Patton,
Platoon, Dances with Wolves, All Quiet on the Western Front
========================================
Cluster 10 details:
--------------------
Key features: [u'despite', u'drop', u'family', u'confront', u'drive']
Movies in this cluster:
The Treasure of the Sierra Madre, City Lights, Midnight Cowboy
========================================
Cluster 11 details:
--------------------
```

```
Key features: [u'discover', u'always', u'feel', u'city', u'act']
Movies in this cluster:
Raging Bull, It Happened One Night, Rain Man, Rebel Without a Cause
========================================
Cluster 12 details:
--------------------
Key features: [u'discuss', u'alone', u'drop', u'business', u'consider']
Movies in this cluster:
Singin' in the Rain, An American in Paris, The Apartment, Annie Hall,
Network
========================================
Cluster 13 details:
--------------------
Key features: [u'due', u'final', u'day', u'ever', u'eventually']
Movies in this cluster:
On the Waterfront, It's a Wonderful Life, Some Like It Hot, The French
Connection, Fargo, Pulp Fiction, North by Northwest
========================================
Cluster 14 details:
--------------------
Key features: [u'early', u'able', u'end', u'charge', u'allow']
Movies in this cluster:
A Streetcar Named Desire, The King's Speech, Giant, The Grapes of Wrath
========================================
Cluster 15 details:
--------------------
Key features: [u'enter', u'eventually', u'cut', u'accept', u'even']
Movies in this cluster:
The Philadelphia Story, The Green Mile, American Graffiti
========================================
Cluster 16 details:
--------------------
Key features: [u'far', u'allow', u'apartment', u'anything', u'car']
Movies in this cluster:
Citizen Kane, Sunset Blvd., The Sound of Music, Out of Africa, Terms of
Endearment, Wuthering Heights, Yankee Doodle Dandy
========================================

# visualize the clusters
In [304]: plot_clusters(num_clusters=num_clusters, feature_matrix=feature_
matrix,
    ...:                 cluster_data=cluster_data, movie_data=movie_data,
    ...:                 plot_size=(16,8))
```

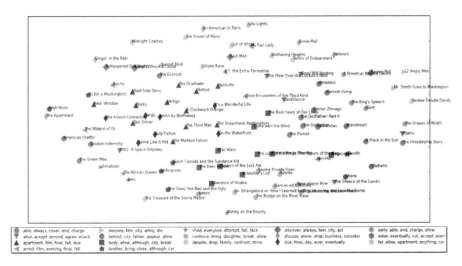

Figure 6-5. *Visualizing the output of Affinity Propagation clustering on IMDb movie data*

The preceding outputs show the contents of the different clusters and their visualization. If the visual text in Figure 6-5 is too small, you can always refer to the file affinity_prop_clustering.png, which contains the plot depicted in higher resolution. You can see from the results that we now have a total of 17 clusters, and there are some similarities where you will see similar movies that were grouped together in k-means clustering are in similar clusters here also, and there are also notable differences where many movies now have their own cluster. Are these clustering results better than the previous one? Well a lot depends on human perspective, and since I have yet to watch several of these movies, I leave this decision to you, dear reader! An important point to note here is that a few keywords from the exemplars or centroids for each cluster may not always depict the true essence or theme of that cluster, so a good idea here would be to build topic models on each cluster and see the kind of topics you can extract from each cluster that would make a better representation of each cluster (another example where you can see how we can connect various text analytics techniques together).

Ward's Agglomerative Hierarchical Clustering

The *hierarchical clustering* family of algorithms is a bit different from the other clustering models we've discussed. Hierarchical clustering tries to build a nested hierarchy of clusters by either merging or splitting them in succession. There are two main strategies for Hierarchical clustering:

- *Agglomerative*: These algorithms follow a bottom-up approach where initially all data points belong to their own individual cluster, and then from this bottom layer, we start merging clusters together, building a hierarchy of clusters as we go up.

- *Divisive*: These algorithms follow a top-down approach where initially all the data points belong to a single huge cluster and then we start recursively dividing them up as we move down gradually, and this produces a hierarchy of clusters going from the top-down.

Merges and splits normally happen using a greedy algorithm, and the end result of the hierarchy of clusters can be visualized as a tree structure, called a *dendrogram*. Figure 6-6 shows an example of how a dendrogram is constructed using agglomerative hierarchical clustering for a sample of documents.

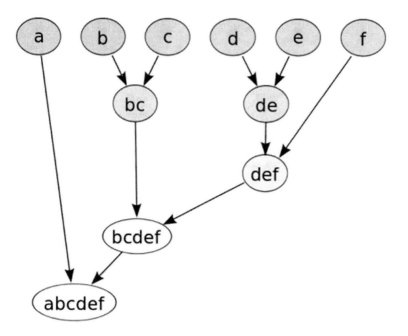

Figure 6-6. *Agglomerative hierarchical clustering representation*

Figure 6-6 clearly highlights how six separate data points start off as six clusters, and then we slowly start grouping them in each step following a bottom-up approach. We will be using an agglomerative hierarchical clustering algorithm in this section. In agglomerative clustering, for deciding which clusters we should combine when starting from the individual data point clusters, we need two things:

- A *distance metric* to measure the similarity or dissimilarity degree between data points. We will be using the Cosine distance/ similarity in our implementation.

- A *linkage criterion* that determines the metric to be used for the merging strategy of clusters. We will be using Ward's method here.

The Ward's linkage criterion minimizes the sum of squared differences within all the clusters and is a variance minimizing approach. This is also known as Ward's minimum variance method and was initially presented by J. Ward. The idea is to minimize the variances within each cluster using an objective function like the L2 norm distance between two points. We can start with computing the initial cluster distances between each pair of points using the formula

$$d_{ij} = d\left(\left\{C_i, C_j\right\}\right) = \left\|C_i - C_j\right\|^2$$

where initially C_i indicates cluster i with one document, and at each iteration, we find the pairs of clusters that lead to the least increase in variance for that cluster once merged. A weighted squared Euclidean distance or L2 norm as depicted in the preceding formula would suffice for this algorithm. We use Cosine similarity to compute the cosine distances between each pair of movies for our dataset. The following function implements Ward's agglomerative hierarchical clustering.:

```
from scipy.cluster.hierarchy import ward, dendrogram

def ward_hierarchical_clustering(feature_matrix):

    cosine_distance = 1 - cosine_similarity(feature_matrix)
    linkage_matrix = ward(cosine_distance)
    return linkage_matrix
```

To view the results of the hierarchical clustering, we need to plot a dendrogram using the preceding linkage matrix, and so we implement the following function to build and plot a dendrogram from the hierarchical clustering linkage matrix:

```
def plot_hierarchical_clusters(linkage_matrix, movie_data, figure_
size=(8,12)):
    # set size
    fig, ax = plt.subplots(figsize=figure_size)
    movie_titles = movie_data['Title'].values.tolist()
    # plot dendrogram
    ax = dendrogram(linkage_matrix, orientation="left", labels=movie_titles)
    plt.tick_params(axis= 'x',
                    which='both',
                    bottom='off',
                    top='off',
                    labelbottom='off')
    plt.tight_layout()
    plt.savefig('ward_hierachical_clusters.png', dpi=200)
```

We are now ready to perform hierarchical clustering on our movie data! The following code snippet shows Ward's clustering in action:

```
In [307]:# build ward's linkage matrix
    ...:linkage_matrix = ward_hierarchical_clustering(feature_matrix)
    ...: # plot the dendrogram
    ...: plot_hierarchical_clusters(linkage_matrix=linkage_matrix,
    ...:                            movie_data=movie_data,
    ...:                            figure_size=(8,10))
```

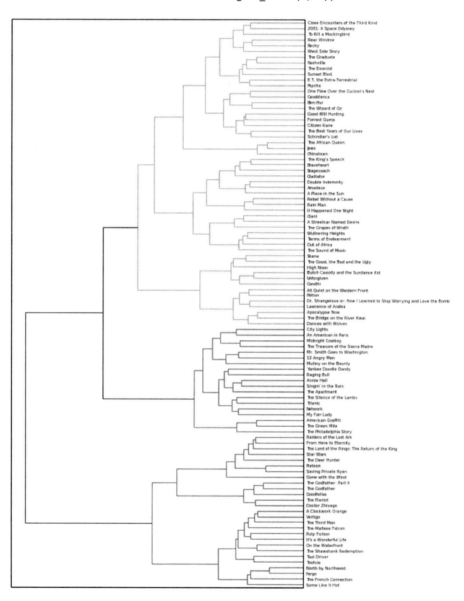

Figure 6-7. *Ward's clustering dendrogram on our IMDb movie data*

The dendrogram in Figure 6-7 shows the clustering analysis results. The colors indicate that there are three main clusters, which further get subdivided into more granular clusters maintaining a hierarchy. (If you have trouble reading the small fonts, look at the file ward_hierachical_clusters.png available with the code files in this chapter). You will notice a lot of similarities with the results of the previous clustering algorithms.

The green colored movies like *Raiders of the Lost Ark, The Lord of the Rings, Star Wars, The Godfather, The Godfather: Part II, Pulp Fiction, A Clockwork Orange,* and *Platoon* are definitely some of the top movies and in fact classics in the *action, adventure, war,* and *crime*-based genres.

The red colored movies include comedy-based movies like *City Lights, The Apartment,* and *My Fair Lady,* and also several movies that belong to the *drama* genre including *Mutiny on the Bounty, 12 Angry Men, Annie Hall, Midnight Cowboy, Titanic,* and *An American in Paris,* with several of them having *romantic* plots too. Several of them are even *musicals,* including *Yankee Doodle Dandy, An American in Paris, Singin' in the Rain,* and *My Fair Lady.* It is definitely interesting indeed that with just movie synopses, our algorithm has clustered movies with similar attributes and genres together!

The blue colored movies give us similar results, in that *Braveheart* and *Gladiator* are *action, drama,* and *war* classics. We also have some classics related to *drama, romance,* and *biographies* like *The Sound of Music, Wuthering Heights, Terms of Endearment,* and *Out of Africa.* Toward the top of the dendrogram you will observe movies related to *science fiction* and *fantasy,* like *2001: A Space Odyssey, Close Encounters of the Third Kind,* and *E.T. the Extra-Terrestrial,* all close to each other.

Can you find more interesting patterns? Which movies do you think do not belong together in the same clusters? Can we build better clusters? Can we recommend similar movies to watch based on clustering movies together? These are some interesting questions to ponder, and I will leave them for you to look at and explore further.

Summary

I would like to really commend your efforts on staying with me till the end of this chapter. We covered a lot here, including several topics in the challenging but very interesting unsupervised machine learning domain. You now know how text similarity can be computed and you learned about various kinds of distance measures and metrics. We also looked at important concepts related to distance metrics and measures and properties that make a measure into a metric. We explored concepts related to unsupervised ML and saw how we can incorporate such techniques in document clustering. Various ways of measuring term and document similarity were also covered, and we implemented several of these techniques by successfully converting mathematical equations into code using the power of Python and several open source libraries. We touched on document clustering in detail, looking at the various concepts and types of clustering models. Finally, we took a real-world example of clustering the top hundred greatest movies of all time using IMDb movie synopses data and used different clustering models like k-means, affinity propagation, and Ward's hierarchical clustering to build, analyze, and visualize clusters. This should be enough for you to get started with analyzing document similarity and clustering, and you can even start combining various techniques from the chapters covered so far. (Hint: Topic models with clustering, building classifiers by combining supervised and unsupervised learning, and augmenting recommendation systems using document clusters—just to name a few!)

CHAPTER 7

■ ■ ■

Semantic and Sentiment Analysis

Natural language understanding has gained significant importance in the last decade with the advent of machine learning (ML) and further advances like *deep learning* and artificial intelligence. Computers and other machines can be programmed to learn things and perform specific operations. The key limitation is their inability to perceive, understand, and comprehend things like humans do. With the resurgence in popularity of neural networks and advances made in computer architecture, we now have deep learning and artificial intelligence evolving rapidly to make some efforts into trying to engineer machines into learning, perceiving, understanding, and performing actions on their own. You may have seen or heard several of these efforts, such as self-driving cars, computers beating experienced players in games like chess and Go, and the proliferation of chatbots on the Internet.

In Chapters 4–6, we have looked at various computational, language processing, and ML techniques to classify, cluster, and summarize text. Back in Chapter 3 we developed certain methods and programs to analyze and understand text syntax and structure. This chapter will deal with methods that try to answer the question *Can we analyze and understand the meaning and sentiment behind a body of text?*

Natural Language Processing (NLP) has a wide variety of applications that try to use natural language understanding to infer the meaning and context behind text and use it to solve various problems. We discussed several of these applications briefly in Chapter 1. To refresh your memory, the following applications require extensive understanding of text from the semantic perspective:

- Question Answering Systems

- Contextual recognition

- Speech recognition (for some applications)

Text semantics specifically deals with understanding the meaning of text or language. When combined into sentences, words have lexical relations and contextual relations between them lead to various types of relationships and hierarchies, and semantics sits at the heart of all this in trying to analyze and understand these relationships and infer meaning from them. We will be exploring various types of semantic relationships in natural language and look at some NLP-based techniques for inferring and extracting meaningful

© Dipanjan Sarkar 2016

D. Sarkar, *Text Analytics with Python*, DOI 10.1007/978-1-4842-2388-8_7

semantic information from text. Semantics is purely concerned with context and meaning, and the structure or format of text holds little significance here. But sometimes even the syntax or arrangement of words helps us in inferring the context of words and helps us differentiate things like *lead* as a metal from *lead* as in the lead of a movie.

Sentiment analysis is perhaps the most popular application of text analytics, with a vast number of tutorials, web sites, and applications that focus on analyzing sentiment of various text resources ranging from corporate surveys to movie reviews. The key aspect of sentiment analysis is to analyze a body of text for understanding the opinion expressed by it and other factors like mood and modality. Usually sentiment analysis works best on text that has a subjective context than on that with only an objective context. This is because when a body of text has an objective context or perspective to it, the text usually depicts some normal statements or facts without expressing any emotion, feelings, or mood. Subjective text contains text that is usually expressed by a human having typical moods, emotions, and feelings. Sentiment analysis is widely used, especially as a part of social media analysis for any domain, be it a business, a recent movie, or a product launch, to understand its reception by the people and what they think of it based on their opinions or, you guessed it, sentiment.

In this chapter, we will be covering several aspects from both semantic and sentiment analysis for textual data. We will start with exploring WordNet, a lexical database, and introduce a new concept called *synsets*. We will also explore various semantic relationships and representations in natural language and we will cover techniques such as *word sense disambiguation* and *named entity recognition*. In sentiment analysis, we will be looking at how to use supervised ML techniques to analyze sentiment and also at several unsupervised lexical techniques with more detailed insights into natural language sentiment, mood, and modality.

Semantic Analysis

We have seen how terms or words get grouped into phrases that further form clauses and finally sentences. Chapter 3 showed various structural components in natural language, including parts of speech (POS), chunking, and grammars. All these concepts fall under the syntactic and structural analysis of text data. Whereas we do explore relationships of words, phrases, and clauses, these are purely based on their position, syntax, and structure. Semantic analysis is more about understanding the actual context and meaning behind words in text and how they relate to other words to convey some information as a whole. As mentioned in Chapter 1, the definition of semantics itself is the study of meaning, and linguistic semantics is a complete branch under linguistics that deals with the study of meaning in natural language, including exploring various relationships between words, phrases and symbols. Besides this, there are also various ways to represent semantics associated with statements and propositions. We will be broadly covering the following topics under semantic analysis:

- Exploring WordNet and synsets

- Analyzing lexical semantic relations

- Word sense disambiguation

- Named entity recognition

- Analyzing semantic representations

The main objective of these topics is to give you a clear understanding of the resources you can leverage for semantic analysis as well as how to use these resources. We will explore various concepts related to semantic analysis, which was covered in Chapter 1, with actual examples. You can refresh your memory by revisiting the "Language Semantics" section in Chapter 1. Without any further delay, let's get started!

Exploring WordNet

WordNet is a huge lexical database for the English Language. The database is a part of Princeton University, and you can read more about it at `https://wordnet.princeton.edu`. It was originally created in around 1985, in Princeton University's Cognitive Science Laboratory under the direction of Professor G. A. Miller. This lexical database consists of nouns, adjective, verbs, and adverbs, and related lexical terms are grouped together based on some common concepts into sets, known as *cognitive synonym sets* or *synsets*. Each synset expresses a unique, distinct concept. At a high level, WordNet can be compared to a thesaurus or a dictionary that provides words and their synonyms. On a lower level, it is much more than that, with synsets and their corresponding terms having detailed relationships and hierarchies based on their semantic meaning and similar concepts. WordNet is used extensively as a lexical database, in text analytics, NLP, and artificial intelligence (AI)-based applications.

The WordNet database consists of over 155,000 words, represented in more than 117,000 synsets, and contains over 206,000 word-sense pairs. The database is roughly 12 MB in size and can be accessed through various interfaces and APIs. The official web site has a web application interface for accessing various details related to words, synsets, and concepts related to the entered word. You can access it at `http://wordnetweb.princeton.edu/perl/webwn` or download it from `https://wordnet.princeton.edu/wordnet/download/`. The download contains various packages, files, and tools related to WordNet. We will be accessing WordNet programmatically using the interface provided by the `nltk` package. We will start by exploring synsets and then various semantic relationships using synsets.

Understanding Synsets

We will start exploring WordNet by looking at synsets since they are perhaps one of the most important concepts and structures that tie everything together. In general, based on concepts from NLP and information retrieval, a synset is a collection or set of data entities that are considered to be semantically similar. This doesn't mean that they will be exactly the same, but they will be centered on similar context and concepts. Specifically in the context of WordNet, a synset is a set or collection of synonyms that are interchangeable and revolve around a specific concept. Synsets not only consist of simple words, but also collocations. *Polysemous* word forms (words that sound and look the same but have different but relatable meanings) are assigned to different synsets based on their meaning. Synsets are connected to other synsets using semantic relations, which we shall explore in a future section. Typically each synset has the term, a definition explaining the meaning of the term, and some optional examples and related lemmas (collection of synonyms) to the term. Some terms may have multiple synsets associated with them, where each synset has a particular context.

Let's look at a real example by using nltk's WordNet interface to explore synsets associated with the term, 'fruit'. We can do this using the following code snippet:

```
from nltk.corpus import wordnet as wn
import pandas as pd

term = 'fruit'
synsets = wn.synsets(term)
# display total synsets
In [75]: print 'Total Synsets:', len(synsets)
Total Synsets: 5
```

We can see that there are a total of five synsets associated with the term 'fruit'. What can these synsets indicate? We can dig deeper into each synset and its components using the following code snippet:

```
In [76]: for synset in synsets:
    ...:        print 'Synset:', synset
    ...:        print 'Part of speech:', synset.lexname()
    ...:        print 'Definition:', synset.definition()
    ...:        print 'Lemmas:', synset.lemma_names()
    ...:        print 'Examples:', synset.examples()
    ...:        print
    ...:
    ...:
Synset: Synset('fruit.n.01')
Part of speech: noun.plant
Definition: the ripened reproductive body of a seed plant
Lemmas: [u'fruit']
Examples: []

Synset: Synset('yield.n.03')
Part of speech: noun.artifact
Definition: an amount of a product
Lemmas: [u'yield', u'fruit']
Examples: []

Synset: Synset('fruit.n.03')
Part of speech: noun.event
Definition: the consequence of some effort or action
Lemmas: [u'fruit']
Examples: [u'he lived long enough to see the fruit of his policies']

Synset: Synset('fruit.v.01')
Part of speech: verb.creation
Definition: cause to bear fruit
Lemmas: [u'fruit']
Examples: []
```

```
Synset: Synset('fruit.v.02')
Part of speech: verb.creation
Definition: bear fruit
Lemmas: [u'fruit']
Examples: [u'the trees fruited early this year']
```

The preceding output shows us details pertaining to each synset associated with the term 'fruit', and the definitions give us the sense of each synset and the lemma associated with it. The part of speech for each synset is also mentioned, which includes nouns and verbs. Some examples are also depicted in the preceding output that show how the term is used in actual sentences. Now that we understand synsets better, let's start exploring various semantic relationships as mentioned.

Analyzing Lexical Semantic Relations

Text semantics refers to the study of meaning and context. Synsets give a nice abstraction over various terms and provide useful information like definition, examples, POS, and lemmas. But can we explore semantic relationships among entities using synsets? The answer is definitely yes. We will be talking about many of the concepts related to semantic relations (covered in detail in the "Lexical Semantic Relations" subsection under the "Language Semantics" section in Chapter 1. It would be useful for you to review that section to better understand each of the concepts when we illustrate them with real-world examples here. We will be using nltk's wordnet resource here, but you can use the same WordNet resource from the pattern package, which includes an interface similar to nltk.

Entailments

The term *entailment* usually refers to some event or action that logically involves or is associated with some other action or event that has taken place or will take place. Ideally this applies very well to verbs indicating some specific action. The following snippet shows how to get entailments:

```
# entailments
In [80]: for action in ['walk', 'eat', 'digest']:
    ...:     action_syn = wn.synsets(action, pos='v')[0]
    ...:     print action_syn, '-- entails -->', action_syn.entailments()
Synset('walk.v.01') -- entails --> [Synset('step.v.01')]
Synset('eat.v.01') -- entails --> [Synset('chew.v.01'),
Synset('swallow.v.01')]
Synset('digest.v.01') -- entails --> [Synset('consume.v.02')]
```

You can see how related synsets depict the concept of entailment in that output. Related actions are depicted in entailment, where actions like *walking* involve or entail *stepping*, and *eating* entails *chewing* and *swallowing*.

Homonyms and Homographs

On a high level, *homonyms* refer to words or terms having the same written form or pronunciation but different meanings. Homonyms are a superset of homographs, which are words with same spelling but may have different pronunciation and meaning. The following code snippet shows how we can get homonyms/homographs:

```
In [81]: for synset in wn.synsets('bank'):
    ...:     print synset.name(),'-',synset.definition()
    ...:
    ...:
bank.n.01 - sloping land (especially the slope beside a body of water)
depository_financial_institution.n.01 - a financial institution that accepts
deposits and channels the money into lending activities
bank.n.03 - a long ridge or pile
bank.n.04 - an arrangement of similar objects in a row or in tiers
...
...
deposit.v.02 - put into a bank account
bank.v.07 - cover with ashes so to control the rate of burning
trust.v.01 - have confidence or faith in
```

The preceding output shows a part of the result obtained for the various homographs for the term 'bank'. You can see that there are various different meanings associated with the word 'bank', which is the core intuition behind homographs.

Synonyms and Antonyms

Synonyms are words having similar meaning and context, and *antonyms* are words having opposite or contrasting meaning, as you may know already. The following snippet depicts synonyms and antonyms:

```
In [82]: term = 'large'
    ...: synsets = wn.synsets(term)
    ...: adj_large = synsets[1]
    ...: adj_large = adj_large.lemmas()[0]
    ...: adj_large_synonym = adj_large.synset()
    ...: adj_large_antonym = adj_large.antonyms()[0].synset()
    ...: # print synonym and antonym
    ...: print 'Synonym:', adj_large_synonym.name()
    ...: print 'Definition:', adj_large_synonym.definition()
    ...: print 'Antonym:', adj_large_antonym.name()
    ...: print 'Definition:', adj_large_antonym.definition()
Synonym: large.a.01
Definition: above average in size or number or quantity or magnitude or
extent
Antonym: small.a.01
```

Definition: limited or below average in number or quantity or magnitude or extent

```
In [83]: term = 'rich'
    ...: synsets = wn.synsets(term)[:3]
    ...: # print synonym and antonym for different synsets
    ...: for synset in synsets:
    ...:     rich = synset.lemmas()[0]
    ...:     rich_synonym = rich.synset()
    ...:     rich_antonym = rich.antonyms()[0].synset()
    ...:     print 'Synonym:', rich_synonym.name()
    ...:     print 'Definition:', rich_synonym.definition()
    ...:     print 'Antonym:', rich_antonym.name()
    ...:     print 'Definition:', rich_antonym.definition()
Synonym: rich_people.n.01
Definition: people who have possessions and wealth (considered as a group)
Antonym: poor_people.n.01
Definition: people without possessions or wealth (considered as a group)

Synonym: rich.a.01
Definition: possessing material wealth
Antonym: poor.a.02
Definition: having little money or few possessions

Synonym: rich.a.02
Definition: having an abundant supply of desirable qualities or substances
(especially natural resources)
Antonym: poor.a.04
Definition: lacking in specific resources, qualities or substances
```

The preceding outputs show sample synonyms and antonyms for the term 'large' and the term 'rich'. Additionally, we explore several synsets associated with the term or concept 'rich', which rightly give us distinct synonyms and their corresponding antonyms.

Hyponyms and Hypernyms

Synsets represent terms with unique semantics and concepts and are linked or related to each other based on some similarity and context. Several of these synsets represent abstract and generic concepts also besides concrete entities. Usually they are interlinked together in the form of a hierarchical structure representing *is-a* relationships. Hyponyms and hypernyms help us explore related concepts by navigating through this hierarchy. To be more specific, *hyponyms* refer to entities or concepts that are a subclass of a higher order concept or entity and have very specific sense or context compared to its superclass. The following snippet shows the hyponyms for the entity 'tree':

```
term = 'tree'
synsets = wn.synsets(term)
tree = synsets[0]
# print the entity and its meaning
In [86]: print 'Name:', tree.name()
    ...: print 'Definition:', tree.definition()
Name: tree.n.01
Definition: a tall perennial woody plant having a main trunk and branches
forming a distinct elevated crown; includes both gymnosperms and angiosperms
# print total hyponyms and some sample hyponyms for 'tree'
In [87]: hyponyms = tree.hyponyms()
    ...: print 'Total Hyponyms:', len(hyponyms)
    ...: print 'Sample Hyponyms'
    ...: for hyponym in hyponyms[:10]:
    ...:     print hyponym.name(), '-', hyponym.definition()


Total Hyponyms: 180
Sample Hyponyms
aalii.n.01 - a small Hawaiian tree with hard dark wood
acacia.n.01 - any of various spiny trees or shrubs of the genus Acacia
african_walnut.n.01 - tropical African timber tree with wood that resembles
mahogany
albizzia.n.01 - any of numerous trees of the genus Albizia
alder.n.02 - north temperate shrubs or trees having toothed leaves and
conelike fruit; bark is used in tanning and dyeing and the wood is rot-
resistant
angelim.n.01 - any of several tropical American trees of the genus Andira
angiospermous_tree.n.01 - any tree having seeds and ovules contained in the
ovary
anise_tree.n.01 - any of several evergreen shrubs and small trees of the
genus Illicium
arbor.n.01 - tree (as opposed to shrub)
aroeira_blanca.n.01 - small resinous tree or shrub of Brazil
```

The preceding output tells us that there are a total of 180 hyponyms for 'tree', and we see some of the sample hyponyms and their definitions. We can see that each hyponym is a specific type of tree, as expected. Hyponyms are entities or concepts that act as the superclass to hyponyms and have a more generic sense or context. The following snippet shows the immediate superclass hyponym for 'tree':

```
In [88]: hypernyms = tree.hypernyms()
    ...: print hypernyms
[Synset('woody_plant.n.01')]
```

You can even navigate up the entire entity/concept hierarchy depicting all the hyponyms or parent classes for 'tree' using the following code snippet:

```
# get total hierarchy pathways for 'tree'
In [91]: hypernym_paths = tree.hypernym_paths()
```

```
    ...: print 'Total Hypernym paths:', len(hypernym_paths)
Total Hypernym paths: 1

# print the entire hypernym hierarchy
In [92]: print 'Hypernym Hierarchy'
    ...: print ' -> '.join(synset.name() for synset in hypernym_paths[0])
Hypernym Hierarchy
entity.n.01 -> physical_entity.n.01 -> object.n.01 -> whole.n.02 -> living_
thing.n.01 -> organism.n.01 -> plant.n.02 -> vascular_plant.n.01 -> woody_
plant.n.01 -> tree.n.01
```

From the preceding output, you can see that 'entity' is the most generic concept in which 'tree' is present, and the complete hypernym hierarchy showing the corresponding hypernym or superclass at each level is shown. As you navigate further down, you get into more specific concepts/entities, and if you go in the reverse direction you will get into more generic concepts/entities.

Holonyms and Meronyms

Holonyms are entities that contain a specific entity of our interest. Basically *holonym* refers to the relationship between a term or entity that denotes the whole and a term denoting a specific part of the whole. The following snippet shows the holonyms for 'tree':

```
In [94]: member_holonyms = tree.member_holonyms()
    ...: print 'Total Member Holonyms:', len(member_holonyms)
    ...: print 'Member Holonyms for [tree]:-'
    ...: for holonym in member_holonyms:
    ...:     print holonym.name(), '-', holonym.definition()
Total Member Holonyms: 1
Member Holonyms for [tree]:-
forest.n.01 - the trees and other plants in a large densely wooded area
```

From the output, we can see that 'forest' is a holonym for 'tree', which is semantically correct because, of course, a forest is a collection of trees. *Meronyms* are semantic relationships that relate a term or entity as a part or constituent of another term or entity. The following snippet depicts different types of meronyms for 'tree':

```
# part based meronyms for tree
In [95]: part_meronyms = tree.part_meronyms()
    ...: print 'Total Part Meronyms:', len(part_meronyms)
    ...: print 'Part Meronyms for [tree]:-'
    ...: for meronym in part_meronyms:
    ...:     print meronym.name(), '-', meronym.definition()
Total Part Meronyms: 5
Part Meronyms for [tree]:-
burl.n.02 - a large rounded outgrowth on the trunk or branch of a tree
crown.n.07 - the upper branches and leaves of a tree or other plant
```

limb.n.02 - any of the main branches arising from the trunk or a bough of a tree
stump.n.01 - the base part of a tree that remains standing after the tree has been felled
trunk.n.01 - the main stem of a tree; usually covered with bark; the bole is usually the part that is commercially useful for lumber

```
# substance based meronyms for tree
In [96]: substance_meronyms = tree.substance_meronyms()
    ...: print 'Total Substance Meronyms:', len(substance_meronyms)
    ...: print 'Substance Meronyms for [tree]:-'
    ...: for meronym in substance_meronyms:
    ...:     print meronym.name(), '-', meronym.definition()
Total Substance Meronyms: 2
Substance Meronyms for [tree]:-
heartwood.n.01 - the older inactive central wood of a tree or woody plant;
usually darker and denser than the surrounding sapwood
sapwood.n.01 - newly formed outer wood lying between the cambium and the
heartwood of a tree or woody plant; usually light colored; active in water
conduction
```

The preceding output shows various meronyms that include various constituents of trees like *stump* and *trunk* and also various derived substances from trees like *heartwood* and *sapwood*.

Semantic Relationships and Similarity

In the previous sections, we have looked at various concepts related to lexical semantic relationships. We will now look at ways to connect similar entities based on their semantic relationships and also measure semantic similarity between them. Semantic similarity is different from the conventional similarity metrics discussed in Chapter 6. We will use some sample synsets related to living entities as shown in the following snippet for our analysis:

```
tree = wn.synset('tree.n.01')
lion = wn.synset('lion.n.01')
tiger = wn.synset('tiger.n.02')
cat = wn.synset('cat.n.01')
dog = wn.synset('dog.n.01')
# create entities and extract names and definitions
entities = [tree, lion, tiger, cat, dog]
entity_names = [entity.name().split('.')[0] for entity in entities]
entity_definitions = [entity.definition() for entity in entities]

# print entities and their definitions
In [99]: for entity, definition in zip(entity_names, entity_definitions):
    ...:     print entity, '-', definition
```

tree - a tall perennial woody plant having a main trunk and branches forming
a distinct elevated crown; includes both gymnosperms and angiosperms
lion - large gregarious predatory feline of Africa and India having a tawny
coat with a shaggy mane in the male
tiger - large feline of forests in most of Asia having a tawny coat with
black stripes; endangered
cat - feline mammal usually having thick soft fur and no ability to roar:
domestic cats; wildcats
dog - a member of the genus Canis (probably descended from the common wolf)
that has been domesticated by man since prehistoric times; occurs in many
breeds

Now that we know our entities a bit better from these definitions explaining them, we will try to correlate the entities based on common hypernyms. For each pair of entities, we will try to find the lowest common hypernym in the relationship hierarchy tree. Correlated entities are expected to have very specific hypernyms, and unrelated entities should have very abstract or generic hypernyms. The following code snippet illustrates:

```
common_hypernyms = []
for entity in entities:
    # get pairwise lowest common hypernyms
    common_hypernyms.append([entity.lowest_common_hypernyms(compared_entity)[0]
                                    .name().split('.')[0]
                            for compared_entity in entities])
# build pairwise lower common hypernym matrix
common_hypernym_frame = pd.DataFrame(common_hypernyms,
                                    index=entity_names,
                                    columns=entity_names)
# print the matrix
In [101]: print common_hypernym_frame
    ...:
           tree       lion      tiger        cat        dog
tree       tree   organism   organism   organism   organism
lion   organism       lion    big_cat     feline  carnivore
tiger  organism    big_cat      tiger     feline  carnivore
cat    organism     feline     feline        cat  carnivore
dog    organism  carnivore  carnivore  carnivore        dog
```

Ignoring the main diagonal of the matrix, for each pair of entities, we can see their lowest common hypernym which depicts the nature of relationship between them. *Trees* are unrelated to the other animals except that they are all living organisms. Hence we get the 'organism' relationship amongst them. *Cats* are related to *lions* and *tigers* with respect to being feline creatures, and we can see the same in the preceding output. *Tigers* and *lions* are connected to each other with the 'big cat' relationship. Finally, we can see *dogs* having the relationship of 'carnivore' with the other animals since they all typically eat meat.

We can also measure the semantic similarity between these entities using various semantic concepts. We will use 'path similarity', which returns a value between [0, 1] based on the shortest path connecting two terms based on their hypernym/hyponym based taxonomy. The following snippet shows us how to generate this similarity matrix:

329

```
similarities = []
for entity in entities:
    # get pairwise similarities
    similarities.append([round(entity.path_similarity(compared_entity), 2)
                         for compared_entity in entities])
# build pairwise similarity matrix
similarity_frame = pd.DataFrame(similarities,
                                index=entity_names,
                                columns=entity_names)
# print the matrix
print similarity_frame
```

```
       tree  lion  tiger   cat   dog
tree   1.00  0.07   0.07  0.08  0.13
lion   0.07  1.00   0.33  0.25  0.17
tiger  0.07  0.33   1.00  0.25  0.17
cat    0.08  0.25   0.25  1.00  0.20
dog    0.13  0.17   0.17  0.20  1.00
```

From the preceding output, as expected, *lion* and *tiger* are the most similar with a value of 0.33, followed by their semantic similarity with *cat* having a value of 0.25. And *tree* has the lowest semantic similarity values when compared with other animals.

This concludes our discussion on analyzing lexical semantic relations. I encourage you to try exploring more concepts with different examples by leveraging WordNet.

Word Sense Disambiguation

In the previous section, we looked at homographs and homonyms, which are basically words that look or sound similar but have very different meanings. This meaning is contextual based on how it has been used and also depends on the word semantics, also called *word sense*. Identifying the correct sense or semantics of a word based on its usage is called *word sense disambiguation* with the assumption that the word has multiple meanings based on its context. This is a very popular problem in NLP and is used in various applications, such as improving the relevance of search engine results, coherence, and so on.

There are various ways to solve this problem, including lexical and dictionary-based methods and supervised and unsupervised ML methods. Covering everything would be out of the current scope, so I will be showing word sense disambiguation using the Lesk algorithm, a classic algorithm invented by M. E. Lesk in 1986. The basic principle behind this algorithm is to leverage dictionary or vocabulary definitions for a word we want to disambiguate in a body of text and compare the words in these definitions with a section of text surrounding our word of interest. We will be using the WordNet definitions for words instead of a dictionary. The main objective for us would be to return the synset with the maximum number of overlapping words or terms between the context sentence and the different definitions from each synset for the word we target for disambiguation. The following snippet leverages nltk to depict how to use word sense disambiguation for various examples:

```
from nltk.wsd import lesk
from nltk import word_tokenize

# sample text and word to disambiguate
samples = [('The fruits on that plant have ripened', 'n'),
           ('He finally reaped the fruit of his hard work as he won the
            race', 'n')]
word = 'fruit'
# perform word sense disambiguation
In [106]: for sentence, pos_tag in samples:
    ...:     word_syn = lesk(word_tokenize(sentence.lower()), word, pos_tag)
    ...:     print 'Sentence:', sentence
    ...:     print 'Word synset:', word_syn
    ...:     print 'Corresponding definition:', word_syn.definition()
    ...:     print
Sentence: The fruits on that plant have ripened
Word synset: Synset('fruit.n.01')
Corresponding definition: the ripened reproductive body of a seed plant

Sentence: He finally reaped the fruit of his hard work as he won the race
Word synset: Synset('fruit.n.03')
Corresponding definition: the consequence of some effort or action


# sample text and word to disambiguate
samples = [('Lead is a very soft, malleable metal', 'n'),
           ('John is the actor who plays the lead in that movie', 'n'),
           ('This road leads to nowhere', 'v')]
word = 'lead'
# perform word sense disambiguation
In [108]: for sentence, pos_tag in samples:
    ...:     word_syn = lesk(word_tokenize(sentence.lower()), word,
                pos_tag)
    ...:     print 'Sentence:', sentence
    ...:     print 'Word synset:', word_syn
    ...:     print 'Corresponding definition:', word_syn.definition()
    ...:     print
Sentence: Lead is a very soft, malleable metal
Word synset: Synset('lead.n.02')
Corresponding definition: a soft heavy toxic malleable metallic element;
bluish white when freshly cut but tarnishes readily to dull grey

Sentence: John is the actor who plays the lead in that movie
Word synset: Synset('star.n.04')
Corresponding definition: an actor who plays a principal role

Sentence: This road leads to nowhere
Word synset: Synset('run.v.23')
Corresponding definition: cause something to pass or lead somewhere
```

We try to disambiguate two words, 'fruit' and 'lead' in various text documents in the preceding examples. You can see how we use the Lesk algorithm to get the correct word sense for the word we are disambiguating based on its usage and context in each document. This tells you how *fruit* can mean both an entity that is consumed as well as some consequence one faces on applying efforts. We also see how *lead* can mean the soft metal, causing something/someone to go somewhere, or even an actor who plays the main role in a play or movie.

Named Entity Recognition

In any text document, there are particular terms that represent entities that are more informative and have a unique context compared to the rest of the text. These entities are known as *named entities*, which more specifically refers to terms that represent real-world objects like people, places, organizations, and so on, which are usually denoted by proper names. We can find these typically by looking at the noun phrases in text documents. *Named entity recognition*, also known as *entity chunking/extraction*, is a popular technique used in information extraction to identify and segment named entities and classify or categorize them under various predefined classes. Some of these classes that are used most frequently are shown in Figure 7-1 (courtesy of nltk and The Stanford NLP group).

Named Entity Type	Examples
PERSON	President Obama, Franz Beckenbauer
ORGANIZATION	WHO, ISRO, FC Bayern
LOCATION	Germany, India, USA, Mt. Everest
DATE	December, 2016-12-25
TIME	12:30:00 AM, one thirty pm
MONEY	Twenty dollars, Rs. 50, 100 GBP
PERCENT	20%, forty five percent
FACILITY	Stonehenge, Taj Mahal, Washington Monument
GPE	Asia, Europe, Germany, North America

Figure 7-1. *Common named entities with examples*

There is some overlap between GPE and LOCATION. The GPE entities are usually more generic and represent geo-political entities like cities, states, countries, and continents. LOCATION can also refer to these entities (it varies across different NER systems) along with very specific locations like a mountain, river, or hill-station. FACILITY on the other hand refers to popular monuments or artifacts that are usually man-made. The remaining categories are pretty self-explanatory from their names and the examples depicted in Figure 7-1.

The Bundesliga is perhaps the most popular top-level professional association football league in Germany, and FC Bayern Munchen is one of the most popular clubs in this league with a global presence. We will now take a sample description of this club from Wikipedia and try to extract named entities from it. We will reuse our normalization module (accessible as normalization.py in the code files) from the last chapter in this section to parse the document to remove unnecessary new lines. We will start by leveraging nltk's Named Entity Chunker:

```
# sample document
text = """
Bayern Munich, or FC Bayern, is a German sports club based in Munich,
Bavaria, Germany. It is best known for its professional football team,
which plays in the Bundesliga, the top tier of the German football
league system, and is the most successful club in German football
history, having won a record 26 national titles and 18 national cups.
FC Bayern was founded in 1900 by eleven football players led by Franz John.
Although Bayern won its first national championship in 1932, the club
was not selected for the Bundesliga at its inception in 1963. The club
had its period of greatest success in the middle of the 1970s when,
under the captaincy of Franz Beckenbauer, it won the European Cup three
times in a row (1974-76). Overall, Bayern has reached ten UEFA Champions
League finals, most recently winning their fifth title in 2013 as part
of a continental treble.
"""


import nltk
from normalization import parse_document
import pandas as pd

# tokenize sentences
sentences = parse_document(text)
tokenized_sentences = [nltk.word_tokenize(sentence) for sentence in
sentences]

# tag sentences and use nltk's Named Entity Chunker
tagged_sentences = [nltk.pos_tag(sentence) for sentence in tokenized_
sentences]
ne_chunked_sents = [nltk.ne_chunk(tagged) for tagged in tagged_sentences]

# extract all named entities
named_entities = []
for ne_tagged_sentence in ne_chunked_sents:
    for tagged_tree in ne_tagged_sentence:
        # extract only chunks having NE labels
        if hasattr(tagged_tree, 'label'):
                entity_name = ' '.join(c[0] for c in tagged_tree.leaves()) #
                get NE name
                entity_type = tagged_tree.label() # get NE category
                named_entities.append((entity_name, entity_type))
# get unique named entities
named_entities = list(set(named_entities))
```

```
# store named entities in a data frame
entity_frame = pd.DataFrame(named_entities,
                            columns=['Entity Name', 'Entity Type'])
# display results
In [116]: print entity_frame
         Entity Name    Entity Type
0            Bayern         PERSON
1        Franz John         PERSON
2   Franz Beckenbauer     PERSON
3            Munich   ORGANIZATION
4          European   ORGANIZATION
5         Bundesliga  ORGANIZATION
6            German            GPE
7           Bavaria            GPE
8           Germany            GPE
9         FC Bayern   ORGANIZATION
10             UEFA   ORGANIZATION
11           Munich            GPE
12           Bayern            GPE
13          Overall            GPE
```

The Named Entity Chunker identifies named entities from the preceding text document, and we extract these named entities from the tagged annotated sentences and display them in the data frame as shown. You can clearly see how it has correctly identified PERSON, ORGANIZATION, and GPE related named entities, although a few of them are incorrectly identified.

We will now use the Stanford NER tagger on the same text and compare the results. For this, you need to have Java installed and then download the Stanford NER resources from http://nlp.stanford.edu/software/stanford-ner-2014-08-27.zip. Unzip them to a location of your choice (I used E:/stanford in my system). Once done, you can use nltk's interface to access this, similar to what we did in Chapter 3 for constituency and dependency parsing. For more details on Stanford NER, visit http://nlp.stanford.edu/software/CRF-NER.shtml, the official web site, which also contains the latest version of their Named Entity Recognizer (I used an older version):

```
from nltk.tag import StanfordNERTagger
import os

# set java path in environment variables
java_path = r'C:\Program Files\Java\jdk1.8.0_102\bin\java.exe'
os.environ['JAVAHOME'] = java_path

# load stanford NER
sn = StanfordNERTagger('E:/stanford/stanford-ner-2014-08-27/classifiers/
english.all.3class.distsim.crf.ser.gz',
                       path_to_jar='E:/stanford/stanford-ner-2014-08-27/
                       stanford-ner.jar')
```

```
# tag sentences
ne_annotated_sentences = [sn.tag(sent) for sent in tokenized_sentences]

# extract named entities
named_entities = []
for sentence in ne_annotated_sentences:
    temp_entity_name = ''
    temp_named_entity = None
    for term, tag in sentence:
        # get terms with NE tags
        if tag != 'O':
            temp_entity_name = ' '.join([temp_entity_name, term]).strip() #
            get NE name
            temp_named_entity = (temp_entity_name, tag) # get NE and its
            category
        else:
            if temp_named_entity:
                named_entities.append(temp_named_entity)
                temp_entity_name = ''
                temp_named_entity = None

# get unique named entities
named_entities = list(set(named_entities))
# store named entities in a data frame
entity_frame = pd.DataFrame(named_entities,
                            columns=['Entity Name', 'Entity Type'])

# display results
In [118]: print entity_frame
         Entity Name    Entity Type
0         Franz John         PERSON
1  Franz Beckenbauer         PERSON
2            Germany       LOCATION
3             Bayern   ORGANIZATION
4            Bavaria       LOCATION
5             Munich       LOCATION
6          FC Bayern   ORGANIZATION
7               UEFA   ORGANIZATION
8      Bayern Munich   ORGANIZATION
```

The preceding output depicts various named entities obtained from our document. You can compare this with the results obtained from nltk's NER chunker. The results here are definitely better—there are no misclassifications and each category is also assigned correctly. Some really interesting points: It has correctly identified *Munich* as a LOCATION and *Bayern Munich* as an ORGANIZATION. Does this mean the second NER tagger is better? Not really. It depends on the type of corpus you are analyzing, and you can even build your own NER tagger using supervised learning by training on pre-tagged corpora similar to what we did in Chapter 3. In fact, both the taggers just discussed have been trained on pre-tagged corpora like CoNLL, MUC, and Penn Treebank.

Analyzing Semantic Representations

We usually communicate in the form of messages in spoken form or in written form with other people or interfaces. Each of these messages is typically a collection of words, phrases, or sentences, and they have their own semantics and context. So far, we've talked about semantics and relations between various lexical units. But how do we represent the meaning of semantics conveyed by a message or messages? How do humans understand what someone is telling them? How do we believe in statements and propositions and evaluate outcomes and what action to take? It feels easy because the brain helps us with logic and reasoning—but computationally can we do the same?

The answer is yes we can. Frameworks like propositional logic and first-order logic help us in representation of semantics. We discussed this in detail in Chapter 1 in the subsection "Representation of Semantics" under the "Language Semantics" section. I encourage you to go through that once more to refresh your memory. In the following sections, we will look at ways to represent propositional and first order logic and prove or disprove propositions, statements, and predicates using practical examples and code.

Propositional Logic

We have already discussed propositional logic (PL) as the study of propositions, statements, and sentences. A *proposition* is usually declarative, having a binary value of being either true or false. There also exist various logical operators like conjunction, disjunction, implication, and equivalence, and we also study the effects of applying these operators on multiple propositions to understand their behavior and outcome.

Let us consider our example from Chapter 1 with regard to two propositions P and Q such that they can be represented as follows:

P: He is hungry

Q: He will eat a sandwich

We will now try to build the truth tables for various operations on these propositions using nltk based on the various logical operators discussed in Chapter 1 (refer to the "Propositional Logic" section for more details) and derive outcomes computationally:

```
import nltk
import pandas as pd
import os

# assign symbols and propositions
symbol_P = 'P'
symbol_Q = 'Q'
proposition_P = 'He is hungry'
propositon_Q = 'He will eat a sandwich'
# assign various truth values to the propositions
p_statuses = [False, False, True, True]
q_statuses = [False, True, False, True]
# assign the various expressions combining the logical operators
conjunction = '(P & Q)'
disjunction = '(P | Q)'
implication = '(P -> Q)'
```

```
equivalence = '(P <-> Q)'
expressions = [conjunction, disjunction, implication, equivalence]

# evaluate each expression using propositional logic
results = []
for status_p, status_q in zip(p_statuses, q_statuses):
    dom = set([])
    val = nltk.Valuation([(symbol_P, status_p),
                          (symbol_Q, status_q)])
    assignments = nltk.Assignment(dom)
    model = nltk.Model(dom, val)
    row = [status_p, status_q]
    for expression in expressions:
        # evaluate each expression based on proposition truth values
        result = model.evaluate(expression, assignments)
        row.append(result)
    results.append(row)
# build the result table
columns = [symbol_P, symbol_Q, conjunction,
           disjunction, implication, equivalence]
result_frame = pd.DataFrame(results, columns=columns)

# display results
In [125]: print 'P:', proposition_P
     ...: print 'Q:', propositon_Q
     ...: print
     ...: print 'Expression Outcomes:-'
     ...: print result_frame
P: He is hungry
Q: He will eat a sandwich

Expression Outcomes:-
       P      Q (P & Q) (P | Q) (P -> Q) (P <-> Q)
0  False  False   False   False     True      True
1  False   True   False    True     True     False
2   True  False   False    True    False     False
3   True   True    True    True     True      True
```

The preceding output depicts the various truth values of the two propositions, and when we combine them with various logical operators, you will find the results matching with what we manually evaluated in Chapter 1. For example, P & Q indicates *He is hungry and he will eat a sandwich* is True only when both of the individual propositions is True. We use nltk's Valuation class to create a dictionary of the propositions and their various outcome states. We use the Model class to evaluate each expression, where the evaluate() function internally calls the recursive function satisfy(), which helps in evaluating the outcome of each expression with the propositions based on the assigned truth values.

First Order Logic

PL has several limitations, like the inability to represent facts or complex relationships and inferences. PL also has limited expressive power because for each new proposition we would need a unique symbolic representation, and it becomes very difficult to generalize facts. This is where first order logic (FOL) works really well with features like functions, quantifiers, relations, connectives, and symbols. It definitely provides a richer and more powerful representation for semantic information. The "First Order Logic" subsection under "Representation of Semantics" in Chapter 1 provides detailed information about how FOL works.

In this section, we will build several FOL representations similar to what we did manually in Chapter 1 using mathematical representations. Here we will build them in our code using similar syntax and leverage nltk and some theorem provers to prove the outcome of various expressions based on predefined conditions and relationships, similar to what we did for PL. The key takeaway for you from this section should be getting to know how to represent FOL representations in Python and how to perform FOL inference using proofs based on some goal and predefined rules and events. There are several theorem provers you can use for evaluating expressions and proving theorems. The nltk package has three main different types of provers: Prover9, TableauProver, and ResolutionProver. The first one is a free-to-use prover available for download at www.cs.unm.edu/~mccune/prover9/download/. You can extract the contents in a location of your choice (I used E:/prover9). We will be using both ResolutionProver and Prover9 in our examples. The following snippet helps in setting up the necessary dependencies for FOL expressions and evaluations:

```
import nltk
import os
# for reading FOL expressions
read_expr = nltk.sem.Expression.fromstring
# initialize theorem provers (you can choose any)
os.environ['PROVER9'] = r'E:/prover9/bin'
prover = nltk.Prover9()
# I use the following one for our examples
prover = nltk.ResolutionProver()
```

Now that we have our dependencies ready, let us evaluate a few FOL expressions. Consider a simple expression that *If an entity jumps over another entity, the reverse cannot happen.* Assuming the entities to be x and y, we can represent this is FOL as $\forall x \, \forall y$ (jumps_over(x, y) → ¬jumps_over(y, x)) which signifies that for all x and y, if x jumps over y, it implies that y cannot jump over x. Consider now that we have two entities fox and dog such that the fox jumps over the dog is an event which has taken place and can be represented by jumps_over(fox, dog). Our end goal or objective is to evaluate the outcome of jumps_over(dog, fox) considering the preceding expression and the event that has occurred. The following snippet shows us how we can do this:

```
# set the rule expression
rule = read_expr('all x. all y. (jumps_over(x, y) -> -jumps_over(y, x))')
# set the event occured
```

```
event = read_expr('jumps_over(fox, dog)')
# set the outcome we want to evaluate -- the goal
test_outcome = read_expr('jumps_over(dog, fox)')

# get the result
In [132]: prover.prove(goal=test_outcome,
     ...:              assumptions=[event, rule],
     ...:              verbose=True)
[1] {-jumps_over(dog,fox)}                    A
[2] {jumps_over(fox,dog)}                     A
[3] {-jumps_over(z4,z3), -jumps_over(z3,z4)}  A
[4] {-jumps_over(dog,fox)}                    (2, 3)

Out[132]: False
```

The preceding output depicts the final result for our goal test_outcome is False, that is, the dog cannot jump over the fox if the fox has already jumped over the dog based on our rule expression and the events assigned to the assumptions parameter in the prover already given. The sequence of steps that lead to the result is also shown in the output. Let us now consider another FOL expression rule $\forall x$ studies(x, exam) $\rightarrow$ pass(x, exam), which tells us that for all instances of x, if x studies for the exam, he/she will pass the exam. Let us represent this rule and consider two students, John and Pierre, such that John does not study for the exam and Pierre does. Can we then find out the outcome whether they will pass the exam based on the given expression rule? The following snippet shows us how:

```
# set the rule expression
rule = read_expr('all x. (studies(x, exam) -> pass(x, exam))')
# set the events and outcomes we want to determine
event1 = read_expr('-studies(John, exam)')
test_outcome1 = read_expr('pass(John, exam)')
event2 = read_expr('studies(Pierre, exam)')
test_outcome2 = read_expr('pass(Pierre, exam)')

# get results
In [134]: prover.prove(goal=test_outcome1,
     ...:              assumptions=[event1, rule],
     ...:              verbose=True)
[1] {-pass(John,exam)}                A
[2] {-studies(John,exam)}             A
[3] {-studies(z6,exam), pass(z6,exam)} A
[4] {-studies(John,exam)}             (1, 3)

Out[134]: False

In [135]: prover.prove(goal=test_outcome2,
     ...:              assumptions=[event2, rule],
     ...:              verbose=True)
```

```
[1] {-pass(Pierre,exam)}                       A
[2] {studies(Pierre,exam)}                     A
[3] {-studies(z8,exam), pass(z8,exam)}   A
[4] {-studies(Pierre,exam)}              (1, 3)
[5] {pass(Pierre,exam)}                  (2, 3)
[6] {}                                   (1, 5)
```

Out[135]: True

Thus you can see from the above evaluations that Pierre does pass the exam because he studied for the exam, unlike John who doesn't pass the exam since he did not study for it.

Let us consider a more complex example with several entities. They perform several actions as follows:

- There are two dogs rover (r) and alex (a)

- There is one cat garfield (g)

- There is one fox felix (f)

- Two animals, alex (a) and felix (f) run, denoted by function runs()

- Two animals rover (r) and garfield (g) sleep, denoted by function sleeps()

- Two animals, felix (f) and alex (a) can jump over the other two, denoted by function jumps_over()

Taking all these assumptions, the following snippet builds an FOL-based model with the previously mentioned domain and assignment values based on the entities and functions. Once we build this model, we evaluate various FOL-based expressions to determine their outcome and prove some theorems like we did earlier:

```
# define symbols (entities\functions) and their values
rules = """
    rover => r
    felix => f
    garfield => g
    alex => a
    dog => {r, a}
    cat => {g}
    fox => {f}
    runs => {a, f}
    sleeps => {r, g}
    jumps_over => {(f, g), (a, g), (f, r), (a, r)}
    """
val = nltk.Valuation.fromstring(rules)
# view the valuation object of symbols and their assigned values
(dictionary)
```

```
In [143]: print val
{'rover': 'r', 'runs': set([('f',), ('a',)]), 'alex': 'a', 'sleeps':
set([('r',), ('g',)]), 'felix': 'f', 'fox': set([('f',)]), 'dog':
set([('a',), ('r',)]), 'jumps_over': set([('a', 'g'), ('f', 'g'), ('a',
'r'), ('f', 'r')]), 'cat': set([('g',)]), 'garfield': 'g'}

# define domain and build FOL based model
dom = {'r', 'f', 'g', 'a'}
m = nltk.Model(dom, val)

# evaluate various expressions
In [148]: print m.evaluate('jumps_over(felix, rover) & dog(rover) &
runs(rover)', None)
False

In [149]: print m.evaluate('jumps_over(felix, rover) & dog(rover) &
-runs(rover)', None)
True

In [150]: print m.evaluate('jumps_over(alex, garfield) & dog(alex) &
cat(garfield) & sleeps(garfield)', None)
True

# assign rover to x and felix to y in the domain
g = nltk.Assignment(dom, [('x', 'r'), ('y', 'f')])

# evaluate more expressions based on above assigned symbols
In [152]: print m.evaluate('runs(y) & jumps_over(y, x) & sleeps(x)', g)
True

In [153]: print m.evaluate('exists y. (fox(y) & runs(y))', g)
True
```

The preceding snippet depicts the evaluation of various expressions based on the valuation of different symbols based on the rules and domain. We create various FOL-based expressions and see their outcome based on the predefined assumptions. For example, the first expression gives us False because rover never runs() and the second and third expressions are True because they satisfy all the conditions like felix and alex can jump over rover or garfield and rover is a dog that does not run and garfield is a cat. The second set of expressions is evaluated based on assigning felix and rover to specific symbols in our domain (dom), and we pass that variable (g) when evaluating the expressions. We can even satisfy open formulae or expressions using the satisfiers() function as shown here:

```
# who are the animals who run?
In [154]: formula = read_expr('runs(x)')
     ...: print m.satisfiers(formula, 'x', g)
set(['a', 'f'])
```

```
# animals who run and are also a fox?
In [155]: formula = read_expr('runs(x) & fox(x)')
     ...: print m.satisfiers(formula, 'x', g)
set(['f'])
```

The preceding outputs are self-explanatory wherein we evaluate open-ended questions like *which animals run*? And also *which animals can run and are also foxes*? We get the relevant symbols in our outputs, which you can map back to the actual animal names (Hint: a: alex, f: felix). I encourage you to experiment with more propositions and FOL expressions by building your own assumptions, domain, and rules.

Sentiment Analysis

We will now discuss several concepts, techniques, and examples with regard to our second major topic in this chapter, sentiment analysis. Textual data, even though unstructured, mainly has two broad types of data points: factual based (objective) and opinion based (subjective). We briefly talked about these two categories at the beginning of this chapter when I introduced the concept of sentiment analysis and how it works best on text that has a subjective context. In general, social media, surveys, and feedback data all are heavily opinionated and express the beliefs, judgement, emotion, and feelings of human beings. Sentiment analysis, also popularly known as *opinion analysis/mining*, is defined as the process of using techniques like NLP, lexical resources, linguistics, and machine learning (ML) to extract subjective and opinion related information like emotions, attitude, mood, modality, and so on and try to use these to compute the polarity expressed by a text document. By *polarity*, I mean to find out whether the document expresses a positive, negative, or a neutral sentiment. More advanced analysis involves trying to find out more complex emotions like sadness, happiness, anger, and sarcasm.

Typically, sentiment analysis for text data can be computed on several levels, including on an individual sentence level, paragraph level, or the entire document as a whole. Often sentiment is computed on the document as a whole or some aggregations are done after computing the sentiment for individual sentences. *Polarity analysis* usually involves trying to assign some scores contributing to the positive and negative emotions expressed in the document and then finally assigning a label to the document based on the aggregate score. We will depict two major techniques for sentiment analysis here:

- Supervised machine learning
- Unsupervised lexicon-based

The key idea is to learn the various techniques typically used to tackle sentiment analysis problems so that you can apply them to solve your own problems. We will see how to re-use the concepts of supervised machine learning based classification algorithms from Chapter 4 here to classify documents to their associated sentiment. We will also use *lexicons*, which are dictionaries or vocabularies specially constructed to be used for sentiment analysis, and compute sentiment without using any supervised techniques. We will be carrying out our experiments on a large real-world dataset pertaining to movie reviews, which will make this task more interesting. We will compare the performance of the various algorithms and also try to perform some detailed analytics besides just analyzing polarity, which includes analyzing the subjectivity, mood, and modality of the movie reviews. Without further delay, let's get started!

Sentiment Analysis of IMDb Movie Reviews

We will be using a dataset of movie reviews obtained from the Internet Movie Database (IMDb) for sentiment analysis. This dataset, containing over 50,000 movie reviews, can be obtained from http://ai.stanford.edu/~amaas/data/sentiment/, courtesy of Stanford University and A. L. Maas, R. E. Daly, P. T. Pham, D. Huang, Andrew Ng, and C. Potts, and this dataset was used in their famous paper, "Learning Word Vectors for Sentiment Analysis." We will be using 50,000 movie reviews from this dataset, which contain the review and a corresponding sentiment polarity label which is either positive or negative. A positive review is basically a movie review which was rated with more than six stars in IMDb, and a negative review was rated with less than five stars in IMDb. An important thing to remember here before we begin our exercise is the fact that many of these reviews, even though labeled positive or negative, might have some elements of negative or positive context respectively. Hence, there is a possibility for some overlap in many reviews, which make this task harder. Sentiment is not a quantitative number that you can compute and prove mathematically. It expresses complex emotions, feelings, and judgement, and hence you should never focus on trying to get a cent-percent perfect model but a model that generalizes well on data and works decently. We will start with setting up some necessary dependencies and utilities before moving on to the various techniques.

Setting Up Dependencies

There are several utility functions, data, and package dependencies that we need to set up before we jump into sentiment analysis. We will need our movie review dataset, some specific packages that we will be using in our implementations, and we will be defining some utility functions for text normalization, feature extracting, and model evaluation, similar to what we have used in previous chapters.

Getting and Formatting the Data

We will use the IMDb movie review dataset officially available in raw text files for each set (training and testing) from http://ai.stanford.edu/~amaas/data/sentiment/ as mentioned. You can download and unzip the files to a location of your choice and use the review_data_extractor.py file included along with the code files of this chapter to extract each review from the unzipped directory, parse them, and neatly format them into a data frame, which is then stored as a csv file named movie_reviews.csv. Otherwise, you can directly download the parsed and formatted file from https://github.com/dipanjanS/text-analytics-with-python/tree/master/Chapter-7, which contains all datasets and code used and is the official repository for this book. The data frame consists of two columns, review and sentiment, for each data point, which indicates the review for a movie and its corresponding sentiment (positive or negative).

Text Normalization

We will be normalizing and standardizing our text data similar to what we did in Chapter 6 as a part of text pre-processing and normalization. For this we will be re-using our normalization.py module from Chapter 6 with a few additions. This mainly includes adding an HTML stripper to remove unnecessary HTML characters from text documents, as shown here:

```
from HTMLParser import HTMLParser

class MLStripper(HTMLParser):
    def __init__(self):
        self.reset()
        self.fed = []
    def handle_data(self, d):
        self.fed.append(d)
    def get_data(self):
        return ' '.join(self.fed)

def strip_html(text):
    html_stripper = MLStripper()
    html_stripper.feed(text)
    return html_stripper.get_data()
```

We also add a new function to normalize special accented characters and convert them into regular ASCII characters so as to standardize the text across all documents. The following snippet helps us achieve this:

```
def normalize_accented_characters(text):
    text = unicodedata.normalize('NFKD',
                                 text.decode('utf-8')
                                 ).encode('ascii', 'ignore')
    return text
```

The overall text normalization function is depicted in the following snippet and it re-uses the expand contractions, lemmatization, HTML unescaping, special characters removal, and stopwords removal functions from the previous chapter's normalization module:

```
def normalize_corpus(corpus, lemmatize=True,
                     only_text_chars=False,
                     tokenize=False):

    normalized_corpus = []
    for index, text in enumerate(corpus):
        text = normalize_accented_characters(text)
        text = html_parser.unescape(text)
        text = strip_html(text)
        text = expand_contractions(text, CONTRACTION_MAP)
        if lemmatize:
            text = lemmatize_text(text)
        else:
```

```
            text = text.lower()
        text = remove_special_characters(text)
        text = remove_stopwords(text)
        if only_text_chars:
            text = keep_text_characters(text)

        if tokenize:
            text = tokenize_text(text)
            normalized_corpus.append(text)
        else:
            normalized_corpus.append(text)

    return normalized_corpus
```

To re-use this code, you can make use of the normalization.py and contractions. py files provided with the code files of this chapter.

Feature Extraction

We will be reusing the same feature-extraction function we used in Chapter 6, and it is available as a part of the utils.py module. The function is shown here for the sake of completeness:

```
from sklearn.feature_extraction.text import CountVectorizer, TfidfVectorizer

def build_feature_matrix(documents, feature_type='frequency',
                         ngram_range=(1, 1), min_df=0.0, max_df=1.0):

    feature_type = feature_type.lower().strip()

    if feature_type == 'binary':
        vectorizer = CountVectorizer(binary=True, min_df=min_df,
                                     max_df=max_df, ngram_range=ngram_range)
    elif feature_type == 'frequency':
        vectorizer = CountVectorizer(binary=False, min_df=min_df,
                                     max_df=max_df, ngram_range=ngram_range)
    elif feature_type == 'tfidf':
        vectorizer = TfidfVectorizer(min_df=min_df, max_df=max_df,
                                     ngram_range=ngram_range)
    else:
        raise Exception("Wrong feature type entered. Possible values:
        'binary', 'frequency', 'tfidf'")

    feature_matrix = vectorizer.fit_transform(documents).astype(float)
    return vectorizer, feature_matrix
```

You can experiment with various features provided by this function, which include Bag of Words-based frequencies, occurrences, and TF-IDF based features.

Model Performance Evaluation

We will be evaluating our models based on precision, recall, accuracy, and F1-score, similar to our evaluation methods in Chapter 4 for text classification. Additionally we will be looking at the confusion matrix and detailed classification reports for each class, that is, the positive and negative classes to evaluate model performance. You can refer to the "Evaluating Classification Models" section in Chapter 4 to refresh your memory on the various model-evaluation metrics. The following function will help us in getting the model accuracy, precision, recall, and F1-score:

```
from sklearn import metrics
import numpy as np
import pandas as pd

def display_evaluation_metrics(true_labels, predicted_labels, positive_
class=1):
    print 'Accuracy:', np.round(
                        metrics.accuracy_score(true_labels,
                                        predicted_labels),
                        2)
    print 'Precision:', np.round(
                        metrics.precision_score(true_labels,
                                        predicted_labels,
                                        pos_label=positive_class,
                                        average='binary'),
                        2)
    print 'Recall:', np.round(
                        metrics.recall_score(true_labels,
                                        predicted_labels,
                                        pos_label=positive_class,
                                        average='binary'),
                        2)
    print 'F1 Score:', np.round(
                        metrics.f1_score(true_labels,
                                        predicted_labels,
                                        pos_label=positive_class,
                                        average='binary'),
                        2)
```

We will also define a function to help us build the confusion matrix for evaluating the model predictions against the actual sentiment labels for the reviews. The following function will help us achieve that:

```python
def display_confusion_matrix(true_labels, predicted_labels, classes=[1,0]):
    cm = metrics.confusion_matrix(y_true=true_labels,
                                  y_pred=predicted_labels,
                                  labels=classes)
    cm_frame = pd.DataFrame(data=cm,
                            columns=pd.MultiIndex(levels=[['Predicted:'],
                            classes],
                                                  labels=[[0,0],[0,1]]),
                            index=pd.MultiIndex(levels=[['Actual:'],
                            classes],
                                                labels=[[0,0],[0,1]]))
    print cm_frame
```

Finally, we will define a function for getting a detailed classification report per sentiment category (positive and negative) by displaying the precision, recall, F1-score, and support (number of reviews) for each of the classes:

```python
def display_classification_report(true_labels, predicted_labels,
classes=[1,0]):
    report = metrics.classification_report(y_true=true_labels,
                                            y_pred=predicted_labels,
                                            labels=classes)
    print report
```

You will find all the preceding functions in the `utils.py` module along with the other code files for this chapter and you can re-use them as needed. Besides this, you need to make sure you have `nltk` and `pattern` installed—which you should already have by this point of time because we have used them numerous times in our previous chapters.

Preparing Datasets

We will be loading our movie reviews data and preparing two datasets, namely training and testing, similar to what we did in Chapter 4. We will train our supervised model on the training data and evaluate model performance on the testing data. For unsupervised models, we will directly evaluate them on the testing data so as to compare their performance with the supervised model. Besides that, we will also pick some sample positive and negative reviews to see how the different models perform on them:

```python
import pandas as pd
import numpy as np
# load movie reviews data
dataset = pd.read_csv(r'E:/aclImdb/movie_reviews.csv')
# print sample data
In [235]: print dataset.head()
                                              review sentiment
0  One of the other reviewers has mentioned that ...  positive
1  A wonderful little production. <br /><br />The...  positive
2  I thought this was a wonderful way to spend ti...  positive
```

```
3  Basically there's a family where a little boy ...  negative
4  Petter Mattei's "Love in the Time of Money" is...  positive

# prepare training and testing datasets
train_data = dataset[:35000]
test_data = dataset[35000:]

train_reviews = np.array(train_data['review'])
train_sentiments = np.array(train_data['sentiment'])
test_reviews = np.array(test_data['review'])
test_sentiments = np.array(test_data['sentiment'])

# prepare sample dataset for experiments
sample_docs = [100, 5817, 7626, 7356, 1008, 7155, 3533, 13010]
sample_data = [(test_reviews[index],
                test_sentiments[index])
                   for index in sample_docs]
```

We have taken a total of 35,000 reviews out of the 50,000 to be our training dataset and we will evaluate our models and test them on the remaining 15,000 reviews. This is in line with a typical 70:30 separation used for training and testing dataset building. We have also extracted a total of eight reviews from the test dataset and we will be looking closely at the results for these documents as well as evaluating the model performance on the complete test dataset in the following sections.

Supervised Machine Learning Technique

As mentioned before, in this section we will be building a model to analyze sentiment using supervised ML. This model will learn from past reviews and their corresponding sentiment from the training dataset so that it can predict the sentiment for new reviews from the test dataset. The basic principle here is to use the same concepts we used for text classification such that the classes to predict here are positive and negative sentiment corresponding to the movie reviews.

We will be following the same workflow which we followed in Chapter 4 for text classification (refer to Figure 4-2 in Chapter 4) in the "Text Classification Blueprint" section. The following points summarize these steps:

1. Model training

    a. Normalize training data

    b. Extract features and build feature set and feature vectorizer

    c. Use supervised learning algorithm (SVM) to build a predictive model

2. Model testing

    a.   Normalize testing data

    b.   Extract features using training feature vectorizer

    c.   Predict the sentiment for testing reviews using training model

    d.   Evaluate model performance

To start, we will be building our training model using the steps in point 1. We will be using our normalization and feature-extraction modules discussed in previous sections:

```
from normalization import normalize_corpus
from utils import build_feature_matrix

# normalization
norm_train_reviews = normalize_corpus(train_reviews, lemmatize=True, only_
text_chars=True)
# feature extraction
vectorizer, train_features = build_feature_matrix(documents=norm_train_
reviews,
                                        feature_type='tfidf',
                                        ngram_range=(1, 1),
                                        min_df=0.0, max_df=1.0)
```

We will now build our model using the *support vector machine* (SVM) algorithm which we used for text classification in Chapter 4. Refer to the "Support Vector Machines" subsection under the "Classification Algorithms" section in Chapter 4 to refresh your memory:

```
from sklearn.linear_model import SGDClassifier
# build the model
svm = SGDClassifier(loss='hinge', n_iter=200)
svm.fit(train_features, train_sentiments)
```

The preceding snippet trainings the classifier and builds the model that is in the svm variable, which we can now use for predicting sentiment for new movie reviews (not used for training) from the test dataset. Let us normalize and extract features from the test dataset first as mentioned in step 2 in our workflow:

```
# normalize reviews
norm_test_reviews = normalize_corpus(test_reviews, lemmatize=True, only_
text_chars=True)
# extract features
test_features = vectorizer.transform(norm_test_reviews)
```

Now that we have our features for the entire test dataset, before we predict the sentiment and measure model prediction performance for the entire test dataset, let us look at some of the predictions for the sample documents we extracted earlier:

```
# predict sentiment for sample docs from test data
In [253]: for doc_index in sample_docs:
     ...:        print 'Review:-'
     ...:        print test_reviews[doc_index]
     ...:        print 'Actual Labeled Sentiment:', test_sentiments[doc_index]
     ...:        doc_features = test_features[doc_index]
     ...:        predicted_sentiment = svm.predict(doc_features)[0]
     ...:        print 'Predicted Sentiment:', predicted_sentiment
     ...:        print
     ...:
     ...:
Review:-
Worst movie, (with the best reviews given it) I've ever seen. Over the top
dialog, acting, and direction. more slasher flick than thriller.With all the
great reviews this movie got I'm appalled that it turned out so silly. shame
on you martin scorsese
Actual Labeled Sentiment: negative
Predicted Sentiment: negative

Review:-
I hope this group of film-makers never re-unites.
Actual Labeled Sentiment: negative
Predicted Sentiment: negative

Review:-
no comment - stupid movie, acting average or worse... screenplay - no sense
at all... SKIP IT!
Actual Labeled Sentiment: negative
Predicted Sentiment: negative

Review:-
Add this little gem to your list of holiday regulars. It is<br /><br
/>sweet, funny, and endearing
Actual Labeled Sentiment: positive
Predicted Sentiment: positive

Review:-
a mesmerizing film that certainly keeps your attention... Ben Daniels is
fascinating (and courageous) to watch.
Actual Labeled Sentiment: positive
Predicted Sentiment: positive

Review:-
This movie is perfect for all the romantics in the world. John Ritter has
never been better and has the best line in the movie! "Sam" hits close to
home, is lovely to look at and so much fun to play along with. Ben Gazzara
was an excellent cast and easy to fall in love with. I'm sure I've met
Arthur in my travels somewhere. All around, an excellent choice to pick up
any evening.!:-)
```

```
Actual Labeled Sentiment: positive
Predicted Sentiment: positive
```

```
Review:-
I don't care if some people voted this movie to be bad. If you want the
Truth this is a Very Good Movie! It has every thing a movie should have. You
really should Get this one.
Actual Labeled Sentiment: positive
Predicted Sentiment: negative
```

```
Review:-
Worst horror film ever but funniest film ever rolled in one you have got
to see this film it is so cheap it is unbeliaveble but you have to see it
really!!!! P.s watch the carrot
Actual Labeled Sentiment: positive
Predicted Sentiment: negative
```

You can look at each review, its actual labeled sentiment, and our predicted sentiment in the preceding output and see that we have some negative and positive reviews, and our model is able to correctly identify the sentiment for most of the sampled reviews except the last two reviews. If you look closely at the last two reviews, some part of the review has a negative sentiment ("worst horror film", "voted this movie to be bad") but the general sentiment or opinion of the person who wrote the review was intended positive. These are the examples I mentioned earlier about the overlap of positive and negative emotions, which makes it difficult for the model to predict the actual sentiment!

Let us now predict the sentiment for all our test dataset reviews and evaluate our model performance:

```
# predict the sentiment for test dataset movie reviews
predicted_sentiments = svm.predict(test_features)

# evaluate model prediction performance
from utils import display_evaluation_metrics, display_confusion_matrix,
display_classification_report

# show performance metrics
In [270]: display_evaluation_metrics(true_labels=test_sentiments,
     ...:                            predicted_labels=predicted_sentiments,
     ...:                            positive_class='positive')
Accuracy: 0.89
Precision: 0.88
Recall: 0.9
F1 Score: 0.89

# show confusion matrix
In [271]: display_confusion_matrix(true_labels=test_sentiments,
     ...:                          predicted_labels=predicted_sentiments,
     ...:                          classes=['positive', 'negative'])
```

```
                  Predicted:
                positive negative
Actual: positive      6770      740
        negative       912     6578
```

```
# show detailed per-class classification report
In [272]: display_classification_report(true_labels=test_sentiments,
    ...:                                 predicted_labels=predicted_
                                         sentiments,
    ...:                                 classes=['positive', 'negative'])
              precision     recall  f1-score    support

    positive       0.88       0.90      0.89       7510
    negative       0.90       0.88      0.89       7490

avg / total        0.89       0.89      0.89      15000
```

The preceding outputs show the various performance metrics that depict the performance of our SVM model with regard to predicting sentiment for movie reviews. We have an average sentiment prediction accuracy of 89 percent, which is really good if you compare it with standard baselines for text classification using supervised techniques. The classification report also shows a per-class detailed report, and we see that our F1-score (harmonic mean of precision and recall) is 89 percent for both positive and negative sentiment. The support metric shows the number of reviews having positive (7510) sentiment and negative (7490) sentiment. The confusion matrix shows how many reviews for which we predicted the correct sentiment (*positive*: 6770/7510, *negative*: 6578/7490) and the number of reviews for which we predicted the wrong sentiment (*positive*: 740/7510, *negative*: 912/7490). Do try out building more models with different features (Chapter 4 talks about different feature-extraction techniques) and different supervised learning algorithms. Can you get a better model which predicts sentiment more accurately?

Unsupervised Lexicon-based Techniques

So far, we used labeled training data to learn patterns using features from the movie reviews and their corresponding sentiment. Then we applied this knowledge learned on new movie reviews (the testing dataset) to predict their sentiment. Often, you may not have the convenience of a well-labeled training dataset. In those situations, you need to use unsupervised techniques for predicting the sentiment by using knowledgebases, ontologies, databases, and lexicons that have detailed information specially curated and prepared just for sentiment analysis.

As mentioned, a lexicon is a dictionary, vocabulary, or a book of words. In our case, lexicons are special dictionaries or vocabularies that have been created for analyzing sentiment. Most of these lexicons have a list of positive and negative polar words with some score associated with them, and using various techniques like the position of words, surrounding words, context, parts of speech, phrases, and so on, scores are assigned to the text documents for which we want to compute the sentiment. After aggregating these scores, we get the final sentiment. More advanced analyses can also be done, including detecting the subjectivity, mood, and modality. Various popular lexicons are used for sentiment analysis, including the following:

- AFINN lexicon

- Bing Liu's lexicon

- MPQA subjectivity lexicon

- SentiWordNet

- VADER lexicon

- Pattern lexicon

This is not an exhaustive list of lexicons that can be leveraged for sentiment analysis, and there are several other lexicons which can be easily obtained from the Internet. We will briefly discuss each lexicon and will be using the last three lexicons to analyze the sentiment for our testing dataset in more detail. Although these techniques are unsupervised, you can also use them to analyze and evaluate the sentiment for the training dataset too, but for the sake of consistency and to compare model performances with the supervised model, we will be performing all our analyses on the testing dataset.

AFINN Lexicon

The AFINN lexicon was curated and created by Finn Årup Nielsen, and more details are mentioned in his paper "A New ANEW: Evaluation of a Word List for Sentiment Analysis in Microblogs." The latest version, known as AFINN-111, consists of a total of 2477 words and phrases with their own scores based on sentiment polarity. The polarity basically indicates how positive, negative, or neutral the term might be with some numerical score. You can download it from www2.imm.dtu.dk/pubdb/views/publication_details. php?id=6010. It also talks about the lexicon in further details. The author of this lexicon has also built a Python wrapper over the AFINN lexicon, which you can directly use to predict the sentiment of text data. The repository is available from GitHub at https://github.com/fnielsen/afinn. You can install the afinn library directly and start analyzing sentiment. This library even has support for emoticons and smileys. Following is a sample of the AFINN-111 lexicon:

```
abandon       -2
abandoned     -2
abandons      -2
abducted      -2
abduction     -2
...
...
youthful       2
yucky         -2
yummy          3
zealot        -2
zealots       -2
zealous        2
```

The basic idea is to load the entire list of polar words and phrases in the lexicon along with their corresponding score (sample shown above) in memory and then find the same words/phrases and score them accordingly in a text document. Finally, these scores are aggregated, and the final sentiment and score can be obtained for a text document. Following is an example snippet based on the official documentation:

```
from afinn import Afinn
afn = Afinn(emoticons=True)

In [281]: print afn.score('I really hated the plot of this movie')
-3.0
In [282]: print afn.score('I really hated the plot of this movie :(')
-5.0
```

Thus you can use the score() function directly to evaluate the sentiment of your text documents, and from the preceding output you can see that they even give proper weightage to emoticons, which are used extensively in social media like Twitter and Facebook.

Bing Liu's Lexicon

This lexicon has been developed by Bing Liu over several years and is discussed in further details in his paper, by Nitin Jindal and Bing Liu, "Identifying Comparative Sentences in Text Documents." You can get more details about the lexicon at https:// www.cs.uic.edu/~liub/FBS/sentiment-analysis.html#lexicon, which also includes a link to download it as an archive (RAR format). This lexicon consists of over 6800 words divided into two files named positive-words.txt, containing around 2000+ words/ phrases, and negative-words.txt, which contains around 4800+ words/phrases. The key idea is to leverage these words to contribute to the positive or negative polarity of any text document when they are identified in that document. This lexicon also includes many misspelled words, taking into account that words or terms are often misspelled on popular social media web sites.

MPQA Subjectivity Lexicon

MPQA stands for Multi-Perspective Question Answering, and it hosts a plethora of resources maintained by the University of Pittsburgh. It contains resources including opinion corpora, subjectivity lexicon, sense annotations, argument-based lexicon, and debate datasets. A lot of these can be leveraged for complex analysis of human emotions and sentiment. The subjectivity lexicon is maintained by Theresa Wilson, Janyce Wiebe, and Paul Hoffmann, and is discussed in detail in their paper, "Recognizing Contextual Polarity in Phrase-Level Sentiment Analysis," which focuses on contextual polarity. You can download the subjectivity lexicon from http://mpqa.cs.pitt.edu/lexicons/subj_ lexicon/, which is their official website. It has subjectivity clues present in the dataset named subjclueslen1-HLTEMNLP05.tff, which is available once you extract the archive. Some sample lines from the dataset are depicted as follows:

```
type=weaksubj len=1 word1=abandoned pos1=adj stemmed1=n
priorpolarity=negative
type=weaksubj len=1 word1=abandonment pos1=noun stemmed1=n
priorpolarity=negative
type=weaksubj len=1 word1=abandon pos1=verb stemmed1=y
priorpolarity=negative
type=strongsubj len=1 word1=abase pos1=verb stemmed1=y
priorpolarity=negative
...
...
type=strongsubj len=1 word1=zealously pos1=anypos stemmed1=n
priorpolarity=negative
type=strongsubj len=1 word1=zenith pos1=noun stemmed1=n
priorpolarity=positive
type=strongsubj len=1 word1=zest pos1=noun stemmed1=n priorpolarity=positive
```

To understand this data, you can refer to the readme file provided along with the dataset. Basically, the clues in this dataset were curated and collected manually with efforts by the above-mentioned maintainers of this project. The various parameters mentioned above are explained briefly as follows:

- **type**: This has values that are either strongsubj indicating the presence of a strongly subjective context or weaksubj which indicates the presence of a weak/part subjective context.

- **len**: This points to the number of words in the term of the clue (all are single words of length 1 for now).

- **word1**: The actual term present as a token or a stem of the actual token.

- **pos1**: The part of speech for the term (clue) and it can be noun, verb, adj, adverb, or anypos.

- **stemmed1**: This indicates if the clue (term) is stemmed (y) or not stemmed (n). If it is stemmed, it can match all its other variants having the same pos1 tag.

- **priorpolarity**: This has values of negative, positive, both, or neutral, and indicates the polarity of the sentiment associated with this clue (term).

The idea is to load this lexicon into a database or memory (hint: Python dictionary works well) and then use it similarly to the previous lexicons to analyze the sentiment associated with any text document.

SentiWordNet

We know that WordNet is perhaps one of the most popular corpora for the English language, used extensively in semantic analysis, and it introduces the concept of synsets. The SentiWordNet lexicon is a lexical resource used for sentiment analysis and opinion mining. For each synset present in WordNet, the SentiWordNet lexicon assigns three sentiment scores to it, including a positive polarity score, a negative polarity score, and an objectivity score. You can find more details on the official web site http:// sentiwordnet.isti.cnr.it, which includes research papers explaining the lexicon in detail and also a link to download the lexicon. The nltk package in Python provides an interface directly for accessing the SentiWordNet lexicon, and we will be using this to analyze the sentiment of our movie reviews. The following snippet shows an example synset and its sentiment scores using SentiWordNet:

```
import nltk
from nltk.corpus import sentiwordnet as swn
# get synset for 'good'
good = swn.senti_synsets('good', 'n')[0]
# print synset sentiment scores
In [287]: print 'Positive Polarity Score:', good.pos_score()
     ...: print 'Negative Polarity Score:', good.neg_score()
     ...: print 'Objective Score:', good.obj_score()
Positive Polarity Score: 0.5
Negative Polarity Score: 0.0
Objective Score: 0.5
```

Now that we know how to use the sentiwordnet interface, we define a function that can take in a body of text (movie review in our case) and analyze its sentiment by leveraging sentiwordnet:

```
from normalization import normalize_accented_characters, html_parser, strip_
html

def analyze_sentiment_sentiwordnet_lexicon(review,
                                           verbose=False):
    # pre-process text
    review = normalize_accented_characters(review)
    review = html_parser.unescape(review)
    review = strip_html(review)
    # tokenize and POS tag text tokens
    text_tokens = nltk.word_tokenize(review)
    tagged_text = nltk.pos_tag(text_tokens)
    pos_score = neg_score = token_count = obj_score = 0
    # get wordnet synsets based on POS tags
    # get sentiment scores if synsets are found
    for word, tag in tagged_text:
        ss_set = None
```

```
        if 'NN' in tag and swn.senti_synsets(word, 'n'):
            ss_set = swn.senti_synsets(word, 'n')[0]
        elif 'VB' in tag and swn.senti_synsets(word, 'v'):
            ss_set = swn.senti_synsets(word, 'v')[0]
        elif 'JJ' in tag and swn.senti_synsets(word, 'a'):
            ss_set = swn.senti_synsets(word, 'a')[0]
        elif 'RB' in tag and swn.senti_synsets(word, 'r'):
            ss_set = swn.senti_synsets(word, 'r')[0]
        # if senti-synset is found
        if ss_set:
            # add scores for all found synsets
            pos_score += ss_set.pos_score()
            neg_score += ss_set.neg_score()
            obj_score += ss_set.obj_score()
            token_count += 1

# aggregate final scores
final_score = pos_score - neg_score
norm_final_score = round(float(final_score) / token_count, 2)
final_sentiment = 'positive' if norm_final_score >= 0 else 'negative'
if verbose:
    norm_obj_score = round(float(obj_score) / token_count, 2)
    norm_pos_score = round(float(pos_score) / token_count, 2)
    norm_neg_score = round(float(neg_score) / token_count, 2)
    # to display results in a nice table
    sentiment_frame = pd.DataFrame([[final_sentiment, norm_obj_score,
                                     norm_pos_score, norm_neg_score,
                                     norm_final_score]],
                                   columns=pd.MultiIndex(levels
                                   =[['SENTIMENT STATS:'],
                                                ['Predicted Sentiment',
                                                 'Objectivity',
                                                 'Positive', 'Negative',
                                                 'Overall']],
                                                labels=[[0,0,0,0,0],
                                                [0,1,2,3,4]]))
                                   print sentiment_frame

return final_sentiment
```

The comments in the preceding function are pretty self-explanatory. We take in a body of text (a movie review), do some initial pre-processing, and then tokenize and POS tag the tokens. For each pair of (word, tag) we check if any senti-synsets exist for the same word and its corresponding tag. If there is a match, we take the first senti-synset and store its sentiment scores in corresponding variables, and finally we aggregate its scores. We can now see the preceding function in action for our sample reviews (in the sample_data variable we created earlier from the test data) in the following snippet:

```
# detailed sentiment analysis for sample reviews
In [292]: for review, review_sentiment in sample_data:
     ...:        print 'Review:'
     ...:        print review
     ...:        print
     ...:        print 'Labeled Sentiment:', review_sentiment
     ...:        print
     ...:        final_sentiment = analyze_sentiment_sentiwordnet_
            lexicon(review,

     ...:
            verbose=True)
     ...:        print '-'*60
     ...:
     ...:
```

Review:
Worst movie, (with the best reviews given it) I've ever seen. Over the top
dialog, acting, and direction. more slasher flick than thriller.With all the
great reviews this movie got I'm appalled that it turned out so silly. shame
on you martin scorsese

Labeled Sentiment: negative

```
    SENTIMENT STATS:
  Predicted Sentiment Objectivity Positive Negative Overall
0           negative      0.83      0.08     0.09    -0.01
------------------------------------------------------------
```
Review:
I hope this group of film-makers never re-unites.

Labeled Sentiment: negative

```
    SENTIMENT STATS:
  Predicted Sentiment Objectivity Positive Negative Overall
0           negative      0.71      0.04     0.25    -0.21
------------------------------------------------------------
```
Review:
no comment - stupid movie, acting average or worse... screenplay - no sense
at all... SKIP IT!

Labeled Sentiment: negative

```
    SENTIMENT STATS:
  Predicted Sentiment Objectivity Positive Negative Overall
0           negative      0.81      0.04     0.15    -0.11
------------------------------------------------------------
```
Review:
Add this little gem to your list of holiday regulars. It is

sweet, funny, and endearing

Labeled Sentiment: positive

```
    SENTIMENT STATS:
  Predicted Sentiment Objectivity Positive Negative Overall
0           positive       0.76      0.18    0.06     0.13
----------------------------------------------------------------
```
Review:
a mesmerizing film that certainly keeps your attention... Ben Daniels is
fascinating (and courageous) to watch.

Labeled Sentiment: positive

```
    SENTIMENT STATS:
  Predicted Sentiment Objectivity Positive Negative Overall
0           positive       0.84      0.14    0.03     0.11
----------------------------------------------------------------
```
Review:
This movie is perfect for all the romantics in the world. John Ritter has
never been better and has the best line in the movie! "Sam" hits close to
home, is lovely to look at and so much fun to play along with. Ben Gazzara
was an excellent cast and easy to fall in love with. I'm sure I've met
Arthur in my travels somewhere. All around, an excellent choice to pick up
any evening.!:-)

Labeled Sentiment: positive

```
    SENTIMENT STATS:
  Predicted Sentiment Objectivity Positive Negative Overall
0           positive       0.75      0.2     0.05     0.15
----------------------------------------------------------------
```
Review:
I don't care if some people voted this movie to be bad. If you want the
Truth this is a Very Good Movie! It has every thing a movie should have. You
really should Get this one.

Labeled Sentiment: positive

```
    SENTIMENT STATS:
  Predicted Sentiment Objectivity Positive Negative Overall
0           positive       0.73      0.21    0.06     0.15
----------------------------------------------------------------
```
Review:
Worst horror film ever but funniest film ever rolled in one you have got
to see this film it is so cheap it is unbeliaveble but you have to see it
really!!!! P.s watch the carrot

Labeled Sentiment: positive

```
   SENTIMENT STATS:
 Predicted Sentiment Objectivity Positive Negative Overall
0           positive        0.79     0.13     0.08    0.05
-------------------------------------------------------------
```

You can see detailed statistics related to each sentiment score and also the overall sentiment and compare it with the actual labeled sentiment for each review in the preceding output. Interestingly, we were able to predict the sentiment correctly for all our sampled reviews as compared to the supervised learning technique. But how well does this technique perform for our complete test movie reviews dataset? The following snippet will give us the answer!

```
# predict sentiment for test movie reviews dataset
sentiwordnet_predictions = [analyze_sentiment_sentiwordnet_lexicon(review)
                            for review in test_reviews]

from utils import display_evaluation_metrics, display_confusion_matrix,
display_classification_report

# get model performance statistics
In [295]: print 'Performance metrics:'
     ...: display_evaluation_metrics(true_labels=test_sentiments,
                                     predicted_labels=sentiwordnet_
                                     predictions,
                                     positive_class='positive')
     ...: print '\nConfusion Matrix:'
     ...: display_confusion_matrix(true_labels=test_sentiments,
                                   predicted_labels=sentiwordnet_
                                   predictions,
                                   classes=['positive', 'negative'])
     ...: print '\nClassification report:'
     ...: display_classification_report(true_labels=test_sentiments,
                                        predicted_labels=sentiwordnet_
                                        predictions,
                                        classes=['positive', 'negative'])
Performance metrics:
Accuracy: 0.59
Precision: 0.56
Recall: 0.92
F1 Score: 0.7

Confusion Matrix:
                Predicted:
                positive negative
Actual: positive     6941      569
        negative     5510     1980

Classification report:
```

	precision	recall	f1-score	support
positive	0.56	0.92	0.70	7510
negative	0.78	0.26	0.39	7490
avg / total	0.67	0.59	0.55	15000

Our model has a sentiment prediction accuracy of around 60% and an F1-score of 70% approximately. If you look at the detailed classification report and the confusion matrix, you will observe that we correctly classify 6941/7510 positive movie reviews as positive, but we incorrectly classify 5510/7490 negative movie reviews as positive—which is quite high! A way to redress this would be to change our logic slightly in our function and relax the threshold for overall sentiment score to decide whether a document will have an overall positive or negative sentiment from 0 to maybe 0.1 or higher. Experiment with this threshold and see what kind of results you get.

VADER Lexicon

VADER stands for Valence Aware Dictionary and sEntiment Reasoner. It is a lexicon with a rule-based sentiment analysis framework that was specially built for analyzing sentiment from social media resources. This lexicon was developed by C. J. Hutto and Eric Gilbert, and you will find further details in the paper, "VADER: A Parsimonious Rule-based Model for Sentiment Analysis of Social Media Text." You can read more about it and even download the dataset or install the library from https://github.com/cjhutto/vaderSentiment, which contains all the resources pertaining to the VADER lexicon. The file vader_sentiment_lexicon.txt contains all the necessary sentiment scores associated with various terms, including words, emoticons, and even slang language-based tokens (like lol, wtf, nah, and so on). There are over 9000 lexical features from which it was further curated to 7500 lexical features in this lexicon with proper validated valence scores. Each feature was rated on a scale from "[-4] Extremely Negative" to "[4] Extremely Positive", with allowance for "[0] Neutral (or Neither, N/A)". This curation was done by keeping all lexical features which had a non-zero mean rating and whose standard deviation was less than 2.5, which was determined by the aggregate of ten independent raters. A sample of the VADER lexicon is depicted as follows:

```
)-:<      -2.2   0.4      [-2, -2, -2, -2, -2, -2, -3, -3, -2, -2]
)-:{      -2.1   0.9434   [-1, -3, -2, -1, -2, -2, -3, -4, -1, -2]
):        -1.8   0.87178  [-1, -3, -1, -2, -1, -3, -1, -3, -1, -2]
...
...
resolved   0.7   0.78102  [1, 2, 0, 1, 1, 0, 2, 0, 0, 0]
resolvent  0.7   0.78102  [1, 0, 1, 2, 0, -1, 1, 1, 1, 1]
resolvents 0.4   0.66332  [2, 0, 0, 1, 0, 0, 1, 0, 0, 0]
...
...
}:-(      -2.1   0.7      [-2, -1, -2, -2, -2, -4, -2, -2, -2, -2]
}:-)       0.3   1.61555  [1, 1, -2, 1, -1, -3, 2, 2, 1, 1]
```

Each line in the preceding lexicon depicts a unique term, which can be a word or even an emoticon. The first term indicates the word/emoticon, the second column indicates the mean or average score, the third column indicates the standard deviation, and the final column indicates a list of scores given by ten independent scorers. The nltk package has a nice interface for leveraging the VADER lexicon, and the following function makes use of the same for analyzing sentiment for any text document:

```python
from nltk.sentiment.vader import SentimentIntensityAnalyzer

def analyze_sentiment_vader_lexicon(review,
                                    threshold=0.1,
                                    verbose=False):
    # pre-process text
    review = normalize_accented_characters(review)
    review = html_parser.unescape(review)
    review = strip_html(review)
    # analyze the sentiment for review
    analyzer = SentimentIntensityAnalyzer()
    scores = analyzer.polarity_scores(review)
    # get aggregate scores and final sentiment
    agg_score = scores['compound']
    final_sentiment = 'positive' if agg_score >= threshold\
                                 else 'negative'
    if verbose:
        # display detailed sentiment statistics
        positive = str(round(scores['pos'], 2)*100)+'%'
        final = round(agg_score, 2)
        negative = str(round(scores['neg'], 2)*100)+'%'
        neutral = str(round(scores['neu'], 2)*100)+'%'
        sentiment_frame = pd.DataFrame([[final_sentiment, final, positive,
                                         negative, neutral]],
                columns=pd.MultiIndex(levels=[['SENTIMENT STATS:'],
                                              ['Predicted Sentiment',
                                               'Polarity Score',
                                               'Positive', 'Negative',
                                               'Neutral']],
                                labels=[[0,0,0,0,0],[0,1,2,3,4]]))
        print sentiment_frame

    return final_sentiment
```

That function helps in computing the sentiment and various statistics associated with it for any text document (movie reviews in our case). The comments explain the main sections of the function, which include text-preprocessing, getting the necessary sentiment scores using the VADER lexicon, aggregating them, and computing the final sentiment (positive/negative) using a specific threshold we talked about earlier. A threshold of 0.1

seemed to work best on an average, but you can experiment further with it. The following snippet shows us how to use this function on our sampled test movie reviews:

```
# get detailed sentiment statistics
In [301]: for review, review_sentiment in sample_data:
     ...:     print 'Review:'
     ...:     print review
     ...:     print
     ...:     print 'Labeled Sentiment:', review_sentiment
     ...:     print
     ...:     final_sentiment = analyze_sentiment_vader_lexicon(review,
     ...:                                                   threshold=0.1,
     ...:                                                   verbose=True)
     ...:     print '-'*60
```

Review:
Worst movie, (with the best reviews given it) I've ever seen. Over the top dialog, acting, and direction. more slasher flick than thriller.With all the great reviews this movie got I'm appalled that it turned out so silly. shame on you martin scorsese

Labeled Sentiment: negative

```
     SENTIMENT STATS:
   Predicted Sentiment Polarity Score Positive Negative Neutral
0            negative             0.03    20.0%    18.0%   62.0%
------------------------------------------------------------
```
Review:
I hope this group of film-makers never re-unites.

Labeled Sentiment: negative

```
     SENTIMENT STATS:
   Predicted Sentiment Polarity Score Positive Negative Neutral
0            positive             0.44    33.0%     0.0%   67.0%
------------------------------------------------------------
```
Review:
no comment - stupid movie, acting average or worse... screenplay - no sense at all... SKIP IT!

Labeled Sentiment: negative

```
     SENTIMENT STATS:
   Predicted Sentiment Polarity Score Positive Negative Neutral
0            negative             -0.8     0.0%    40.0%   60.0%
------------------------------------------------------------
```
Review:
Add this little gem to your list of holiday regulars. It is

sweet, funny, and endearing

Labeled Sentiment: positive

```
      SENTIMENT STATS:
  Predicted Sentiment Polarity Score Positive Negative Neutral
0            positive         0.82    40.0%    0.0%   60.0%
----------------------------------------------------------
```
Review:
a mesmerizing film that certainly keeps your attention... Ben Daniels is
fascinating (and courageous) to watch.

Labeled Sentiment: positive

```
      SENTIMENT STATS:
  Predicted Sentiment Polarity Score Positive Negative Neutral
0            positive         0.71    31.0%    0.0%   69.0%
----------------------------------------------------------
```
Review:
This movie is perfect for all the romantics in the world. John Ritter has
never been better and has the best line in the movie! "Sam" hits close to
home, is lovely to look at and so much fun to play along with. Ben Gazzara
was an excellent cast and easy to fall in love with. I'm sure I've met
Arthur in my travels somewhere. All around, an excellent choice to pick up
any evening.!:-)

Labeled Sentiment: positive

```
      SENTIMENT STATS:
  Predicted Sentiment Polarity Score Positive Negative Neutral
0            positive         0.99    37.0%    2.0%   61.0%
----------------------------------------------------------
```
Review:
I don't care if some people voted this movie to be bad. If you want the
Truth this is a Very Good Movie! It has every thing a movie should have. You
really should Get this one.

Labeled Sentiment: positive

```
      SENTIMENT STATS:
  Predicted Sentiment Polarity Score Positive Negative Neutral
0            negative        -0.16    17.0%   14.0%   69.0%
----------------------------------------------------------
```
Review:
Worst horror film ever but funniest film ever rolled in one you have got
to see this film it is so cheap it is unbeliaveble but you have to see it
really!!!! P.s watch the carrot

Labeled Sentiment: positive

```
    SENTIMENT STATS:
  Predicted Sentiment Polarity Score Positive Negative Neutral
0              positive            0.49    11.0%   11.0%   77.0%
-------------------------------------------------------------
```

The preceding statistics are similar to our previous function except the Positive, Negative, and Neutral columns indicate the percentage or proportion of the document that is positive, negative, or neutral, and the final score is determined based on the polarity score and the threshold. The following snippet shows the model sentiment prediction performance on the entire test movie reviews dataset:

```
# predict sentiment for test movie reviews dataset
vader_predictions = [analyze_sentiment_vader_lexicon(review, threshold=0.1)
                 for review in test_reviews]

# get model performance statistics
In [302]: print 'Performance metrics:'
     ...: display_evaluation_metrics(true_labels=test_sentiments,
     ...:                            predicted_labels=vader_predictions,
     ...:                            positive_class='positive')
     ...: print '\nConfusion Matrix:'
     ...: display_confusion_matrix(true_labels=test_sentiments,
     ...:                          predicted_labels=vader_predictions,
     ...:                          classes=['positive', 'negative'])
     ...: print '\nClassification report:'
     ...: display_classification_report(true_labels=test_sentiments,
     ...:                               predicted_labels=vader_predictions,
     ...:                               classes=['positive', 'negative'])
Performance metrics:
Accuracy: 0.7
Precision: 0.65
Recall: 0.86
F1 Score: 0.74

Confusion Matrix:
                  Predicted:
                  positive negative
Actual: positive      6434     1076
        negative      3410     4080

Classification report:
                precision    recall  f1-score    support

    positive         0.65      0.86      0.74       7510
    negative         0.79      0.54      0.65       7490

avg / total          0.72      0.70      0.69      15000
```

The preceding metrics depict that our model has a sentiment prediction accuracy of around 70 percent and an F1-score close to 75 percent, which is definitely better than our previous model. Also notice that we are able to correctly predict positive sentiment for 6434 out of 7510 positive movie reviews, and negative sentiment correctly for 4080 out of 7490 negative movie reviews.

Pattern Lexicon

The `pattern` package is a complete package for NLP, text analytics, and information retrieval. We discussed it in detail in previous chapters and have also used it several times to solve several problems. This package is developed by CLiPS (Computational Linguistics & Psycholinguistics), a research center associated with the Linguistics Department of the Faculty of Arts of the University of Antwerp. It has a sentiment module associated with it, along with modules for analyzing mood and modality of a body of text.

For sentiment analysis, it analyzes any body of text by decomposing it into sentences and then tokenizing it and tagging the various tokens with necessary parts of speech. It then uses its own subjectivity-based sentiment lexicon, which you can access from its official repository at `https://github.com/clips/pattern/blob/master/pattern/text/en/en-sentiment.xml`. It contains scores like polarity, subjectivity, intensity, and confidence, along with other tags like the part of speech, WordNet identifier, and so on. It then leverages this lexicon to compute the overall polarity and subjectivity score associated with a text document. A threshold of 0.1 is recommended by `pattern` itself to compute the final sentiment of a document as positive, and anything below it as negative.

You can also analyze the mood and modality of text documents by leveraging the mood and modality functions provided by the `pattern` package. The mood function helps in determining the mood expressed by a particular text document. This function returns `INDICATIVE`, `IMPERATIVE`, `CONDITIONAL`, or `SUBJUNCTIVE` for any text based on its content. The table in Figure 7-2 talks about each type of mood in further detail, courtesy of the official documentation provided by CLiPS `pattern`. The column Use talks about the typical usage patterns for each type of mood, and the examples provide some actual examples from the English language.

Mood	Form	Use	Example
INDICATIVE	none of the below	fact, belief	*It rains.*
IMPERATIVE	infinitive without *to*	command, warning	*Don't rain!*
CONDITIONAL	*would, could, should, may,* or *will, can + if*	conjecture	*It might rain.*
SUBJUNCTIVE	*wish, were,* or *it is +* infinitive	wish, opinion	*I hope it rains.*

Figure 7-2. *Different types of mood and their examples (figure courtesy of CLiPS pattern)*

Modality for any text represents the degree of certainty expressed by the text as a whole. This value is a number that ranges between 0 and 1. Values > 0.5 indicate factual texts having a high certainty, and < 0.5 indicate wishes and hopes and have a low certainty associated with them. We will define a function now to analyze the sentiment for text documents using the pattern lexicon:

```
from pattern.en import sentiment, mood, modality

def analyze_sentiment_pattern_lexicon(review, threshold=0.1,
                                      verbose=False):
    # pre-process text
    review = normalize_accented_characters(review)
    review = html_parser.unescape(review)
    review = strip_html(review)
    # analyze sentiment for the text document
    analysis = sentiment(review)
    sentiment_score = round(analysis[0], 2)
    sentiment_subjectivity = round(analysis[1], 2)
    # get final sentiment
    final_sentiment = 'positive' if sentiment_score >= threshold\
                      else 'negative'
    if verbose:
        # display detailed sentiment statistics
        sentiment_frame = pd.DataFrame([[final_sentiment, sentiment_score,
                                       sentiment_subjectivity]],
                                       columns=pd.MultiIndex(levels
                                       =[['SENTIMENT STATS:'],
                                                   ['Predicted Sentiment',
                                                    'Polarity Score',
                                                    'Subjectivity Score']],
                                                    labels=[[0,0,0],
                                                    [0,1,2]]))
        print sentiment_frame
        assessment = analysis.assessments
        assessment_frame = pd.DataFrame(assessment,
                                columns=pd.MultiIndex(levels=[['DETAILED
                                ASSESSMENT STATS:'],
                                                    ['Key Terms', 'Polarity
                                                    Score',
                                                    'Subjectivity Score',
                                                    'Type']],
                                                    labels=[[0,0,0,0],
                                                    [0,1,2,3]]))
                                                    print assessment_frame
                                                    print

    return final_sentiment
```

We will now test the function we defined to analyze the sentiment of our sample test movie reviews and observe the results. We take a threshold of 0.1 as the cut-off to decide between positive and negative sentiment for a document based on the aggregated sentiment polarity score, based on several experiments and recommendations from the official documentation:

```
# get detailed sentiment statistics
In [303]: for review, review_sentiment in sample_data:
     ...:       print 'Review:'
     ...:       print review
     ...:       print
     ...:       print 'Labeled Sentiment:', review_sentiment
     ...:       print
     ...:       final_sentiment = analyze_sentiment_pattern_lexicon(review,
     ...:
threshold=0.1,
     ...:
verbose=True)
     ...:       print '-'*60
```

```
Review:
Worst movie, (with the best reviews given it) I've ever seen. Over the top
dialog, acting, and direction. more slasher flick than thriller.With all the
great reviews this movie got I'm appalled that it turned out so silly. shame
on you martin scorsese

Labeled Sentiment: negative

    SENTIMENT STATS:
  Predicted Sentiment Polarity Score Subjectivity Score
0           negative         0.06                0.62
  DETAILED ASSESSMENT STATS:
                 Key Terms Polarity Score Subjectivity Score  Type
0                 [worst]           -1.0               1.000  None
1                  [best]            1.0               0.300  None
2                   [top]            0.5               0.500  None
3                [acting]            0.0               0.000  None
4                  [more]            0.5               0.500  None
5                 [great]            0.8               0.750  None
6              [appalled]           -0.8               1.000  None
7                 [silly]           -0.5               0.875  None
```

```
------------------------------------------------------------
Review:
I hope this group of film-makers never re-unites.
```

Labeled Sentiment: negative

     SENTIMENT STATS:
  Predicted Sentiment Polarity Score Subjectivity Score
0   negative   0.0   0.0
Empty DataFrame
Columns: [(DETAILED ASSESSMENT STATS:, Key Terms), (DETAILED ASSESSMENT
STATS:, Polarity Score), (DETAILED ASSESSMENT STATS:, Subjectivity Score),
(DETAILED ASSESSMENT STATS:, Type)]
Index: []

Review:
no comment - stupid movie, acting average or worse... screenplay - no sense
at all... SKIP IT!

Labeled Sentiment: negative

     SENTIMENT STATS:
  Predicted Sentiment Polarity Score Subjectivity Score
0   negative   -0.36   0.5
  DETAILED ASSESSMENT STATS:
                Key Terms Polarity Score Subjectivity Score Type
0   [stupid]   -0.80   1.0 None
1   [acting]   0.00   0.0 None
2   [average]   -0.15   0.4 None
3   [worse, !]   -0.50   0.6 None

Review:
Add this little gem to your list of holiday regulars. It is

sweet, funny, and endearing

Labeled Sentiment: positive

     SENTIMENT STATS:
  Predicted Sentiment Polarity Score Subjectivity Score
0   positive   0.19   0.67
  DETAILED ASSESSMENT STATS:
                Key Terms Polarity Score Subjectivity Score Type
0   [little]   -0.1875   0.5 None
1   [funny]   0.2500   1.0 None
2   [endearing]   0.5000   0.5 None

Review:
a mesmerizing film that certainly keeps your attention... Ben Daniels is
fascinating (and courageous) to watch.

Labeled Sentiment: positive

```
    SENTIMENT STATS:
  Predicted Sentiment Polarity Score Subjectivity Score
0          positive          0.4              0.71
  DETAILED ASSESSMENT STATS:
              Key Terms Polarity Score Subjectivity Score  Type
0          [mesmerizing]      0.300000           0.700000  None
1           [certainly]       0.214286           0.571429  None
2          [fascinating]      0.700000           0.850000  None
```

Review:
This movie is perfect for all the romantics in the world. John Ritter has never been better and has the best line in the movie! "Sam" hits close to home, is lovely to look at and so much fun to play along with. Ben Gazzara was an excellent cast and easy to fall in love with. I'm sure I've met Arthur in my travels somewhere. All around, an excellent choice to pick up any evening.!:-)

Labeled Sentiment: positive

```
    SENTIMENT STATS:
  Predicted Sentiment Polarity Score Subjectivity Score
0          positive         0.66              0.73
    DETAILED ASSESSMENT STATS:
                Key Terms Polarity Score Subjectivity Score  Type
0            [perfect]        1.000000           1.000000  None
1             [better]        0.500000           0.500000  None
2             [best, !]       1.000000           0.300000  None
3             [lovely]        0.500000           0.750000  None
4           [much, fun]       0.300000           0.200000  None
5            [excellent]      1.000000           1.000000  None
6              [easy]         0.433333           0.833333  None
7              [love]         0.500000           0.600000  None
8              [sure]         0.500000           0.888889  None
9           [excellent, !]    1.000000           1.000000  None
10              [:-)]         0.500000           1.000000  mood
```

Review:
I don't care if some people voted this movie to be bad. If you want the Truth this is a Very Good Movie! It has every thing a movie should have. You really should Get this one.

Labeled Sentiment: positive

```
    SENTIMENT STATS:
  Predicted Sentiment Polarity Score Subjectivity Score
0          positive              0.17               0.55
  DETAILED ASSESSMENT STATS:
                 Key Terms Polarity Score Subjectivity Score  Type
0                    [bad]          -0.7            0.666667  None
1          [very, good, !]           1.0            0.780000  None
2                 [really]           0.2            0.200000  None
```

Review:
Worst horror film ever but funniest film ever rolled in one you have got
to see this film it is so cheap it is unbeliaveble but you have to see it
really!!!! P.s watch the carrot

Labeled Sentiment: positive

```
    SENTIMENT STATS:
  Predicted Sentiment Polarity Score Subjectivity Score
0          negative             -0.04               0.63
  DETAILED ASSESSMENT STATS:
                 Key Terms Polarity Score Subjectivity Score  Type
0                  [worst]     -1.000000                 1.0  None
1                  [cheap]      0.400000                 0.7  None
2      [really, !, !, !, !]      0.488281                 0.2  None
```

The preceding analysis shows the sentiment, polarity, and subjectivity scores for
each sampled review. Besides this, we also see key terms and emotions and their polarity
scores, which mainly contributed to the overall sentiment of each review. You can see
that even exclamations and emoticons are also given importance and weightage when
computing sentiment and polarity. The following snippet depicts the mood and modality
for the sampled test movie reviews:

```
In [304]: for review, review_sentiment in sample_data:
     ...:     print 'Review:'
     ...:     print review
     ...:     print 'Labeled Sentiment:', review_sentiment
     ...:     print 'Mood:', mood(review)
     ...:     mod_score = modality(review)
     ...:     print 'Modality Score:', round(mod_score, 2)
     ...:     print 'Certainty:', 'Strong' if mod_score > 0.5 \
     ...:                         else 'Medium' if mod_score > 0.35 \
     ...:                         else 'Low'
     ...:     print '-'*60
```

Review:
Worst movie, (with the best reviews given it) I've ever seen. Over the top
dialog, acting, and direction. more slasher flick than thriller.With all the
great reviews this movie got I'm appalled that it turned out so silly. shame
on you martin scorsese
Labeled Sentiment: negative
Mood: indicative
Modality Score: 0.75
Certainty: Strong

Review:
I hope this group of film-makers never re-unites.
Labeled Sentiment: negative
Mood: subjunctive
Modality Score: -0.25
Certainty: Low

Review:
no comment - stupid movie, acting average or worse... screenplay - no sense
at all... SKIP IT!
Labeled Sentiment: negative
Mood: indicative
Modality Score: 0.75
Certainty: Strong

Review:
Add this little gem to your list of holiday regulars. It is

sweet, funny, and endearing
Labeled Sentiment: positive
Mood: imperative
Modality Score: 1.0
Certainty: Strong

Review:
a mesmerizing film that certainly keeps your attention... Ben Daniels is
fascinating (and courageous) to watch.
Labeled Sentiment: positive
Mood: indicative
Modality Score: 0.75
Certainty: Strong

Review:
This movie is perfect for all the romantics in the world. John Ritter has
never been better and has the best line in the movie! "Sam" hits close to
home, is lovely to look at and so much fun to play along with. Ben Gazzara
was an excellent cast and easy to fall in love with. I'm sure I've met
Arthur in my travels somewhere. All around, an excellent choice to pick up
any evening.!:-)

```
Labeled Sentiment: positive
Mood: indicative
Modality Score: 0.58
Certainty: Strong
---------------------------------------------------------------
Review:
I don't care if some people voted this movie to be bad. If you want the
Truth this is a Very Good Movie! It has every thing a movie should have. You
really should Get this one.
Labeled Sentiment: positive
Mood: conditional
Modality Score: 0.28
Certainty: Low
---------------------------------------------------------------
Review:
Worst horror film ever but funniest film ever rolled in one you have got
to see this film it is so cheap it is unbliaveble but you have to see it
really!!!! P.s watch the carrot
Labeled Sentiment: positive
Mood: indicative
Modality Score: 0.75
Certainty: Strong
---------------------------------------------------------------
```

The preceding output depicts the mood, modality score, and the certainty factor expressed by each review. It is interesting to see phrases like "Add this little gem…" are correctly associated with the right mood, which is an *imperative*, and "I hope this…" is correctly associated with *subjunctive* mood. The other reviews have more of an *indicative* disposition, which is quite obvious since it expresses the beliefs of the review who wrote the movie review. Certainty is lower in cases of reviews that use words like "hope", "if", and higher in case of strongly opinionated reviews.

Finally, we will evaluate the sentiment prediction performance of this model on our entire test review dataset as we have done before for our other models. The following snippet achieves the same:

```
# predict sentiment for test movie reviews dataset
pattern_predictions = [analyze_sentiment_pattern_lexicon(review,
                    threshold=0.1)
                        for review in test_reviews]

# get model performance statistics
In [307]: print 'Performance metrics:'
     ...: display_evaluation_metrics(true_labels=test_sentiments,
     ...:                             predicted_labels=pattern_predictions,
     ...:                             positive_class='positive')
     ...: print '\nConfusion Matrix:'
     ...: display_confusion_matrix(true_labels=test_sentiments,
     ...:                             predicted_labels=pattern_predictions,
     ...:                             classes=['positive', 'negative'])
```

```
...: print '\nClassification report:'
...: display_classification_report(true_labels=test_sentiments,
...:                                predicted_labels=pattern_
                                    predictions,
...:                                classes=['positive', 'negative'])
Performance metrics:
Accuracy: 0.77
Precision: 0.76
Recall: 0.79
F1 Score: 0.77

Confusion Matrix:
              Predicted:
              positive negative
Actual: positive    5958    1552
        negative    1924    5566

Classification report:
          precision   recall  f1-score   support

positive       0.76     0.79      0.77      7510
negative       0.78     0.74      0.76      7490

avg / total    0.77     0.77      0.77     15000
```

This model gives a better and more balanced performance toward predicting the sentiment of both positive and negative classes. We have an average sentiment prediction accuracy of 77 percent and an average F1-score of 77 percent for this model. Although the number of correct positive predictions has dropped from our previous model to 5958/7510 reviews, the number of correct predictions for negative reviews has increased significantly to 5566/7490 reviews.

Comparing Model Performances

We have built a supervised classification model and three unsupervised lexicon-based models to predict sentiment for movie reviews. For each model, we looked at its detailed analysis and statistics for calculating sentiment. We also evaluated each model on standard metrics like precision, recall, accuracy, and F1-score. In this section, we will briefly look at how each model's performance compares against the other models. Figure 7-3 shows the model performance metrics and a visualization comparing the metrics across all the models.

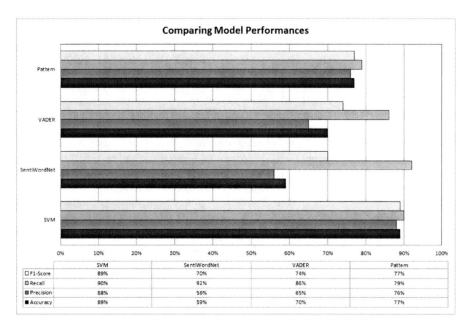

Figure 7-3. Comparison of sentiment analysis model performances

From the visualization and the table in Figure 7-3, it is clear that the supervised model using SVM gives us the best results, which are expected because it was trained on 35,000 training movie reviews. Pattern lexicon performs the best among the unsupervised techniques for our test movie reviews. Does this mean these models will always perform the best? Absolutely not. It depends on the data you are analyzing. Remember to consider various models and also to evaluate all the metrics when evaluating any model, and not just one or two. Some of the models in the chart have really high recall but low precision, which indicates these models have a tendency to make more wrong predictions or false positives. You can re-use these benchmarks and evaluate more sentiment analysis models as you experiment with different features, lexicons, and techniques.

Summary

In this final chapter, we have covered a variety of topics focused on semantic and sentiment analysis of textual data. We revisited several of our concepts from Chapter 1 with regard to language semantics. We looked at the WordNet corpus in detail and explored the concept of synsets with practical examples. We also analyzed various lexical semantic relations from Chapter 1 here, using synsets and real-world examples. We looked at relationships including entailments, homonyms and homographs, synonyms and antonyms, hyponyms and hypernyms, and holonyms and meronyms. Semantic relations and similarity computation techniques were also discussed in detail, with examples that leveraged common hypernyms among various synsets. Some popular techniques widely used in semantic and information extraction were discussed, including word sense disambiguation and named entity recognition, with examples. Besides semantic relations, we also revisited concepts related to semantic representations, namely propositional logic and first order logic. We leveraged the use of theorem provers and evaluated actual propositions and logical expressions computationally.

Next, we introduced the concept of sentiment analysis and opinion mining and saw how it is used in various domains like social media, surveys, and feedback data. We took a practical example of analyzing sentiment on actual movie reviews from IMDb and built several models that included supervised machine learning and unsupervised lexicon-based models. We looked at each technique and its results in detail and compared the performance across all our models.

This brings us to the end of this book. I hope the various concepts and techniques discussed here will be helpful to and that you can use the knowledge and techniques from this book when you tackle challenging problems in the world of text analytics and natural language processing. You may have seen by now that there is a lot of unexplored territory out there in the world of analyzing unstructured text data. I wish you the very best and would like to leave you with the parting thought from Occam's razor: *Sometimes the simplest solution is the best solution.*

Index

▓ M

Get the eBook for only $4.99!

Why limit yourself?

Now you can take the weightless companion with you wherever you go and access your content on your PC, phone, tablet, or reader.

Since you've purchased this print book, we are happy to offer you the eBook for just $4.99.

Convenient and fully searchable, the PDF version enables you to easily find and copy code—or perform examples by quickly toggling between instructions and applications.

To learn more, go to http://www.apress.com/us/shop/companion or contact support@apress.com.

CPSIA information can be obtained
at www.ICGtesting.com
Printed in the USA
LVOW08s0225280217
525566LV00008BA/53/P